T0247749

UNPRECEDENTED **ASSAULT**

www.amplifypublishinggroup.com

Unprecedented Assault: How Big Government Unleashed America's Socialist Left

For more information, please contact:
RealClear Publishing, an imprint of Amplify Publishing Group
620 Herndon Parkway, Suite 220
Herndon, VA 20170
info@amplifypublishing.com

Library of Congress Control Number: 2024909268

CPSIA Code: PRF0724A

ISBN-13: 979-8-89138-129-2

Printed in Canada

To my wife Jennifer, without whose support and patience this book could never have been written.

UNPRECEDENTED
ASSAULT

HOW BIG GOVERNMENT UNLEASHED
AMERICA'S SOCIALIST LEFT

J.T. YOUNG

RealClear
Publishing

CONTENTS

CONTENTS

INTRODUCTION

America is enduring the greatest leftist uprising in our history. It is unprecedented in its virulence—not even during the turbulent 1960s or the anarchistic uprising at Chicago's Haymarket a century earlier has America seen leftists act with such a depth and breadth of hostility. It shows no sign of ending, and if it is up to the socialist Left, it will not until they have recreated America in their own embittered image of hatred.

This uprising is also unprecedented in its scope. And it is an uprising—a guerilla action of sorts—even if the leftists have not always declared it as such, and even if the rest of America does not recognize it. Seemingly every significant arena in American society is now a battleground. Even the casual observer sees this, and many have encountered it first-hand. Examples are pervasive, but to list a few: The leftists' radical climate agenda favors ideology over energy. Their Social Justice Initiative claims to combat America's implicit racism but does so with its own explicit racism. In schools, they pursue indoctrination over education. In health care, leftists want to replace America's private health care system with a government-run one under the rubric of Medicare for All. Instead of upholding America's foundational standard of individual freedom, they seek to allot rights through identity-group politics and segment the nation. To pay for their excessive spending on such items as the multi-trillion-dollar Green New Deal, leftists pursue revolutionary and confiscatory wealth taxes. Their Defund the Police movement has turned many inner cities into lawless war zones, because leftist officials place a higher value on protecting criminals than on defending citizens—leaving the former on the streets, while the latter are driven into their homes. With their support, unenforced immigration laws invite illegal entry, while Left-run sanctuary cities block the removal of illegal immigrants apprehended there.

Unprecedent in virulence and scope, the assault that America is enduring is also unprecedented in its source: socialist ideology. Today's socialist Left is different from America's traditional Left, which formed around a panoply of causes spanning the left side of America's ideological spectrum for generations. Conversely, the socialist Left is Marxist at its core, which means that it seeks state control of as much as possible, and ultimately its control of the state. Hidden for decades within America's broader, traditional Left, the socialist Left is now ascendant within it and insurgent within America.

Rather than try to hide these connections, many within the socialist Left explicitly embrace the socialist label, even elected officials like Vermont's self-described democratic socialist senator Bernie Sanders and several members of Congress. Many more implicitly embrace the label by refusing to reject it[1]. Still others embrace its means of centralizing power in the federal government and away from individuals. What this means is that a huge swath of those Democrats with decision-making power support (or at least do not reject) an agenda that extends far beyond creating yet another liberal government program. It aims for a redistribution of society's resources. Although it may appear under an array of more palatable names (e.g., "progressive" and the various "justice" movements—social, racial, environmental, etc.), or the guise of a particular cause, ultimately their goals cannot be fully realized without implementing socialism. Everything they do, then, is a veneer for gaining control of government at the local, state, and federal levels. Today's socialist Left burst into the national spotlight with Senator Bernie Sanders's 2016 campaign for the Democrat Party's presidential nomination. It has only gathered momentum since.

Equally important to understanding today's socialist Left is understanding who it is not. Today's socialist Left does *not* comprise all those who participate in the causes it seeks to control. The socialist Left is not every person who sympathizes with Black Lives Matter, for example, despite its being founded by two women with admitted socialist ideology.[2] It is not all Democrats, despite the socialist Left's increasing influence within that party. It is not every teacher, despite the socialist Left's increasing influence within America's two largest teachers' unions. If the goal is to defeat this unprecedented uprising, the last with clients to be serviced."[18] Decades earlier, President Ronald Reagan summed up well the insidious problem of federal bureaucracy in perpetuity when he attributed immortality to it: "A government bureau is the nearest thing to eternal life we'll ever see on this earth!"

But that is what the socialist Left wants: bigger and more overreaching government. In turn, they are telling the American people that this is what *they* want, too. In addition to its successful leveraging of America's traditional Left and the Democrat Party to gain increasing influence over the foundation of resources that a massive federal government offers, the socialist Left has lately benefitted from America's changed perception of socialism itself. Besides the tens of millions of Americans who are now direct dependents of federal government programs, a diminishing number of Americans have any negative memories of organized socialism, due both to these organizations' miniscule impact and the fact they effectively disappeared long ago.[19]

Diminishing too are memories of when the socialist regimes of the USSR and its Warsaw Pact allies were America's adversaries in the Cold War, or in hot ones like Korea or Vietnam. Long gone is the fearsome post-WWII Iron Curtain, despite its having lasted through the 1980s. While communism seemed on the march for most of the 20th century, it has been in retreat for over a generation now. Absent China, today's other communist governments—North Korea, Cuba, Vietnam, and Venezuela—are largely laughable relics. And while China certainly could someday present the same potential problem that the USSR once did for America's socialist Left, it does not yet. China's emergence as America's chief adversary is still relatively new, and thus far, this relationship has also lacked the distinctive ideological conflict of the Cold War. This is because, until recently, China's government outwardly downplayed its communist character to an extent unimaginable from the old USSR.

Whether America's perception of China's communist government continues to be so neutral in COVID's wake (amid persistently increasing evidence of the Chinese government's role in it) and Xi Jinping's aggressive internal and external moves remains to be seen. But even if China's government serves to broadly discredit socialism in America again, communism's prolonged "out of sight, out of mind" respite has further allowed America's socialist Left a chance to rehabilitate and reinvent itself at home. In America's forgetfulness, the socialist Left has gone from fascist to fashionable.

With the massive size and scope of the federal government enabling the socialist Left to offer billions in tangible benefits to millions, its frequently successful leveraging of the broader American Left and through it the Democrat Party, and Americans' changed perception of socialism, the socialist Left is now pursuing its policies and programs as never before. Identifying these is not straightforward because, with the exception of a still small but growing number of elected officials, the socialist Left prefers to travel *incognito*. America's establishment media only facilitates this obfuscation through its use of code words like "progressive," "far left," or simply leaving it undifferentiated within "the Left"—anything to describe it without labeling it truly Marxist. Likewise, its policies.

Rare are the programs and movements that are identified with the socialist Left directly. Founders of the Black Lives Matter movement had socialist roots and have publicly acknowledged those. However, absent such direct identification (and often even with it), the bulk of socialist Left policies will continue to fly beneath the establishment media's radar and the public's perception. The most comprehensive way to identify socialist Left policies and programs is to find those that fracture American society in order to separate it from its foundational principles, and those that increase government control of, and involvement in, the private sector. The Communist Party USA's embrace of Michigan's repeal of its right to work law is a prime example. With every Democrat in the legislature supporting repeal, the CPUSA posted on X on March 10. 2023: "We're proud to join with our union members and our friends in the labor movement to #RestoreWorkerFreedom & put an end to so-called 'Right to Work laws.'" The socialist Left knows all too well where its interests lie.

America is only beginning to recognize the areas where socialist Left policy has been adopted by the Biden administration. But the shift is there: teachers' unions successfully lobbying for continued school closures; environmental organizations' cozy relationship with energy regulators and policymakers; and administration efforts to censor dissenters to its COVID policies.

More broadly, the push for vastly increased federal spending, while still insufficient for the socialist Left's goals, was still welcomed. The same applies to the push for greatly increased taxes, especially wealth taxes,[20] that are being increasingly aimed at accumulated wealth at both the state and national level—taxes that had previously been spectacular failures in Europe.[21]

Tax policy perfectly underscores the fundamental difference between America's traditional Left and its socialist Left. In contrast to traditional liberals, who seek higher taxes to pay for their desired higher spending, the socialist Left seeks higher taxes for their own sake. Higher taxes are not a means to an end for the socialist Left, but *the* end in themselves. For the socialist Left, higher taxes do not exist to fund a preferred program, as they do for traditional liberals, they *are* a program—its program of bringing more resources under the public sector's control. For the socialist Left, targeting the rich for taxation reduces income inequality by redistributing income. Thus, even if its programs were paid for and the federal budget balanced, today's socialist Left would *still* favor higher taxes as a means of redistributing society's resources in accordance with its criterion of "fairness."

If the socialist Left's policies are often obscured from easy identification by the establishment media, and even the socialist Left's adherents themselves, the failures that have stacked up since 2016 stand out starkly. Although broadly mentioned earlier, the low points warrant a quick enumeration.

First, many of America's inner cities have become war zones under policies espoused by the socialist Left. Entire areas of many are virtually lawless. A "deep blue" colors the failures of Chicago, Seattle, Portland, New York, San Francisco, Los Angeles. The list goes on, but it always begins on the left. From defunding their police, these cities have gone to high crime and violence—from shoplifting to riots to homicide spikes to New York's governor deploying the National Guard in the New York City's subway in March 2024.

The socialist Left has insisted that America's southern border be ungoverned, too. As a result of the current administration's acquiescence to these wishes, our Mexican border now has little more meaning than a line on a map. For those who manage to cross our porous border, but are somehow apprehended internally, the socialist Left has led the charge to abolish ICE (US Immigration and Customs Enforcement), prevent the border-crossers' removal, and then offer them government benefits. Whenever ICE does apprehend individuals, governments in America's deep blue cities often refuse to cooperate with them on detention and deportation. Organizations influenced and supported by the socialist Left then work for their release through the courts, often using federal tax dollars to do so.

Perhaps the biggest opportunity seized—and fumbled—by the socialist Left was the global COVID-19 pandemic of 2020. Naturally, COVID prompted a government response, and the socialist Left's institutional assault was nowhere more apparent than in the locking down of America's public-school system, locking out pupils from in-classroom learning and parents from school board decisions. Leftist teacher unions fought nationwide against reopening over two school years. The specter of the aptly named "remote learning" (where learning is only a remote possibility) still haunts America's parents as, sadly, evidence continues to mount that the consequences of these lockouts will harm these children and America for years to come.[22]

The nationwide COVID lockdowns also echoed the socialist Left's zeal for total control. Their origins in the blue strongholds of California and New York typified their connection with the socialist Left: they were championed by the national teachers' unions, where the socialist Left has made great inroads; at their insistence they were pursued harder and lasted longer where the socialist Left was strongest politically and governments bluest. In "A Final Report Card on the States' Response to COVID-19," an April 2022 National Bureau of Economic Research Working Paper, Phil Kerpen, Stephen Moore, and Casey Mulligan measured state economic and education performance. In its measurement of "cumulative in-person education percentage," of the lowest twenty-one, nineteen were blue states; the only red states were Kentucky at 39, and North Carolina at 34. In its measurement (adjusted for "unemployment and GDP changes for industry composition") of the "combined economic performance scores of the states," fifteen of the lowest performing twenty were blue states; the only red states were Louisiana at 43, Alaska at 39, Wyoming at 37, Oklahoma at 36, and Ohio at 34.[23]

The socialist Left's imprint of failure is also evident in America's fiscal policy. The onset of COVID was quickly embraced as a means of justifying the socialist Left's desire to draw more resources to the government through its profligate predilection for taxing and spending. Spending increased by 50 percent, the deficit jumped more than threefold, and debt soared during the first year of the pandemic. Yet this was not enough for the socialist Left. As soon as Joe Biden took office, his administration championed a new $1.9 trillion spending bill. Once this was enacted, President Biden unveiled plans for over $4 trillion more in so-called "infrastructure spending" to be offset by, yes, higher taxes. Even this stratospheric amount was insufficient for the socialist Left; its champion,

Senator Bernie Sanders of Vermont, sought $6 trillion.[24]

Enhanced unemployment benefits during COVID serve as another case study in socialist Left-supported policy. These resulted in the contradictory coexistence of large numbers of unemployed workers and record levels of job openings—all while labor-force participation dropped. The reason was simple: since the public sector doesn't have to worry about making a profit or running deficits, its benefits could—and did—easily exceed the private sector's ability to pay wages. This dysfunctional dichotomy was not short-lived. It will be a national and human tragedy if socialist Left policies have converted many workers into client recipients of government benefits—even those linked to the pandemic—who as a result now eschew long-term upward mobility from free-market participation.

The result of the socialist Left's approach to massively offset the economic effects of the COVID lockdowns it championed was a veritable neutron bomb of a recovery. It helped spur inflation at levels unseen for decades and precipitated a string of interest-rate increases, while the nation's economy shrank in the first two quarters of 2022. Although the economy's macroeconomic numbers returned, the workforce was diminished as millions ceased participating in it—at the encouragement of the socialist Left. The result of the socialist Left encouraging the lowest skilled workers (where unemployment is almost always highest) to abandon work for enriched unemployment benefits could mean these workers' potentially permanent replacement by others more willing to work, or by businesses simply eliminating positions entirely. Of course, the purveyor of this policy interpreted the fallout from its misguided efforts as evidence that its policies were not only needed but should be extended further.

Sadly, even if exhausting to hear, this litany of leftist lunacy is hardly exhaustive. Examples are replete in every area in which socialist Left policies have been pursued, and in each case, the results remain the same: an assault on common sense and the status quo that results in failure.

The reason for socialist Left policy failures is inherent to its approach. To paraphrase the renowned economist Ludwig von Mises, when fully implemented, socialism is simply monopoly administered by government. In every sphere it can, it controls. And ultimately, the socialist Left seeks to control all spheres; this is what explains the broad, unprecedented assault America is now enduring. The result of this insatiable overreach is equally predictable. Economically, public-sector control is less productive than private-sector control. Whether a single program or sector-wide, the results are more expensive, less efficient, and unpopular. How fast a socialist Left-backed program drains the economy's resources, and the public's goodwill, are merely a factor of how far it is pursued.

However, simply awaiting the inevitable collapse of the socialist Left's policies and its support is not a solution. To do so is to sentence Americans to endure it. And like the Titanic's sinking, many innocents will go down with it. After all, failure is not a deterrent to the socialist Left; it is justification for increasing its misguided policies.

So, how can such an unprecedented assault, one precipitated by a massive government and pursued by ideological zealots, be defeated? The 18th century conservative statesman and philosopher, Edmund Burke, stated: "When bad men combine, the good must associate, else they will fall, one by one, an unpitied sacrifice in a contemptible struggle."[25] Today, the rest of America must be "the good," because conservative principles and policies are the only way to beat the socialist Left.

If the pain from the socialist Left's current and continuing assault is insufficient incentive, then conservatism's promise of opportunity should suffice. America's increasing demand for conservative policies in response to the socialist Left's assault offers not only the opportunity to defeat the socialist Left, but to discredit America's broader Left and return it to the irrelevance it endured in presidential politics from the 1970s until Obama resurrected it.

If resistance from Americans outside traditional conservative ranks seems too good to be true, consider the examples already occurring.

During intra-party debate over President Biden's Build Back Better $3.5 trillion tax and spending package, Senator Bernie Sanders ran an October 15, 2021, opinion piece attacking Democrat Senator Joe Manchin in his home state of West Virginia, calling him out as one of two Democratic senators not giving their support for the legislation. Manchin's response underscored the divide the socialist Left is opening, rankling first that "an out-of-stater" had any right to tell West Virginians what is best for them, then saying that " ... Congress should proceed with caution on any additional spending and I will not vote for a reckless expansion of government programs. No op-ed from a self-declared Independent socialist is going to change that."[26]

Manchin is not alone. There are many American liberals and Democrats who in no way join the socialist Left in its means or goals. In October 2022, former House Representative and Democrat presidential candidate Tulsi Gabbard resigned from the Democrat Party over what she called its "cowardly wokeness." In an October 11, 2022, video posted on Twitter, Gabbard accused the party of "racializing every issue, stoking anti-white racism [and] actively working to undermine our God-given freedoms enshrined in our Constitution."[27]

Nor are these rebellions individual initiatives. In 2021, Republican Glenn Youngkin beat former governor and longtime Democrat operative Terry McAuliffe in Virginia's gubernatorial election with a 7 percentage-point improvement over Republicans' 2020 presidential outcome. On October 7, 2023, the world watched in horror as Hamas unleashed a premeditated terrorist assault on Israeli civilians. In contrast, America's socialist Left celebrated.[28] Americans now find themselves doubly repulsed: at terrorism's horror abroad and at the socialist Left's ideological inroads here at home—especially at America's so-called elite universities. And in a January 2024 *CBS News* poll, 67 percent of Independents disapproved of President Biden's job performance, while 20 percent of Democrats did so.[29] Six months later, this trend drove Biden to abandon his reelection bid.

Clearly, in a contest between policies, not simply personalities, conservative approaches can win—even outside conservative circles.

However, beating the socialist Left requires more than simply winning elections. The very dynamic that has allowed the socialist Left to wage its unprecedented assault must be reversed by bringing competition and choice as much as possible into all government programs.

Though the COVID emergency provided quick inroads for the socialist Left to reach the American populace, it also required flexibility from the suffocating control that had blocked long overdue reforms aimed at putting patients' needs first. How? By putting competition in place. The Trump administration instituted many waivers that showed what could happen in health care where competition was allowed in. A January 2023 Heritage Foundation paper by Robert Moffit and Doug Badger detailed how "federal agencies reviewed, revised, or suspended many regulatory restrictions that inhibited the flexibility of medical profes- sionals in treating the virus. This resulted in numerous innovations in health care delivery that were beneficial to doctors and patients alike, such as rapid expansion of telehealth."[30] This is not surprising. The popularity and efficacy of competition in health care has already been shown in the addition of Medicare

Advantage, private plans that compete to offer more than traditional Medicare. As Grace-Marie Turner of the Galen Institute observes, Medicare Advantage already has 28 million voluntary enrollees—over half the Medicare population—while Medicare's Part D prescription drug program "is the only government health program to come in under budget, with premiums averaging about the same as they were when the program started in 2006—around $30 a month."[31]

Both areas show something America too often forgets: supply creates its own demand. The socialist Left knows this all too well; it is why they block competition and choice at every turn. Once the public gets a taste of competition and choice's superiority, they develop an appetite for them.

The socialist Left has benefitted from a dynamic where big government begat even bigger government. Where the supply of subsidized subsistence from government benefits has conditioned a demand for more because recipients knew nothing *other* than the subsidized, subservient, subsistence to which they had been relegated. Just as that dynamic preceded the socialist Left and created the conditions for it, one of competition and choice will run in favor of conservatives, leading to increased demand for a conservative approach.

To defeat the socialist Left, we must specifically sever it from the federal programs that sustain it and advance its policies. In this effort, America's souring view of Communist China is an apt analogy.

Decades ago, America and the West believed that bringing Communist China into our world through such means as WTO (World Trade Organization) membership would influence it to adopt the ways of the West, primarily respect for human rights and intellectual-property rights. The decades have proved us wrong. Now awake to the fact that China has no intention of adhering to the West's rules of trade or competition, the danger that China presents is clear. With this clarity has come a growing call for strategic decoupling: reducing America's dependence on China for vital resources and blocking China's access to America's strategic assets.

The same lesson about decoupling should be learned and applied to the federal government and the socialist Left. Marxism's real threat to America does not lie in China; it lies here at home. As the socialist Left and government are drawn invariably closer together, with government bureaucracy enticed by the pursuit of its own enlargement, the only way to diminish the socialist Left's power is to decrease government's size and scope—particularly the programs and bureaucracies which it so successfully uses to advance its agenda.

There has always been a left to America's political spectrum. Those groups we recognize today as the Left—the traditional Left—were largely created during the 1960s, in the wake of the Johnson administration's Great Society program that aimed to organize precisely this part of the political spectrum. While the socialist Left is a part of the traditional Left collectively, its embrace of socialism sets it apart ideologically. However, is there overlap? Unquestionably. There are policies of the traditional Left that the socialist Left will support as an advancement of its own agenda. There are also policies of the socialist Left that the traditional Left will support because the full threat of the socialist Left—complete state control—is not immediately clear.

Today's socialist Left certainly believes the state should control the meaningful means of production; however, as we have seen from its recent upheavals in every area of our society, it envisions state control over even more: from the means of production of goods to the distribution of goods, and even to the production and distribution of ideas and values. While much is still beyond the socialist Left's reach, that will not last if it is not stopped.

Socialist regimes abroad and across history have aimed at comprehensive state monopolies—exigencies arising from their failures—and nearly all have devolved into authoritarian ones. What sets America's socialist Left apart from the traditional Left in America is its intent on establishing comprehensive state monopoly at its very inception. As the first chapter of this book will show, what the Obama administration did for America's traditional Left (returning it from its forty years of exile in presidential politics and using the imprimatur of the federal government to make it respectable), the Biden administration is doing for the socialist Left today. The socialist Left is now more able and most willing to wage a conflict with America's right-of-center status quo than at any time in our history. Absent a change in these factors, particularly the economic, political, and electoral power provided by a massive federal government, the socialist Left will not stand down. Our expectation should be for their internal ideological assault to continue and intensify.

Only if Americans grasp the threat and accept their role will today's socialist Left assault of America end. The objective of this book and America's imperative align: to attest that the socialist Left for the first time meaningfully exists in America; to document its origins and the intentions of its current assault; and to explain what America must do to end it. To start, Americans must lead; to lead they must understand the socialist Left and where it will take America if not stopped.

CHAPTER ONE

THE RISE OF AMERICA'S SOCIALIST LEFT

SECTION I
Introduction

The socialist Left's rise in America, most notably since 2016, is the result of a symbiotic relationship. Over the last 90 years, the growth of the federal government's reach and resources has now provided the socialist Left the fundamental means it has historically lacked. This, combined with the socialist Left's increasing access to this enlarged federal government, especially since 2021, has given it the greatest accumulation of power in its history, yielding its unprecedented assault on America. Although the long-term trend is the more important and enduring, there is importance in the short-term, too. It is also the more easily discernible. Like a powder keg's sizzling fuse, it has ignited America's socialist Left. This chapter examines the lighting of this fuse.

Despite Democrats' defeat in the 2016 presidential election, both the traditional Left and the socialist Left benefitted from their campaign. Senator Bernie Sanders's strong challenge to Hillary Clinton demonstrated definitively how far both had come. More than just an unabashed liberal, Sanders willingly embraced (and still embraces) the label of "democratic socialist," the acceptance of which signaled a turning point in American politics.

The virulent opposition of even the traditional Left—the broad, historical amalgamation of groups and individuals on the left of America's political spectrum—to the Trump administration signaled their receptivity to a far more radical Left. These were no longer voters and politicians playing the passively quiescent role of "limousine liberals" of yore. Increasingly leaders in the traditional Left had roots in the socialist Left, and they took aim, not just at Trump, but America itself. By 2018, when Democrats retook the House, it was clear that the socialist Left, which had dramatically increased in influence well beyond its own size in the intervening years, was also now increasingly influencing the Democrat Party. This meaningful access to a major party was the socialist Left's greatest historical success in America. Although through others, it had some past successes—notably during the Populist Era and the New Deal—and policy achievements that incrementally advanced its agenda—such as the Great Society programs of the 1960s and more recently Obamacare—these were far outweighed by its historical failures.

As the 2020 presidential campaign began, the shift in influence that had occurred in the Democrat Party was clear. In 2016, the Sanders campaign was the vehicle for a motivated minority rising up from within the traditional Left against the Democrat establishment. Four years later, the Democrat Party field was dominated by those candidates on the far left of the political spectrum. With the exception of Sanders, all the candidates who excited Democrats—Elizabeth Warren, Pete Buttigieg, Kamala Harris, Michael Bloomberg—were new. And all ran well to the left of Joe Biden. In contrast, Biden was old news and old-school: an establishment politician who had been a fixture in Washington for half a century and had failed badly in two previous attempts at the nomination. Ultimately, their multiplicity of contenders prevented the Left from coalescing around a single candidate. This fracturing of the Left let the historically moderate Joe Biden win the nomination—but not before he too was forced to acknowledge the socialist Left's importance within the Democrat Party. Events of 2020—the COVID pandemic, nationwide lockdowns, the economy's abrupt plunge, George Floyd's death, and riots erupting across the country—accelerated the socialist Left's rise, and produced the most leftwing administration in American history, giving the socialist Left unprecedented influence.

This chapter traces the socialist Left's ascent within both the traditional Left and the Democrat Party as a whole. This significant influence on a major party, requisite under America's two-party system, was necessary for the socialist Left

January 2017 quoted one such, www.impeachdonaldtrumpnow.org:

> The nation is now witnessing a massive corruption of the presidency, far worse than Watergate," the campaign's website says. "From the moment he assumed the office, President Donald Trump has been in direct violation of the U.S. Constitution. The President is not above the law. We will not allow President Trump to profit from the presidency at the expense of our democracy.[10]

Unhinged reactions like this from the Left increased and extended from Trump's upset victory through his departure from office and beyond. Over time, things also grew increasingly confrontational. Early on, Vice President Pence and his family were treated to an extended show of political theatrics at an encore after a performance of *Hamilton* on Broadway. Antics like these would escalate substantially and would also shift from impromptu altercations to planned ones. Even elected Democrats started to join in. On June 23, 2018, Representative Maxine Waters of California called for specific targeting of Trump administration officials. *NBC* reported the following: "If you see anybody from that Cabinet in a restaurant, in a department store, at a gasoline station, you get out and you create a crowd and you push back on them, and you tell them they're not welcome anymore, anywhere."[11] This would only prove a springboard for more organized and serious efforts.

SECTION VI
The 2018 Midterms

The extent of how far left the Democrat coalition had shifted became clear in the 2018 midterms when Democrats won control of the House after eight years in the minority. The Left's resistance went from seemingly informal to clearly institutionalized. Again, the socialist Left led the way.

According to *NBC*'s reporting at the time, Democrats' 9.5 million total popular vote margin (53.4 percent to Republicans' 44.9 percent) in the House races was the largest ever, surpassing the previous record of 8.7 million in the 1974 Watergate-dominated midterm.[12] They gained 41 House seats and also won three Senate seats, narrowing the Republican majority to a scant single seat following a December special election.

Democrats' numbers were not just quantitatively different, they were qualitatively different too. They were no longer simply Left, but radically Left. No longer simply in attendance in their ranks, the socialist Left was in the forefront. Nothing epitomized the change like "The Squad," who egged on House Democrats to pursue a vendetta in the form of investigations and hearings, calling for impeachment —something the House would soon do not once, but an unprecedented twice, despite neither attempt having any chance of removing the president from office, and the last taking place just days before his term ended.

The name "The Squad" was coined by Alexandria Ocasio-Cortez, a newly-elected Representative from New York's 14th district. She was first joined by three other first-term women: Ilhan Omar (MN-5), Ayanna Pressley (MA-7), and Rashida Tlaib (MI-13). The replacement of old-line liberals by the socialist Left was literal in the cases of Cortez and Pressley. Both had defeated Democrat incumbents in primaries on their path to Congress. The Squad's determined opposition to the status quo made them instant celebrities.

In a gushing August 8, 2019 *New York Times* opinion piece on the Squad, Barbara Ransby, "a historian who specializes in black politics and social movements" summed up the four women, and the new socialist Left in the House Democrat Caucus in general:[13]

> ... They insist on bringing the concerns of historically marginalized communities into the rooms where decisions are made, even when that is seen as impolite or inappropriate. This is evident through their politics, priorities and style—not only their presence. Consider Rashida Tlaib's "Lift + Act" bill, which comes as close as any to advancing the radical economic principle of universal guaranteed income that Martin Luther King Jr. so eloquently advocated some 50 years ago. They're exposing the false belief that American foreign policy is infallible. This is exemplified by their critique of Washington's unconditional support for Israel ...

"Maurice Mitchell, who now runs the Working Families Party, sees them as central to a seismic shift in electoral politics post-2016. "This moment has radicalized liberals and electoralized radicals," he told me. Meaning there are new political actors with new agendas and expectations ...

Well, the squad members, all with varying activist backgrounds, are a part of that generation. They are products of the Movement for Black Lives, #MeToo, Occupy Wall Street and an increasingly militant immigrant rights movement. These bold, game-changing social movements are led by a cohort of savvy young women organizers who are not afraid to speak truth to power and upset business as usual ...

They are wisely acting as if they represent the demographic and political majority that their generation will become. It is significant that a majority of millennials polled by Harvard researchers in 2016 rejected capitalism and leaned toward the left politics that these four congresswomen represent ...

If there is any doubt as to what the Squad stands for, Justine Medina, a former aide to Rep. Ocasio-Cortez, was listed belonging to the "Executive Committee of the New York State Communist Party" in May 2023. According to a *New York Post* article at the time, Democrat Queens Councilman Bob Holden is quoted as saying: "It's frightening. They're coming out of the woodwork. Communism has failed in so many places that it is mind-boggling that AOC's constituents keep electing her. This is kind of like a smoking gun that these elected officials and congresspeople are out and out communist.'"[14]

Just as no one embodied the socialist Left in the Democrat Caucus like the Squad, nothing typified the Squad's and the socialist Left's policies like the Green New Deal. Introduced by Rep. Cortez (and Senator Ed Markey, D-MA), the Green New Deal would make the original New Deal green with envy, with a towering list of demands. It included changes for everything from cutting greenhouse-gas emissions to net zero in just a decade to guaranteeing jobs for all. According to the *Washington Post*, its prominent backers were all "liberal and environmental groups," as well as Democrats running for president, including Sens. Cory Booker (NJ), Kirsten Gillibrand (NY), Kamala D. Harris (CA), Amy Klobuchar (MN) and Elizabeth Warren (MA). The *Post* noted, too, that "Republicans say it's a non-starter that reeks of socialism." So large was the Green New Deal, that contention immediately arose over what was, and was not, in it. The *Washington Post* Fact Checker stepped in on February 11, 2019[15] to try to clear things up, saying that the "10-year national mobilization" would include:

- Guaranteeing a job with a family-sustaining wage, adequate family and medical leave, paid vacations, and retirement security to all people of the United States.
- Providing all people of the United States with—(i) high-quality health care; (ii) affordable, safe, and adequate housing; (iii) economic security; and (iv) access to clean water, clean air, healthy and affordable food, and nature.
- Providing resources, training, and high-quality education, including higher education, to all people of the United States.
- Meeting 100 percent of the power demand in the United States through clean, renewable, and zero-emission energy sources.

Naturally the Green New Deal's expansiveness led to questions about its expensiveness. The Aspen Institute published an estimate by Doug Holtz-Eakin, president of American Action Forum, a non-profit center-right think tank, former Chief Economist of the President's Council of Economic Advisers, and former director of the Congressional Budget Office: "If one adds up the low end of the range, the total is $52 trillion (over the next 10 years); at the high end it is $93 trillion."[16]

For context, the Bureau of Economic Analysis determined that US GDP in 2021's Q3 was $23.2 trillion.[17] Assuming a midpoint estimate ($72.5 trillion) of Holtz-Eakins's cost estimate, imposing the Green New Deal over a decade would require 31 percent of all US GDP. That is almost one out of every three dollars America's entire economy produced![18] And because much of the Green New Deal contains ongoing programs, such costs would continue in perpetuity. Paying for such an astronomical undertaking would require an unimaginable tax burden on the American people—hiking the combined marginal income and employment tax rate well over the 2023 rate of 41.6 percent for those in the top bracket, and comparatively increasing rates for all individuals—to even begin approaching the Green New Deal's price tag. With sights set so high, it is no wonder, that the socialist Left is eying wealth taxes as future sources of revenue.

The new socialist Left-infused Democrat House hit the ground running in 2019. According to the law firm of Gibson, Dunn and Crutcher, LLP,[19] it armed itself with greatly increased investigative powers. Bolstering the formidable arsenal it already possessed, it took immediate aim at the Trump administration in the halls of Congress with investigations, hearings, and legislation. In May 2019, just a few months into the new Democrat majority, *NBC News* reported: "At least 14 Democrat-led House committees have been investigating various aspects of President Donald Trump's businesses, campaign, and his presidency since the beginning of this year ... In all, those committees have launched at least 50 probes into Trump world."[20]

As bad as the socialist Left-led Democrats made 2019 for the Trump White House, 2020 made things even worse for the administration ... and America. The COVID pandemic and then George Floyd's death on May 25, 2020, gave the socialist Left unparalleled opportunities to pursue its agenda both nationally and locally.

When coronavirus, or COVID-19, landed in the United States,[21] it gave the socialist Left an opportunity to push control over facets of society to a hitherto unimaginable extent. In a word: lockdowns. By March 15, 2020, states had begun issuing shutdown orders, including the New York City public school system, the nation's largest. Almost overnight, additional lockdowns spread— California Governor Gavin Newsom issuing a statewide stay-at-home order on March 19— telling residents to leave home only when necessary and closing all but essential businesses. They would continue to spread through much of the nation. The shorthand is simple: the lockdowns that occurred first, lasted longest, and were most severe where the Left was strongest. Routinely, the bluer the government, the worse the lockdown. After California issued the first statewide stay-at-home order on March 19, Illinois, New Jersey, New York, and Connecticut quickly followed, issuing their own orders just days later. With the effective closing of much of America, the economy crashed. America's GDP fell 5.1 percent in 2020's Q1 and an astounding 28 percent in Q2.[22] Unemployment peaked at 14.8 percent in April 2020, with 20.6 million unemployed during 2020's Q2.[23]

The socialist Left loved the power that lockdowns extended to government—

and the opportunity it gave to the socialist Left to influence blue governments. The second order of business was to call for vast aid to compensate for the lockdowns. In all, roughly $5.3 trillion would be spent by the federal government in just over a year. Additionally, the Federal Reserve held interest rates at near-zero levels and beginning in June 2020, pumped massive amounts of liquidity into the system through its monthly purchases of $120 billion in government-backed securities.[24]

Combined federal government spending and Federal Reserve action during this period put more than $11 trillion into the US economy.[25] This amounted to roughly half of America's 2021 annual GDP. As to be expected, this massive increase in money, and its increased velocity of circulation through massive government spending, triggered inflation in 2021. By December, inflation was running at a 7 percent clip —the highest annual rate since 1982 (it would peak at 9.1 percent the following year).

What COVID did for the socialist Left's advancement through government, the video of George Floyd's tragic death in Minneapolis, Minnesota, at the hands of a White police officer did for it in the streets. The rise of the Black Lives Matter Movement was the perfect cover for the socialist Left to make moves here. The association of BLM's leaders with the socialist Left has been well documented, often by their own admission.[26] Always the socialist Left's first home, protest, civil disobedience, and rioting remain its most familiar outlets, and these would prevail in unprecedented fashion throughout the remainder of 2020.

Once again, blue jurisdictions set the pace. A 2020 report on incidents from May 25 through July 31 by police chiefs of major metropolitan cities stated: "The level of civil disobedience that began in late May and continued for many months was significant and unprecedented for most major city law enforcement agencies."[27] It was also unprecedented for most Americans. In some areas, like Portland, Minneapolis, and Seattle, it seemed almost perpetual. Both Portland and Seattle would see "autonomous zones" declared by militants and allowed to remain in place by city authorities for extended periods of time. Seattle's CHAZ (Capitol Hill Autonomous Zone) would last almost a month. The Major Cities Chiefs Association report counted 8,700 protests during the 68-day period it covered: "While the vast majority of these protests were peaceful, a large portion did include non-violent acts of civil disobedience such as the takeover of a roadway or disruption of commerce." There were also "574 protests that involved acts of violence, some of which were severe." Although just seven percent of the protest total, violent protests were occurring at a rate of just under nine a day, and in 79 percent of the report's cities. Almost half of protests involved either civil disobedience or violence.[28]

In just over two months of coverage, the report found protests occurring at a rate of almost 130 per day. Los Angeles and New York each had over one thousand protests during this time. Sixty-two percent of the reporting agencies experienced looting, 56 percent had incidents of arson, 26 percent had police cars burned, and 72 percent had officers injured. Out-of-state participation in the protests was common, with 90 percent of agencies reporting it. Twenty-nine percent of the jurisdictions even discovered that protesters were being paid. When infiltration by violent extremists was determined, the Left was identified 50 percent more often than the Right.[29]

Like the lockdowns, the protests were centered in blue jurisdictions. In these jurisdictions, elected leaders frequently did not support their own law enforcement, and often did not prosecute those arrested in the disturbances. Fifty-three percent of agencies reported their "District Attorney's Office elected not to prosecute protest-related cases," and "approximately 52 percent of major city law enforcement agencies reported having to re-arrest suspects at least once at different protest-related events."

The socialist Left's aims at this time were clearly advanced by BLM movement supporters who advocated defunding the police. Former Department of Housing and Urban Development Secretary Ben Carson said that the movement has become a "Marxist-driven organization" that "espouses things like taking down the model of Western family structure."[30] Conservative commentator Carol Swain stated: "They [BLM] are using Black people to advance a Marxist agenda."[31]

By the time of the November 2020 presidential election, the socialist Left had attained unimaginable advances—there was now no way they were going to passively return to being a silent partner in the new Democrat triumvirate of White House, Senate, and House control.

SECTION VII
The 2020 Election

The 2020 Democrat nomination contest showed the reversal that had taken place within the Party in just four years. Where only Bernie Sanders had been in 2016, speaking for the socialist Left as a minority, in 2020, the majority of candidates seeking the Democrat nomination embraced much of those policies, even if they were not adopting the label of "democratic socialist." When John Hickenlooper, the former Colorado governor, denounced socialism at the 2019 California state party annual convention, he was booed.[32]

This sudden popularity, however, was not necessarily good for the party as a whole, and the number of far-Left Democrat candidates espousing elements of the socialist Left's agenda ironically worked *against* their ability to achieve ultimate success within the Democrat Party. In the past, its agenda had stalled because none embraced it; in 2020, it was hindered when *too many* did so. The larger base of support was split between those who espoused socialist Left-supported policies and those who wanted to let the Democrat establishment back in.

Joe Biden was essentially alone in running as less-left and more-establishment, and it was this alignment that allowed him to squeak through the early contests, while the further-left candidates knocked each other out. Had Biden's opposition consisted of just one far-Left candidate instead of many, he would likely have been eliminated in the campaign's initial contests—he nearly was even in the crowded field. Simply, Biden was not the first choice of a Democrat majority until essentially no alternative remained. Democrats clearly and consistently wanted a nominee to the left of Biden, so, despite his effectively being the sole establishment representative in the Democrat field, Biden was hardly immune from having to run hard to the left in order to succeed. His attempts at accentuating his establishment credentials failed miserably with Democrat voters. Among the most notable rebukes was delivered early by his future Vice President in June of 2019. California Senator Kamala Harris implicitly labeled him a racist (while explicitly exonerating herself from calling Biden one) in perhaps the hardest blow landed in the countless Democrat debates:

> I'm going to now direct this at Vice President Biden. I do not believe you are a racist. I agree with you when you commit yourself to the

importance of finding common ground. I also believe … It's personal. It was actually hurtful to hear you talk about the reputations of two United States senators who built their reputations and career on the segregation of race in this country. It was not only that but you also worked with them to oppose busing. There was a little girl in California who was part of the second class to integrate her public schools. She was bused to school every day. That little girl was me. I will tell you that on this subject it cannot be an intellectual debate among Democrats.[33]

This point only reinforced how far left the Democrat field had moved in just four years. The sole (and perhaps quintessential) establishment representative could not win by running as an establishment candidate. He could not, because there were not enough establishment, moderate Democrats to appeal to. Biden had to run much further to the left than Hillary Clinton had in 2016 (e.g., the reversal of his long-time opposition to using federal money to pay for abortions).[34] For Clinton, her leftward move was strategic; for Biden, it was existential.

Even after Biden had safely secured the nomination, he had to continue left to keep the Democrat base motivated. No clearer evidence of this exists than his running-mate decision. To avoid rebuke, the socialist Left's criteria had to be honored. First, bowing to the reality of identity-group politics, his choice must not resemble him in any way. Not White, not male, not old, and not establishment.[35] While the Democrat primary field he had faced offered him ample options for meeting one or more of these "musts," only one offered him them all. So in the end, Biden had to stoop to conquer; he chose the Democrat primary challenger who had delivered the most personal and damaging insult to him of the entire contest—whom Biden's wife had said after the Democrat debate's "racist" exchange that Harris could "go fuck herself," according to Edward-Isaac Dovere's book *"Battle for the Soul: Inside the Democrats' Campaigns to Defeat Trump,"* and for which Biden himself took extreme offense, whispering at the time to fellow-debater Pete Buttigieg, "Well, that was some fucking bullshit."[36]

Once Harris was taken on board, his campaign opted for the transparent strategy of sequestering Biden away from the public to help eliminate his predilection for public gaffes. More opaque but equally important (and why this strategy is relevant here), it also helped reduce his need to take extreme-left positions that would hurt him in the general election when he would need to appeal to swing voters as well as those more traditional Democrats. Unable to minimize the demands of 2020's radicalized Left, Biden's campaign could only try to minimize their candidate's opportunities to respond to them.

Even with the nomination clinched, the "correct" running mate chosen, and his strategy of keeping a low profile, Biden could never garner personal support from his party. According to *RealClearPolitics'* average of 2020 national polling numbers, Biden started at 29 percent midway through December 2018 and finished 2019 at 28.4 percent. By mid-February 2020 and facing early elimination, he had plummeted to just 16.5 percent. Even in early April, with the race over (Sanders having dropped out the same day), Biden's support stood at only 60.8 percent.[37] The point is clear: he was the default choice of the Left-dominated Democrat electorate: a perpetual presidential consolation prize. Biden was the place the Democrats ended up, not where they wanted to go. This had enormous implications for Biden throughout the 2020 race. He could never take his support for granted because so few granted it to him personally. He followed, rather than led his party, and had to continue to move further still to the left. He tapped for Vice President the person who had leveled the harshest personal attack toward him during the primaries because she was the least threatening representative of the far Left that he could find.

Even when he won the general election and the total popular vote by 4.5 percentage points, his popular vote margins in the six states (Arizona, Georgia, Michigan, Nevada, Pennsylvania, and Wisconsin) were thin: just 77,000 votes spread across four of them (Arizona, Georgia, Nevada, and Wisconsin) kept him from electoral college defeat. Thus, Biden could never afford to alienate any of his fragile base—even his socialist Left one. Necessity had made Biden pliable, and this would work in the socialist Left's favor once he took office.

SECTION VIII
The Biden Administration 2021-Present

The tenuous nature of the Democrats' tripartite control only strengthened the socialist Left's hand within the Democrat Party. The House had been greatly same one that the socialist Left is using now to justify its proposed social spending programs by the Biden administration. The misguided strategy of centrally-planned, massive government spending that lured Johnson into a huge buildup in Vietnam, is the same one that Democrats are embracing on behalf of the socialist Left's spending and tax programs today.[48] And it is the very failure of big-government programs to beat poverty that is ultimately the implicit justification for pouring trillions more today into more big-government efforts to do what its earlier programs have miserably failed to do.

As long as the socialist Left holds influence in the Democrat Party, the Democrat Party will pursue the increase of government through every means available. Biden's numerous multi-trillion dollar spending and tax proposals are prime examples. Even with rising inflation pressures in the wake of earlier massive COVID spending responses, the first objective of both the administration and many congressional Democrats is to spend and tax more. The goal is to put in place far-Left and far-reaching social spending. Such spending might be professed to be temporary, but it's the socialist Left's clear intent to maintain them into perpetuity. Their hope, as proved by their efforts to extend Obamacare premium subsidies and the enhanced child tax credit, is that they will prove politically impossible to eliminate due to benefitted constituencies' support for them.

As later chapters will show, even if the socialist Left ultimately retreats back into the shadows, the foundational trajectory that was set into place decades earlier will accelerate government growth and propel it to continue growing on its own. This is the socialist Left's long-term economic foundation—the powder keg on which its success rests—and it will do all it can to increase and uphold this spending trajectory.

Today's political factors—the fuse lighting the socialist Left's current ascent—will also continue for the immediate future. Although seemingly counterintuitive, this will not only occur despite the negative fallout resulting from the socialist Left's current rise, but because of it. The root cause of this is a carryover from Democrats' 2020 nomination contest. As discussed, Biden has little core support of his own—as *Rasmussen*'s daily polling shows, Biden's strong support is roughly half of his strong opposition. To give more dimension to this, on the one-year anniversary of his presidential win, *Rasmussen*'s daily tracking poll gave Biden an overall negative job approval rating of 55 percent.

As bad as this was, it paled in comparison to the discrepancy between Biden's strong approval and strong disapproval rating of 23 percent to 47 percent. Three years later on January 19, 2024, the numbers were essentially unchanged.[49]

This is not surprising, of course, as it's been discussed that Biden has been the perpetual last choice for many Democrat supporters. Thus, the core Democrats Biden should be able to strongly count on—as evidenced by *Rasmussen's* low strong approval rating— in today's tough times are not behind him. As his administration moved further left and floundered, the more moderate voters deserted; the more they deserted, the more dependent Biden became on the socialist Left. And the socialist Left remained behind him only because it saw him as a useful vehicle for its agenda.

Over time, the socialist Left's agenda will produce a Democrat delegation that moves ever more to the left. Even should the Democrat Party lose numbers absolutely, the socialist Left will grow proportionally within its ranks and exert more influence in a smaller Democrat Party.

SECTION X

Conclusion: The Biden Administration's Legitimization of the Socialist Left

America's perpetual two-party system always presented the socialist Left with a dual—and until today, unsolvable—problem. To have a direct impact on American politics, a group must either be one of the two major parties, or it must have influence in one of the two major parties. As a minority within a minority, the socialist Left found this hurdle insurmountable throughout American history. What finally has bridged this hurdle for the socialist Left was the traditional Left's takeover of the Democrat Party between 2008 and 2016, followed quickly by the socialist Left's ascension within the traditional Left from 2016 through 2023.

Despite the long time and the long-shot odds of the minority socialist Left arriving at their current pinnacle of political power within the traditional Left and the Democrat Party, the socialist Left's influence in the traditional Left and than the unified, working-class approach. The socialist Left's splintering into specific groups that embraced these causes— causes that an earlier socialist Left would have rejected as diversions from the true class struggle—would accelerate during the 1960s and later, The socialist Left had also lowered its sights. Gone was the fundamental quest to capture government through a separate party approach. Despite this often being successful abroad, in the US this had been a disastrous failure. Now its victories were sought in the judicial system and through succor from government programs.

While these shifts had a positive effect on the socialist Left, they did not come by choice, but through weakness. There is a parallel in Saul Alinsky's citation of Lenin. The quintessential leftist organizer and agitator of the 1960s, Alinsky perfectly sums up the new socialist Left: "The essence of Lenin's speeches prior to the Revolution was 'They have the guns and therefore we are for peace and for reformation through the ballot. When we have the guns then it will be through the bullet. And it was.'"[10] In other words, America's socialist Left had to adapt to its American conditions. The new Left sought refuge in the causes and groups of the broader Left. Realistically, it had nowhere else to go.

Although Alinsky himself was not chronologically a "new Lefter," nor did he get along well with its leadership, his idea of grassroots action was the heart and soul of the new Left's direction. And its dispersion could not have come at a more propitious time. Because as the socialist Left dispersed, a tidal wave of federal spending would soon flow to the grassroots.

SECTION IV
The Emergence of Today's Traditional Left

The story of today's Left, the traditional Left that we recognize today and have known for decades, stretches back to the early 1960s. It begins on a high note, but not due to the traditional Left's victory, but to conservatives' implosion.

It was the ascension of Lyndon Johnson to the presidency—first following Kennedy's 1963 assassination, but more so following the 1964 presidential election—that opened the door for an extremely liberal agenda. During the campaign season, Democrats had been able to broadly define the Republican nominee, Arizona Senator Barry Goldwater, as an extremist. Goldwater said in his July 16 nomination acceptance speech: "I would remind you that extremism in the defense of liberty is no vice ... And let me remind you also that moderation in the pursuit of justice is no virtue."[11]

Two months later in September, Democrats unleashed their now-infamous "Daisy Girl" ad. It first depicted a girl counting as she pulled petals from a daisy, then switched to a male voice counting down to a nuclear explosion that was superimposed over the girl. Aired only once, the ad's point and its effect were unmistakable. The Democrats' extremist charge had stuck with an electorate still shaken by Kennedy's recent assassination. America elected Democrat Lyndon Johnson in a landslide; he won by 15 million popular votes and 486 to 52 in electoral votes.

The Johnson landslide also delivered overwhelming majorities in Congress. Democrats won two Senate seats and thirty-seven seats in the House, bringing their majorities to their largest totals since the late 1930s and very early 1940s[12]. Legislatively, there was little that Johnson could not do if he desired to. What Johnson historian Robert Caro writes in *Master of the Senate*, his history of Johnson's twelve Senate years, also holds for his presidency: "Throughout Lyndon Johnson's life, there had been hints of what he might do with great power, should he ever succeed in attaining it."[13] Hints were all that existed, however, because there was no precursor for what came. As later chapters will describe in greater detail, Johnson's goal was to recreate an enlarged New Deal with a much more leftist lean. LBJ and his Great Society programs catalyzed the traditional Left through the auspices—the legislation, the funding, the organization, and the imprimatur—of the federal government. This genesis was exogenous and brief, but it was crucial. Through its funding, the federal government pumped vast sums into the traditional Left, far more money than these groups could ever have raised on their own. This money came as a result of legislation such as the Economic Opportunity Act, which also worked to organize the unorganized, creating new groups in places where they had not existed before; groups that would soon comprise the traditional Left.

Passed in July 1964, the EOA was the spearpoint of Johnson's War on Poverty. Federal entitlement historian John Cogan writes: "The landmark law's centerpiece, and ultimately a major source of its undoing, was Title II, which the 1980 landslide for Reagan and conservativism, Democrats would run from the liberal label—not with it—until 2008. Reagan's vice president, George H.W. Bush, would win his own presidential race in 1988 by painting Massachusetts Governor Mike Dukakis as too liberal. As his state's high tax burden became known, derogatory calls of "Taxachusetts" arose—and stuck. When Democrat Bill Clinton won in 1992, it was not on the strength of being liberal. In the mold of Carter, Clinton was a governor from a conservative southern state, Arkansas. He won because Reagan's conservative coalition had split nationally between the incumbent President Bush, who had broken his pledge to not raise taxes, and third-party candidate Ross Perot, who siphoned away 19.7 million votes by focusing on the national deficit.

Even with a Democrat in the White House, being labeled as liberal was still a political disadvantage. Following a large tax hike and the failure to pass First Lady Hillary Clinton's healthcare reform plan (dubbed derisively "Clinton Care"), Democrats suffered landslide losses in the 1994 midterms. For the first time since Truman's presidency, Democrats lost control of the House and the Senate. Seeing the anti-Left political reality and facing an aggressive Republican Congress, Bill Clinton quickly disavowed his earlier liberal approach—infuriating Washington's traditional Left holdovers in the process. In October 1995, Clinton stated at a public gathering: "Probably there are people in this room still mad at me because you think I raised your taxes too much. It might surprise you to know that I think I raised them too much, too."[19]

As he prepared for re-election, Clinton moved even more deliberately center-ward. In his 1996 State of the Union speech in front of Republican Senate and House majorities, he uttered the famous line stating that the "era of big government is over," confessing his own rhetorical recalibration in hopes of bringing himself into line with the nation's anti-Left mood. Far from a simple *mea culpa*, it was a full confession:

> We know big government does not have all the answers. We know there's not a program for every problem. We have worked to give the American people a smaller, less bureaucratic government in Washington. And we have to give the American people one that lives within its means.
>
> The era of big government is over. But we cannot go back to the time when our citizens were left to fend for themselves ...

I believe our new, smaller government must work in an old-fashioned American way, together with all of our citizens through state and local governments, in the workplace, in religious, charitable and civic associations.[20]

The official Republican response by Senate Majority Leader Robert Dole kept the conservative pressure on the President:

The President has chosen to defend with his veto a welfare system that no one can defend, for it is a daily assault on the values of self-reliance and family ... President Clinton has chosen to defend and increase a tax burden that has pushed countless families into their own personal recessions. And unfortunately he has chosen to veto the first balanced budget in a generation, offering only a fantasy in its place.[21]

In late August, just months before the 1996 election and after having vetoed two earlier versions, Clinton signed into law the Republican Congress's welfare reform bill. The Personal Responsibility and Work Opportunity Reconciliation Act ended welfare as an entitlement, capped an individual's participation in the program, and instituted work requirements. Two high-ranking members of Clinton's Department of Health and Human Services resigned in protest. The traditional Left was in full retreat—literally as well as figuratively.

Just as Clinton had been reluctant to accept welfare reform, he was brought kicking and screaming to accept a balanced budget by the Republican Congress. In true Clinton fashion, he later came to embrace it and take credit for its success. Altogether, Clinton's change of course worked, and he won re-election. And the traditional Left remained politically buried nationally.

In the following two elections, neither Democrat nominee, Vice President Al Gore in 2000 or Massachusetts Senator John Kerry in 2004, dared to run as *bona fide* liberals—though George W. Bush's campaigns certainly cast them as such. Instead, Gore's emphasis was on his role in the Clinton administration and as a Senator from Tennessee, while Kerry's campaign tried to accentuate his role as a decorated veteran in the Vietnam War. Still, both lost to Bush, who ran in 2000 as a "compassionate conservative"—the optimal word remaining "conservative."

SECTION VII
The Return of America's Traditional Left Under Obama

Democrats' three presidential election victories between 1968 and 2004 all occurred in *spite* of the traditional Left rather than because of it. In 1976, they won with Watergate and a weak economy, and with a candidate from a conservative southern state who had led the charge against McGovern within the party four years earlier. In 1992, another governor from a conservative Southern state won with the help of a third-party candidate who split the conservative coalition, and in 1996, the same candidate, now an incumbent, won after he disavowed liberalism, declaring "the era of big government is over."

Gallup polling testifies to the traditional Left's political exile. As late as 1992, just 17 percent of Americans identified themselves as liberals, compared to 36 percent who self-identified as conservatives and 43 percent as moderates. Not until the middle of the next decade did liberals' figure reach 21 percent (versus 37 percent for conservatives and 38 percent for moderates). Even in 2020, liberals' highwater mark over the 1992-2020 period, the liberal score only hit 25 percent (versus 36 percent for conservatives and 35 percent for moderates).[22]

Yet as much a minority as they remained at the national level, liberalism was growing. The number of those identifying as liberals had increased by almost 50 percent— a dramatic improvement in a relatively short time. And they retained pockets of power at the national level, notably in Congress—especially prior to the Republicans' 1994 midterm tidal wave. Perhaps the biggest indicator of change occurred with Barack Obama taking office in 2008.

The charges of liberalism against Obama did not stick to the young senator with the scant record, as they had against previous Democrat presidential candidates. Even his association with the leftwing pastor of Chicago's Trinity United Church of Christ, Reverend Jeremiah Wright, whose anti-US statements brought national media attention and eventually drove Obama to withdraw his church membership in May 2008, failed to derail him.

Once in office, the Obama administration's reactions to fallout over its liberal policies were markedly different than when the Clinton administration had to answer to the same. When faced with criticism, Obama never disavowed his tax hikes or Obamacare, even when confronting a strong Republican resurgence after the 2010 midterm elections, or when seeking his second term in

2012. In contrast, Bill Clinton did both. A small change in rhetoric signaled a bigger one in Democrats and America. It underscored the start of the traditional Left's rehabilitation.

Both Clinton and Obama suffered huge midterm defeats. During Clinton's first midterm election in 1994, Democrats lost the House and the Senate. During Obama's first midterm in 2010, Democrats lost the House; four years later, they lost the Senate too. Obviously, these defeats had different circumstances. Clinton saw Republicans take control of both bodies of Congress simultaneously for the first time in decades. Obama saw Republicans retake a single body of Congress in successive midterms. Republicans' having held each body just years earlier—not decades ago—reduced the shock. Further, Obama had signed Obamacare into law; he thus was in far less of a position to walk away from his health care reform than was Clinton, who had seen Clinton Care fail. Finally, Clinton's double rebuff came two years *before* he was to seek re-election; contrastingly, Obama did not face a fully Republican Congress until *after* he had been re-elected and had only two years remaining in office.

Obama was both responsible for and a beneficiary of the traditional Left's rehabilitation, so even as the 2010 midterm defeat was a decisive rebuke (Obama himself termed it "a shellacking"), he did not back down from his more left-leaning policies, despite having seemingly ample political incentive to do so. While he implied that his own administration had lost touch when he said, "sometimes we lose track of the ways that we connected with folks that got us here in the first place," Obama did not, and certainly not to the extent seen with Bill Clinton, renounce liberalism or big government.[23] Because even while posing as a moderate to the general electorate, Obama *was*, at his core, far more to the left than Clinton. The traditional Left was perceived very differently by that time, in no small part due to Obama himself. It is these reasons, too, that underscore the traditional Left's rehabilitation—both in general and in the person of Obama.

Obama was the embodiment of the traditional Left; in truth he embodied its ideals more than he emphasized them in his campaigns for president. In style, the 2008 campaign resembled Kennedy's in 1960: Obama was a political newcomer, a Black JFK in a contest against an establishment Republican a generation older. But while Obama ran as a moderate, he governed as a liberal—even as he did so in a more incremental fashion than President Clinton had attempted at first. This campaigning as a moderate and governing as a liberal was crucial to the traditional Left and rehabilitated it in style and in substance to many Americans.

Obama included the traditional Left in his administration, adding its personnel and pursuing its policies. He included in his cabinet liberal Senator Tom Daschle as Secretary of Health and Human Services and of course Hillary Clinton as Secretary of State. And where Bill Clinton had failed with comprehensive health care reform, Obama succeeded in the more incremental version of Obamacare. In addition to influence within the executive branch and throughout the federal government, this gave a home to the traditional Left and invaluable government experience. And, very similar to the creation of the traditional Left through the Great Society's EOA, under Obama's administration the federal government lent its legitimacy to what for decades had been a marginalized political sector in presidential elections.

But what Obama did, which LBJ could never do, was to lend his personal charisma to the traditional Left. That proved invaluable to both: rehabilitating the traditional Left, whose increased legitimacy in turn helped Obama in office. The reemergence of the traditional Left—rehabilitated in both substance and style—was also crucial for today's socialist Left, because it was there that it resided, incubating for over half a century.

SECTION VIII
The Socialist Left's Ascent Will Continue Within the Traditional Left

Paralleling the traditional Left's rise within the Democrat Party over the last half century, the socialist Left will continue its own rise within the traditional Left, propelled by the same dynamic discussed in the previous chapter: the sacrifice of the middle.

The more the socialist Left continues to gain ground and assert itself—its leaders, its methods, and its policies—within the groups of the traditional Left, the more the less-extreme members of those groups will be driven out. Although less focal than the effect of losing political elections is for the Democrat Party, the effect will be no less real. The socialist Left will increase relatively, if not absolutely, within the groups of the traditional Left. This dynamic will further increase the socialist Left's power and influence by giving it the greatest access to formal organizations it has ever had, organizations that it has never been able to form on its own—or under its own name. In addition to the increased channels through which to pursue its policies, these groups of the traditional Left will also invaluably cover the socialist Left's policies from the sight of many Americans. They will also provide enhanced fundraising opportunities—both private and public—for socialist policies that could or would never be funded directly.

SECTION IX
Conclusion

Over the last six decades, three defining events have shaped the federal government and America's Left: the Johnson administration creating the traditional Left that we know today; the Obama administration rehabilitating the traditional Left; and the Biden administration legitimizing the socialist Left, as discussed in Chapter One. For roughly two-thirds of this period, the traditional Left wandered in America's political wilderness. Having abandoned its orthodox Marxist approach and dispersed into the traditional Left, the socialist Left became a political afterthought, and was therefore in no position to have a significant impact on American politics. For the radical socialist Left to have any chance at reemerging politically, the less-extreme traditional Left first had to be rehabilitated.

This rehabilitation was possible because while the traditional Left had been exiled at the level of national presidential elections, it had retained its local champions. This was particularly true of Congress and the Democrats in it. Despite Nixon's two impressive victories, for example, success did not extend to Republicans as a whole. In 1968, Republicans gained just five House seats and amazingly, none in 1972, leaving them a 193-242 minority in the House.

In 1968, they gained 7 Senate seats, but this only brought them to a 43-57 minority there; in 1972, they gained no Senate seats. Thus, in spite of losing seven of ten presidential elections from 1968 through 2004, Democrats retained full control of Congress until 1980, and then again from 1987 through 1994. This control was crucial. As Charles Blahous of the Mercatus Center at George Mason University, an expert on federal entitlements, noted in recent testimony before Congress on the federal government's budget problems:

> Nearly three-fifths of the federal government's long-term fiscal imbalance, or 59 percent, was enacted during a particularly eventful period of federal legislation during the brief span of 1965 to 1972. During this period, both Medicare and Medicaid were enacted (in 1965) and later expanded (Medicare in 1972, Medicaid in 1971 and 1972). Social Security was also dramatically expanded in 1972 and subjected to new automatic growth mechanisms ... Legislation enacted from 1965 through 1972 actually did more to create the current federal fiscal imbalance than all subsequent legislative actions combined.[24]

All this legislation embodied and implemented traditional Left policies. It shows just how effective the traditional Left were in gaining and maintaining control of the Democrat Party in Congress and just how effective these Democrats were in funding and institutionalizing the traditional Left.

The political rehabilitation that the traditional Left underwent in 2008 with Obama's presidential victory accelerated under eight years of what was the most leftwing administration in American history up to that point. It was a rising tide, lifting all the organizations and movements that comprised them—including the socialist Left within them. It also provided cover for the socialist Left's further advancement within this broader group. By moving with and within them, the socialist Left was able to hide how extreme it actually was.

Despite the long-shot odds of the minority socialist Left's arrival at its current pinnacle of political power within the Democrat Party, the socialist Left's influence is likely to increase in the near term. In his 2018 book, *Where We Go from Here: Two Years in the Resistance*, Bernie Sanders wrote: "All over the world, traditional left parties are in rapid decline. Facing major crises, these parties have not responded effectively. The old political leadership and their ideas have grown stale and have alienated working-class and young people who have historically supported them."[25] The parallel of this sentiment to the 1960s' new Left's rhetoric is striking. Today, the socialist Left is straining against the constraints of both the Democrat Party and the traditional Left establishment—just as the new Left did against the old Left it faced.

This is leading to the sacrifice of the middle. The excising of those less-extreme members of the Democrat Party is obvious. However, this is not just a political phenomenon. It will occur within any group the socialist Left infiltrates. As it starts to happen within the traditional Left, the socialist Left will continue to gain greater access within American society more broadly. The socialist Left will rise in proportional strength within these organizations—unions, social action groups, and political action committees (PACs)—that comprise the traditional Left and support the Democrat Party.

This is unquestionably an immediate opportunity for the socialist Left, who will be able to advance under the guise of traditional Left organizations—environmental groups, civil rights groups, unions—that they could never have successfully formed under their own aegis, promoting policies they could never have successfully pursued under their own name. This will gradually result in these groups' increasing radicalization by the socialist Left (just as the traditional Left pushed the broader Democrat Party further to the left). Because the socialist Left aims for a truly revolutionary restructuring of American society—it does not wish to simply add new programs. Ultimately, this will result in an abandonment of the infiltrated groups by many of those who refuse to go along with this radicalization.

The sacrifice of the middle is a long-term curse for whatever hosts the socialist Left. The longer the socialist Left remains in any group it infects, the more it will drive away or silence those who oppose it. Its minority status makes it an aggressor to all who refuse to accept its leadership, and it therefore thrives on the division of its opponents. Therefore, revolution is not simply a tactic (as when the McGovernites drove elements of the New Deal coalition out of the Democrat delegations at the 1972 presidential convention) of the socialist Left; it is a way of life. It is the socialist Left's reason for being, the result of its ideology.

This ideology cannot be turned on and off; it is who the socialist Left is, even when its results clearly weaken its coalition. To see it, look no further than the current fracturing of the traditional Left and the Democrat Party over Israel's right to defend itself, and even exist, as the socialist Left leads rallies ostensibly in support of Palestine, but with ends clearly helpful to Hamas. Such a rally took place in New York City, just a day after Hamas' October 7, 2023, terrorist attack on Israel. The rally was organized by the Democratic Socialists of America's (DSA) New York chapter, which has also sometimes been the party of Rep. Alexandria Ocasio-Cortez (D-NY) and Rep. Jamaal Bowman (D-NY), both members of the Squad.[26]

While this is a recent example (as of this book's writing), it is hardly the only one. Democrats have long posed as champions of the working class, but the cost of the socialist Left's radical environmental agenda (to name just one issue) penalizes America's working class the most—in higher costs and lost jobs. The women's movement, long a mainstay of the traditional Left, sees women's rights being jeopardized by the socialist Left's radical transgender policies. At the same time, urban minorities who have long voted overwhelmingly Democrat, and are the purported beneficiaries of countless policies of the traditional Left, are now victims of the socialist Left's Defund the Police agenda.

Because the socialist Left is composed of ideologues and historically accustomed to minority status, it is quite willing to sacrifice the Biden presidency, the Democrat Party, and the traditional Left to its agenda's advancement. From its perspective, it is playing with "house money," its winnings from "drawing to an inside straight" in America's game of political poker and winning the biggest jackpot it has ever seen.

To appreciate how far the socialist Left has penetrated into the Democrat Party, imagine how previous Democratic presidents would have fared in 2020's race. Would Jimmy Carter or Bill Clinton—and perhaps even Barack Obama—espousing the political stances that won them their presidencies have had a chance? To understand its penetration into the traditional Left, ask who has been the most prominent leader on civil rights over the last several years: the NAACP or Black Lives Matter? The damage the socialist Left is doing to the traditional Left and the Democrat Party they control is as clear as is the damage it is doing to America *through* its traditional Left and Democrat hosts.

While this evisceration of traditional Left groups and the Democrat Party through the sacrifice of the middle is a great opportunity for the socialist Left, it is an even greater one for conservatives. The socialist Left's purge of moderates from the traditional Left offers conservatives the greatest opportunity since Reagan: to not simply defeat the socialist Left, but to return the traditional Left to the exile from national politics that they endured for four decades.

Whatever is in store for the future, the socialist Left is not going away quickly or quietly. As the remainder of this book will show, what seems like an explosion is due to the confluence of the long-term factor of enormous federal government growth (and the resources that provides), and the short-term factor of ideal political circumstances. Combined, these have given the socialist Left unprecedented access within this enlarged government. The former is the powder keg, the latter the fuse; the socialist Left is determined that, once ignited, its explosion will not subside.

What we are left with is a question: how do we combat a virulent parasite that devours its host? Once in, how is it removed? The best way to understand how to defeat the socialist Left is to look back at the successful model that kept it out for so long: America. The principles on which this country was founded and the structure those principles erected are blueprints. Their effectiveness also explains why the socialist Left is so insistent on expunging them from our history—and even more from current practice. Chapter Three will begin the explanation of how these principles and their structures came to be and how they so effectively functioned.

CHAPTER THREE

THE ORIGINS OF AMERICAN EXCEPTIONALISM

SECTION I
Introduction

America's history, predating even its formal founding, shows how antithetical the socialist Left is to our country's prevailing ideals. It is the fact of American exceptionalism that, until now, has shut the socialist Left out of having any significant impact in America. This is also why the socialist Left is so intent on denying that exceptionalism. The logic is simple: if the socialist Left is to play a meaningful role in America, as it does in other countries, it must make America like other countries. The first steps are to deny, and then rewrite, the very history which proves America's exceptionalism.

Not only does the socialist Left understand itself and its weaknesses extremely well, but it also understands (far better, it can be posited, than the American mainstream does) how the very founding of America created the strengths that have held it at bay. For the socialist Left to force itself onto America now, it must overturn America's institutions, and to do that, it must first overturn America's past. If the socialist Left is to be defeated, America must understand its past, how exceptional it truly is, and the importance of what this exceptionalism has wrought.

America's exceptionalism existed before its birth as an independent country.

In the late 17th century, America's first English colonists were living with an amalgamation of important circumstances that together made them unique. To name the most important: English government tradition, their New World location (which provided separation from their mother country), a middle-class population, and their capitalist economy. These circumstances, especially as an amalgamation, would make the colonists adept at, and pre-disposed to, self-government and later independence. When crises arose with their mother country, they were inherently prepared—politically and economically—to take matters into their own hands.

Primary among the American colonies' special attributes was the fact that they were *English* colonies. The government tradition from which they arose was centuries old and uniquely rich. With the English Bill of Rights ratified in 1689, pronounced limits were set on their hereditary monarch's power, expanding on what had been developing for over four centuries. England had a robust representative legislative body that made laws and controlled the crucial ability to tax. And there was a thorough and meaningful judicial system. All these components had been honed by sustained practice and solid theoretical justifications into a well-functioning system that was institutionally unto itself. Thus, as English subjects, the colonists transported this rich government legacy and system to America. The institutions they constructed, then, replicated the sophisticated English government system under which they had lived—and saw themselves as still living under—thousands of miles away.

Each of the thirteen colonies existed in one of three forms: As a proprietary colony (essentially land grants from the Crown to individuals, such as Pennsylvania and Maryland), a royal colony (owned and administered by the Crown, such as Rhode Island and Connecticut), or a self-governing colony (charter grants from the Crown to a joint-stock company that operated its own independent governing system—subject to the Crown's ultimate approval, of course—such as Virginia and Massachusetts).[1] Despite these differences, by the time of the American Revolution the colonies' governmental systems all mimicked England's with its executive (royal governors), legislative (representative assemblies), and judicial branches. They were in essence "little Englands," made up of English subjects living under English forms of government. As products of this well-established government, these colonies were expected to function in a manner that agreed with that system—and they did. This made them exceptionally suited for self-government.

As robust as it was, it was not the practice of government alone that fitted America's English colonies for self-rule. A rich body of political theory existed around the English government system and had served as a guide during tumultuous periods when that government system was in upheaval. More important, these theories aided the colonies as they charted their own course, providing extensive literature and ready sources for the colonists' debates. This meant that they neither had to start from scratch nor search far to begin their work. It also gave them ready means to judge the English system—both at home and in the colonies.

At the two ends of the monarchical question stood the English philosophers Thomas Hobbes and the inestimable John Locke. The former's ideology was the standard American colonists sought to refute, the latter what they sought to attain. Put simply, Hobbes's core principles were top-down, while Locke's were bottom-up: Hobbes saw government centered on the monarch's right to govern; Locke saw government centered on the people's consent. Of course, Locke prevailed to the point that the philosopher Isaiah Berlin called him "the father of the central philosophical and political tradition of the Western world, especially in America ... "[2]

Additionally, there were choruses on both sides of the debate over the king's proper power in a government system. As the historian Bernard Bailyn points out, the influence of the Whig press, both in England and the colonies, is often overlooked today. The Whigs[3] were forever suspicious against any encroachment of the monarchy on its subjects and the government on its citizens. In the colonies especially, the critiques of England's foibles and failings that the Whigs posited were made all the clearer by the colonists' physical distance from them. These ideas were also echoed and expanded upon in a vibrant colonial press.

That isolation of the American colonies from England—and even from each other, given the difficulty of travel internally—reinforced their inherent inclination to a large degree of self-government. The colonies were three thousand miles away from Great Britain, separated by an ocean that could be treacherous even in good weather. A round trip, between request for and response to instruction, could take months—not including the time it took for a decision to be reached at either end. Even communication between the colonies was daunting, which aided the development of governments within the colonies, requiring each to be relatively self-sufficient. The advantage this establishment of thirteen separate government systems gave the colonies was that it expanded participation. Each colony brought their own colonists into the governing and public process. When the time for declaring independence came, the colonies had all been "practicing" self-government to a great degree and involving a relatively large number of their citizens in the process. The economist Adam Smith, writing at the time of the American Revolution attested to it: "The government of the English Colonies is perhaps the only one which, since the world began, could give perfect security to the inhabitants of so very distant a province."[4]

The immensity of England's colonies in America also offered another advantage to the colonists: land. In this regard, physical immensity equaled political opportunity. The thirteen American colonies encompassed 430,000 square miles and stretched over 1,000 miles of coastline. In contrast, England measures just 50,000; the whole United Kingdom today measures just 95,000 square miles. The colonies were also vastly less populated than England. In 1700, the colonial population was just 250,000; in contrast, England, Wales, and Scotland had about 6.5 million people—600,000 in London alone.[5]

This was important because political participation in the English system was restricted to "free men," a status closely linked to owning land. Meeting this qualification was extremely difficult in England, but comparatively simple in its American colonies. Indentured servitude was extremely common in the American colonies because of the need for laborers to work—and because land was so plentiful, even indentured servants could reasonably expect to be landholders themselves once their indentures ended.

This meant that over time, America's colonial government grew to be far more representative of the actual population, more accurately reflecting the average colonist's thoughts. This made them far more invested in their own colonial government, and far more versed in government participation too. They not only voted in far greater percentages than their English counterparts, but a far greater proportion of them served in government. Americans, then, were more citizens than subjects. It is one thing to have rights (as did males in England); it was another to habitually exercise them. For American colonists, their government was not remote—they *were* the government.

The colonies' rich political legacy and opportunity combined with an auspicious economic one. One would influence the other, taking each to places neither had been before—ones that no other country had replicated so seemingly effortlessly or effectively. First, the colonies were *founded* with an eye on economics, and thus were born of mercantilism. They existed to a large degree to make money for those involved. Even religious refugees like the Pilgrims came to make a worldly success, even as they pursued a godly one. John Locke's assertion that government was instituted to protect property was not just political theory in America; it was personal aspiration and expectation.

Mercantilism erroneously saw economic relations between countries as a zero-sum affair: the country with the biggest positive balance of trade was the winner. As a result, English colonies (in America and worldwide) were expected to make money for the mother country, to provide cheap raw materials that the home country lacked, as well as lucrative markets for the home country's finished products—thereby improving England's balance-of-payments ledger. In America, when England's mercantilist demands constrained the colonies' pursuit of prosperity, there was an immediate resistance as the two parties' expectations collided.

The early years of the American colonies also coincided with the flowering of *laissez faire* capitalism. It is worth noting that Adam Smith, the economist most associated with capitalism, published his seminal work, *The Wealth of Nations*, in March 1776—just four months before the signing of the Declaration of Independence. Yet, as influential as Adam Smith is taken to be, capitalism did not spring fully formed from Smith's head, as did Athena from Zeus's. Rather, in addition to being prophet and proselytizer, Smith was foremost a shrewd observer, describing a new economic development already occurring. It was taking root, especially in England, at the same time as the colonies were taking off. The capitalism that was straining against pre-existing barriers in England found far fewer limitations in England's American colonies.

The colonies' rapid growth underscored the success of all of these factors found in America. While, as previously noted, the colonies were far smaller in population than England, their numbers were growing with startling rapidity, expanding tenfold to 2.7 million from 1700 to 1780.[6] This rapid growth owed to the fact that America's isolation from England meant it was also isolated from England's (and Europe's) upheavals over the 17th century. The American colonies escaped the cataclysmic period between the English Civil War and the Glorious Revolution. Undoubtedly, the colonists did not regret it. While

England was convulsed, at home and abroad, her American colonies were comparatively untouched.

Under the impetus of all these fortuitous advantages—one the colonists themselves would have called "providential"—it is unsurprising that England's American colonies became to England what England was to the rest of the world.

SECTION II
Mayflower Compact

It cannot be stated enough that Americans were exceptional even before they set foot on America's shores. This is no oxymoron—despite the colonists not yet seeing themselves as American but transplanted Englishmen first—since it was their English heritage that planted the seeds of what would grow rapidly into American exceptionalism. No document is better evidence of this than what has long been known as the Mayflower Compact.

After two aborted attempts to cross, and then over two months of sailing in heavy seas, the one-hundred-and two English passengers and crew of the Mayflower finally saw land in early November of 1620. Unfortunately for them, the land they saw was hundreds of miles from the land they had hoped to see near the mouth of the Hudson River. Having already survived numerous crises on their voyage, they now faced a new one within their ship.

The colonists' patent for their "particular plantation," or settlement, was from the Virginia Company of London. The Mayflower Pilgrims had crossed the ocean on a charter grant for a specific place in a vast new world. Yet the land they spied from Provincetown Harbor was not in their intended location, but in in the Council for New England's jurisdiction. This meant their patent from the Virginia Company was no longer valid.[7] In addition to the Pilgrims onboard, there were also passengers hired by the London merchants bankrolling the Pilgrims' endeavor, there to provide essential assistance to the new colony. This "hired help," whom the Pilgrims called "strangers," now no longer felt themselves bound by their original agreement and stated by "discontented and mutinous speeches ... that when they came ashore they would use their own liberty; for none had power to command them, the patent they had being for Virginia and not for New England, which belonged to another government … "[8] With winter fast approaching and exhausted from their voyage, if the Pilgrims wanted to make a landing, a new document was necessary to replace their now invalidated authority.

Just two hundred words long, what would only years later be dubbed the Mayflower Compact addressed the immediate question as to how those onboard would order themselves once ashore. The document underscores the Pilgrims' intent for their settlement, mentioning God four times and faith twice. Yet as they were acutely made aware by the "strangers'" objections, they also had to make it a consensus document for governing the group. To that point, the Mayflower Compact's core is:

> We … in the presence of God, and one of another, covenant and combine our selves together into a civil body politic, for our bettering ordering and preservation and furtherance of the ends aforesaid, and by virtue hereof to enact, constitute, and frame such just and equal laws, ordinances, acts, constitutions and offices, from time to time, as shall be thought most meet and convenient for the general good of the Colony, unto which we promise all due submission and obedience.

Almost all the Mayflower's males, forty-one in all, signed the short document. Six months later, only twenty were still alive, but this small group constituted the freemen who would govern the colony, largely following the Compact's plan. They elected their governor William Bradford (then reelected thirty-one times), a secretary, and a few other positions. As the historian Samuel Eliot Morison wrote:

> They also met at least once a year in a general court or assembly, which passed laws, acted as a supreme judicial court, and, after the colony had begun to spread out, set up a representative system. In 1636, the general court adopted a body of laws called the 'general fundamentals,' which included a bill of rights. But the Compact seems to have been at the bottom of everything; we have evidence from the records that it used to be read aloud when the assembly met.[9]

Over time, the Compact would take on an almost mythological status in American history and Morison correctly raises "the question of the Compact's influence outside Plymouth." Yet how the Compact should be viewed as historical progenitor is really beside the point. For our purposes, the Compact's real importance is as a testament to how the colonists saw themselves and their role. It speaks with undiminished eloquence four centuries later of their immediate intention and ability for self-government within the parameters of English tradition. Morison quotes Bradford about the Compact's origins: "[it] might be as firm as any patent, and in some respects more sure."[10] In other words, far from reducing their governmental authority, the Compact's signers saw their own action as increasing it.

The Compact succinctly underscores the uniqueness of the American experience from its earliest origins. As English Americans, the Mayflower Pilgrims combined unique characteristics and circumstances. Their experience was imbued with the influence of an English government and legal tradition that was unequalled—a point that the Constitution's drafters still recognized even after their break from Britain. This tradition was transported to a vast expanse that was without a pre-existing government or social structure that the colonizers or the colonists recognized. This unimaginably vast expanse was also extremely remote, with no possibility of timely contact with England. Those who ventured to this vast remoteness formed a truncated version of English society—one without either aristocracy or poverty (at least for very long). Finally, the colonies were planted in a virtual economic nursery; they were mercantilist endeavors, but at a time when the *laissez faire* approach of capitalism was flowering.

SECTION III
Magna Carta

By the time the Mayflower Compact was written, the English political system from which it sprung was already four centuries old—the same distance in time to the Pilgrims as their Compact is to us. That system was one rich in both the

governments consisted of a governor, or deputy or lieutenant governor in the case of proprietary colonies or when a vacancy existed, an upper house, and a lower house."[19]

Governors were appointed by either the king (except in Connecticut and Rhode Island, where they were elected by the colonies' freemen) or, if a proprietary colony, by the proprietor (dependent on the Crown's agreement).[20] Colonial legislatures were bicameral (except in unicameral Pennsylvania). Upper houses were generally comprised of royal appointees who had been recommended by the colony's governor; the exceptions were again Connecticut and Rhode Island, where freemen elected them, and Massachusetts, where the lower house elected them. The colonies' lower houses were elected by freemen.

Two things stand starkly out in the colonial governments. One is that the colonies were indeed "little Englands," governed in strict parallel to the English government system, which also underscores the colonists' expectation of English rights—which themselves originated well before the English Bill of Rights. Also important is the high level of consent by those governed —higher, even, than in England itself. Not only were the lower houses elected by the people, but so too governors in two colonies and the upper house in three (or by the people's lower-house representatives in the case of Massachusetts).

Just how jealously the colonists guarded their rights as Englishmen is described by Samuel Eliot Morison: "They objected to the governor's instructions from the crown being considered mandatory. If the governor was energetic and conscientious, these instructions involved him in a row with the assembly, which naturally did not think it compatible with the liberty of British subjects that they should inflexibly obey directions from England."[21]

Morison describes a similar conflict over the appointment of judges. The fight was over their tenure, whether it should extend "during good behavior" or "during the king's pleasure." The former prevailed in England while the latter did in the colonies. Then, the death of King George II in 1760 voided all royal commissions and required new ones from King George III. In an effort to assert their rights as Englishmen, the colonies sought the "good behavior" condition, too, and throughout the colonies judges refused to accept appointments except under this proviso. The Crown, however, refused to *make* appointments except for "during the king's pleasure." As Morison states, "in one colony after another, except North Carolina, which preferred to go without courts for several years rather than submit, the crown won this controversy, and in so doing caused a resentment which is expressed in the Declaration of Independence."[22]

And again, the colonists not only held tight to their rights as Englishmen, they had a much greater exercise of them in voting. As Rabushka asserts: "Eligibility to vote in the colonies far exceeded [that] in Great Britain. No more than one in twelve adult males were eligible to vote in Britain during the 18th century … Much broader land ownership in the colonies enabled half or more of the adult male population to meet voter requirements, proportionally six times higher than the eligibility rate in Britain."[23]

On the threshold of revolution, the colonists were insisting that the colonies were thirteen "little Englands," while they, themselves were fully Englishmen. As Morison sums up, with the exception of "foreign affairs, war and peace, and overseas trade," by 1763, "Americans had acquired home rule."[24] They had in fact realized more of the promise of the English Bill of Rights, and at virtually no cost, than their counterparts in England itself.

SECTION VI
Political Thought

The English Civil War no less shaped political thought than it had shaped political practice. As touched upon briefly, Thomas Hobbes and John Locke demarcated England's theoretical spectrum. Written in 1651, Hobbes's *Leviathan* was a product of the Civil War from which it emerged. In contrast, *The Second Treatise on Government* by Locke gave voice to the new order under the English Bill of Rights when it appeared in 1689. That the American colonists so completely chose Locke as their philosophical lodestar indicates their perception of government and society. The threats that they feared the most were not the ruin and rapine of civil war, as Hobbes had; instead, they shared Locke's fear of an autocratic executive who denied their fundamental rights.

Hobbes became the philosophical whipping boy for the colonists who opposed what they saw as English government overreach, although as Bernard Bailyn points out, he was also viewed as an "[opponent] of Enlightenment rationalism" and was "denounced as frequently by loyalists as by patriots … "[25]

It is unsurprising that Hobbes's view of government would find little resonance in the American colonies who had avoided the horrific carnage of the English Civil War. Despite having landed into what they might call a state of nature in America, Hobbes's view of the "state of nature"—human existence prior to the institution of government—was utterly foreign to them: "Whatsoever therefore is consequent to a time of Warre, where every man is Enemy to every man; the same is consequent to the time wherein men live without other security, than what their own strength, and their own invention shall furnish them … And which is worst of all, continuall feare, and danger of violent death; And the life of man, solitary, poore, nasty, brutish, and short."[26]

To avoid this chaos, Hobbes theorizes that people are willing to lay down liberty to a sovereign who will protect them, as C.B. MacPherson states in his commentary on *Leviathan*[27] Hobbes sums up the civil compact: "being thereby bound by Covenant … therefore, they that are subjects to a Monarch cannot without his leave cast off Monarchy, and return to the confusion of a disunited multitude; nor transferre their Person from him that beareth it, to another Man or other Assembly of men … "[28] In other words, subjects could not simply unilaterally sever the compact with their ruler.

For the American colonists, this was too stiff, and deemed to be a wholly unnecessary price to pay. They vastly preferred Locke's governmental view— the complete opposite of Hobbes's. Truthfully, it would be hard to overestimate Locke's contribution to the American colonies' political thought or to America's eventual foundation. Bailyn writes: "In pamphlet after pamphlet, the American writers cited Locke on natural rights and on the social and governmental contract … "[29] Regarding Locke's enormous influence, Thomas Peardon, Professor of Political Science at Barnard College, in his introduction to *The Second Treatise*, states: "But it was in America that Locke met with the most resounding response. Early in the 18th century his books were being circulated in the colonies, while many Americans learned about them at British universities."[30] Instead of Hobbes's Civil War pessimism, Locke embodies Glorious Revolution optimism. Locke views the state of nature as peaceful compared to Hobbes's chaos. He therefore views government's role as bettering the positive rather than ameliorating the negative. Locke literally spoke to the American colonies' condition: "Thus in the beginning all the world was America … "[31]

Rather than relinquishing freedom, "the end of law is not to abolish or restrain but to preserve and enlarge freedom ... "[32]

For Locke, consent of the governed was requisite to government's legitimacy. "Men being ... by nature all free, equal, and independent," he stated in *Second Treatise*, "no one can be put out of this estate and subjected to the political power of another without his own consent."[33] And this consent is given for only one reason: "[O]nly with an intention in every one the better to preserve himself, his liberty and property—for no rational creature can be supposed to change his condition with an intention to be worse ... " The end of government was therefore clear: "to be directed to no other end but the peace, safety, and public good of the people."[34]

Finally, "legislative power" was at the center of Locke's government system. "[T]he first and fundamental positive law of all commonwealths is the establishing of the legislative power ... "[35] It must also be foremost: "In all cases, while the government subsists, the legislative is the supreme power; for what can give laws to another must needs be superior to him ... the legislative must needs be the supreme, and all other powers in any members or parts of the society derived from and subordinate to it."[36]

Locke's governmental view appealed to the American colonists on several levels. First, he spoke to the American condition. His view of the state of nature resembled theirs, which had not been jaundiced by the English Civil War's horrors and chaos. Second, Locke's view that government existed to preserve property resonated with the widespread access to property holding that existed in the American colonies. Equally significantly, Locke took a very expansive view of "property"—considerably broader than simply possessions. "By property I must be understood here, as in other places, to mean that property which men have in their persons as well as goods." This was extremely important for the American colonists; such a broad interpretation of "property" could be found in the English Bill of Rights and would be even more defined in the American Constitution. (Locke's expansive view of property is also a significant point for our examination of the socialist Left's current undermining of America's foundation, because its attack on property writ large is one of its assault's most subversive elements.)

Third, Locke's requirement for the consent of the governed was crucial to the American colonists. In general, consent functions as a block against arbitrary rule, but in the American colonies' case it was even more so, in both theory and practice. Consent could *only* come from the legislative branch, the means by which American colonists participated in their colonial government system (and central to Locke's ideal, too). In other words, consent was not just a theoretical political safeguard, it was practical and personal in the colonies.

Bailyn points out two other important sources of English political thought that influenced the American colonies. One was " ... the writings of a group of prolific opposition theorists, 'country' politicians and publicists [who,] more than any other single group of writers ... shaped the mind of the American Revolutionary generation."[37] The other was the Whig opposition to Walpole's administration in Parliament.[38] Together, in the words of Bailyn, these "decried the corruption of the age and warned of the dangers of incipient autocracy."[39] And if they were just a spark in England, they were a wildfire in the American colonies: "Opposition thought, in the form it acquired at the turn of the 17th century and in the early 18th century, was devoured by the colonists."[40]

As Bailyn asserts, these writers were not original, but they were strident and insistent. So, while their concepts of natural rights, of society and government's contractual bases, and of England's "mixed constitution" were ordinary, their emphasis of them was extraordinary. They "studied the processes of decay, and dwelt endlessly on the evidences of corruption they saw about them and the dark future these malignant signs portended."[41]

These laments were captured by the English poet Oliver Goldsmith. In *The Deserted Village*, Goldsmith mourns the passing of the English countryside and its simple sturdy virtues at the hands of decadent wealth. Goldsmith opens by describing the bucolic idyll that once was England's countryside:

Sweet Auburn! Loveliest village of the plain,

Where health and plenty cheered the laboring swain ... [42]

But he quickly moves to the fact that this countryside no longer exists, "and desolation saddens all thy green":

Ill fares the land, to hastening ills a prey,

Where wealth accumulates and men decay ... [43]

When he writes "far, far away, thy children leave the land," American colonials would have known to where they had fled. Like Locke, these "country" and opposition politicians spoke to the American colonists. The colonies *were* the transported English countryside; what was being lost in the mother country was being recreated in her offspring. Thus, the American colonists saw themselves as the repository of the ancient virtues that England was now not just losing but threatening to extirpate.

The colonists knew that they were seen as inferior to Englishmen in so many obvious ways—as the song *Yankee Doodle* popularly and derisively attested—but they took heart in the self-flattering belief that they were superior in the traits to which England ultimately owed her superiority—the "ancient" ones that truly mattered. As for the unoriginality of the key concepts—natural rights, the contractual basis of society and government, the uniqueness of England's liberty-preserving "mixed constitution"—these were even more important to the American colonists. In the colonies, these were not just theoretical barriers, but practical ones to England's encroachment on their government. While these assurances of English rights may have meant less for the majority of the population in England itself—many of whom lacked property and the voting eligibility it granted—they were crucial in the American colonies where these were much more broadly enjoyed and universally aspired to.

Essentially, as the English saw themselves in relation to the rest of the world—uniquely free by virtue of age-old rights (the English Bill of Rights cites the English people as "vindicating and asserting their ancient rights and liberties")—the American colonists saw themselves in relation to England. English political thought further added an intellectual foundation for this sense of apartness that geography and their colonial governments fostered.

SECTION VII
Economics and the American Colonies

The American colonies were no less exceptional in their economic circumstances than in their political ones. Creating wealth was at the heart of their origins and remained in the soul of their being. This is not meant to diminish the religious roots that also existed, but to underscore that even in these, they were expected to make of themselves a worldly success as well as a godly one. This economic consideration is evident even in the charter of the Mayflower's primary passengers: their overtly religious venture was after all bankrolled by English investors.

When it came to the colonies, there were basic economic considerations. Simply, the Crown wanted to make money from the colonies and the colonists wanted to make money in the colonies. That the latter were far more successful than the former was just another reason for the rising friction and the eventual rupture between the two.

SECTION VIII
Economic Thought

The American colonies were born in the heart of, and arguably owed their very existence to, what economists call the Mercantilist Period. Defining mercantilism, the economic historian Murray Rothbard explains in his history of economic thought: "'Mercantilism' is the name given by late 19th century historians to the politico-economic system of the absolute state from approximately the 16th to the 18th centuries … [I]t was a comprehensive system of state-building, state privilege, and what might be called 'state-monopoly capitalism.'"[44]

Mercantilism's most prominent feature from an economic standpoint was its myopic focus on trade surpluses. Its adherents were convinced that trade in particular was a zero-sum game, the winner of which was the nation that gained the largest positive balance of trade. To advance this objective, barriers to imports and subsidies for exports were frequently imposed. In England, the Navigation Act of 1651 was "a mercantilist measure for the subsidizing and privileging of English shipping."[45] The law's purpose was to keep trade within the realm: forcing the colonies and mother country to trade with each other and discouraging the trade of both with foreign nations. Another hallmark was its frequent reliance on government-sanctioned trade monopolies; in

England there were many of these, among the most prominent being the East India Company, which was "chartered in 1600 with a monopoly of all trading to the East Indies."[46]

Mercantilism's focus on trade also had a strong influence on foreign policy, with a premium on colonies.[47] Colonies were intended to serve as low-cost suppliers of raw materials and purchasers of finished goods. It was a system of vertical integration on a state-scale—materials and goods purchased from a colony kept money within the nation's trading system and prevented "leakage" of precious bullion. Anything that furthered this integration was fair game.

Naturally, the mercantilist system had a major impact on the American colonies. It unquestionably shaped their relationship with England from their founding to their separation. Less obviously, it influenced their relations with the French Empire too. Jean-Baptiste Colbert (1619-1683) is widely considered the quintessential mercantilist. As First Minister of State to King Louis XIV, "the Sun King," Colbert functioned as a "virtual economic czar"[48] and set his nation on a colonial course that brought France into North American conflict with England and her colonies. Beginning in the late 17th century and extending until 1763, this North American colonial conflict would profoundly shape the American colonies' relationship with both empires.

The more lasting and beneficial influence, economically, on the American colonies was the rise of mercantilism's competing school of economic thought: capitalism. In capitalist theory, the individual entrepreneur is the engine of economic dynamism. Entrepreneurs could be found everywhere in the colonies; they were not bound by class constraints or specific economic sectors (such as land and agriculture, as the economic Physiocrats had once insisted). Virtually all economic contributions were valued and seen to create value, with less regard given to who or where they came from. It was capitalism's guiding ethos of *laissez faire* that unshackled economic activity from the impeding control of state and society. Anyone with a modicum of money could use it as capital, instantly transforming himself into an entrepreneur. As capitalism continued its rise, the two conflicting economic systems would increasingly collide, and nowhere more than in America. As Murray Rothbard writes about Colbert's view: "Trade was war and conflict."[49] Fittingly, in North America, France and England would have both.

It was more than just coincidence that America and Adam Smith's *An*

Inquiry into the Nature and Causes of the Wealth of Nations were each born in 1776. Both were products of the most powerful economic force in human history. Capitalism's rapid and irresistible growth propelled the first and inspired the second. Smith, who mercilessly attacked mercantilism, noted: "Between whatever places foreign trade is carried on, they all of them derive two distinct benefits from it. It carries out the surplus part of the produce of their land and labor for which there is no demand among them, and brings back in return for it something else for which there is a demand."[50] Therefore, any obstacles to this process reduced economic benefits.

Beyond mercantilism's limits on trade's benefits, state intervention in the economy was in general suspect. "No regulation of commerce can increase the quantity of industry in any society beyond what its capital can maintain. It can only divert a part of it into a direction which it might not otherwise have gone; and it is by no means certain that this artificial direction is likely to be more advantageous to the society..."[51]

Left to their own devices, Smith posited that anyone could be a capitalist and would make the best use of his capital for the simple reason that he would "endeavor to employ it in the support of that industry of which the produce is likely to be of the greatest value."[52] Motivated only by his own self-interest, Smith believed the entrepreneur would produce this positive economic benefit unknowingly and even without a desire to do so.[53]

Smith asserted that the state harmed itself when it interfered with this natural economic process. Instead, the government played its best role in the economy when it was limited, operating through, and under, known laws. This limited role was vital to capitalism: Smith's analysis is straightforward and cogent. First, he took on the prevailing mercantilist system, and emphasized free trade, instead of mercantilism's state-managed trade. This emphasis on freedom permeated capitalism's general approach regarding the state's optimal role in its economy, giving the most important role in the economy to the individual, unencumbered capitalist. Allowing this free play of entrepreneurs yielded the optimal economic outcome, even though it was unknown to the entrepreneurs, nor even consciously desired. The economy and the government had to work hand in hand, however, and they worked best when the economy was free, and the government's involvement limited.

Despite the common tendency to link Smith to the rise of capitalism, especially among conservatives, the former did not create the latter. Economics is the study of real circumstances, and such was the case for Smith, who was an early and wildly successful examiner of forces that were already sweeping Britain. Rather than creating capitalism, Smith was a keen observer who noticed what was happening around him. This does not diminish his impact, but rather validates it. Smith gave voice to a system already ascending in practice; by analyzing early capitalism's rapid emergence, he called attention to its importance.

Nowhere was capitalism's impact more obvious and surging than in the American colonies. Smith specifically, repeatedly, and favorably mentions the colonies in *Wealth of Nations. "In every thing, except their foreign trade, the liberty of the English colonists to manage their own affairs their own way is complete. It is in every respect equal to that of their fellow-citizens at home ...* "[54] He noted that "there is more equality, therefore, between the English colonists than among the inhabitants of the mother country."[55]

It helped that in America, capitalism was largely unencumbered from the governmental and societal forces that still constrained it in Britain. Capitalism's *laissez faire* theory was perfectly suited to the American colonies' circumstances. Capitalism promoted entrepreneurs, and the colonies were essentially populated entirely by them, or those who aspired to be one of them. And there were countless ways to become an entrepreneur in the colonies. As already noted, there was no real landed aristocracy to impede land purchase, nor were there any meaningful quit-rent payments.[56] Together this afforded colonists increased land availability *and* profitability in comparison with England. The result was that as soon as colonists had money, they had land or entry as a small business owner into whatever occupation their talents directed them.

What there was a shortage of was labor, which manifested itself in innumerable ways. What resulted, as historian Richard Hofstadter has shown, was the rise of a middle-class American empire. "In the colonies goodly numbers of those starting life below the middle class not only shared its aspirations but had a significant chance to realize them within a lifetime. And in this America was supreme."[57] Perhaps most interestingly, despite capitalism's rapid development and enrichment of many, the American colonies' mores remained middle class. "Hence the philosophy, the political values, the moral commitments of the townspeople, even into the upper ranks, remained middle class."[58]

As the colonists were gaining wealth, the colonies themselves also flourished economically—in just seventy-odd years from 1700 to the mid-1770s, their "gross product" was around $25 million annually, nearly one-third the figure of the mother country (where it had been a trifling 4 percent of Britain's gross product in 1700).[59] Yes, the population grew enormously and rapidly, but according to Professor Edwin Perkins of the University of Southern California in his study of the colonial economy, non-population factors accounted for almost 25 percent of the colonies' economic growth in the 18th century.[60] Further, population growth had historically resulted in a *decrease* in per capita resources. Not so in the colonies. As Perkins observes, "Despite the rapid rise in population, the typical colonial household was able to maintain its already very high material standard of living and even made some improvements … Indeed, food surpluses were so great in the late colonial period that overseas exports of wheat and rice were roughly on a par with the great southern staple—tobacco."[61]

The colonial living standards that Perkins references were also unequaled. According to his book *The Economy of Colonial America*, "the material standard of living enjoyed by the typical white family unit in the thirteen mainland colonies was almost certainly the highest in the world by the 1770s."[62] This in turn led to a high level of health that "was unrivaled in the 18th century if measured on the basis of low infant mortality and adult death rates."[63] Those high living standards also extended to those without land who worked in cities.[64] This was important; it meant that those arriving in the colonies could effectively start with nothing but their labor and still build capital to move upward. This upward mobility is precisely what occurred in the colonies as children married and bought farms of their own.[65]

While capitalism grew in the colonies, the mercantilist approach still prevailed in the English government. This was antithetical to the colonies' interests. It trapped them on either side, limiting both the markets in which they could sell and in which they could buy. In between, they encountered monopolies. All were due to the English government, and all hurt them financially. The colonies may have been borne on an English mercantilist tradition, yet it was rising capitalism that propelled them to leapfrog over its limitations. Once the colonies were self-sustaining, the collision of economic ideologies drove their departure to independence. It is impossible to see how in the absence of England's demands that the colonies would have separated from the mother country if simply allowed to remain in a condition of effective home rule. For evidence of this one need look no further than the reluctance with which the colonies separated even after suffering what they considered to be unendurable demands for a prolonged period of conflict—including a year of open warfare with England.

What set the colonies on the road to self-sustainment in an incredibly short period of time was the unimpeded growth of capitalism within the English government system as put into practice in America. Far more than in England itself, the driver of unparalleled economic prosperity in America was capitalism. There were virtually no barriers to it and the colonies bridled at any that England tried to implement. Evidence of capitalism's magic was everywhere in America. Its population exploded, far surpassing even England's rapid increase. That population was immediately swept into capitalism's development as small entrepreneurs who rapidly prospered. The result was that the American colonies' standard of living and economic growth were unequaled. By any measure, the colonies were an economic miracle for the period.

SECTION IX
Conclusion

Crisis shaped the colonies' political development, even when it did not directly occur there. Four centuries before them, the conflict between King John and his barons yielded the Magna Carta that formed the foundation from which the unique English government system grew and was transplanted to America. Over four centuries later, the cataclysmic English Civil War brought forth the English Bill of Rights that codified the constitutional monarchy. This further advanced the English government system and, most important for our purposes, the colonial governments relative to England's government.

The English Civil War irrevocably changed Britain; it also changed the American colonies, which disproportionately benefited without significantly suffering. Politically, it enhanced the American colonies' self-government, bolstering it in practice and justifying it (at least in the colonists' minds) in theory.

Opportunity shaped the colonies' economic development first at the macro level, in the form of England's mercantilist approach, through which the colonies were founded. Mercantilism also guaranteed England's continued attention to the colonies' well-being in their formative and vulnerable beginnings. Second, opportunity came at the micro level to individual colonists in the form of capitalism, of which England was the most advanced practitioner. This was the reason for the colonies' unrivaled success and growth—and most important for our examination, it drove the colonists and became embedded in them and everything they did.

These unique political and economic factors were applied to a vast, comparatively peaceful, environment at a remote distance from the mother country. Any one of these elements of America's origins would have made it unusual; all of them combined made our country a veritable black swan. Beyond a *rara avis*, it became the bird hitherto unseen. And this was only the beginning of its uncharted course. Thus, even before America was America—the United States of America, that is—it was exceptional. It was not America that produced its exceptionalism—though it would certainly continue to expand on it—but exceptionalism that produced America.

CHAPTER FOUR

CAPITALISM, REPUBLICANISM, AND CONSTITUTION

SECTION I
Introduction

It's been made clear that the political and economic circumstances under which Britain's American colonies existed made them inherently exceptional—and this is what pushed them into conflict with, and ultimately independence from, their mother country.[1] Economically, a mercantilist mindset brought Britain and France into greater conflict for North America. After Britain's victory, mercantilism goaded the mother country to begin demanding that her now secured colonies provide a return for her substantial investment on their behalf—demands that were, to the colonies, an unnecessary expense on their burgeoning capitalist economies. Politically, the conflict between Britain and France changed the relationship between Britain and her American colonies. In war's aftermath, the American colonies expected their previous status quo—which had essentially been home-rule—to return. Britain, however, saw the opportunity to integrate her colonies more fully and profitably into her empire. The new conflict would be one of home-rule (America) versus rule from home (Britain).

93

Today, we distill the conflict between the American colonies and Britain down to one over taxation. Unquestionably this *was* a central issue. Yet the conflict was deeper and more nuanced, going well beyond just a quantitative question of *how much* the colonies should be taxed, to a qualitative one over *how* they should be taxed, and specifically, by *whom*. Did this right to tax lie with Parliament, as it did in Britain? Or did it lie with the colonial legislatures as it had since their inception? Where did the undisputed legislative right to tax reside?

Elemental as taxation is to governance, this dispute naturally grew to the larger one of how and by whom the colonies should be governed. It is not surprising that this debate would lead eventually to armed resistance, then to revolution, and finally to independence. As discussed in the previous chapter, the English philosopher John Locke had observed and the colonists believed, property and its protection lay at the core of government's proper function. A threat to the former led inevitably to a question about the latter.

Writ large, the end of Britain and France's external conflict in North America brought a prolonged period of internal conflict: First, between Britain and her American colonies; then among the newly created states. Though the conflict between the states was certainly in a milder form, it threatened them no less than had the one with Britain. It also raised the same question: how should they be governed? It was a question that would not be resolved until the Constitution's ratification. This unparalleled document would codify the economic and political exceptionalism that had driven the colonies to revolution and independence. It also would give a framework for their successful continuation with a central government of strictly limited powers that left America's citizens and economy largely unfettered.

SECTION II
The Colonial Wars with France

In the late 17th century, Britain's European wars began to extend to North America. Fortunately for Britain, there were relatively few competing European colonies there, and only two of real consequence, colonies of France and Spain. Of these, France was England's primary adversary, colliding in North America after each had pursued and built their empires. The result was a succession of intermittent conflicts that raged roughly seven decades, from 1689 to 1763. Significantly, this meant that the colonists who would determine America's destiny had no memory of a prolonged period in which the colonies had not been threatened.

North America's conflicts were no less ferocious despite the lack of countries or combatants involved. Historian Howard Peckham, in his history of these colonial wars, notes that these conflicts occurred "on the fringes of settlement" in the wilderness. "[U]nder these different circumstances and from the lack of professional armies," he writes, "the body of rules generally accepted in Europe was largely ignored. Although discipline was more slack, warfare was more cruel."[2] Accounts of these battles bear a resemblance to Hobbes's "nasty and brutish" state of nature. This gave these wars a visceral quality for the colonial Americans; it also sharpened their view of the lack of support they frequently felt from the British government.

In Europe, wars were marked by the formalities of the period—declarations of war, truces, and treaties. Not so in North America. Many engagements took place outside formally declared wars, including several in which George Washington featured prominently. In Britain's American colonies, these wars were known as King William's War (1689 to 1697), Queen Anne's War (1702 to 1713), King George's War (1744 to 1748), and the French and Indian War (1756 to 1763). As Peckham points out, because Europe's wars had not reached North America, Britain's American colonists had no "education in arms. No military tradition took root in the colonies."[3] Therefore, when war did come, the colonies felt particularly dependent on the mother country. However, as early as King William's War, England's American colonies learned two things: a mistrust of how much—or how little—Britain would help in conflicts and "that the only way to achieve permanent peace was to push the French off the continent."[4]

The colonies found themselves left far too often to their own defense. While certainly not to their liking, this reinforced their reliance on self-government: to it they added defense. From this grew an increasing cooperation between the individual colonies to compensate for the lack of assistance they received from Britain. Along with the responsibility for their own defense came the necessity of paying for it. During King William's war, the colonies issued paper currency for the first time, which, as Peckham states, "continued during (and perhaps made possible) the successive French and Indian wars."[5]

Britain's choice to leave the colonies to defend themselves underscores the mercantilist aspect of her relationship to them. Peckham writes regarding the aftermath of King William's War: "The Lords of Trade, on whom responsibility for colonial affairs had been thrust, were convinced that the colonies had men and means to drive the French out of Canada … "[6] The mercantilist focus was driven home in the French and Indian War, which itself differed in several important aspects from its predecessors. Peckham writes:

> The previous colonial wars were largely echoes of European conflicts which had started first. Now in the final struggle for empire, hostilities began in America and spread slowly to the home countries. What made this war even more significant was the viewpoint of William Pitt, who came to have the management of it as secretary of state. He held the new and strange conviction that France could be best reduced in power and influence by taking away her colonies rather than by trying for the fourth time to defeat her big army at home.[7]

Thus, the French and Indian War was larger, more expensive, and involved a fundamental strategic change. Altogether, this resulted in a concerted British effort in the conflict, and the eventual successful elimination of France in North America, the colonies' greatest security threat. This was something the colonists had desired for three generations, yet once established as a new point of focus, it would prove impossible for the colonies to remove themselves from the British government's attention. For the first time in generations, they had peace … but also very little need for British government. In contrast, England had her great debt and her greatest opportunity to profit from her now seemingly secure American colonies.

SECTION III
From External to Internal Conflict

Though they were victorious, the British government exited the French and Indian War with a massive debt and much larger expectations for her American colonies. Historian Colin Bonwick states:

> In anticipation of a continuing struggle against France and in the
> interest of economic development it was also thought necessary to
> strengthen imperial authority in America. Logic as well as policy
> suggested the desirability of stronger central direction, and the subor-
> dination of local colonial interests to the greater good of the empire as a
> whole. Necessarily, it was assumed, overall command and responsibility
> for formulating general policy would rest with the British government
> in London ... [There was also] widespread horror at the increase of
> the national debt to 130 million pounds, much of which was due in
> British eyes to recent campaigns in America ... [8]

The British government wasted little time in seeking to address its heightened debt and expectations and turned to the American colonies to do so. At the
same time, the colonies were turning away. They had proven to themselves that
they had very little need for Britain's direct involvement—especially its soldiers,
which were both the greatest cost and the most visible evidence of Britain on the
colonies' soil. As noted in the last chapter, Adam Smith observed that Britain's
American colonies effectively had home rule.[9] The only real safety threat to
the American colonists was from American Indians on the frontier—and the
removal of the French had greatly reduced that threat as well. The colonists
participated in their own government to a far greater extent than their British
counterparts and had no standing army to threaten their domestic peace—a
fear British in Europe and North America alike shared.

Even their tax burden was far smaller than that existing in Britain. Rarely
did the colonists' taxes approach even 50 percent of England's.[10] There was
no reason the colonists would want that to change, and there was equally no
way that any intrusion on these extensive advantages would go unnoticed.
The colonies had almost complete freedom, so it also follows that they would
chafe at the point where their freedom was most constrained. When Britain
made her first moves to exert control on trade, this accentuated the colonies'
frustration. Their response was immediate and beyond any expectation of the
British government.

The British government took several actions that the colonies saw as intrusive. It prohibited new settlement west of the Appalachian watershed. Also, and in contrast to how little military assistance had been offered in the earlier colonial wars with France, the British government for the first time permanently stationed twenty battalions in America.[11] Enforcement of the collection of trade duties on colonial imports was strengthened. Colonial issuance of paper money (the means by which they had financed the costs of their earlier defense against the French) was also banned.

Most inflammatory of all was the Stamp Act of 1765. The Stamp Act was designed to offset the cost of colonial defense by means of duties placed on a wide range of items including legal documents and newspapers. Colonial umbrage was twofold. First, they saw this cost as unnecessary (having already proven they could defend themselves against their Indian threat), and second, the means—an internal tax rather than duties levied on imported goods—was viewed as a violation of their assemblies' sole right to tax them. Opposition was universal (only Georgia's stamp distributor was not forced out by year's end) and often violent.[12]

The elements of crisis were now in place—the British government's determination to assert what it saw as its right, and the colonies' determination to protect their rights as exercised by their assemblies. Over the next decade, the particulars of the various conflicts would differ, but the principles remained fundamentally the same. And at the heart of them all was the same question: who had the right to govern the colonies? Each side would reassert its position as the crisis escalated.

The Stamp Act also added one other crucial element to the crisis: coordination between the colonies. Sons of Liberty groups appeared throughout, and a Stamp Act Congress was held in New York with nine colonies sending representatives. Although this gathering only passed a few resolutions and certainly did not exert enough influence to have factored in the Stamp Act's 1766 repeal, it signaled a growing level of coordinated action.[13] Such action had been taken during the colonial wars with the French, but only at the point of the most serious threat to safety and only among the colonies directly threatened. Now coordination was occurring on a more widespread level and in response to a legal, rather than a lethal, danger. These efforts demonstrate the seriousness with which they took the British government's actions and show the colonies' growing self-awareness of their shared condition.

· The Stamp Act's repeal did not end the confrontation between Britain and her American colonies, because neither side abandoned the principle that had driven it to confrontation in the first place. On the same day Parliament repealed the Stamp Act in 1766, it passed a Declaratory Act that "reasserted parliament's right to legislate for the colonies in all cases whatsoever ... "[14] Parliament's prideful Parthian shot left no doubt as to where the colonies stood: "that the said colonies and plantations in America have been, are, and of right ought to be, subordinate unto, and dependent upon the imperial crown and parliament of Great Britain."[15] In turn, the colonists did not budge from their position that only their colonial legislatures could tax them. This made the post-Stamp Act situation more truce than peace. If anything, the colonists' position was hardening. Where earlier they had sought to distinguish between Parliament's right to tax if related to trade and the colonial legislatures' right to tax internally, now, the evolving position was that their legislatures alone—in any circumstance—had the right to tax them.

As each side held to its principles, the confrontation escalated until another blow fell on the colonial legislatures. With the Townshend Acts in 1767, the British government sought new duties on several imported products—glass, paper, printers' colors, and red and white lead—with the most notable being tea. The money raised was used again for defense, but also to pay British government representatives in the colonies. This removed them from dependency on—and no little control by—the colonial legislatures that had formerly paid them.[16]

In 1768, the Massachusetts assembly sent a Circular Letter drafted by Samuel Adams to the other colonial assemblies calling for coordinated action against the British government's intrusion on the colonists' rights under the English constitution: the colonies were not being taxed by their representatives, but instead by Parliament where they were not represented. Britain ordered the Massachusetts governor to direct the assembly to rescind the Circular Letter, and the other colonial governors to dissolve their legislatures if they followed recommendations from Massachusetts. The Massachusetts assembly did not rescind the letter, the colony's governor dissolved the assembly, and British troops arrived in Boston. Other legislatures followed Massachusetts's lead, sent their own circular letters, and ceased the import and consumption of British goods.

In 1770, the British government once more repealed duties, which were largely ineffective anyway, but retained the one on tea. Again, they were holding to their asserted right to tax the colonies. The effect was to focus the colonies' assertion of their right (that they could be taxed only by their legislatures) on a single product. As time passed, additional perceived infringements by the British government were added to the colonies' list of grievances, but tea remained the focal point. More coordinated colonial action also occurred: notably, committees of correspondence organized by colonial towns, then more formal ones established by the colonial legislatures.

On December 16, 1773, the Boston Tea Party broke a stalemate between colonists and the royal governor over the unloading of taxed tea from British ships when colonists boarded the ships, broke open hundreds of chests of tea, and dumped their contents into Boston Harbor. It also lit the fuse to the ultimate conflagration. The British government responded in 1774 with what the colonials termed the "Intolerable Acts," which closed Boston harbor until the destroyed tea was paid for; imposed a Crown-appointed council in place of the one elected by Massachusetts's lower house; permitted trials for royal officials outside Massachusetts; and authorized governors to lodge troops in unoccupied private buildings, without first obtaining a justice's consent. Along with these came three regiments of British soldiers and a military governor for Massachusetts.[17]

The colonial legislatures responded by calling an all-colonies congress, and Virginia's legislature raised the stakes by calling for this congress to meet annually. The resulting First Continental Congress met in Philadelphia from September 5 to October 26; only Georgia failed to send representatives. Ostensibly the most notable achievement of the First Continental Congress was the passing of the Suffolk Resolves, which outlined the colonies' perception of the growing conflict and their proposed responses to it. The *real* accomplishment of the Congress, however, was its escalation and expansion of the conflict. Rather than engaging in separate conflicts responding to isolated incidents between individual colonies and the British government, bringing the colonies together in the First Continental Congress meant this was now a single conflict between the colonies as a whole and the British government.

The Suffolk Resolves also effectively marked the last attempt by Massachusetts to retain allegiance to the king, if not Parliament. The Resolves recognized the king as ruling by virtue of a compact with "the English colonies in America," while simultaneously denying Parliament's right to legislate on issues involving them. It urged those officials who had been appointed, by virtue of Parliament's usurpation of Massachusetts's right to legislate, to resign and for the people to disregard any laws passed by this usurpation. It also urged a boycott of all goods—"especially of East-India teas and piece goods"—from Britain. And ominously, to begin military preparation for the colony's defense.

By collectively adopting the Suffolk Resolves, the First Continental Congress joined Massachusetts in going halfway to independence from Parliament, though not yet the king.[18] The Congress also issued its own Declaration of Colonial Rights and Grievances. The Declaration asserted the colonial legislatures' sole right to make laws and levy taxes on their citizens; it also listed thirteen parliamentary actions that had violated colonial rights since 1763. Finally, the Congress approved a three-stage economic attack on Britain: ceasing to import, then ceasing to consume, and finally ceasing to export.

It was a bold step—and one of the last peaceful ones the colonies would take. Less than a year later, shots were fired at Lexington, and the colonies were moving toward demanding full independence. Between the First Continental Congress and "the shot heard round the world"[19] at Lexington, there would be further escalating actions by Britain. Four thousand more soldiers were sent, and Parliament extended its restraint on colonial trade, first to New England, then to all the colonies except New York, North Carolina, and Georgia. By March, Parliament declared Massachusetts to be in rebellion. The colonies responded with greater resistance to British government actions and greater preparation for military defense. On April 19, 1775, British troops marched from Boston to capture colonial military supplies in Concord and open warfare erupted.

The pace of unravelling was astonishing. Just two years after 1763 came the resistance to the Stamp Act. Five years after that, the Boston Massacre occurred. Just twelve years after the English colonies' greatest assurance of external peace, they were convulsed in internal war with their mother country. Just thirteen years after 1763, they declared their independence.

Only mighty forces could have led to such a rapid and complete reversal from peace to war. Economically, British government action was led by the hand of mercantilism, while the colonies' capitalism demanded resistance to economic restrictions. Politically, the long practice of self-government was evident in the colonies' willingness and ability to resist so quickly and ably. As big and precipitous as their plunge seems, the colonies were both economically and politically prepared for it—even if they themselves were not consciously aware of this. They were exceptionally well prepared for the step they took—uniquely so.

SECTION IV
The Declaration of Independence

As already shown, Britain's American colonies were superior to the mother country in many ways, such as their greater equality as noted by Adam Smith, and the colonies' higher average living standard. There were more economic and social opportunities for advancement, which led to greater political participation. A higher percentage of the male population could vote and the developed governmental structure in each of the colonies created a large number of political offices in which they could serve. The colonies were also growing faster in both population and in their collective economy. Finally, the colonies saw themselves as superior in the ancient virtues that had favorably and uniquely shaped Britain but were now being dissipated by corruption and a general dissolution.

Yet for all this evidence of superiority, both real and self-perceived, the colonies were clearly inferior in two fundamental areas. Despite having been effectively self-governing since their founding, this was true only in practice, and not on paper, as Britain's assertion of its claimed legislative right in 1763 demonstrated all too painfully. Much of Britain's reassertion of its political rights also proved that the colonies did not control their economies either.

Enlightenment thought reinforced the colonies' political idea that they should be neither inferior nor subservient. As Locke argued, no free men should or could be governed without their consent. Less consciously, but no less conspicuously, the rise of capitalism was breaking the old mercantilist bonds holding it back, and nowhere was the strain between capitalism's economic dynamism and mercantilism's despotism more visible than in the American colonies.

The conflict that resulted from the British government's political reassertion against the political and economic aspirations to which the American colonies believed themselves entitled was thus inevitable. By 1776, however, the ultimate step of independence had still not been taken. Because as inevitable as the break was to some, such as firebrands like Boston's Samuel Adams, it remained undesirable to most—a Rubicon they loathed to cross.

Just how reluctant the colonists were to declare independence is shown by the seriousness of the events that took place in the fifteen months between the shots fired in Lexington and the Independence declared in Philadelphia on July 4, 1776. Despite being willing to fight, the colonies were still unwilling to dissolve their bond with Britain. The Second Continental Congress, which convened on May 10, 1775, in Philadelphia, voted to raise troops and money, and in June, it put in charge of their defense the ablest military leader they believed the colonies had: George Washington. Even so, less than three weeks after the battle at Bunker Hill, the Second Continental Congress adopted the Olive Branch Petition on July 5, 1775, reaffirming their loyalty to the king. On the other side, the British government began employing German mercenaries against their own colonists, whom the king had declared to be in rebellion. By March of 1776, these "rebels" numbering in the thousands, had driven the British soldiers out of Boston, and British government authority was effectively collapsing in the colonies.

Yet despite all this, the thirteen colonies remained just that, officially still part of the British empire with whom they were waging a still unofficial war.

As summer approached, the final break did, too. On May 15, 1776, Virginia, the largest and richest colony, finally instructed their delegates to vote for separation, and the die was cast. The only question that remained regarding independence was whether the colonies would be united in their declaration of it. On June 7, Richard Henry Lee of Virginia made the motion "That these United Colonies are, and of a right ought to be, free and independent states, that they are absolved from all allegiance to the British Crown, and that all political connection between them and the state of Great Britain is, and ought to be, totally dissolved."[20] After vigorous debate, a final vote was delayed for twenty days so that all the delegations could be fully instructed from home. On July 2, twelve delegations voted for independence—with only New York in abstention—thus allowing the document to begin: "The unanimous Declaration of the thirteen United States of America."[21]

The task of drafting the Declaration of Independence had been given earlier to a committee of five. John Adams, a senior statesman at the Congress, had precedence, but succinctly summed up why Thomas Jefferson should write it: "Reason first: you are a Virginian and a Virginian ought to appear at the head of this business. Reason second: I am obnoxious, suspected and unpopular. You are very much otherwise. Reason third: You can write ten times better than I can."[22]

The document, purely Locke throughout, showed how much the colonies had been influenced by his and the Enlightenment's thinking. Jefferson, intent on treading old ground to a new destination, stated: "Neither aiming at originality of principle or sentiment ... it was intended to be an expression of the American mind, and to give to that expression the proper tone and spirit called for by the occasion."[23]

This was appropriate because as Barnard College professor of government Thomas Peardon points out, Locke himself was not an original thinker, but instead "gave clear and reasonable expression to beliefs that were the product of centuries of political experience and the stock-in-trade of liberty-loving Englishmen and Americans in the 17th and 18th centuries."[24] It was in both authors' pursuit of what they asserted to be fundamental truths that the force of their argument lay. One need look no further than Locke's statement in his *Second Treatise of Government to sum up the patriots' position as well as the case they had to make in the Declaration of Independence:*

> ... [S]uch revolutions happen not upon every little mismanagement in public affairs. Great mistakes in the ruling part, many wrong and inconvenient laws, and all the slips of human frailty will be borne by the people without mutiny or murmur. But if a long train of abuses, prevarications, and artifices, all tending the same way, make the design visible to the people, and they cannot but feel what they lie under and see whither they are going, it is not to be wondered that they should then rouse themselves and endeavor to put the rule into such hands which may secure to them the ends for which government was at first erected, and without which ancient names and specious forms are so far from being better that they are much worse than the state of nature or pure anarchy—the inconveniences being all as great and as near, but the remedy farther off and more difficult.[25]

The Declaration's preamble is a theoretical justification for what the new states were doing. The former colonies, now states, were acting "to dissolve the political bands" and by doing so, they cast themselves back into Locke's state of nature. Therefore, entitled under "the Laws of Nature and of Nature's God," they could fully govern themselves. Governments exist to secure mankind's "unalienable Rights" and derive "their just powers from the consent of the governed."

Overlooked today, the Declaration's real crux was its proof that the king—no longer just Parliament—had broken the compact with the colonies, thereby freeing them to form their own government. The new states saw this as a violation of their rights: "whenever any Form of Government becomes destructive of these ends, it is the Right of the People to alter or abolish it, and institute a new Government." In doing so, the Declaration of Independence does not just look ahead, but backward to the foundational documents of the English government—Jefferson's retreading of old ground. Similar to the English Bill of Rights, the Declaration lists the transgressions of the king, thereby justifying the action being taken. In the case of King James II in 1689, he actually had abdicated his throne; in the case of King George III, the Declaration of Independence posited that he had figuratively abdicated his legitimate role. Several of the Declaration of Independence's extensive list of transgressions violated freedoms that stretched back to the Magna Carta.

The Declaration lists twenty-seven separate offenses that justify the colonies' independence. The first six—and fourteen, overall—are violations of legislative rights. If violations of judicial rights are included, then there are eighteen violations of the legitimate functioning of the law. Of course, for Locke, the legislative function was at government's core, because: "[T]he end of law is not to abolish or restrain but to preserve and enlarge freedom."[26] The new Americans saw things similarly; additionally, their colonial legislatures had been their particular form of self-government *within* Britain. Britain's violations of legitimate functioning laws, from legislating to adjudicating, here were both theoretically and practically offensive to the Americans. In their eyes, and in what they hoped would be the eyes of the world, they sought to convince that they had no choice but to seek independence. To this point, the American historian Samuel Eliot Morison explained: "Make no mistake; the American Revolution was not fought to obtain freedom, but to preserve the liberties that

Americans already had as colonials."[27]

Notably, the tax and trade transgressions against the colonies, the two things referred to most commonly today as the reasons for the American Revolution, were mentioned only briefly and appear as 16th and 17th on the list of Britain's offenses. Again, the issue was not how *highly* the colonies had been taxed, but in *how* they had been taxed: by Parliament and not their own legislatures. Too, it has already been touched upon how lightly the colonies were taxed compared to the mother country. Perkins writes that after 1764, the colonial contribution to meeting defense costs in North America was virtually nil."[28] Rabushka points out that the British taxes after 1763 also produced very little revenue: "[T]oo, the amount was only a small fraction of the several hundred thousand pounds annual cost of maintaining British troops in the colonies."[29]

This discrepancy reinforces the Declaration's overarching point: that the Americans viewed what had occurred as a general violation of the fundamental compact between the British government in the person of the king, and the colonies. With the compact violated, the Americans were justified in withdrawing their consent and exercising their natural rights to form a new government.

The real genius of the Declaration of Independence, though, was not in its thought, but in its action. The colonists were putting into practice—for the first time on a statewide scale and on the world stage—what had only before been written, spoken, and debated. When they concluded the Declaration with "we mutually pledge to each other our Lives, our Fortunes and our sacred Honor," and then affixed their signatures to it, they were doing just that—precisely *because* they were self-consciously putting into action what could have been simply and more safely left as mere words. Every man who had been party to taking this step from words to the action of declaring independence knew well the penalty for treason: death by hanging. Benjamin Franklin therefore was not speaking off-handedly when he purportedly said as the fateful step was being taken, "we must, indeed, all hang together, or most assuredly we shall all hang separately."[30]

Although today's socialist Left dismisses the Declaration of Independence as anything but revolutionary, it truly was. It fully overturned the government under which Americans lived. The British government ceased to function in its former colonies, and the now thirteen new states instituted their own individual governments. Further, these separate governments immediately joined into a confederation to work together in their own defense.

The socialist Left also seeks to discredit the Declaration of Independence as not being societally revolutionary, claiming that it did not overturn the social order. This, too, is wrong. America's new society was far different from that of Britain. It was consciously middle-class, gladly excluding aristocracy and expecting poverty to be only a temporary condition. It was startling in its comparative equality and even more in this equality being its accepted norm. Even where equality did not exist—and even ardent patriots such as John Adams recognized that it did not in many cases—the prevailing relationship between such "unequals" was one of equality. There was a shared *aspiration of equality, so equality became the standard that governed America in its formal government and in its broad society. It also became the theoretical norm at which they aimed when it did not exist in practice.*

Regarding America's move to independence, Pulitzer Prize-winning American historian Gordon Wood writes in *The Radicalism of the American Revolution:*

> [the American Revolution] was as radical and as revolutionary as any in history ... In fact, it was one of the greatest revolutions the world has known, a momentous upheaval that not only fundamentally altered the character of American society but decisively affected the course of subsequent history ... In our eyes the American revolutionaries appear to be absorbed in changing only their governments, not their society. But in destroying monarchy and establishing republics they were changing their society as well as their governments, and they knew it.[31]

The American patriots sought change by looking both backward—to reestablishing the old virtues and principles they felt Britain itself was abandoning—and forward to self-government in a form that they well knew had never existed in history before.

The socialist Left's real problem with the Declaration of Independence and the American Revolutionary War that followed is not that society wasn't transformed, but that American society was not transformed according to its current wishes. It was not therefore America's lack of radicalism, but the absence of the exact form of radicalism that today's socialist Left desires—the one it now seeks to enforce by discrediting, erasing, and rewriting America's actual revolutionary history. Understanding this is vital to recognizing how far today's socialist Left is from America's history and the principles that underlie it.

SECTION V
The Revolutionary War

"No nation ever voluntarily gave up the dominion of any province, how troublesome soever it might be to govern it, and how small soever the revenue which it afforded might be in proportion to the expence (sic) which it occasioned. Such sacrifices, though they might frequently be agreeable to the interest, are always mortifying to the pride of every nation ... "[32]

Adam Smith had to look no further than his own Britain to make this observation when he wrote these words in 1776.

There can be many appraisals of America's war for independence but only one verdict: Despite all odds, America won. And America won because Britain finally reached the conclusion that there was nothing left in America to save. This conclusion was not reached easily or quickly. It took seven years and enormous resources—far more in men, money, and material than it could have ever hoped to recoup from its former colonies—to realize that all was lost.

It is important to recognize that it was not war that drove America's resistance to British rule, or its desire for independence; war only reinforced them. Despite the fighting that had taken place before July 4, 1776, and the far more extensive fighting that would take place in the following years, war was a byproduct of the colonies' struggle with Britain. Refusal to accept Britain's encroachments on their liberty was the heart of America's revolutionary war struggle. Without that heart, the new American states could not have endured so long and so one-sided a conflict.

If the spirit of liberty was the heart of the patriots' resistance, its head was unquestionably George Washington. American historian Richard Ketchum in his introduction to Lancaster's history of the war writes: "If any one man can be said to have been the American Revolution, it was George Washington, who willed his little army to endure."[33] Throughout the independence movement and across its range of participants, Washington repeatedly emerges in virtually all accounts—from those of modern historians to the reminisces of former combatants, from officers to foot soldiers—as the essential person without whom America's effort could not have succeeded. Simply, without Washington, the struggle could not have been waged over seven years, let alone won.

Washington embodied the army he led. Both started with no appreciable experience for the tremendous task they faced: building an ability from scratch and defeating one of Europe's premier armies. Both had to learn in the heat of conflict—failing frequently—and both kept developing until eventually matching and then surpassing their opponent. Washington outlasted four British commanders in chief, despite dealing with infinitely more hardships than any of them, while the American army had begun going toe-to-toe with British regulars relatively early in the war.[34] Looking back, we take these feats for granted, if not as inevitable. The first should not be, because the latter was anything but.

The Continental Army, Washington's pride and joy, was the skeleton that held the war effort together, the militia its flesh. As Washington expressed often, a long-term professionally trained army was essential to successfully fighting the British regulars. That men did so against all odds and often without regular pay or meals while facing an enemy who had abundant resources is astounding (private Joseph Plumb Martin's account of his war experiences should be required reading). Yet, the story of the frequently discounted militia is also one of heroism and no less a testament to the American will for independence. Time and time again, American militia units made up of temporary volunteers reported to battle with little more than the material they supplied themselves, knowing they were militarily outclassed by the British regulars they often faced.

The Revolutionary War was the most serious crisis America had faced since the colonies' founding. It was undoubtedly costlier in every aspect than all the previous wars with the French combined. The threat the new independent states faced was real—as reinforced by the treatment meted out by the British on those patriots they captured. Even non-belligerents fared poorly as the British passed through what they saw as rebel territory. And it also could have lasted beyond its seven long years. Despite Yorktown's fall, British strongholds remained in New York and Charleston. If the British government had not accepted the obvious—that the colonies could only be retained by great and continuous force—they had the resources to keep going.

During the war, the British pursued a strategy of division. Their belief, or at least their hope, was that the rebellion was isolated—to Boston, then to Massachusetts, and then to New England. They sought—and failed—to militarily cut out the cancer. First, it was aimed at the north. British General John Burgoyne's defeat in October 1777 at Saratoga came from an attempt to cut New England off from the rest of the colonies. Later, a strategy to save the southern colonies was pursued. Both rested on the false assumptions that the rebellion was isolated and that loyalists were, if not a majority, at least sufficiently large to maintain British rule.

From 1763 to 1775, the British miscalculated that its American colonies would pay to remain in the empire. In reality, the colonists felt they were already paying too high a price, via restricted trade and western expansion restrictions, even before the British attempted to impose higher taxes and tariffs. Then, from 1776 to 1783, the British miscalculated the degree of loyalty remaining in its former colonies. The ensuing war was a demonstration that the British government could only militarily enforce loyalty. As soon as the British military left any region, loyalty and British authority crumbled, too—the same circumstance that had prevailed just prior to the fighting at Lexington.

In the end, neither side really knew the war they had embarked upon. For Britain it was one of conquest instead of the one of preservation they had imagined. Confoundingly, the more they fought the more they lost—even as they won battle after battle. Only after Yorktown did they acknowledge the obvious. When informed of the defeat, British Prime Minister Lord North is cited as "crying out wildly as he paced to and fro, 'Oh, God, it is all over!'"[35] Of course, all was not really; the British still held major strongholds with large garrisons; King George III even promised to continue the war. But the real objective was lost: bringing America back in as a collective colony. When the final treaty (the Treaty of Paris) was signed on September 3, 1783, this conclusion had been clear for some time.

For America, the war for independence was one of attrition. Some such as John Adams foresaw this (Adams wrote to his wife that he knew well the "toil and blood and treasure that it will cost us to maintain this declaration"[36]), but most did not, unable to imagine seven years of horror and sacrifice unlike anything they or their forebears had ever known. They had always seen themselves as equal citizens to the British, which meant that theirs was a desire for freedoms they believed they already rightfully possessed, and that the British should already recognize and respect. The British did not reciprocate. Their view of the colonies was colored by their mercantilist mindset: to them, the colonies were the tree branches, Britain the trunk.

Thus, the real crux of the conflict was one of competing and contradictory visions, both political and economic: equality as declared in the Declaration of Independence and embedded in the capitalism they embraced versus colonial subservience inherent in the mercantilist mindset. The American path offered a way forward to republicanism. The British path offered only a way backward to colonialism.

SECTION VI
The Articles of Confederation

Ironically, independent America in 1783 found itself in the same position Britain had been in 1763: Deeply in debt. Truthfully, America was worse off, because America had less ability to reduce, or even service, its debt. America had endured an existential struggle for seven years on its soil, with all the horrors and destruction that this entailed. Further, it now faced punitive restrictions within the British trading system on which it had been dependent, and which was the world's largest. Superseding all of this was the weakness of the American government. Under the Articles of Confederation, America's federal government could not tax nor in any way interfere with the thirteen states' commerce.

After the Declaration of Independence, the Second Continental Congress's next order of business had been to assign a committee to draft a plan of confederation. The subsequent delay in its affirmation was an omen for its existence. Reported from committee in July 1776, Congress did not approve it until November 1777; by February 1779, twelve states had ratified it, but Maryland would not do so until March 1781. Samuel Eliot Morison called the Articles of Confederation "the best instrument of federal government adopted anywhere up to that time."[37] America's experience with earlier, less formal, colonial confederations aided it in this achievement, but it is for their limitations that the Articles are remembered today.

The Articles were essentially an international treaty, "a league of friendship" between "The United States of America," which were thirteen sovereign states that each jealously guarded their sovereignty. Article II states: "Each state retains its sovereignty, freedom, and independence, and every power, jurisdiction, and right, which is not by this confederation expressly delegated to the United States, in Congress assembled." Each state in the new confederation had a single vote and nine states had to agree in order to take any action, while it took unanimous agreement of the state legislatures to amend the Articles themselves.

The Articles also tightly circumscribed the area for Congress's action. As Morison observed,[38] the Articles only gave to Congress an authority to act in those areas which the states felt had been the legitimate powers the king and Parliament should have had in colonial America: war and trade. And as the colonies' resistance progressed, really only war. Trade authority was severely circumscribed by the stipulation in Article IX that "no treaty of commerce shall be made whereby the legislative power of the respective states shall be restrained from imposing such imposts and duties on foreigners, as their own people are subjected to, or from prohibiting the exportation or importation of any species of goods or commodities whatsoever."

Finally, the Articles gave Congress no power to tax, at least not directly, which in reality meant no taxing power at all. From Article VIII: " ... [E]xpenses that shall be incurred for the common defense or general welfare, and allowed by the united states in congress assembled, shall be defrayed out of a common treasury, which shall be supplied by the states in proportion ... [and] the taxes for paying that proportion shall be laid and levied by the authority and direction of the legislatures of the [13] states ... "

The Articles of Confederation's limitations were recognized during the Revolution, but the exigencies of war allowed no chance for change. Then, after the war, victory's euphoria allowed the Articles' limitations to be ignored temporarily. Shays' Rebellion in Massachusetts helped focus attention on the lack of a true federal authority. Farmers in western Massachusetts led by Daniel Shays, a former captain in one of the state's Revolutionary War line regiments, rebelled against the state's taxes; when the state appealed to the Confederation for help, Congress could offer none.[39] Writing in 1786, James Madison summed up the Articles' failing: "A Sanction is essential to the idea of law as coercion is to that of Government. The federal system being destitute of both, wants the great vital principles of a political constitution."[40]

Prompted by trade issues, Virginia's legislature invited the states to send delegates to Annapolis, Maryland, to "'take into consideration the trade of the United States.'"[41] The September 1786 convention in Annapolis attracted delegates from just five states, but it did yield a report to Congress by James Madison and Alexander Hamilton that contained the recommendation for a general convention of all the states to meet "'to devise such further provisions as shall appear to them necessary to render the constitution of the federal government adequate to exigencies of the Union.'" Congress in turn invited the states to send representatives to Philadelphia in May 1787 "'for the sole and express purpose of revising the Articles of Confederation … '"

Far from revising the Articles, which was essentially impossible under their condition for unanimity in amendments, the Philadelphia convention would replace them entirely. The delegates who would attend the Constitutional convention in Philadelphia in 1787 were drawing on unique experience and insight pertinent to the task at hand.

SECTION VII
The Constitution

The Constitution is the most important document in American history, if not modern political history. The Americans who undertook its creation intended it to be and treated it as such. As a result, its creation is also extremely well documented. James Madison seemingly took dictation of the proceedings. The preeminent compiler of the convention's proceedings, Max Farrand, quotes Madison in his three-volume collection of all participants' notes: "I chose a seat in front of the presiding member, with the other members, on my right and left hand. In this favorable position for hearing all that passed I noted … what was read from the Chair or spoken by the members … "[42] Yet while Madison's effort was without equal, he was not alone. Farrand used notes taken by six others in attendance, as well as official vote tallies. All attest to the importance that those present ascribed to the convention's work.

To say America and those at the Constitutional Convention were prepared for the task at hand is an understatement. No people and no men were more so or have been since. Of course, they had Britain's practical and theoretical legacy, but America had been building on both for generations. They had their prolonged colonial experience of what had largely been self-government. Then for a generation they had moved toward actual self-government in the individual states, particularly in the state constitutions written after 1776. To this, they added experience at the collective level through the Articles of Confederation. They had been schooled by success and failure alike. And that schooling spanned two generations of men who had been intensively thinking about, and involved in the practice of, these self-governing efforts. America's best thinkers and doers of governing converged on Philadelphia to put into practice what they had been practicing for their whole adult lives. They knew what they were doing and were uniquely qualified to do it.

Perhaps the most important and most American innovation that they brought with them was a shared spirit of republicanism. The further they diverged from Britain, the more the colonists were pushed back into the American condition that shaped them. The overarching similarity was an ethos of equality. Despite their differences—and the convention accentuated several—this sense of equality bound them together and separated them from the rest of the world and history. From it, republicanism took root, and it was the Americans' adoption of it that created a norm that drove American society even more toward equality. It became a self-reinforcing cycle. "State politics showed that the language of equality, consent, and individual liberty quickly acquired a persuasiveness and legitimacy that conferred an advantage on those who could employ it most effectively."[43]

As constitutional scholars Kelly, Harbison, and Belz point out in their seminal work, *The American Constitution:* "In the received wisdom of the day republics were disdained as small, weak, and ineffective; the word *republican* was derisive, a term of opprobrium. With the abolition of monarchy in America, however, the perception of republican government changed."[44] As these authors explain, there were two branches of republicanism. One was "corporatist" and accentuated the collective over the individual. This, they emphasize, was demonstrated in the many mass actions taken under the republican banner before and during the Revolutionary War. The exigencies of organized resistance and then war itself, as they have under similar circumstances but different eras, undoubtedly promoted this branch.

The other branch of republicanism was "individualist," accentuating the individual's rights, and was expressed in a limitation on government's powers. In the aftermath of resistance and war, individualist republicanism won out. As Kelly, Harbison, and Belz write: "[G]uarantees of property rights and protection of individual liberty against arbitrary power acquired precedence in constitution writing and in the conduct of American politics."[45]

This precedence prevailed in Philadelphia. Delegates began arriving for the Constitutional convention on May 14, 1787. Not until May 25 did formal meetings begin; the convention "remained in continuous session until September 17, with the exception of one adjournment of two days over the Fourth of July and another of ten days, from July 26 to August 6 to allow the Committee of Detail to prepare its report."[46] The convention's first order of business was to choose a president; George Washington was unanimously elected. Although he is rarely recorded as speaking, Washington nonetheless gave the convention an unimpeachable imprimatur. Despite divisions amongst delegates— between large and small, slave and non-slave states—the shared elements overrode, or at least allowed compromises to be reached. The product that emerged was one of republicanism and capitalism, limited government and equality of rights.

The Constitution is a directive for limited government. While the Articles of Confederation are often viewed as the comparable predecessor to the Constitution, the fact is that the Articles were more treaty than constitution—a far less comprehensive structure laying out a far less centralized government. Therefore, the proper point of comparison would be other centralized governments of the day—and even so, the American Constitution was thoroughly unprecedented in its starting from limitations on centralized governmental power. In England, and others that would follow in the Old World, it went the other direction, with marginal limitations imposed on strong central governments, and restrictions added as conditions warranted and permitted. This was the pattern from the Magna Carta on. What the English had achieved over almost 600 years, the Americans surpassed in one fell swoop.

The clearest example of this intent to limit government power, in addition to all the Constitution's explicit limitations, is its deposit of the bulk of what power was allotted to government into the legislative branch, i.e., into the people's hands through their representatives. This original intent might seem alien to us today, after seeing the executive branch's ascent over much of the last century, yet it is nonetheless clear.

The Constitution perfectly fit republicanism and capitalism, just as these two perfectly fit each other. The Constitution was also perfectly designed to advance both. Capitalism needs free individuals to play its central role of entrepreneurs and thrives most where its market is freest. Conversely, government authority is capitalism's biggest long-term threat. The Constitution unfettered individuals and markets by fettering government within strictly defined limits. In sum, American exceptionalism produced the Constitution. The Constitution then secured the free rein for American exceptionalism to continue.

Still, the Constitution was not a foregone conclusion. There were several junctures during the convention when the outcome appeared to hang in the balance. Even at the convention's conclusion, several prominent delegates refused to sign it. As the *Federalist Papers* (and the now largely overlooked *Antifederalist Papers*) attest, there were many heated debates in the states over ratification. The Constitution was not secured until almost a year later, June 21, 1788, when New Hampshire became the ninth state to ratify it (as per the Articles, nine were needed for it to take effect). Then the question was whether Virginia, America's largest and wealthiest state, would ratify. Finally, the question became one of unanimity, which took another two years, when Rhode Island became the last of the thirteen states to ratify in 1790.

The opposition to the Constitution came not from those who thought it too weak, but from those who thought it too strong. As Patrick Henry stated before Virginia's Ratifying Convention: " ... we should not have been brought to this alarming transition, from a Confederacy to a consolidated Government ... Here is a revolution as radical as that which separated us from Great Britain."[47] Even the Federalists, who wanted a true central government, not a mere confederation, wanted to strictly limit its area of operation. The best evidence of this lies in the biggest outcome of the ratification process: the insertion of the first ten amendments to the Constitution, the Bill of Rights, which further delineated the limitations of the new central government. This limited central government is what the convention in Philadelphia achieved over the summer of 1787.

SECTION VIII
Conclusion

At the highest level, it was the exceptionalism of Britain's American colonies that set the stage for a revolutionary reordering of America into the United States of America in a single generation. This reordering followed a distinct pattern, from capitalism to republicanism to Constitution, with the last being both the product of the other two, as well as a powerful fillip to their strengthening. This combination set America on a course from which it has not seriously threatened to diverge until today's assault from the socialist Left.

Yet to truly appreciate what transpired in America from the late 17th to the late 18th century, it's crucial to take an even closer look. The insulation America enjoyed from Britain's turmoil could not last forever. Although spared the internal upheaval of England's Civil War, eventually Britain's external wars with France spilled into their North American colonies. The largest of these, the French and Indian War, proved to be the last. Britain's victory in 1763 resulted in France's complete removal from North America and offered Britain's American colonies seemingly permanent peace. It also left the American colonists with a sense of their own abilities—something a young colonial officer named George Washington from Virginia personified.

With the French no longer a threat in North America, the stage was set for the conflict between England and her colonies there. While the British victory gave the American colonies a substantial sense of security, it left the British government with a significant debt. The mercantilist mindset, whereby the colonies should benefit the mother country, sent Britain to her colonies in America for what she saw as her due. Of course, the colonies saw things differently. With the French threat gone, there was no longer a need for an enlarged defense, so they believed things should return to the way they had always been before in America: effectively self-governed.

Of course, things did not return to their pre-war status. Instead, they descended into a sequence of taxes-protests-reprisals that ultimately triggered the American revolution. That tax fight, though, was not primarily about how *much*, but about *how* and *by whom* the colonies were taxed. The colonists felt the power to tax them resided in their own colonial legislatures, not Britain's Parliament. The escalating conflict over this question expanded into one of who would govern them, uniting the thirteen colonies against the British government.

For the American colonists, the heart of the matter was that their rights as British subjects were being denied, prompting them to establish their own rights as Americans. When the conflict over taxes and authority finally came, the American colonies had been uniquely prepared throughout their existence to act on it. Thus, the French and Indian War's successful conclusion gave the colonies security while also opening the way for an even greater conflict with Britain.

America's drive to independence was astonishingly rapid. British mercantilism directly confronted American capitalism in 1763. Born of its widespread and unparalleled equality of conditions—and even more, its equality of aspirations—America's political resistance formed quickly around a clear ideology of republicanism. By 1776, republican leaders, with all options at reconciliation exhausted, declared America independent. Thirteen newly independent states formed a confederacy and successfully waged a war against the world's greatest military power. Victorious, but feeling again inhibited by their political system—this time by its weakness—the thirteen states again reordered it. All this occurred from 1763 to 1789, a single generation. Equally remarkable: exactly a century passed from the English Bill of Rights in 1689 to its apotheosis in the operation of the US Constitution in 1789.

That this chain of events was forged so quickly and successfully against such odds is a powerful testament to the economic and political forces that linked them and the men embodying them. It is understandable why Americans felt Providence was at work; the Declaration of Independence mentions God four times in four forms ("God," "Creator," "Supreme Judge," and "Divine Providence") in its short span.

The Declaration of Independence was the theory and proof of America's exceptionalism. The Constitution was the implementation of that exceptionalism. Both product and paradigm of capitalism and republicanism, the Constitution was a "Goldilocks" achievement between the constraints of British rule and the weakness of the Articles of Confederation. That the Constitution would be a framework for promoting America's capitalist development is hardly surprising. Nor is it surprising that America had leapfrogged the world in developing such a framework. The Constitution took the stage because of America's existing capitalist achievement, and it set the stage for greater capitalist development in accordance with America's growing aspirations.

America's Constitution is a blueprint for uniquely limited government. America also took a unique route to its limited government. Old World nations with existing strong central governments could only attempt to pare back their authority at the margins, in fits and starts over time. Britain was a case in point. In contrast, America constructed a limited government from the start, and because of this *de novo* origin, it was able to progress much further and faster than other nations in placing those limits. This also allowed America's government to endure, in comparison to France's nearly concurrent revolutionary effort. Further, America's limited government allowed its economy to surge ahead. Finally, as the next chapter will demonstrate, this combination of limited government and surging economy foreclosed any significant or sustained openings for the socialist Left and its calls for an overarching, overseeing, and overbearing state.

SECTION IX
Implications for the Socialist Left

There are many implications, both past and present, for today's socialist Left in America. An obvious one is the inability of political theories to long thwart their economic realities.

In the mid-18th century, despite capitalism's rapid economic success, mercantilism still held sway in the political sphere. The British government fatefully lagged its economy, which unleashed a chain of events that led first to the conflict with France for control of the American colonies, and then between Britain and the colonies it could no longer control. It is an apt warning for policymakers today—though this 250-year-old lesson is also certain to fall on deaf ears within the socialist Left because this imposition of ideology by government is precisely what America's socialist Left wants to do today.

There is enormous irony that Marx premised the communist ideology he unleashed on the world on an inexorable economic chain of events that would produce communism from capitalism. It was, according to Marx, uncontrollable. Yet capitalist economies on their own have shown no signs of evolving to communism. Instead, communism and socialism have had to be politically thrust on capitalist economies. When this has transpired, attempts to take socialism to its greatest extent of full state control over economic forces have universally foundered—specifically their own economies. Despite the full force of political power at their disposal, even to the point of totalitarianism, socialist states have always found themselves overmatched by economics and their economies' inexorable efforts to move to capitalism. Faced with this conundrum, the socialist Left has always chosen the path of most resistance: to forcefully impose itself on resistant economies. America's socialist Left is seeking to do nothing less today.

It therefore follows that America's socialist Left seeks to refute our historical legacy, particularly the nation's founding, by every means available. The socialist Left aims to change Americans' historical narrative because it does not support the result this history has produced, and because it seeks to change the course our economy and society are following. It is opposed to capitalism and a freely functioning economy. It is equally opposed to rights being assigned directly to people as individuals, rather than allotted by the state through groups. Opposed to a free-market economy, the socialist Left sees any outcome from such an economy as inherently illegitimate. Opposed to the assignation of rights on an individual basis, the socialist Left sees such individual liberty as producing inherently illegitimate outcomes.

The apotheosis of America's revolutionary history, the Constitution, offers no place for the statist approach that the socialist Left seeks. The socialist Left's opposition is not just ideological but practical as well. The American product is due to the American paradigm; America is not an accident but an achievement. Capitalism did not flower elsewhere in the world to the extent it did in America because other states did not so limit their government's ability to interfere with it. This American prosperity in turn reinforced the legitimacy of its limited government, and effectively barred the socialist Left from a historically meaningful role in America.

The socialist Left knows that to change the product (capitalism and individual liberty), it must change the paradigm. It must nullify the Constitution, the history that created it, and the later history that the Constitution shaped. The most direct way for the socialist Left to do this is to delegitimize those histories. It therefore seeks to rationalize any and every means to do so.

America mistakenly misperceives those of the socialist Left as simple ideologues pursuing a simple ideological assault on our history and that America's history is something that the socialist Left *wants* to change. The socialist Left *needs* to change America's history. There is a very practical intention to its assault. If it is to reshape American society, it must first overturn the foundations that support our society. In order to change America's present, the socialist Left must change America's past.

CHAPTER FIVE

AMERICA'S SMALL-GOVERNMENT MODEL

SECTION I
Introduction

Throughout its colonial history, during its independence under the Articles of Confederation, and even under the Constitution's federal government, up until well into the 20th century, America lived under small, limited, central governments. It was all those first Americans had ever known, and when they came together to create their own government, they produced a small one. This was not by accident, but by precedence and preference.

Of course, there followed episodes when the federal government assumed great power and great size. But these were all periods of crisis: exceptions to the rule. Wars and economic recessions have regularly occurred throughout American history, but the two truly calamitous events of the Constitution's first 140 years were the Civil War and World War I. These wars were not simply crises—small waves on an otherwise calm sea—but tidal waves that rocked the ship of state.

One need not even look in a history book to find evidence of the effects of the Civil War and World War I (as well as lesser adverse events). A simple review of America's financial records reveals them. Like a seismograph reading, the jolts to America's landscape can be detected by spikes of significant increases in federal spending and significant decreases in revenues. Smaller crises would jar either or both; the two truly serious crises significantly rocked both. More important, in addition to quantitative effects, these serious crises provoked qualitative shifts in the federal government itself. During each war, the federal government broadened its scope of operations and increased its powers within this larger scope.

Such qualitative changes put the federal government in a position to permanently assume this expanded role, bringing it right up to—and giving it the power and the means to cross—this threshold. And yet, as this chapter shows, the federal government returned to its small government roots each time.

SECTION II
Colonial Government

America's small government heritage began not only with its origins, as Chapter Four discussed, but with its inhabitants. American colonists did not come to America to be closely governed, and in fact, the colonies were largely self-governed, and that government was largely focused on self-defense. Obviously, there was more nuance to America's colonial government than this, but these two essential traits stand out.

Alvin Rabushka, in his monumental study of colonial taxation in America, makes a point commonly recognized by historians: Americans were lightly taxed by any European standard. And they liked it that way: "[T]hat the overwhelming majority of the colonists resented paying even low taxes is evident from reports and laws dealing with noncompliance, arrears, and even the occasional violent rebellion."[1]

What is overlooked in this often-recognized fact is that Americans' love of low taxes was an effect, not a cause. Americans were lightly taxed because they were lightly governed. Americans were only taxed out of necessity to fund their government, and government only existed out of necessity for specific services, like defense. Government spending, then, fluctuated based on threats to the colonies' safety.[2] Rabushka points out that this reflected "the preferences of the colonists." Small government was endemic to America because it was innate to the colonists, and it was innate to the colonists because for those immigrating from Europe, government was at worst synonymous with chaos, and at best a restriction on their freedom.[3]

The best benchmark for measuring the colonial governments' small size is a comparison of revenues with that of the mother country. In 1688, America's taxes amounted to a mere 0.6 percent of Britain's on a per capita basis.[4] A generation later in 1714, the same applied: those in Britain paid a per capita tax almost ten times higher than the American colonialists.[5] By 1739, British citizens were paying a per-capita rate almost 31 times greater than the colonists.[6]

In each of these periods, colonial taxes would spike in times of conflict and then return to their normally low levels.[7] Government size depended on necessity, and to the colonies, necessity equated to safety. Despite the notable frequency of these conflicts—even during the watershed of the French and Indian War—colonial taxes remained low.[8]

America's colonies were not just accustomed to light taxes compared to Britain, they were lightly governed as well. This is true in both absolute and in relative terms. That they were lightly taxed—absolutely and relatively—is accepted, and taxes are often seen as the focal point of the fight for independence. But that they were lightly governed—and that the British government was increasing in size in the colonies—is almost entirely overlooked. Britain's attempt to exert greater—and more external—governmental control, and thereby greater government, on the colonies was more than they were willing to bear, and a fact that would have enormous implications for America's own future government. Even without the increased taxes, and even if the greater government had originated from within the colonies themselves, Americans would have been unlikely to have found it any more tolerable.

Americans wanted their government small and cheap; after all, it was all they had ever known or sought.

SECTION III
1790-1860

The American federal government essentially began where its earlier colonial governments had: at zero. When the Constitution was written, there was no central structure to take control of, as once the British government in America failed altogether, thirteen *separate* state governments arose. Without Britain, which had been the central authority in the colonies previously, there was no structure to inherit. Even the Articles of Confederation outlined a weak central government which deferred to the new state governments in virtually every domestic instance, and once that collapsed, what followed was only the confederation of thirteen new states. Thus, in many respects, there effectively *was* no central government in the newly declared independent America. (In fact, there truly was no central government at all from November 1, 1788, until the first week of April 1789 when the Congress was organized and Washington inaugurated.)[9]

As the 19th-century French political scientist and philosopher Alexis de Tocqueville wrote: "[A]s soon as peace was concluded, the defects of this legislation stood revealed: the state seemed to dissolve all at once."[10]

America's history of light government fostered a resentment of the more rigorous government of the type imposed by Britain after the French and Indian War. It is little wonder, then, that when the Constitution installed a new central government, it was one with very limited and delineated powers. As de Tocqueville wrote: "Therefore the attributes of the federal government were carefully defined, and it was declared that everything not contained within that definition returned to the jurisdiction of state governments. Hence state authority remained the rule and the federal government the exception."[11]

But before the federal government could be even an "exception," it first had to come into being. As the American historian Samuel Eliot Morison writes in the second volume of his three-volume monograph: "This new government had to create its own machinery."[12] Doing so meant building from scratch. Per Morison, "the American Confederation left nothing but a dozen clerks with their pay in arrears, an empty treasury, and a burden of debt."[13] Of course, the smallness of the preceding Confederation government and the decamping of the earlier British one meant there also was no appreciable reserve of administrative talent from which to draw. As Morison states: "No successful leader of a revolution has been so naked before the world as Washington was in 1789."[14]

And what was one of the first things this new limited and unstaffed federal government did? Pass a Bill of Rights that further curtailed the central government's authority *vis-à-vis* its citizens and their state governments. These limitations are particularly evident in the Ninth and Tenth Amendments, which together explicitly reserve rights not mentioned in the Constitution for the people and the states. The new Congress's initial effort is a reminder that the anti-federalists, of whom there were a substantial number, wanted a government even more curtailed than the very limited one already provided by the Constitution.[15] Thus, the Constitution's belt and suspenders approach to limiting the new central government was a prudent choice considering the people it hoped to govern.

A quick recounting of the new government's first-year agenda gives a sense as to how unprepared it was for the task at hand. The House and then the Senate were both organized in April 1789. After counting the electors' votes for President, Washington was informed he had won (and was sworn in two weeks later, on April 30). Not until July 4 did Congress pass a tariff bill (8.5 percent on certain items, which were assessed at 10 percent less if they were imported in American ships) to fund itself. It would not create a means for collecting the tariff for another two months, and President Washington did not appoint Alexander Hamilton to head the Treasury Department until September 11, 1789. On January 14, 1790, Hamilton submitted to Congress his Report on the Public Credit, which aimed to unwind the Gordian knot of America's complicated financial predicament. Hamilton's plan—to pay America's past debts at par and assume the states' war debts—would take six months to pass (in four bills on July 29).[16] Only then were America's debt issues, and the means for paying these debts, settled. In short, America's new central government was not intended, equipped, or funded to be anything but small, and it continued on this way for seven decades.

In 1789-92, the federal government took in $4.4 million in receipts, spent $4.3 million, and had a total public debt of $77.2 million.[17] By 1811, its revenue had increased to $14.4 million, its spending $8.1 million, and its total public debt fallen to just $45.2 million. (Within this period, the federal government ran sixteen surpluses.) The War of 1812 (1812-1815) saw receipts drop and spending surge to $20.3 million, the highest in the federal government's history to that point. Regardless, by 1817 receipts more than tripled their wartime numbers, hitting $33.9 million, and spending dropped to $21.8 million (lower than any of the previous four years). By 1834, there was essentially no public debt.[18] America's war with Mexico and its aftermath saw a repetition of the

1812 fiscal pattern.[19] In 1860, on the threshold of the Civil War, the total public debt was $64.8 million ($54.2 million of this came during the three years of war with Mexico).

The composition of the federal government's fiscal record was equally stable. Almost all its receipts came from customs, and almost all payments went either to the military or interest on its debt.[20] To modern eyes, America's federal government remained amazingly small and stable for its first three generations. Of course, at the time, this was not amazing at all; it was exactly what had been intended. The government increased in times of war, but it either retrenched absolutely (as its spending dropped) or relatively (as America's economy outpaced it) in peacetime. When recessions caused deficits, economic rebounds quickly wiped those deficits out. Where it had civilian employees, almost all were employed in the nation's post offices[21] and almost all federal employees were located outside Washington. And if the government seemed small in absolute terms, it was even more so in relation to others; in comparing America to France, de Tocqueville wrote: "[T]he king of France disposes of eleven times as many places as the President of the United States, although the population of France is only one and a half times as great as that of the Union."[22]

SECTION IV
Civil War: 1861-1865

Still the most cataclysmic event in American history, the Civil War was a five-year fratricidal war that virtually spanned the American continent, utterly devastating the southern states. The conflict was also a prescription for a vastly increased federal government.

Under the Constitution, war directs federal government functions toward the president as commander in chief. This increased responsibility flows through the executive branch that supports the president, and thereby to an overall increase in government. This pattern of surge had shown itself in the War of 1812 and the Mexican-American War. Of course, the Civil War itself was of an altogether different magnitude and duration; while as president, Abraham

Lincoln was willing to take more power than any of his predecessors. As a result, the federal government grew massively larger and its power more expansive than ever before.

In his opening on the Civil War, Morison writes:

> Lincoln wielded a greater power throughout the war than any other President of the United States prior to Franklin D. Roosevelt ... Contemporary accusations against him of tyranny and despotism read strangely to those who know his character, but not to students of his administration. Lincoln came near to being the ideal tyrant of whom Plato dreamed, yet nonetheless he was a dictator from the standpoint of American constitutional law.[23]

Lincoln's aggregation of power in the executive branch—at times he effectively assumed the operations of both the judicial and legislative branches as well—was matched by an unimaginable increase in federal government power and size.

Before the combatants came to grips with the magnitude that the nascent conflict would reach, federal spending in 1861 increased surprisingly little, just about five percent. Conversely, the South's secession caused federal receipts to plunge, falling almost 27 percent, to the lowest level since 1849. This combination set off what would become a wartime trend of uncontrolled federal deficits and debt. The deficit more than tripled from 1860's, hitting $25 million—surpassing the entire 1845 federal budget. Concomitantly, the federal debt jumped almost 40 percent, reaching $90.6 million, the highest level since 1823.

Naturally, the federal government's greatly increased spending needs demanded increased revenue. Despite this, America's taxes still never rose that high. Even in 1865, at the height of federal government spending, receipts only reached $333.7 million, just 3.3 percent of GDP.[24]

To collect the additional taxes it *did* raise, Congress responded with the Internal Revenue Act of 1862. Enacted on July 1, 1862, America's first income tax imposed a 3 percent tax on incomes between $600 and $10,000 and 5 percent on those over $10,000. Additionally, it imposed taxes on virtually everything it could reach. David A. Wells, chairman of the US Revenue Commission in 1865, summarized the federal government's approach: "Whenever you find an article, a product, a trade, a profession, or a source of income, tax it!"[25] These monthly taxes, licenses, and stamp duties were applied to as wide an array of products and services as possible. Housed in the Treasury Department, a new Office of the Commissioner of Internal Revenue oversaw the tax collection. Through a series of executive orders, Lincoln added a host of collection districts (no more than one per congressional district), each with an assessor and a collector.[26] Over the course of the war, the new income tax would raise almost $55 million, boosting revenue, but still not keeping pace. Spending reached $474.8 million, exploding 1858's previous record of $74.2 million. The deficit hit $422.7 million, and the federal debt almost quintupled to $524.2 million, easily exceeding 1815's previous high of $127.3 million.

In 1863, the government grew even more. Receipts more than doubled from the previous year, but spending outpaced it. The deficit increased precipitously and the debt doubled, breaking the billion-dollar barrier for the first time. The exploding demand for more revenue spurred Congress to increase income-tax rates and penalties in the Internal Revenue Act of 1864. Now any income between $600 and $5,000 was taxed at 5 percent and any over $5,000 at 10 percent; additionally, luxury items (such as gold watches and family billiard tables) were taxed.[27] Still, revenues continued to fall well short. Although 1864 saw revenues double again, spending still rose more, ballooning the debt to $1.8 billion.

Across the fiscal board, 1865 exceeded all the previous war years. Tax receipts hit $333.7 million, almost six times what they had been in 1860. Spending exceeded $1 billion for the first time, larger than the entire federal debt of 1863. The deficit rose to roughly twice 1862's total debt, and the debt increased to $2.7 billion, almost 50 percent higher than in the previous year.

In just five years, the federal government had grown to a comparative behemoth. It had amassed unimaginable power, including some powers deemed unconstitutional—such as the income tax, which as we will see later, was ruled unconstitutional in 1895. It was also spending and raising unprecedented sums, and now had a gargantuan federal debt that had to be serviced. All the components and all the justifications for an enlarged federal government were in place—the debate that had begun at the nation's origins between state and federal government authority had been settled by the sword. And all were elements that had provoked Britain to increase government and taxes in its American colonies a century earlier.

SECTION V
Postwar: 1866-1914

The Civil War left the federal government more powerful—quantitatively larger and qualitatively more expansive—than it had ever been. It did not simply use more resources to do what it had done before; it used more resources to do what it had *never* done before, crossing a threshold to become far bigger in American life—*vis-à-vis* both the states and its citizens.

De Tocqueville had predicted a generation earlier: "[I]f the people of the United States are ever involved in serious difficulties, taxes there will soon be found to rise as high as in most of the aristocracies or monarchies of Europe."[28] But America proved him wrong. Despite having crossed all its boundaries, the federal government retreated. Even at the height of this unprecedented increase in size, scope, resources, and concentration of power in the executive branch, the federal government retrenched after the war's conclusion. It did not return to its former size, but it did return to a level far below its wartime peak. And this occurred in both its size and authority. This seems unimaginable now, when the federal government only grows, and when once begun programs never cease, but unbelievably the federal government shrank, and programs ended. Rapidly.

The reason was noted by de Tocqueville a generation earlier: "The parties that threaten the Union rely not on principles but on material interests. In so vast a land these interests make the provinces into rival nations rather than parties."[29] These "rival nations" were now forcibly combined into one United States. Yet as de Tocqueville had noted, these rival nations had not contended over the principles of limited government laid out in the Constitution, but over slavery, tariffs, and free trade. Limited government alone had remained above the terrible fray. As Morison observed, Americans remained "averse from increasing the power of government."[30]

After reaching a high of $1.3 billion in 1865, federal spending plummeted by almost two-thirds ($800 million) in a single year. And it kept falling. Federal spending dropped in almost every consecutive year until 1878 when it hit $237 million—over $1 billion less than its former all-time high. Place these federal spending numbers relative to a booming economy, and it is clear federal spending was falling proportionally more. As a percentage of GDP, by 1916, federal spending was slightly below where it had been in 1861 (1916's 1.422 percent versus 1861's 1.424 percent). The 1916 level was also below the spending-to-GDP ratio of 1851 (1.7 percent), 1841 (1.6 percent), 1831 (1.4 percent), and 1821 (2.1 percent).

Notably, federal government spending over this five-decade period was not an aberration. It exhibited the same wartime cycle as it had in the earlier and smaller conflicts of the War of 1812 and Mexican-American War. During the brief Spanish-American War that followed, spending in 1898 jumped almost $80 million (over 20 percent) from 1897, and in 1899 leapt another $160 million; however, by 1900 it fell $85 million and then leveled off.

Despite the nominal spending over pre-Civil War levels, federal deficits dropped, too. In 1865, the federal deficit was a staggering $938 million—a sum larger than combined federal spending from 1840 through 1860. Yet just a year later, the 1866 federal budget recorded a $37 million surplus—an astounding $1 billion swing to the positive. The surplus in 1867 was almost $100 million larger again. The federal government would run surpluses in every year from 1866 through 1893, when only that year's severe financial panic ended the twenty-eight-year run in 1894.

Sustained federal budget surpluses had a pronounced effect on the debt. From its high of $2.7 billion in 1865, the federal debt dropped by almost two-thirds by 1893, reaching $961.4 million. Compared to the nation's GDP, the federal debt had fallen even more precipitously. In 1865, the federal debt was 26.7 percent of GDP; by 1881, it stood at 17 percent, and by 1891, 6.3 percent. It continued to fall each decade until 1916, when the federal debt amounted to just 2.4 percent—matching its 1851 level.

The most interesting fiscal variable of the fifty-year period is found in its taxes. From the positive performance of deficits and debt, a logical assumption would be that the federal government should retain its wartime Big Government approach in the tax code. Specifically, one might assume that it was the retention of 1862's income tax and other wartime taxes that produced the other positive fiscal effects. This was not the case. The enhanced wartime tax regime lasted only a few short years.

After the war, critics of an income tax of any kind grew. As Steven Weisman of the *New York Times* writes in his history of the period, *The Great Tax Wars*, "Though the tax was paid by only a tiny percentage of Americans, it was widely criticized in the press and among influential opinion leaders on various grounds. Many argued that the revenue was no longer needed and that graduated rates were fundamentally unfair. Still others detested the publication of tax returns, calling it an invasion of privacy, and claimed that the tax was administered inefficiently."[31]

So, Congress whittled away at the income tax. In 1870, with only 100,000 Americans still subject to it, the rate was lowered to 2.5 percent on incomes over $2,500, the publication of tax returns was ceased, and the tax extended for only two more years.[32] President Grant sponsored repeal of the income tax and most other "emergency" taxes in 1872.[33] Over its 1862-72 life, America's first income tax generated $376 million (peaking at $73.5 million in 1866), accounting for 24 percent of federal revenues in 1867 and one-fifth of federal revenues during the war.[34] As a percentage of GDP, receipts fell from their wartime peak of 3.3 percent in 1865 to 2.5 percent in 1891, to 2 percent in 1911, and to 1.5 percent in 1916.

Tax policy would continue to be extremely volatile for the next fifty years—going from eliminating the income tax to enshrining it in the Constitution. Bigger than the quantitative change in federal receipts was the qualitative one. With rapidly reduced spending, the federal government did not need *more* revenues, but a growing contingent supported a shift of the revenue burden: away from the general population (as tariffs were seen to impose) and toward the wealthy (as the income tax had done). Thus, although the income tax's critics prevailed after the Civil War, its supporters never vanished. The Populist Party included it in their 1888 platform, and it was introduced in Congress dozens of times following Grant's 1872 repeal.[35] Amidst the fallout of the financial Panic of 1893, an income tax was included in the Wilson-Gorman Tariff Act of 1894. Along with a corporate tax on net profits, the reborn income tax took effect in 1895 with a 2 percent rate on net incomes over $4,000 (there was no corporate exemption, though certain businesses were excluded). It would last five years, would affect only 2 percent of Americans, and would raise $75 million over that time (compared to $73.5 million in 1866 alone).[36]

The paltry amount collected by the tax spurred the critics. Despite having lost in the courts in the past, opponents again sued, arguing that the income tax was unconstitutional. In *Pollock v. Farmers' Loan and Trust Company* (1895), opponents made three arguments: First, that it was effectively a land tax and constitutionally "must be levied among the states according to population." Second, that it was only levied against individuals and corporations earning more than $4,000 and therefore violated Article I, Section 8, of the Constitution, "which required that all taxes must be uniform throughout the United States." Third that it was "invalid insofar as it was levied upon the income of state and municipal bonds."[37] In a final 5-4 verdict in May 1895, the Supreme Court declared the entire income tax unconstitutional. As a result of the *Pollock* ruling, an income tax would require a constitutional amendment.

Supporters again went to work. Against what at first seemed impossible odds, the Sixteenth Amendment enshrined the income tax in the Constitution in 1913.[38] Support was bipartisan. Theodore Roosevelt, who was president at the time, called for "a graduated income tax" in his 1906 annual message to Congress, and the Democrat Party included it in their 1908 presidential platform.[39] The language that became the Sixteenth Amendment passed the Senate 77-0 and the House 318-14; the states voted for ratification 42 to 6.[40]

Democrats wasted no time in using the opening. On October 3, 1913, President Wilson signed into law the Underwood-Simmons tariff bill that contained America's first permanent income tax—a 1 percent tax on net income above $3,000 (rates moved up until reaching a maximum 6 percent rate above $500,000).[41] Its proximity to World War I often causes a misidentification of the income tax as a war measure. Certainly, it generated revenue during the war, yet this income tax was fundamentally different from its earlier iteration, which had *intentionally* generated revenue for the Civil War. America's new permanent income tax existed due to a qualitative change, not a quantitative necessity. There was no rush to action. It took years to achieve, bipartisan support, and a constitutional amendment. It addressed no crisis; World War I would not begin until 1914 and America would not enter it until November 1917. That this income tax measure could be achieved over time and without a crisis was due to a conscious and prolonged desire to shift the source—at least to some extent—from which America's revenues were obtained. That shift was multifaceted. It was a shift in kind, from tariffs to income. It was a geographic shift, from South and West to North and East. It was a demographic shift, from rural to urban. It was a class shift, from middle class and working class to the wealthy. And finally, it was qn economic shift, from consumption to earnings.

For these shifts, there was overwhelming support from both parties, support that existed because of what the new income tax was *not*. It was *not* intended to be a means to fund a bigger government. It was *not* meant to be a means to redistribute income or to be punitive to the wealthy. Democrat Senator John Sharp Williams of Mississippi, a leader on the income tax in the Senate Finance Committee stated: "No honest man can make upon great fortunes per se. The Democratic Party never has done it; and when the Democratic Party begins to do it, it will cease to be the Democratic Party and become the socialistic party of the United States; or, better expressed, the communistic party, or quasi communistic party, of the United States."[42]

Unquestionably, the new income tax created a portal through which further policy and ideological changes could proceed. Still, despite the profound change that the new income tax represented, and the profound changes that it would later present, the American paradigm of small federal government prevailed. It prevailed despite the financial collapse of 1893, despite the Spanish-American War, despite new permanent sources of revenue—corporate, income, and estate taxes—and despite the change in party control in Washington.

SECTION VI
World War I

Two generations after the Civil War, America entered another conflict that enlisted the nation in a total war effort. It was led by Woodrow Wilson, the first Democrat to win two consecutive presidential terms since Jackson in 1832. Ironically, Wilson won his second term largely on the strength of keeping America out of the war that he ultimately would lead it through.

Confronted once more with an all-consuming conflict, America turned first to examples from its prior one—retaining many and discarding some government actions. Taken in the biggest of pictures, the federal government quickly grew more expansive and expensive again, though Wilson's aim was to keep the government's growth informal and, most important, temporary. Like the nation itself, a sense of voluntarism pervaded the federal government's wartime approach.

Unlike his initial presidential victory in 1912, won only by virtue of the dominant Republican Party splitting between Taft and Roosevelt, Wilson's victory in 1916 was his own. But it was close. Wilson beat the Republican Charles E. Hughes by less than 600,000 popular votes; this translated to an even narrower electoral vote margin of 277-254. At this stage, World War I had been raging for two years, producing unimaginable carnage in Europe. It was the campaign's dominant issue and America's predominate sentiment to stay out. "He kept us out of war" was Wilson's biggest accomplishment in the eyes of many Americans, built on his Declaration of Neutrality from August 4, 1914: "The United States must be neutral in fact, as well as in name, during these days that are to try men's souls. We must be impartial in thought, as well as action, must put a curb upon our sentiments, as well as upon every transaction that might be construed as a preference of one party to the struggle before another."[43] Yet by the time he was sworn in for his second term in March 1917, Wilson's—and America's—hope of neutrality was diminishing by the day.

From its outset, the war had been close and crept ever closer to America. On May 17, 1915, a German submarine sank the British steamship *Lusitania*, killing almost 1,200 people, over one-hundred of them Americans. Germany issued an apology and paid reparations, but the sea war continued to affect America. During his 1916 campaign, Wilson issued an ultimatum demanding Germany stop its indiscriminate submarine warfare. Germany agreed, but on January 31, 1917, reneged on its promise, laying the course for hostile relations with America.

On February 3, Germany sank several US ships and America severed relations. At the beginning of March, the Zimmerman telegram[44] further pushed relations to the brink, and on March 4, (privately, and then publicly the next day) Wilson was inaugurated. On March 12, legislation was passed that US merchant ships were to be armed. On March 18, three US ships were torpedoed by German submarines. On March 20, Wilson's cabinet unanimously advised going to war. On April 2, Wilson spoke before a joint session of Congress, which overwhelmingly voted for a declaration of war that Wilson signed on April 6.

And so, just five months after winning re-election for having kept the US out of war, Wilson had taken America into the very conflict he had hoped to avoid.

America's response to being at war was equally swift. Prior to World War I, America's Army had been equivalent in size to those of smaller nations such as Chile and the Netherlands.[45] On May 18, about six weeks after Wilson signed the declaration of war, Congress passed the Selective Service Act and 24.2 million men registered.[46] Six months after that, on November 30, the first American units arrived in France; just under a year later, the war ended with the Armistice on November 11, 1918. Within this short timeframe, America would deploy two million men to France—with another two million awaiting deployment at home.[47] The massive infusion of fresh manpower proved decisive in a conflict that already had bled the other combatants white.[48]

At home, the federal government prepared itself for combat no less swiftly and aggressively. In just thirteen months, it extended its reach throughout society and the economy. It gave itself extensive power to curtail civil liberties (passing the Espionage Act on June 15, 1917; the Trading with the Enemy Act on October 6, 1917; the Sabotage Act on April 20, 1918; and the Sedition Act on May 16, 1918). It also gave the federal government almost unlimited power over the economy (legislation fixing prices was passed on August 10, 1917; on December 18, 1917, it took control of the rails). Assuming control of the War Industries Board on March 4, 1918, Barnard Baruch coordinated large sections of the economy; on April 8, 1918, the National War Labor Board began overseeing workforce disputes. Internally, the Overman Act on May 20, 1918, gave President Wilson carte blanche to reorganize the federal government as he deemed necessary.[49]

Not surprisingly, the federal government's vast effort was reflected in unprecedented spending. In 1917, federal spending rose $1.2 billion—an amount that almost equaled its all-time total spending peak reached in 1865, the last year of the Civil War. In 1918, it rose roughly $10 billion more, hitting $12.7 billion. And in 1919, it easily eclipsed the previous two years combined, climbing 50 percent to $18.5 billion.

Financing this massive expenditure in such a short time was a mammoth undertaking. President Wilson's Treasury Secretary, William G. McAdoo scoured the Civil War for lessons and came away with "a pretty clear idea of what not to do."[50] Instead of simply printing money, McAdoo was determined to rely predominantly on loans, and not just from normal investors but average citizens, too. Passed on April 24, 1917, the Liberty Loan Act would raise $20 billion. The first Liberty Loan for $2 billion in May 1917 attracted four million subscribers. A second $3 billion issue in October 1917 was oversubscribed by more than 50 percent.[51] "Eventually at least half of American families subscribed, with Americans of moderate incomes (under $2,000 a year) purchasing nearly a third of the bonds."[52]

Even with McAdoo's predetermined loan-to-tax ratio of three-to-one,[53] federal revenues had to rise dramatically. To achieve this, the administration and Congress pushed through three large tax increases between 1916 and 1919.[54] A combination of income and corporate taxes, these particularly targeted upper incomes and "war" and "excess" corporate profits (as an example, 1918's Revenue Act aimed to raise roughly four-fifths of its estimated $6 billion from "taxes on incomes, war profits, excess profits and estates.")[55] It also broadened the base by lowering exemption levels. To administer all these new taxes, IRS personnel increased from 4,000 in 1913 to 15,800 in 1920.[56]

And it worked: federal revenues exploded. In 1917, receipts increased almost 50 percent, exceeding $1 billion for the first time. In 1918 revenues tripled to $3.6 billion—more than the entire public debt of 1917. In 1919, revenues hit $5.1 billion and in 1920, $6.6 billion. Even with the huge new revenues, Treasury Secretary McAdoo's disproportionate reliance on loans meant deficits exploded too: $900 million in 1917; $9 billion in 1918; and $13.4 billion in 1919. Simultaneously, federal debt also skyrocketed. In 1917 it hit the highest level in history up to that time—$2.975 billion—and increased dramatically from there. In 1918, it quadrupled to $12.5 billion, doubling again in 1919 to $25.5 billion.

World War I left the federal government at its peak—not just fiscally in spending, taxes, deficits, and debt, but arguably in power as well. By having fully institutionalized and broadened its income and corporate tax base, the federal government now had unprecedented means to remain at these peaks. In 1919, spending stood at 23.4 percent of GDP, versus 13 percent in 1865. Federal receipts stood at 6.5 percent of GDP, versus 3.3 percent in 1865. The federal deficit stood at 16.9 percent of GDP, versus 1865's 9.6 percent; 1919's federal debt was 32.2 percent of GDP, versus 1865's 26.7 percent. The federal government emerged from World War I far larger than it had left the Civil War—and it had achieved this in far less time.

Yet for all the government's enhanced power—much of which now resided with the president and executive branch—Wilson himself did *not* institutionalize most of it. As Wilson biographer Kendrick Clements writes of his wartime approach: " ... During World War I he resisted dramatic extensions of federal and executive power in favor of an attempt to mobilize the economy by voluntary cooperation among government, business, and labor."[57] Quoting Wilson, Clements writes that the president feared the government was "in danger of creating too much machinery."[58]

The examples of Wilson's reliance on a voluntary approach—rather than formal government structures that could become institutionalized—are many. The American Protective League was given "quasi-police powers" to supplement the Bureau of Investigation's limited means to investigate despite enhanced authority to do so.[59] The War Industries Board (1917), the Food Administration (1917), the Fuel Administration (1917), and the Railroad Administration (1917), were all "run by 'dollar-a-year' businessmen who volunteered their services [and] the new agencies also depended on voluntary methods ... "[60] Even within the government, "Wilson made little use of the Overman Act," despite its broad authority "to make such redistribution of functions among executive agencies as he may deem necessary."[61]

SECTION VII
1919-1929

Thus, the federal government entered the post-World War I period larger than it had ever been, both quantitatively and qualitatively. It was well positioned to exist this way permanently—but Americans were not prepared for it to do so.

World War I ended in 1918, and the federal government spent $12.7 billion in that year alone, four times more than the entire national debt the year before. It took in $3.6 billion in receipts, almost double its total spending in 1917. This made the federal government's bigness quantifiably undeniable. Yet it was the *qualitative* extension of its authority that most prepared the federal government for a permanently expanded role. By dint of the war, the government now extended into virtually every aspect of American life. Nowhere was this clearer than in its power to tax. In addition to raising receipts through tariffs, a power on which it had relied almost exclusively since its inception, remember that the federal government now had the constitutional power to tax income. The federal government therefore not only was much larger, but it also had a fundamentally expanded ability to finance a vastly larger government in perpetuity.

Having experienced this vastly expanded size and scope, the federal government stood in the same position as the American soldiers now returning from France. In the words of a popular song of the era: "How ya' gonna keep 'em down on the farm after they've seen Paree?"

As it turned out, America returned its federal government to "the farm" with surprising ease. The signs that the nation was eager to do so were clear. Of course, the most obvious example was Wilson's stinging defeat over the League of Nations, despite his national barnstorming—an effort that caused the president's collapse and came close to costing him his life. Just a year after the 1918 Armistice, a Senate majority rejected America's membership in this international intergovernmental body on November 19, 1919. A year later, ratification failed again in the Senate.[62]

Other Wilson post-World War I transition proposals were similarly rejected: "Wilson recovered enough to propose setting up public works programs and farm irrigation projects to ease the transition, but the climate for a muscular federal government had disappeared with the war."[63]

Democrats—Wilson's party—had been steadily losing seats in Congress since 1916, and in 1920, they lost a whopping 61 House seats and 10 Senate seats. Then, the 1920 presidential election epitomized the ultimate rejection of Wilson and the embrace of a return to small government. Warren G. Harding, a relatively unknown senator from Ohio who would be best remembered for scandals in his subsequent administration, conducted a front-porch campaign based on "normalcy," citing "America's present need" was for "normalcy" and "not revolution, but restoration; not agitation, but adjustment; not surgery, but serenity; not the dramatic, but the dispassionate; not experiment, but equipoise; not submergence in internationality, but sustainment in triumphant nationality."[64]

He would go on to win in a landslide, the biggest in Republican history up to then. Harding was against "war taxes" without a war and opposed to the lower tariffs enacted during the Wilson presidency, which he believed would trigger a recession.[65] These two issues were the central points of his administration.[66] Harding's tax cutting would continue throughout the post-World War I decade; Congress cut taxes five times in the 1920s: in 1921, 1924, 1926, 1928, and 1929.[67]

Calvin Coolidge, who became president following Harding's death in 1923, would continue the momentum on downsizing the federal government. As Morison observed: "[T]here was no change in political or economic policy between the Harding and the Coolidge administrations. Policies of high tariff, tax reduction, and government support to industry were pushed to extremes, and a high plateau of prosperity was attained."[68] Known as "Silent Cal," Coolidge was an exemplar of what Americans wanted from their federal government: "Frugality, unpretentiousness, and taciturnity."[69] Walter Lippmann's remarks about Coolidge summed up this overlooked President, who would become one of Ronald Reagan's favorites.

> Mr. Coolidge's genius for inactivity is developed to a very high point. It is far from being an indolent inactivity. It is a grim, determined, alert inactivity which keeps Mr. Coolidge occupied constantly. Nobody has ever worked harder at inactivity, with such force of character, with such unremitting attention to detail, with such conscientious devotion to the task. Inactivity is a political philosophy and a party program with Mr. Coolidge, and nobody should mistake his unflinching adherence to it for a soft and easy desire to let things slide. Mr. Coolidge's inactivity is not merely the absence of activity. It is, on the contrary, a steady application to the task of neutralizing and thwarting political activity wherever there are signs of life.[70]

Coolidge himself said as much, though as to be expected, more succinctly: "It is much more important to kill bad bills than to pass good ones."[71] When Coolidge prepared to leave office and hand the presidency to Herbert Hoover, his final address to Congress in 1928 captured America's unparalleled condition in its opening lines: "No Congress of the United States ever assembled, on surveying the state of the Union, has met with a more pleasing prospect than that which appears at the present time. In the domestic field there is tranquility and contentment, harmonious relations between management and wage earner, freedom from industrial strife, and the highest record of years of prosperity."[72]

In 1928, Democrats faced the hopeless task of confronting Republicans' record—Will Rogers summed it up with "You can't lick this Prosperity thing"—and saw Hoover win in a landslide.[73]

Overall, the economy's performance from 1919 to 1929 was astounding. According to MeasuringWorth, from 1919 through 1929, America's real GDP rose a staggering 40 percent. On a per capita basis, it increased 21 percent in just over a decade.[74]

As the economy grew and prosperity flowed, the federal government shrank. In 1918, World War I's last year, federal spending was more than the entire federal debt. Due to massive US aid to Europe, on top of the loans already extended to the Allies, spending would rise another 50 percent in 1919—but from there it plummeted. From 1920 on, it fell each year by large amounts until 1924, when it remained essentially flat through 1929.[75]

Driven by five tax cuts over the decade, receipts followed spending. Following the post-war drop in 1920, federal receipts fell by 15 percent to $5.6 billion in 1921, by 29 percent to $4 billion in 1922, and slightly in 1923, remaining essentially flat through 1929. It should be noted that even so, 1929's receipts of $3.9 billion still surpassed 1917's federal debt.

With spending falling more rapidly than receipts, even as taxes were being cut, record deficits turned quickly into surpluses. From a 1919 deficit of $13.4 billion, the budget swung to a $291 million surplus in 1920, and only continued to grow. In 1927, it hit an unprecedented $1.2 billion, higher than the entire public debt of 1915. These surpluses, which ran every year from 1920 through 1930, quickly pared back the federal government's debt, dropping it by a full third in just ten years.

In nominal terms, the federal government was admittedly larger than it had ever been. But benchmarked to the economy, it was small. In 1929, as a percentage of GDP, federal spending was smaller than it had been eleven years after the Civil War—amounting to just under 3 percent of GDP versus 3.1 percent in 1876. At the same time, its receipts were only slightly larger (3.7 percent versus 3.5 percent), and its budget surplus almost twice as large. And its debt was appreciably smaller—16 percent versus 25 percent. This should also be viewed in perspective: America had not only funded its World War I costs but a substantial amount of the Allies' costs too; additionally, it had provided significant assistance to Europe after the war.

SECTION VIII
Conclusion

For almost one-and-a-half centuries America had a small federal government. While this may shock Americans today, it was simply a continuation of the norm of the time. Because except for intermittent crises, America had no precedent for anything else. America's colonial government had been small. It was Britain's attempt to enlarge it that precipitated America's revolution and independence. Absent the fillip of an increased British government, increased British taxes to pay for it, and increased British government intrusion into areas that American colonists thought rightfully theirs—or beyond the right of any government—the Declaration of Independence would have been impossible to imagine in 1776.

The Articles of Confederation gave Americans a smaller government still. Arguably there was essentially no central government at all, little more than a league of newly independent small states. When experience proved to the newly independent Americans that a central government was essential, they severely constrained it with the Constitution. An important and often overlooked aspect of America's new central government was that it was designed to not just be constrained, but also to be small.

De Tocqueville had correctly foretold that crises would increase government taxes. Yet what he had not foreseen was that after these crises ended, those increased taxes and enlarged federal government would shrink back. After both the Civil War (which was brutal and waged almost entirely on American soil) and World War I (which required America's full level of participation in money, material, and men), as well as several other crises of lesser magnitude, America's federal government returned to its previous small size. And it did so quickly—so quickly that it left no residual larger government still in place to be built on in the next crisis. Nor did returning to a small federal government provoke any crisis of its own—something that could easily have happened had those in power sought to retain their power. That the federal government returned to its previously small size so quickly and so easily—or that those who benefitted from the increase did not more strongly resist its decrease—simply reflects the widely shared acceptance, both inside and outside government, that this was its proper role and that small was its proper size.

Henry David Thoreau's observation in 1849 "that government is best that governs least" was a sentiment that greatly predated him. It existed from America's earliest origins and extended throughout the colonial period. It would also postdate him, extending forward well into the 20th century.

Over and over against repeated opportunities to retain or grow it, America's federal government was not permanently enlarged for 140 years. Despite having increased quantitatively (in manpower and money) and qualitatively (in function and power), small prevailed, even after a short-term enlarged government had proven itself effective in a crisis. Its paradigm of smallness held. And as America's small government paradigm held, the socialist Left continued to be shut out in America, as Chapter Six will show. Chapters Seven and Eight therefore pose dual questions. How in the face of contrary precedent did America's federal government grow into today's behemoth? How in the face of contrary precedent did today's socialist Left reach its current size and level of insurgency?

CHAPTER SIX

THE SOCIALIST LEFT'S HISTORY IN AMERICA

SECTION I

Introduction

Born of capitalism, republicanism, and Constitution, once independent and free, America did not stop at its self-creation. Almost immediately, it began re-creating itself on an expanded and accelerated scale. This was made possible by the new nation's small government model that protected individuals, states, and the economy alike. In so doing, the socialist Left was also shut out of operating on any significant scale in America for over two centuries.

America blocked the socialist Left's ability to take root on all fronts: Economically, through prosperity; politically, through the Constitution; and societally, through republicanism. Both politically and societally, America nurtured capitalism, which in turn spurred the prosperity that economically stifled the socialist Left, creating walls to block it that grew as the nation did. It is for these reasons that, unlike what has been observed in other similar democratic nations, the socialist Left has never had a significant sustained presence in America.

This is not to say that the socialist Left never existed in America. From America's earliest beginnings there was a socialist Left on its soil. Most of England's early colonies—Jamestown, Plymouth, and Massachusetts Bay—were owned by English merchants and staffed by their employees. Effectively operated as company property, the land was held under communal ownership,[1] and socialization of the means of production is the capstone of socialist Left ideology. Too, Rhode Island and Providence Plantation were founded by, in historian Samuel Elliott Morison's words, "left-wing Puritans."[2]

Indeed, the socialist Left has a long and complicated history in America. Yet despite its continuity and variety, each iteration shares a common element: failure. This repeated failure also explains why various movements and organizational structures that have been misconstrued as indications of the socialist Left's influence in America—such as unions and cooperatives—were not. It is a failure so uniformly utter and rapid that it tends to overshadow the socialist Left's very presence. As a result, rather than having been written in chapters, the history of America's socialist Left is more aptly recorded in footnotes.

This chapter focuses on the history of the socialist Left in America. It examines the socialist Left's various iterations and aims, as well as each attempt's reasons for failure. No matter its form, the socialist Left was antithetical to America's foundational principles and Americans' aspirations, and therefore unacceptable to the population's overwhelming majority.

Because this chapter will observe the socialist Left in a variety of forms, time periods, principles, and participants, a basic question is raised: What do we mean by "the socialist Left" in America? There is a temptation to fall into Justice Potter Stewart's subjective dictum on pornography: "I know it when I see it." The question of what defines the socialist Left is not uniquely America's. It is one that has bedeviled the socialist Left itself. Much of Karl Marx's writing and most virulent criticism is directed at those socialists that he identified as falling short ideologically. Within the Marxist school this same internecine warfare has continued. Invariably, Marxist leaders—from Lenin to Stalin to Mao to Castro to Ho Chi Minh to Pol Pot to infinity—wind up recreating Marxism in their own image.

As Ludwig von Mises, a leader in the Austrian school of economics, wrote: "It is a matter of dispute whether, prior to the middle of the 19th century, there existed any clear conception of the socialist idea."[3] It could be argued that a century-and-a-half later there is still no clear conception of what the socialist Left is, even among the socialist Left itself.

For our purposes in examining the socialist Left in America, however, we will do so through von Mises's definition of socialism: "By which is understood the socialization of the means of production with its corollary, the centralized control of the whole of production by one social or, more accurately, state organ."[4] Abridging private property rights is therefore a good litmus test for what constitutes the socialist Left. Of course, the protection of property was what John Locke saw as government's primary purpose, and Locke in turn was the primary influence on those who declared America's independence and wrote our Constitution. It is no wonder then that the socialist Left was, and remains, fundamentally out of step with the American political, societal, and economic status quo.

Many groups within the broad Left, which are often identified as predecessors to today's socialist Left, could never bring themselves to cross the Rubicon on curtailing private property rights. A case in point is the "radical" Depression-era farm organization, the Farmers' Holiday Association, which forcibly blocked foreclosure actions on farmers in Iowa. Whatever its other ideals may have been, at its core, the FHA's actions were intended to retain the farmer's private property, to keep it from shifting to banks or the government. Such examples exist throughout American history—as mentioned earlier, including Shays' Rebellion that increased calls for a stronger central government in the late 18th century.

In examining the socialist Left's long history of failure in America, this chapter will briefly review the most prominent groups through which the socialist Left attempted—or which are commonly misidentified as attempting to—advance its agenda. These include: the early antebellum commune attempts; the late 19th century Populists and the early 20th century Progressives; Eugene Debs and the Socialists; the Communists; and the post-World War II split of the new Left from the old Left. While each of these groups differs in form and principle, those that were truly socialist Left each exhibit the same defining trait: a diametrical opposition to America's founding principles and the status quo that embodies them. This rejection is an important reason why the socialist Left has failed throughout its American history—either in its attempts to advance its ideology or in its being barred from the organizations it tried to use to do so. Equally important has been the socialist Left's inability to offer Americans an adequate return for joining them in rejecting the status quo. Historically, there has never been any real benefit to Americans for supporting the socialist

Left, and consequently, the socialist Left could never get a significant portion of Americans to join it in any type of organization.

Finally, the socialist Left's failure became so pronounced that by the latter half of the 20th century it had to not only forsake trying to advance itself as a separate party, but from seeking to explicitly advance socialism at all. Instead, it had to sublimate itself entirely, to pursuing goals through separate *ad hoc* movements within the broad collection of groups on the left side of America's ideological spectrum. Rather than seeking to advance itself as "the Movement," as the socialist Left had done successfully abroad, America's socialist Left resorted to hiding itself within the various movements of what we recognize today as the traditional Left. In a political, societal, and economic sense, the socialist Left's history until well into the 21st century was one of being effectively inconsequential.

As example is often the clearest teacher, specifically, this chapter will examine the socialist Left's failed attempts to directly implement its agenda, such as through the early 19th-century Owenite communes and the early 20th-century attempts at running as an independent third party in national elections. It will also examine the broad occupational groups of agriculture and manufacturing from which, according to socialist theory and practice, it should have arisen. This chapter recounts the American experience with the socialist Left: that it did not exist where it "should" have—or where many mistakenly believe it did—and that where it *did* exist, it never existed long or amounted to much.

The socialist Left did not fail because Americans were reluctant to join organizations, not motivated by economic concerns, or because there was a total absence of socialist opportunities. Americans have always been avid joiners, and highly motivated by economic concerns. And while some socialist organizations did exist in various forms, in various places, in various periods (though never for long), the overwhelming majority of Americans rejected the socialist Left because it offered them nothing—either tangible or intangible. This is shown—and will be examined here—throughout its history, from its very beginnings to the disintegration and dispersion as the old Left and emergence as a new Left following the Port Huron Statement of the 1960s. These attempts include both socialist and communist organizations, which as von Mises points out is a distinction without a difference—they are one and the same. "In the terminology of Marx and Engels the words communism and socialism are synonymous … No Marxian ever ventured, before 1917, to distinguish between communism and socialism."[5]

This chapter will also examine the occupational organizations of American workers in agriculture and manufacturing. These are, after all, the groups which socialists identify as leading the way to socialism from capitalism, and the groups which successful socialist Left leaders abroad (Lenin, Mao, and more) have used as the basis for their socialist states.[6] Yet in neither the direct attempts, nor in the occupational groups—farm organizations or manufacturing unions—did America's socialist Left succeed.

SECTION II
America's Origins to the Civil War: The Socialist Left Seeks to Separate

Even as America itself was just beginning, the socialist Left was on a course to failure. Of the early colonies of Jamestown, Plymouth, and Massachusetts Bay, Samuel Eliot Morison wrote: "In no one of these colonies was private ownership of land permitted until communal ownership proved to be a failure."[7] It proved so in short order.

Conservative author Daniel Flynn quotes Plymouth governor William Bradford on the colony's three-year attempt at communal ownership: "The strong, or man of parts, had no more division of victuals and clothes than he that was weak and not able to do a quarter the other could; this was thought injustice."[8] It was the decision to switch to private ownership that "made all hands very industrious."[9] Over the next three centuries, its opposition to private property would regularly undermine America's socialist Left.

Once capitalism took over, America took off. As seen in Chapter One, even before it became an independent nation, America boasted the world's highest living standard. And once it shed the shackles of Britain's mercantilism and colonial policies, and its own Articles of Confederation, the new nation grew even faster and richer.

From 1790 to 1815, America added five states to its original thirteen, and its population more than doubled from 3.9 million to 8.4 million. According to MeasuringWorth, an invaluable calculator of America's historical GDP, nominal GDP quintupled from $193 million to $935 million, while its real GDP (measured in constant 2017 dollars) more than tripled from $5 billion to $15.7 billion. With economic growth outpacing the population's, real GDP per capita (the true yardstick for personal prosperity) rose by almost 50 percent (from $1,266 to $1,863).[10]

The second generation of post-independence America also prospered. From 1815 to 1840, America added eight more states and its population again more than doubled (from 8.4 million to 17.1 million). America's nominal GDP grew 70 percent (from $935 million to $1.6 billion), while its real GDP jumped almost 150 percent (from $15.7 billion to $38.5 billion). And again, real GDP per capita grew too (over 20 percent, from $1,863 to $2,246).

America's third post-independence generation bettered its predecessor economically yet again. From 1840 to 1860, America added seven states and its population grew over 80 percent (from 17.1 million to 31.5 million). Nominal GDP almost tripled ($1.6 billion to $4.4 billion) and real GDP grew 160 percent (from $38.5 billion to $99.8 billion). Once more, real GDP per capita grew sharply, rising over 40 percent (from $2,246 to $3,168).

In just over seven decades, America had added twenty additional states, and its population was over eight times larger. Economically, it also experienced astonishing growth. Nominal GDP was twenty-three times larger, and real GDP twenty times. As for personal living standards, on a real GDP per capita basis, America's living standard was two-and-a-half times greater than the already world-class standard set by colonial America. No American generation had known anything but prosperity.

Amidst all of this growth came the Industrial Revolution, which caused America's population to undergo a huge shift from farm to factory. According to US Census statistics, in 1790 just 202,000 Americans lived in urban areas, while 3.7 million lived in rural areas. By 1860, although America's population was still overwhelmingly rural (25.2 million), 6.2 million lived in urban areas.[11]

This is the America Alexis de Tocqueville described in his monumental book, *Democracy in America*. Beginning in 1831, he traveled extensively throughout every region of the country, before publishing *Democracy* in 1835.

Writing in his foreword to the 1848 edition, de Tocqueville described post-independence America as having "increased in population, territory, and wealth; and, let it be noted, throughout that period it has been not only the most prosperous but also the most stable of all the peoples in the world."[12]

To de Tocqueville, America's overriding trait was unmistakable:

> No novelty in the United States struck me more vividly ... than the equality of conditions. It was easy to see the immense influence of this basic fact on the whole course of society. It gives a particular turn to public opinion and a particular twist to the laws, new maxims to those who govern and particular habits to the governed. I soon realized that the influence of this fact extends far beyond political mores and laws, exercising dominion over civil society as much as over the government; it creates opinions, gives birth to feelings, suggests customs, and modifies whatever it does not create.[13]

De Tocqueville's countryman, J. Hector St. John de Crèvecoeur, had made the same observation in 1782 in *Letters from an American Farmer*: "We are all animated with the spirit of industry which is unfettered and unrestrained, because each person works for himself ... We are the most perfect society now existing in the world. Here man is as free as he ought to be, nor is this pleasing equality so transitory as many others are."[14]

What both were describing in general (and de Tocqueville would go on to describe in minute detail in *Democracy*) was the continuation of what had driven America toward independence decades earlier: capitalism and republicanism, both now enshrined in the Constitution. The three reinforced each other, driving America ever onward and upward.

To the question of why there was no socialist Left movement in America as existed in European countries, de Tocqueville saw the answer in its "equality of conditions," which in America, was formalized in the government. As de Tocqueville wrote of America's government: "The people reign over the American political world as God rules over the universe. It is the cause and the end of all things; everything rises out of it and is absorbed back into it ... In America the people are a master who must be indulged to the utmost possible limits."[15]

Because the people had an "equality of conditions" and governed themselves through representatives who were of the same encompassing equality, there was "no class hatred because the people is everything, and nobody dare[d] to struggle against it."[16] Additionally, de Tocqueville observed "there is no public distress to exploit because the physical state of the country offers such an immense scope to industry that man has only to be left to himself to work marvels."[17]

In short, equality, self-government, and prosperity prevailed. There simply was nothing to rebel against. "As men equal among themselves came to people the United States, there is as yet no natural or permanent antagonism between the interests of the various inhabitants."[18] And there was nothing the socialist Left could do to encourage it, because, as de Tocqueville observed, "there are no proletarians in America. Everyone, having some possession to defend, recognizes the right to property in principle."[19]

Of course, despite his thorough examination, de Tocqueville was wrong[20]. There was a socialist Left in America—or at least there tried to be. But that it could escape such scrutiny as de Tocqueville's speaks to its completely inconsequential nature.

As Flynn recounts, the socialist Left of this period retreated from America into its own communal societies. But even America's communal movement only lasted a moment, with Robert Owen's effort as the most prominent example. A transplant from Britain, Owen brought with him a vision of living completely at odds from what de Tocqueville observed everywhere else in America. With an ardent gift for self-promotion, Owen attracted a great deal of publicity and attention, including from American leaders.[21] He also attracted a few followers. Owen tried to realize his utopian vision of shared work and shared returns in several communes in America, most famously in New Harmony, Indiana.[22] Or rather "infamously," because it failed miserably and quickly. While there were a few salacious, smaller reasons for its failure, the main sticking point was the same as had been for its early colonial predecessors: in the long view, people will only work hard for themselves. Flynn details several such communal attempts,[23] and they all equaled failure. By the time of the Civil War, the commune movement, which sought to voluntarily separate from American ideals and provide an example of socialist Left principles' success, was gone.[24] So fleeting was it that de Tocqueville missed it, and few today know it ever occurred.

SECTION III
1865-1900: Social Upheaval and Populism—
The Socialist Left Organizes

When examining America and the socialist Left, it makes sense to review post-Civil War America in three categories: agriculture, manufacturing, and the socialist Left. As de Tocqueville observed, America's political parties relied "not on principles but on material interests." In the same vein, the socialist Left's Marxist foundation also sees material interests as society's driver. Given these two foundations, and the great transition from farm to factory that was occurring at the time, the best review of the socialist Left in this era is by how Americans worked: agriculture and manufacturing. Both would be fundamentally altered by the injection of capital on a greatly increased scale. According to Marx, such an injection of capital—and with it, capitalism—should have been a breeding ground for the socialist Left. Yet Americans on farms and in factories did not turn to the socialist Left any more than they did to the earlier Owenite communes.

Like its predecessors, this generation saw continued growth and prosperity for the most part. America continued to grow, both economically and in population. From 1865 to 1900, America's population (34.2 million to 76.1 million) and real GDP per capita (from $3,741 to $6,857) both more than doubled.[25] This prosperity continued to be more attractive than socialism and Americans adopted new organizational forms to pursue it more successfully.

SECTION IV
Cooperatives and Unions: 1865-1900

In both agriculture and manufacturing, the influx of capital changed the way America worked. It also changed the relationship *within* American work, spurring both farmers and workers to begin to organize on a large scale. Although cooperatives and unions had existed in America for some time, the latter half of the 19th century is when they really exploded. Loosely defined, a cooperative is comprised of members who seek to advance their common interests in buying and selling particular goods, and a union is comprised of members who seek to advance the common interests of their occupation. The cooperatives and unions of the time offered tangible benefits to their members, such as goods sold at discount and life and burial insurance. They also sought to meet the economic powers their members faced with their own countervailing power.

Agriculture historians trace American cooperatives back to the American farmers' adoption of the Rochdale model, which originated in Britain in 1844.[26] By 1900, there were an estimated one-thousand cooperatives operating in America.[27]

Whether the function was buying or selling, the goal of agricultural cooperatives was the same: get (or save) more money for its members. In the case of selling, cooperatives came to perform some functions of middlemen, and sometimes even sought to withhold crops from the market to drive up prices.[28] Ultimately this failed—the free-rider problem (those who reap the benefits of an action or organization without contributing in any meaningful way) ultimately undermined efforts to control supply and prices for farm crops.[29] Nevertheless, cooperatives proved extremely popular, and farmers demanded that farm organizations operate them. This was due to cooperatives' focus on economic efficiency. The shift to efficiency and away from market control, demonstrates that cooperatives and their members had firmly accepted capitalist fundamentals.[30] It is also important to ensure that the focus cooperatives had on market reform—whether buying or selling—is not mistaken for an attempt at social reform. These were economic operations and although they assuredly had social aspects, social *reform* was not one of them.

Union efforts in cities and non-agricultural labor broadly reflected the same. Many worker institutions offered benefits to their members, and though they differed slightly from one another, they were all "infused with a spirit of mutuality."[31] In fact, union benefits often included cooperatives which, like their agricultural counterparts, had no interest in overturning the social order. The goal of the earliest national union, the Knights of Labor, was conciliation rather than confrontation in the workplace.[32]

SECTION V
Agriculture and Labor Organizations: 1865-1900

While American agriculture and labor organizations both sought to improve their members' conditions within the markets, neither ever sought to overturn those markets—let alone the economic order. They even pursued similar actions to achieve their goals. In agriculture, it was the withholding of crops with the (ultimately unsuccessful) goal of increasing prices. In labor, it was the withholding of labor—the strike—to increase wages, reduce working hours, and alter working conditions.

On the agricultural side, a parade of farm organizations, many scarcely remembered today, moved through this period.[33] Reflecting the great diversity in American agriculture, these groups arose all over the country—and reflecting the vagaries of agriculture, many were transitory, lasting only a few short years before vanishing.

The first large national agricultural organization was called the Grange. Founded in 1866 as a social and educational organization, the Grange became a success when it embraced cooperatives[34] at the insistence of its members. The Grange's popularity led to the Farmers Alliance, which existed as three separate Alliances—Northern, Southern, and Colored.[35] The Alliance was an economic movement from the start and it immediately embraced cooperatives, which proved a big draw.[36] The Southern Alliance had over one million members by 1890.[37]

On the manufacturing side of things, labor unions representing a multiplicity of trades such as shoemaking, construction, coal mining, and iron production proved the most resilient and active, staging large-scale strikes for an eight-hour workday. Despite early popularity, these unions were effectively wiped out by 1873's recession, and it took until 1877 for a union to enter the public's consciousness in a significant way.

The Knights of Labor, a general union not confined to a single trade, used rituals to bond and shield their members. When the Knights held their first General Assembly in 1878, Terence Powderly, the former mayor of Scranton, Pennsylvania, was elected as its leader, or Grand Master Workman. While the general perception of this era is one of continuous violent conflict between workers and employers, the Knights actually opposed strikes in principle, as

Powderly abhorred their destructiveness.[38] Still, the Knights did sanction strikes as needed, such as when employers refused arbitration, or its members were "victimized."[39]

One issue Powderly consistently cautioned his membership to avoid was the burgeoning movement for an eight-hour day.[40] Eight-Hour Leagues sprouted nationwide in the 1880s, and on May 1, 1886, a wave of parades filled many major American cities. Three days later on May 4, a protest called by anarchists in Chicago's Haymarket Square resulted in multiple deaths when anarchists were accused of throwing a bomb that instigated a riot in which eight people were killed.

Despite the Knights of Labor's attempts to disassociate itself from socialism, anarchism, and even the eight-hour movement, one of the four anarchists tried, convicted, and hanged for the Haymarket explosion was a Knight of Labor. Thus, the way was open for a new national union. Led by Samuel Gompers, a British immigrant cigarmaker, the American Federation of Labor was created in 1886 as a conservative counter to the Knights of Labor. The AFL too sought cooperation with business leaders, and a place in America's industrial order.

Still, major strikes persisted. These were enlarged by "sympathy strikes," where unions not directly engaged in the initial strike would join in support.[41] Eugene Debs, then head of the American Railway Union, lauded sympathy strikes as "the hope of civilization and the supreme glory of mankind."[42] He would soon unleash its most spectacular manifestation—one that would ultimately prove to be his union's demise.

The period's biggest sympathy strike involved the Pullman Car Company and the American Railway Union boycotting all Pullman cars on any trains. The ARU action spiraled into a shutdown of the rails in the Midwest and Far West. Using the Sherman Antitrust Act, which had been enacted to promote competition in commerce, an injunction was issued against the ARU. Troops were dispatched to protect railway lines, martial law was declared in Chicago where the Pullman company was located, and the ARU's president (and future socialist presidential candidate) Eugene Debs was jailed along with other ARU leaders.

Although the frequent violence gave the appearance of revolutionary upheaval, neither the Knights of Labor nor the AFL were sympathetic to, or welcoming of, the socialist Left. Their goals remained centered on their members' betterment *within* the existing economic system. ARU president Eugene Debs' radicalization in prison would personify what occurred: individuals might be swayed by the socialist Left but the broad mass of workers were not.

SECTION VI
Populist Party

Arguably the most important political occurrence of the latter quarter of the 19th century was the national third-party effort of the People's Party. A "people's party" immediately calls to mind the socialist Left, but once again, there is no connection. Dubbed the Populist Party, it was a mass of contradictions and characters, as well as an amalgamation of the old Greenback Party (an earlier third-party effort that aimed at an inflationary "easy money" policy, among other things) and the Farmers Alliance. During the 1890s, it also constituted the most important third-party movement since 1860 and was one of the more significant in American history. It was the period's second combination of agriculture and labor in a third-party effort (the Greenback Party, which received just over 300,000 votes in the 1880 election, being the first).

The Populists' platform called for government ownership of railroads ("The railroad corporations will either own the people or the people must own the railroads"), telephones and telegraphs, unlimited use of silver as money, a graduated income tax, an eight-hour day for labor, and various electoral reforms.[43]

In the 1892 presidential election, the Populists' candidate, James B. Weaver, won one million votes (over eight percent of the popular vote), 22 electoral votes (in six states, four of which they carried); the party also garnered seven House seats and six Senate seats. Four years later in 1896, the Populist Party endorsed William Jennings Bryan, the Democrats' presidential nominee. Bryan had emerged from the field at the Democrats' convention in Chicago where he electrified delegates with his Cross of Gold speech. Vilifying President Cleveland and his adherence to the gold standard, Bryan exclaimed: "Having behind us the commercial interests and the laboring interests and all the toiling masses, we shall answer their demands for a gold standard by saying to them, you shall not press down upon the brow of labor this crown of thorns. You shall not crucify mankind upon a cross of gold."

Yet in the end, it was the Populist Party that died. The Democrat Party having taken on their issues, and the Populists in turn having given their presidential endorsement to the Democrats' nominee, there was no reason for the Populist Party to continue. The Democrats in turn were soundly defeated in the general election.

American historian Norman Pollack states that the Populist Party considered itself a class movement,[44] but Richard Hofstader, a leftist Pulitzer Prize-winning American historian, correctly observed that it was not really so radical.[45] While Populists certainly believed government should be more than a neutral observer, saw farmers as more a class than an occupation,[46] and were, according to Hofstadter, the first modern political movement of significance to assert government's responsibility to proactively work for the common good, these did not make it the socialist Left. Rather, Populism is more accurately described by Hofstadter as "American entrepreneurial radicalism."[47]

The specific case of the Populist Party serves as a general explanation of the period. It unquestionably attests to the development of a Left in American agriculture and labor. And while there *were* sprinklings of the socialist Left within this broader Left, this broad Left was still a far cry from a true socialist Left.

The true socialist Left came to America from Europe in the aftermath of the failed European socialist revolutions of 1848. The first English publication of Marx's *Communist Manifesto* appeared in America in 1871—almost a generation after it was first published in London in German.[48] Still, these true socialists never amounted to more than agitators working within larger movements that were not of their creation, such as the Eight-Hour League. Further, these larger Left movements did not want the socialist Left's help. Powderly himself expressed animosity toward the attempts of the "mouthers and spouters of bolshevism" to infiltrate the Knights of Labor.[49] Despite that the period after the Civil War saw the development of America's Left, the socialist Left barely registered—not even within this broad American Left, much less within American society as a whole.

Americans in both the agricultural and non-agricultural sectors joined the many organizations that existed at this time—both on the left and the right. They did so for a variety of benefits. The organizations that offered these benefits grew, like the Grange and the Farmers Alliance through their cooperatives; those that did not, died. The goals and transactional nature of these organizations reflected the economic motivation of their members. Agriculture organizations sought higher prices for what their members produced. Labor organizations sought higher wages for the hours their members worked. It should be noted that even in organizations that were to the left politically, their programs did not seek to overturn the prevailing capitalist system. At most they might call for switching ownership of the monopolies that they faced to the state (e.g., the railroads, telegraphs, and telephones, in the case of the Populists[50]), but they had no interest in sweeping away private property, least of all from their members.

When these organizations did pursue politics, it was only as a means to realize their basic economic goals. In the case of the Populists, the period's biggest and most ambitious political movement, the decision to pursue political action occurred only after both of the two major parties had embraced policies they opposed—President Cleveland's "sound money" and President Harrison's high tariffs. And even in this most focal of efforts, the Populists still won less than 10 percent of the popular vote and effectively died after just two presidential elections.

The socialist Left that had begun to emigrate from Europe in mid-century still remained foreign in every sense of the word. It was a follower within, not a leader of, America's broad Left—continually, and unsuccessfully, seeking entry. The closest America came to realizing a socialist Left at the time was epitomized by Eugene Debs's transformation—which also epitomized its plight and fate. Jailed for his role in the Pullman Strike, Debs entered prison as a member of the overall Left and exited an ardent socialist. He ran for president five times in the early 1900s on the Socialist ticket—and failed resoundingly each time.

SECTION VII
1900-1929: The Progressive Era

Known historically as the "Progressive Era," this label now seems a misnomer because of the contemporary Left's misappropriation of the term "progressive."

There was little of today's "progressive" in the era that bears its name. The Temperance Movement featured prominently, and eugenics was the day's pathbreaking science.[51] Even the socialist Left, which then came out of society's shadows, held views at odds with those of today's self-declared "progressives." It opposed immigration, which it saw as undermining America's own working class, and the pursuit of women's rights was viewed as fracturing the unity of class struggle.

Several prominent features of the Populist Period's upheaval passed into the Progressive Era, but many did not make it out. For example, violence was still used as a means of pursuing economic and political ends, but even that at a much lower rate. A third party arose, too—the Progressive Party—but by the era's end, third parties would also be abandoned as meaningful political attempts.

A bigger change was the switch from confrontation to integration among the predominant groups of agriculture and labor. In agriculture, this was embodied in the newly founded Farm Bureau, which pursued gains for its members through greater economic efficiency. In labor, it was the American Federation of Labor which, with the demise of the Knights of Labor, became America's leading union and pursued a collective bargaining strategy. Both sought legislation—notably to address the Sherman Antitrust Act being turned against them—through the existing political and two-party system.

While this was the time when socialist and communist parties started to gather momentum abroad, these decades saw the socialist Left in America limp out of them. By 1930, the communists had been discredited by their allegiance to the USSR instead of the USA. And while the Socialist Party would appear on the ballot and win increasing popular vote totals over the era, it would endure a steady comparative diminution within America's political system.

Even the impetus for organizing was reversed in the early 20th century in America. Where hardship had driven the earlier organizations' creation, now it was affluence. The Progressive Era did not organize around distress but around America's growing middle class. During this time, from 1900 to 1929, America's population surged from 76 million to 122 million. Again, the economy grew even faster: nominal GDP rose fivefold ($21 billion to $105 billion) and real GDP more than doubled ($522 billion to $1.2 trillion). As a result, real GDP per capita rose over 40 percent ($6,857 to $9,773).[52] Simultaneously a dramatic shift away from agriculture was occurring. Between

1900 and 1930, the percentage of Americans living on farms fell from 39.3 percent to 24.8 percent.

SECTION VIII
Agriculture: 1900-1929

It can be broadly said that the prosperity seen in the new century ended the farm revolts that closed out the previous one.[53] The 1897-1920 period was one of sustained agricultural price increases,[54] which in turn spurred increased investment: The value of farm machinery rose from $750 million in 1900 to $3.6 billion in 1920.[55] Even in this new era, agriculture had its populist holdovers,[56] but these quickly disappeared.

Naturally, the transition from protest to prosperity did not happen overnight or even uniformly.[57] Cooperatives also remained hugely popular. The major farm organizations supported them, as did President Theodore Roosevelt and other political leaders.[58] As agriculture's primary economic tool, cooperatives were viewed through two lenses. The first saw cooperatives as a means to control supply; the other saw them as a means to enhance economic efficiency.[59] As mentioned earlier, the latter would prevail.

As American political scientist David Truman observed, American farmers of the time had more political than economic power.[60] They therefore gradually sought to use their political power to pursue economic leverage. However, rather than seeking to do so through a third party, they worked through the existing two-party system. A clear example is the effort from 1913 to 1921 in which farmers worked to thwart the use of the Sherman Antitrust Act against cooperatives.[61] Their influence in Congress won passage of the Capper-Volstead Act, which protected farmer marketing cooperatives from antitrust actions.[62] Agriculture's greatest political success was the Farm Bloc, a bipartisan group of Senators who pursued agriculture's legislative interests. The Bloc twice passed the McNary-Haugen Act, which proposed to buy surplus crop production and sell it abroad. Only two vetoes by President Coolidge prevented its enactment.[63]

SECTION IX
Labor: 1900-1929

The continued shift from farms to factories saw union strength grow. Union membership rose from 447,000 to 2.1 million in the seven years between 1897 and 1904, while confrontation from the rawer Populist Period persisted.[64] Violence between unions and employers, was especially prevalent in the mining areas out West and in West Virginia.[65] In some places, dynamite attacks and nothing short of pitched battles occurred, often resulting in deaths.[66] In an effort to quell the violence, companies tried to resist independent unions with the creation of their own "company unions."

It took World War I to raise the stakes for achieving labor peace. For the war effort, the country needed uninterrupted production—i.e., no strikes. To appease the unions, President Wilson requested, and received, legislation instituting an eight-hour workday for railroads. In December 1917, he took over the railroads' operation with wages set by a government board and no discrimination against union membership.[67] When strikes persisted throughout the economy, Wilson set up the National War Labor Board. Equally composed of employer and union representatives, it instituted a ceasefire in the labor conflict. It declared there would be no strikes or lockouts, guaranteed the right to unionize, ensured no coercion to join or resign from unions, and prohibited coercive tactics by unions in seeking their goals.

After the war, employers felt unions had been allowed to gain too much ground and pushed for "open shops," meaning union membership was optional for employees. Employer court action against unions proved fruitful. Earlier, the Pullman strike had shown the effectiveness of antitrust actions in limiting strikes' impact and ultimately ending them. Now a series of court rulings determined that employers could terminate workers for union membership and employers could compel workers to sign "yellow dog" contracts stating employees would not join a union. Such court actions, and employers' determination to apply them, had a predictable effect on membership. From 1920 to 1923, union membership dropped by almost one-third, from 5.1 million to 3.6 million.[68]

SECTION X
The Socialist Left: 1900-1929

Unlike in agriculture, real attempts at socialist organizations were made in American labor. The most notable was the Industrial Workers of the World. Founded by Eugene Debs and a host of socialist Left luminaries in 1905 and nicknamed the "Wobblies," the IWW advocated an end to capitalism and the creation of industrial unions. The IWW did not last long or accomplish much, but they were loudly vocal while they existed. They were also roundly rejected by workers, employers, the public, and political leaders. Its members were jailed in large numbers for opposing World War I; it also alienated workers (by opposing employer concessions), employers (by refusing to hold to its agreements with them), and the public (by supporting violence).[69]

The Progressive Era is when America's socialist Left clearly emerged in organized forms. No longer limited to isolated agitators, or seeking influence in others' movements, as in the Populist period, the socialist Left strode out on its own. And no longer were the individuals themselves just foreign transplants. Flynn cites estimates that by 1908, American-born socialists outnumbered foreign by seven to three, a reversal from one in ten of the 1870s and roughly three in ten of the 1890s.[70] Flynn credits much of this "Americanization" to J.A. Wayland's *Appeal to Reason*, a paper published in Girard, Kansas, that put socialism into the American vernacular. Despite its changed accent, American socialism would still be beset by in-fighting—both within its own ranks and with various American communist parties. Americans' perception of the "foreignness" of the socialist Left would be reinforced by its opposition to World War I; then after the USSR's creation, by American communists' actual adherence to Moscow's dictates (and dollars).[71] The subtleties of the difference between socialists and communists were undoubtedly lost on many Americans and further contributed to a general rejection of the socialist Left.[72] This rejection can be easily quantified by looking at the failure of America's leading socialist, Eugene Debs. As has been noted, he ran for president and lost five times—in 1900, 1904, 1908, 1912, and 1920. In all five combined, Debs never won a single electoral vote. Although he won progressively more votes in each election, his largest total amounted to just 3.5 percent of total votes cast.

SECTION XI
The Progressive Party

Of course, the most prominent third-party effort of the era was the one that took its name from the era itself: the Progressive Party. Yet absent Theodore Roosevelt using it as a personal vehicle to strike at Taft in 1912—thereby splitting the Republican base, finishing second, and giving the election to Woodrow Wilson—the Progressive Party proved of limited consequence.[73] Nor was the Progressive Party a party of the socialist Left. In fact, Richard Hofstadter termed it more *regressive* than *progressive*.[74] Progressivism arose amidst times of plenty, and according to Hofstadter, few reform movements have been so based on support from the wealthy.[75] Hofstadter also correctly observed that there were strong elements of nativism in the Progressive Party, whose real goal was to give government a countervailing power, rather than remake society; at most, it was a middle way between Left and Right.[76] By today's socialist Left standards, its platform was milquetoast: allowing labor to organize and bargain collectively, aiding farm cooperatives and reducing tariffs and rail rates, public ownership of the railroads, and tax increases on the wealthy, but "limiting tax exactions strictly to the requirements of the government administered with rigid economy."[77]

Far from heralding a rise of the socialist Left, the Progressive Era saw its emergence and then descent, as the socialists and communists were effectively extinguished. In agriculture and industry, the ascendant groups were conservative: the Farm Bureau and the American Federation of Labor, both of which arose to counter more confrontational groups. Farmers and workers sought more favorable integration in America's economy through cooperatives and unions—not the economy's overturning. Politically, too, the leading agriculture and labor groups pursued their goals *through* the prevailing two-party system rather than by creating their own or combined parties (as with the Greenback and Populist parties). Their goal was to pass legislation within the system, not to overthrow that system. By the end of the 1920s, the third-party route had been relegated to mere symbolic status, one in which the socialist Left—personified by Debs—languished and would continue to do so.

SECTION XII
1929-1945: Depression, New Deal, and World War II

These years comprise the longest period of severe stress in American history: The nation's longest and deepest depression, capped with its greatest military mobilization. The magnitude of the Great Depression is almost incomprehensible. Nominal and real GDP fell for four consecutive years (1930 through 1933) and real GDP would not return to its 1929 level until 1936;[78] 12.8 million were unemployed by 1933, a quarter of the workforce. It took America entering World War II to end it, and even so, full employment would not return until 1942, thirteen years after Wall Street's 1929 collapse.

Such prolonged national calamity would seem an ideal opening for America's socialist Left. Orthodox Marxism theorizes that capitalist economic development leads to a growing proletariat, which then becomes increasingly immiserated, leading ultimately to revolution. Prior to the Depression, America was at its highest level of economic development (with a world-leading economy) and had its largest industrial workforce (both absolutely and comparatively). With both thrown suddenly into their greatest economic crisis for a prolonged period, one might expect the socialist Left to step into prominence.

Further, the government during this crisis had an almost free hand to take unprecedented aggressive action, and in Franklin Roosevelt, a leader willing to do so. In his March 4, 1933, inaugural address, Roosevelt summed up his perceived mandate: "This nation calls for action, and action now. Our greatest primary task is to put people to work." The result was a greatly (and permanently) expanded state that met little effective political opposition (save early on from the Supreme Court, though this, too, dissolved over time). This rapid increase in government and government power brought in legions of new people, many of whom had leftist leanings and were placed in positions within organizations with great influence over America's workforce—notably the USDA and the Department of Labor.[79] Yet despite these golden opportunities for America's socialist Left, nothing came of them. The socialist Left had less impact than either the short-lived FHA or the Bonus Marchers in Washington—neither of which were socialistic. This section will examine why.

SECTION XIII
Agriculture: 1929-1945

Along with real GDP, real GDP per capita fell for four consecutive years, plunging almost a third from its 1929 level (from $9,773 to $6.981), a point it would not reach again for a decade.[80] Farmers who had borrowed heavily to buy land and machinery were now squeezed as falling prices left them unable to repay their loans. Just as low prices and high debt had spurred farmers to action in the 19th century, they did so again during the Depression, most notably in the Farmers' Holiday Association. On its surface, the FHA is another organization that could be mistaken for the socialist Left; however, as with its farm protest predecessors, closer examination reveals that it was not.

A midwestern organization, the FHA has been termed the century's most militant agricultural movement. Founded by the farmer populist Milo Reno, a president of the Iowa Farm Union, and centered in Iowa (where 13 percent of farmland had been sold at foreclosure between 1921 and 1933), the FHA was both a formal farm organization and a movement of spontaneous action to prevent farm foreclosures.[81] FHA's approach was a combination of strike and boycott: "Stay at home—buy nothing—sell nothing!"[82] The movement spread to other midwestern states and grew in militancy. It became famous (or infamous) for anti-foreclosure actions known as "penny auctions" and "Sears-Roebuck" sales. In a final, unsuccessful effort it tried to consolidate radical farm groups (including the communist Sharecroppers' Union and the socialist Southern Tenant Farmers' Union) to join with labor.

What stole the FHA's thunder was the creation of the Agricultural Adjustment Administration, which was enacted in the Agricultural Adjustment Act during Roosevelt's first hundred days. The AAA made direct payments to agricultural landowners in exchange for not planting on portions of their land; thus the infusion of federal money solved the farmers' cash constraints—and ended the FHA's reason for being. (Even after the Supreme Court overturned the Agricultural Adjustment Act in 1936, payments were still made to farmers under the guise of conservation payments.)

Ironically, while the AAA undermined the need for militancy and the potential for radicalization, under Roosevelt, the USDA that administered it housed some of the New Deal's most radical personnel with a decided interest in emphasizing social reform. Nowhere was this social reform mission clearer than in the creation of the Farm Security Administration in 1937. Aimed at addressing rural poverty, it was arguably the most significant social effort up to that point in America's history.[83] Unlike the farm movements that preceded it, the FSA originated not within the agriculture community but within the USDA and was staffed by a dedicated group of leftist social reformers there.[84]

All of this—the impetus for action from the country, the president's willingness to act aggressively, and a dedicated group of leftists within USDA—should have led to the socialist Left prospering, if not prevailing, but their opportunity for action within government was short-lived. Many leftists were famously purged from the USDA in 1935 and the social reformist FSA was killed in 1946—both by the hands of overwhelming conservative resistance and a lack of public resonance.

SECTION XIV
Labor: 1929-1945

America's cataclysmic economic collapse hit the nonagricultural workforce equally hard. Not only was unemployment severe, but under-employment was as well. Work-sharing became common and was embraced by industries, unions, and the Hoover administration in a desperate attempt to confront mounting unemployment. To give an idea of just how bad it was: In 1929, the United States Steel Corporation had 224,980 full-time workers; in 1930, 211,055; in 1931, 53,619; in 1932, 18,938; and on April 1, 1933, 0—all its remaining workers were part-time and even these were only half 1929's total workforce.[85]

And as in agriculture, the desperate times triggered a workforce response. Many took to the road in attempts to find work, only to find migrant camps—"Hoovervilles." The most prominent of such migrations was made by the Bonus Marchers, World War I veterans seeking early payment of promised adjusted compensation for their service. From Portland, Oregon in May 1932, 300 veterans hopped freight trains headed for Washington, DC. Press coverage drew thousands more until over 40,000 arrived and set up an enormous encampment. Despite Congress failing to pass the sought relief in June, they stayed until July 28, when a military force led by General Douglas MacArthur (and including Dwight Eisenhower and George Patton) forcibly evicted them and burned the shanties. The Bonus bill would not be passed for another four years (over FDR's veto and giving the veterans an average payment of $583).

SECTION XV
The New Deal

In response to the rampant abject poverty and millions out of work, the Roosevelt administration rushed a host of federal programs into existence— the Federal Emergency Relief Act, the National Recovery Administration, the Public Works Administration, the Civil Works Administration (formed from the PWA), the Civilian Conservation Corps, the Works Progress Administration—to combat unemployment. The administration also pushed through the National Industrial Recovery Act. Because the NIRA allowed businesses to join collectively, at the AFL's insistence authority was granted to workers to organize, bargain collectively, and be protected from employer reprisal for doing so. Large strikes in 1934 led to further union gains from 1935's National Labor Relations Act. Also known as the Wagner Act,[86] it guaranteed employees "the right to self-organization, to form, join, or assist labor organizations, to bargain collectively through representatives of their own choosing, and to engage in concerted activities for the purpose of collective bargaining or other mutual aid and protection." It also outlawed company unions, set legal guidelines for electing union representatives, and required companies to bargain collectively with certified unions. It applied to all employers involved in interstate commerce except airlines, railroads, agriculture, and government. Later, the 1938 Fair Labor Standards Act established a national minimum wage and 40-hour work week.

Even with these unprecedented efforts to address unemployment and meet union demands, millions were still left out of work. In 1939, ten years after the

Crash, there were still almost 9.5 million unemployed—an unemployment rate over 17 percent.[87]

SECTION XVI
The Socialist Left: 1929-1945

Despite all these factors favoring its advance, America's socialist Left was no closer to resonance with Americans, let alone power, than it had been before the Depression. Still, the New Deal's great and rapid government expansion did give the socialist Left an opening to surreptitiously slide some of its sympathizers in. Daniel Flynn lists several—including Frances Perkins (Labor), Adolph Berle (State), Henry Morgenthau (Treasury), and advisers Harold Ickes, Rexford Tugwell, and Harry Hopkins, while others, most notably Henry Wallace, took a decidedly leftward turn once in the Roosevelt administration.

Contrary to popular thought, Franklin Roosevelt, who perhaps had the most patrician background of any American president, was decidedly not one of these. Richard Hofstadter incorrectly labeled the New Deal era as the first in America's history when the leader of a reform movement took power during an economic crisis.[88] But Roosevelt would not have considered himself this way. Rather, Roosevelt was an astute politician, not an ideologue, and only sought to lead an effort to address a crisis—and politically capitalize on it. As preeminent Roosevelt biographer Conrad Black writes: "In all circumstances Roosevelt would remember where the majority of the votes were and how to produce as little division as possible in the nation as a whole ... Roosevelt never wavered in his determination to maintain the political center as a position of strength ... "[89] Far from novel, crisis was well known to Democrats: crisis was the only thing that had yielded them presidential power over the last three generations—amounting to just 16 of the previous 72 years. This is what FDR was responding to—not answering a battle cry of the socialist Left.

Thus, the socialist Left's direct impact on America during this time was no more—and was arguably less—than in any preceding periods. As deep and prolonged as the crises of Depression and World War II were, they were still not sufficient to elevate America's socialist Left to power or even to take advantage of the openings the New Deal gave it. Its actions amounted to footnotes at best. In California, while there were large communist-led strikes by agricultural workers, few permanent unions resulted.[90] In the mid-1930s, communists had a major influence in the National Maritime Union, which organized a series of violent strikes;[91] however, the union was comparatively small. And in 1941, despite that communist-led local unions shut down plants in Milwaukee and Inglewood, California,[92] these were not as consequential as the FHA or Bonus Marchers, neither of which were of the socialist Left.

The socialist Left's lack of influence in an era that seemed tailor-made to foster it is less surprising when one considers the overall minimal quantitative impact of the Left itself. In Eugene Debs's final presidential run in 1920, he garnered less than one million votes. In 1924, La Follette's Progressive Party won 4.8 million votes. At its 1939 apex, America's Communist Party totaled just 90,000 members.[93] By comparison, Roosevelt—a Democrat, but hardly of the socialist Left—won by 7 million votes in 1932 and by 11 million in 1936. In contrast, Socialist Norman Thomas won 900,000 votes in 1936 and 187,000 in 1936; the Communists won only 70,000 votes in 1932 and just 80,000 in 1936.

America was not particularly attuned to the socialist Left, and thus, neither was Roosevelt. Roosevelt's New Deal governing coalition had huge margins and was comprised of equally huge constituencies, of which the socialist Left was a miniscule fraction. Simply, America's socialist Left did not contribute much to the latter because they were not part of the former. Nor did the Depression grow their number. As a result, when the socialist Left caused friction within the New Deal coalition—such as within the USDA— Roosevelt did not hesitate to excise it or allow it to be eliminated.[94]

Rather than relying on the socialist Left, or even the broad Left, the New Deal in its haste to address the economic crisis relied on existing groups to direct its efforts—particularly the Farm Bureau and the AFL. As the prior periods showed, these groups were the conservative ones within their respective sectors.

America's socialist Left amounted to surprisingly little during what should have been its most auspicious moment. While it amounted to more in the New Deal apparatus than in society generally, it did not last long enough there to have any real impact—its mere presence aroused conflict with conservative New Deal coalition partners, and thus, the socialist Left had to go.

SECTION XVII
Post-War: 1946-2008—From Explicit to Implicit Socialist Left

As bad as things were for America's traditional Left before World War II, they became even worse in the post-war years. As the perennial runt of the litter, things were worst for the socialist Left, which died—if not in name, then by its own definition of leading the proletariat's cause in the class struggle. Only by renouncing its very essence was the socialist Left able to continue at all.

At the opening of the 20th century, Werner Sombart had posed "The Question" to the socialist Left with his book *Why is There No Socialism in the United States*? Sombart succinctly attributed its failure to prosperity, saying that, "All Socialist utopias came to nothing on roast beef and apple pie."[95] By mid-century, the socialist Left's failure was utterly complete, and it was in large part due to Sombart's thesis, along with the socialist Left's own history of cumulative failure. Put simply, there was effectively no membership and no organization to sustain it. The socialist Left's adoption of the hostility foreign communists had for America became yet another reason for its failure. Unsurprisingly, Americans reciprocated the animosity. With America engaged in a Cold War with the USSR and China, and in hot wars with communists in Korea and Vietnam, failure of the socialist Left abroad only further discredited it at home. Khrushchev revealed Stalin's atrocities to the world in 1956, while the contemporary practices of other communist countries compounded the lesson for Americans. And, as Sombart theorized, had even these overwhelming problems not been enough, America's prosperity would have wiped out the socialist Left single-handedly.

Thus, to survive at all, America's socialist Left had to implicitly renounce itself and everything it had once proclaimed to stand for. The semantics of identifying a new Left to replace an old Left is a transparent dodge. The old Left, the true socialist Left, at least had some coherence. The new Left's existence was simply an admission of failure: The Movement was dead; a pursuit of movements replaced it. Instead of revolution it went for incrementalism. This shift is inscribed in Saul Alinsky's *Rules for Radicals*, his 1971 testament of the old Left's resignation and roadmap for the new Left. "Remember we are talking about revolution, not revelation ... As an organizer I start from where the world is, as it is, not where I would like it to be. That we accept the world as it is does not in any sense weaken our desire to change it into what we believe it should be ... "[96] For America's socialist Left, during this period starting "from where the world is, as it is, not where I would like it to be" meant accepting that the socialist Left in its orthodox and historical form had no place in America.

Globally, the period was marked by three events: The Cold War, the USSR's collapse, and China's embrace of limited capitalism for survival. In America, the period for the socialist Left was marked by: its forsaking explicit Marxism and politics as its primary message and means of agenda advancement; its switch from the overarching Cause, where its goal of revolution was explicit, to specific causes where its goal was implicit—such as the antiwar movement, women's rights, environmentalism, civil rights, and anti-poverty; and the Democrats' 1972 political fiasco when they embraced an extreme-Left platform.

SECTION XVIII
1946-2008: Agriculture

Substituting capital for labor in American farming, a practice that had been underway for decades, accelerated after World War II. According to US Census

Board in Washington to increase interest rates. Instead, the board vetoed rate hikes in New York. Russell Leffingwell saw a Greek tragedy unfolding … At the worst possible moment, the system was undercut by bureaucratic feuding. When the discount rate was belatedly raised in August 1929 from 5 to 6 percent, it was too late to cool off the boom.[7]

The curtain went up on the so-called Greek tragedy in late October 1929. At the New York Stock Exchange's opening on Thursday, October 24, share prices began to fall and trading volumes broke records. By 11:30am, panic had set in and the ticker tape increasingly lagged actual transactions. Investment bankers meeting at J.P. Morgan & Company agreed to intervene; millions of dollars were used to purchase stocks and prices firmed. After a relatively calm Friday, when the market opened on Monday October 28, prices again fell; this time there was no intervention. On Tuesday, October 29, panic-selling prevailed, and the ticker tape fell over two hours behind actual transactions. A then-record 16,410,030 shares were traded with 880 stocks reporting losses. The *New York Times* reported that losses exceeded $8 billion.[8] To put that into perspective: The 1929 federal budget was $3.1 billion; the entire federal debt was $16.9 billion;[9] and the increase in GDP from 1928 to 1929 was just over $6 billion.[10] Wall Street's losses were incomparable and incomprehensible.

After the Crash, the mistakes kept coming and compounding. In the midst of the crisis, the federal government raised taxes,[11] cut spending, and raised tariffs to their highest levels. But the biggest mistakes lay with the Federal Reserve, namely its constriction of the money supply at a time when additional liquidity was desperately needed. Nobel Prize-winning economist Milton Friedman and Anna Schwartz painstakingly detailed the fiasco in their study of America's monetary policy in *A Monetary History of the United States, 1867-1960*:

> At all times throughout the 1929-33 contraction, alternative policies were available to the System by which it could have kept the stock of money from falling, and indeed could have increased it at almost any desired rate. Those policies did not involve radical innovations. They involved measures of a kind explicitly contemplated by the founders of the System to meet precisely the kind of banking crisis that developed in late 1930 and persisted thereafter. They involved measures that were

actually proposed and very likely would have been adopted under a slightly different bureaucratic structure or distribution of power, or even if the men in power had had somewhat different personalities.[12]

If the point is somehow still missed: "To consider still another alternative: if the pre-1914 banking system rather than the Federal Reserve System had been in existence in 1929, the money stock almost certainly would not have undergone a decline comparable to the one that occurred."[13] In short: No Fed, no Depression. Instead of increasing, as it should have: "By early 1933, when the monetary collapse terminated in a banking holiday, the stock of money had fallen by one-third—the largest and longest decline in the entire period covered by our series."[14] Nor was this the only restrictive action taken by the Federal Reserve during the Depression; in 1936-37 they "doubl[ed] reserve requirements in three stages" and the "strictly monetary changes associated with those actions were equally sharp and distinctive."[15] And as we shall see later, a severe economic downturn followed in the wake.

Add to the central bank's failure a run on the nation's banks in 1932. Herbert Hoover biographer Glen Jeansonne describes the scene as America awaited FDR's move to the White House: "Rumors gathered that the new president planned to devalue gold-backed money or abandon the gold standard entirely, which provoked the greatest bank panic of the Depression, eclipsing 1929 and 1931 ... Banks and repositories were drained of assets and toppled like children's blocks ... " Occurring during the prolonged period between FDR's election and his inauguration "some three-fourths of the withdrawals occurred during the week before FDR's inauguration, more than half during the final three days."[16]

Thus, rather than ameliorating circumstances, the Federal Reserve in particular, and the government in general, exacerbated them. In so doing, a crisis became a catastrophe, and a recession became the Great Depression.

Up to this point, the economic downturn nearest in severity to the Depression was the aforementioned Panic of 1893, and it really wasn't so close at all. According to MeasuringWorth's estimates, America's GDP dropped just under 6 percent in nominal and real terms from 1892 to 1893 and roughly 8 percent in nominal terms and 5 percent in real terms from 1893 to 1894. By 1895, it had begun recovering in both nominal and real terms; by 1897 it had recovered in real GDP and essentially so in nominal GDP. In contrast, during the Depression, America's GDP fell in both nominal and real terms for four consecutive years—the duration of almost the entire decline *and* recovery of 1893's Panic. Over 1930 through 1933, nominal GDP fell 45 percent and in real terms 26 percent.[17] In nominal terms, US GDP did not regain its 1929 level until 1941—and absent the buildup of World War II, it is unclear when America would have recovered.[18] Often forgotten, too, is the fact that the economy fell again in 1937.[19] Jeansonne describes the carnage: "In the summer of 1937 the economy plummeted, the worst sudden debacle in history, eclipsing the 1929 crash ... Between September of 1937 and the following June, industrial production plunged 33 percent, national income plummeted 13 percent, profits fell by an enormous 78 percent, payrolls eroded by 35 percent, and industrial stocks lost more than 50 percent in value."[20]

Because the Depression was so unprecedented, precedent also unnecessarily inhibited the federal government's response. As previously shown, during wartime crisis, the small-government model routinely bent (as it had during the Civil War and World War I), only to return to its previous state (as measured relative to GDP) after the crisis had passed. In comparison, during the Panic of 1893, federal spending barely moved—increasing by roughly 10 percent in 1893 and then slightly decreasing over the next three years.[21] While federal receipts rose in 1893, they stayed below that level until 1898. Historically, the federal government had not responded to economic problems; it attempted to do so during the Depression, albeit in occasionally conflicting ways. Federal government action simply could not compensate for the Federal Reserve's draconianly constrictive policies—it could lessen the impact, not address the cause.

However, the conventional wisdom of the political system—both Republican and Democrat alike—was not prepared for an unprecedented economic crisis brought on by the government itself. That a Republican—Herbert Hoover—was in office gives no reason to believe that Democrats would have approached the unfolding crisis differently, either, given that Democrat Grover Cleveland was president during the Panic of 1893 and Democrats held majorities in both houses of Congress at the time. It should also be remembered that as FDR biographer Conrad Black points out, Democrats' 1932 platform called for a "balanced budget [and] reduced federal expenditures."[22] Still, it is a common misperception—and one cultivated by Roosevelt's campaign—that Hoover and Republicans who controlled the federal government fiddled while Rome burned. While federal outlays (i.e., federal spending in a given year) in 1930 remained at 3.4 percent and receipts at 4.1 percent of GDP, remember that the economy had only just begun its contraction (a year after the Wall Street collapse). Outlays did increase in the following years, but still could not offset the economic damage that the Federal Reserve's constriction of the money supply was causing.[23]

Further evidence of conventional wisdom being exercised in the face of the decidedly unprecedented is supplied by Roosevelt himself, who entered office in 1933 determined to reduce the federal budget deficits, which he saw as having exacerbated the economy's fall.[24] To accomplish his goal, Roosevelt took aim at veterans' pensions, successfully passing "An Act to Maintain the Credit of the United States Government." Known simply as "the Economy Act," its "reduction in the veterans' pensions program is the largest ever taken in any entitlement program in U.S. history."[25] As it continued and worsened, the Depression's pronounced impact would challenge not just partisan mindsets, which were remarkably similar up to then, but the nation's—and with it the prevailing small-government model.

The Crash that signaled the start of the Depression occurred just seven months after President Hoover's inauguration, striking directly at his wunderkind reputation, and was perfectly timed to inflict maximum political damage on his administration and the Republicans. As presidential historian Leuchtenburg writes: "Few presidents have entered office so highly acclaimed as Herbert Hoover."[26] A self-made multi-millionaire at a young age, he had been pressed into organizing food relief in Belgium and then in German-occupied northern France. Once America entered the war, his work expanded to America and the Allies as a whole; then, after the war, throughout Europe—including Russia. By the time he was finished, Hoover had fed tens of millions for years and averted untold deaths. He had also become recognized as an administrator without equal. Like the rest of America, which had seen Hoover succeed at everything he had done administratively in World War I, Franklin D. Roosevelt said in 1920: "he is certainly a wonder, and I wish we could make him President of the United States. There would not be a better one."[27]

Hoover continued to ascend, becoming Secretary of Commerce for Presidents Harding and Coolidge. He was no less successful there, expanding the reach of what up until then had been a backwater government agency.

Somewhat presciently, Hoover worried about the downside of his many accolades as he waited to take office in 1929: "I have no dread of the ordinary work of the presidency. What I do fear is the … exaggerated idea the people have conceived of me. They have a conviction that I am a sort of superman, that no problem is beyond my capacity … If some unprecedented calamity should come upon the nation … I would be sacrificed to the unreasoning disappointment of a people who expected too much."[28] Hoover was uncannily clairvoyant.

No person was more qualified to encounter a crisis as president than Hoover. Yet no president had ever encountered what Hoover did, and no president up to that point could have been expected to address it any differently. And Hoover did try to address it. Leuchtenburg writes that following Wall Street's collapse, Hoover "moved briskly to cope with the crisis. He summoned businessmen and labor leaders to the White House for the Conference on Continued Industrial Progress, urged employers to maintain wage rates, asked Congress to approve a tax cut and to appropriate funds for public works, and prodded the Federal Reserve Board to expand the money supply."[29]

Nor were Hoover's efforts limited to simply jawboning. He signed an income-tax cut in December 1929 that was estimated to save taxpayers $160 million. In December 1930, with 4.5 million Americans already unemployed, Hoover called on Congress to spend between $100 million and $150 million on public works.[30] To try to ease the global economic crisis, which was rebounding back on America, in 1931 he declared a one-year reprieve on European war debt payments to the US in exchange for their moratorium on Germany's reparation payments to them. He also signed into law the Reconstruction Finance Corporation, which was chartered to lend large sums to banks to keep them afloat.[31] Jeansonne describes the RFC as: "a landmark shift toward a more powerful government." The legislation creating it "included direct money and bonds of some $2 billion," and was "the largest relief bill passed by Congress up to that point." Over eight years, it would lend $50 billion.[32] In July 1932, Hoover signed the Emergency Relief Act, which provided $300 million in loans to states for relief, quickly followed by the Federal Home Loan Bank Act to spur residential home construction.[33]

Still, the crisis escalated beyond anything anyone had ever seen. As a result, federal spending increased as well: to 3.4 percent of GDP in 1930, 4.2 percent in 1931 (even as revenues fell absolutely and relative to GDP) and rose over 60 percent in 1932 to 6.8 percent of GDP (even after receipts fell again in actual dollars by over one-third).[34] In 1931, the federal government ran its first deficit since 1919; in 1932, it ran its largest peacetime deficit ever: $2.7 billion. It would run deficits every year until 1947. Despite the 1893 precedent that prompted the federal government to not address economic crises like it did wartime ones, the federal government did, under both Hoover and FDR, but could not offset the money supply being reduced by one-third. The New Deal's failure to rescue the economy over the next eight years would only further confirm this.

SECTION III
New Deal

It's evident that Roosevelt was well aware that he was bluffing when he said, famously, at his inauguration: " … the only thing we have to fear is fear itself—nameless, unreasoning, unjustified terror which paralyzes needed efforts to convert retreat into advance." The truth was that at this time, Americans had a lot to fear—Hoover had been vainly trying to reassure America throughout his presidency. Far from "nameless," however, Americans' terror had all too many names. The economy had shrunk every year since 1929; unemployment was epidemic, affecting one-third of the workforce;[35] many families' savings had been wiped out; there was no money; prices had fallen; and the banking system was in tatters, with 2,294 banks having failed in 1931 and nearly $1 billion in withdrawals in the two weeks preceding FDR's inauguration in 1933.[36] What *was* "nameless" was the cause of the catastrophe, and its solution.

FDR's big advantage before the election was that his opponent was doomed to pay the conventional price for economic calamity; FDR's big advantage after the election was that every conventional means of addressing the calamity had been exhausted by the time he took office, almost four years into the Depression.

Even before the implementation of the New Deal, the federal government had been growing as a result of the Depression. From spending just under 3 percent of GDP in 1929, it had more than doubled that level to 6.8 percent by 1932 (while running a deficit equal to 4 percent of GDP).[37] FDR's administration, therefore, had ready precedents for a concerted federal government response in the form of the New Deal—certainly the takeover of large sections of the economy in World War I, but also actions in the Hoover administration. And there was a real demand for such a response. Entering a fifth year of the Depression, it was becoming clear that this crisis was not transient, as America's earlier ones had been. Many Americans in the 1930s had lived through the Panic of 1893, and so had ample points of comparison for what recovery should look like. Had the Depression followed the recovery timeline of the Panic of 1893 (the economy was, by contrast still shrinking in the fifth year after the Crash), a strong argument could be made that there would have been no FDR landslide or need for the New Deal, and that the small-government model would have continued to prevail as it had throughout the nation's history.

By 1933, however, it was clear that the Depression was decidedly unlike any economic crisis before it. This led to a demand for—or at least an acceptance of—a bigger, more concerted government response, which in turn set off a chain reaction that would fundamentally change the federal government. The federal-government programs that arose during the New Deal era were marked by their transfer of government resources (money and authority) to individuals both as beneficiaries and bureaucrats. As the Depression continued, these formal government responses continued, too—even as particular programs changed. This transformed beneficiaries into clients, thus creating a base of support to demand the continuation of particular programs that benefitted them—some of these programs ultimately became permanent.

Nowhere was this permanence more embodied in policy than in Social Security, which was unprecedented at the time. As FDR biographer Conrad Black writes in his definitive monograph on Roosevelt:

> Social Security was an idea whose hour had come. At a time when the United States had been stricken by an economic crisis that had left nearly a third of the country destitute, it gave promise of an imminent time when there would be emergency support for everyone. This measure raised the hope of the nation that it would never again be defenseless against the vagaries of economic fortune, which had shown

itself more capricious and dangerous than most Americans had ever imagined possible.[38]

A product of the so-called second New Deal, which occurred over 1935 and 1936, Social Security became the most revolutionary program of the entire New Deal era. Riding the wave of midterm victories that increased Democrats' already substantial congressional majorities, and the prodding from left-wing populists within his own party, Social Security was the result of Roosevelt's aim to take the New Deal further in the wake of the Depression's persistence. As a concept, Social Security was not new—academics and politicians had been discussing it since shortly after World War I—so when FDR created the Committee on Economic Security, composed of top advisers to study it in 1934, the conversation was already there. From this Committee came, "[a] mixed plan ... combining pay-as-you-go, deferred funding from general revenues, and a partial reserve." This plan was intended to cover "both unemployment and old-age insurance and recommend[ed] increased aid to the states for dependent children and public health assistance."[39]

Social Security was proposed to Congress on January 17, 1935, and signed into law on August 14, taking the federal government well beyond its prior assistance programs. Wilson had proposed aid to the unemployed and Hoover had provided it, and Roosevelt's early New Deal had offered employment pro- grams on a massive scale through an army of acronym agencies such as the CCC (Civilian Conservation Corps) and the WPA (Works Progress Administration). But Social Security was entirely different from these temporary responses to crisis. While Social Security unquestionably was meant to aid in the recovery from the Depression, it was also intended to prevent future hardships for the aged—not just in crises but as a government-run quasi-insurance plan. Most private-sector workers, 60 percent of America's total workforce, were required to participate. Beginning in 1937, both employees and employers were taxed at a 1 percent rate (rising to 3 percent in 1949) on the covered employee's first $3,000 in earnings. To be covered, an employee would have to have "worked at least five years in jobs covered by the program, and earned total wages of at least $2,000 in those jobs, before they reached age 65."[40] Social Security taxes were deposited into an Old-Age Reserve Account, from which the first benefits would be paid in 1942. Beneficiaries of the program would be permanently entitled to these benefits and an enormous beneficiary base was immediately created—including individuals who would receive benefits from a worker's estate in the event the covered worker died.[41] Thus was born the federal government's enhanced and permanent entitlement system.

During the New Deal era, federal government spending skyrocketed: in 1929, federal outlays amounted to $3.1 billion; in 1937, they were $7.6 billion—even as the country was enduring deflation.[42] Spurred on again by the Lend-Lease Act of 1941, which hastened America on the path of war spending, it rose further still, hitting $13.7 billion in 1941. In the process, it ran substantial deficits from 1931 through 1946, with the deficits routinely approaching or exceeding what annual federal spending had been as recently as 1930. There was no peacetime precedent for the federal government's size, spending, and deficits.[43]

It must be remembered that despite dramatically increasing the federal government's size, the New Deal did not end the Depression: World War II did.[44] It was massive American war spending that finally put an end to the Depression—first to supply the Allied forces, and then its own tremendous needs. Simultaneously, massive conscription soaked up unemployment so effectively that it created a labor shortage. Just how soon wartime spending began to have an effect on America's economy is also often forgotten. Late in 1939 Congress repealed the arms embargo clause of the Neutrality Act of 1937 and allowed belligerents to purchase arms on a cash-and-carry basis (with their own money and in their own ships—a step that only aided the Allies who controlled the seas and had available money). In January 1940, FDR requested $1.8 billion for defense, and then $1.3 billion more in May. On January 8, 1941, eleven months before America's formal entry into the war, FDR submitted a $17.5 billion budget, with 60 percent allotted for defense.[45] Finally, in June 1943, the WPA closed its doors, having spent $11 billion over eight years and employing 8.5 million people.

In retrospect, it can be said that both Hoover's efforts and Roosevelt's New Deal addressed the effects, not the causes of the Depression.

SECTION IV
World War II

If the Depression had grown the federal government, and the New Deal had done so significantly more, World War II would grow it far larger still. Unlike World War I, World War II was truly a worldwide conflict for America. Through America's heavy material assistance to the Allies, its involvement had begun well before Americans went into combat, and by the time the war ended 405,000 Americans had lost their lives, with many more wounded, and 16 million having worn uniforms: here at home, across the Pacific, throughout the Atlantic, onto North Africa, up into southern Europe, onto the beaches of Normandy, and across the European continent.

Beginning with Roosevelt's signing of the Lend-Lease Act in March 1941, America became "what our people have proclaimed it must be—the arsenal of democracy." The president was granted roughly $13 billion to use with wide discretion to help the Allies (for perspective, entire federal spending in 1940 amounted to just $9.5 billion).[46] Over the course of the war, almost $49 billion would be distributed to almost 40 nations.[47]

America had already been on a quasi-war footing before it was formally drawn into it following Japan's December 1941 sneak attack on Pearl Harbor—a date which still lives on "in infamy." The Selective Service Training and Service Act had instituted the first peacetime draft in 1940 and the Office of Production Management had been established to handle defense production and aid shipments to the Allies.[48] As early as March 1941, America was producing over 1,200 planes a month.[49] So when war finally came, the federal government was already ramped up for it. It is not surprising then that it so surpassed previous levels of spending.

Unlike the unprecedented Depression and the equally unprecedented response of the New Deal, the federal government had ample precedents for a response to World War II. The expansion and extension of federal-government power and its centralization in the executive branch were hallmarks of America's general wartime pattern. During wars, America frequently saw receipts fall, and it always saw spending and deficits rise. As discussed earlier , just a generation earlier, World War I had taken this pattern of expansion, extension, and centralization to new heights. This gave the federal government fresh blueprints to follow when it created the War Production Board and the War Manpower Commission in 1942. What was unprecedented, then, was not the federal government's greatly increased spending but its magnitude and duration.

Federal spending in 1941 already amounted to 11.7 percent of GDP, not far behind 1865's Civil War peak of 13 percent. In 1942, the first full year of America's involvement in World War II, spending more than doubled as a percentage of GDP, hitting a record-high of 23.8 percent. In 1943, this figure almost doubled again, reaching 42.6 percent, and then continued to edge up. Even after America's 1944 production had proved so abundant that difficulties arose dispensing it, spending stayed at 41 percent of GDP in 1945.[50]

For three consecutive years, the federal government was spending over two-fifths of America's total production. This was roughly twice the previous high, which had occurred in only a single year (1919). Funding this meant running enormous deficits. In 1942, the deficit was 13.9 percent of GDP, higher than both 1865's total wartime spending and the federal government's spending in 1941—and would continue to break records over the next four years.[51] By the end of World War II, Americans were accustomed to a federal government of far greater magnitude and for a far longer duration than anything it had ever experienced.

SECTION V
Post-War: Cold War to 1964

Post-World War II, America's unprecedented experiences continued to stack up. In Eastern Europe, the devastation of the war created a power vacuum that authoritarian communism and the USSR were only too eager to fill. As America alone had the military and economic might to prevent its spread, the nation had no reasonable alternative to assuming the global role thrust upon it.

Recall that after World War I, America returned to its pre-war "normalcy." The broader world order did as well; power was not so much extinguished as shifted between World War I's combatants (though not all) and many empires still stood. At that time, America had refused to assume the larger global role that was available, eschewing a place in the League of Nations. America was an important provider of much-needed financial and material resources for rebuilding and humanitarian purposes, preferring to project its economic power over its military power.

America's post-World War II experience, however, was very different. The federal government's failure to return to its pre-Depression levels was on one hand a product of its large growth during the New Deal and World War II: its floor had been significantly raised far beyond anything ever experienced either in peace or war. And on the other hand, there were extenuating circumstances. Rather than the multi-polar world post-World War I, America now faced a bipolar one. Politically, the world was split between democracy and authoritarianism, and economically between capitalism and communism. And in terms of military power, it was split between the US and the USSR. Eastern Europe was immediately incorporated into the authoritarian, communist, USSR camp, as Churchill so eloquently described it: "From Stettin in the Baltic to Trieste in the Adriatic, an iron curtain has descended across the continent." He went on to say that "[t]he Communist parties, which were very small in all these Eastern States of Europe, have been raised to pre-eminence and power far beyond their numbers and are seeking everywhere to obtain totalitarian control. Police governments are prevailing in nearly every case, and so far ... there is no true democracy."[52] And other European nations, like France, Italy, and Greece, were threatened as well. Czechoslovakia's democratic government was toppled by a coup in February 1948 and a communist government installed. Just four months later, on June 24, a nearly year-long blockade of West Berlin began embodying the threat that communism and the USSR posed to the world. Just as only an extraordinary airlift effort that delivered 2.3 million tons of supplies to the residents of East Berlin could thwart Stalin's aggression, so only a concerted American effort could stop communism globally.[53]

And communism's threat was truly global. Both Turkey (in 1945) and Iran (in 1946) were in its crosshairs. Rapidly China, then regularly throughout the Cold War, other nations—North Korea, North Vietnam, and Cuba—would fall behind communism's curtain, while others—South Korea and South Vietnam—would be attacked.

As a result of America's newly assumed global role, the federal government encountered obvious defense and international obstacles that prevented it from following its precedent of post-conflict government retrenchment. The first evidence of this changed international perspective was the Senate's adoption of the UN Charter in July 1945. In contrast to the rejection of the League of Nations after World War I, the UN Charter was adopted 89-2. Further (huge) evidence was quick in coming: The Marshall Plan's massive aid to rebuild Europe. Finally, America's commitment to foreign defense was formalized by the Senate's 82-13 ratification of the NATO Treaty: "Never before had the United States gone so far in a peacetime promise to fight under certain conditions, or to recognize a frontier extending far overseas."[54] This, of course, cost money—a lot of money.[55] A review of international, defense, and Social Security and retirement spending of the time shows the significant impact these areas had on growing the government from its already elevated base.

In 1940, federal defense spending was $1.7 billion, jumping to $13.7 billion in 1950, and $48.1 billion in 1960. By 1964, it was $54.8 billion. Over the same decades, federal spending on international affairs was $51 million in 1940, leaping to $4.7 billion in 1950. It dropped to $3 billion in 1960, but then leapt up and surpassed previous numbers to $4.9 billion in 1964. In 1940, the federal government spending on Social Security and retirement was $129 million. This amount rose to $1 billion in 1950, $11.7 billion in 1960, and by 1964, it was $16.9 billion.[56]

With these newly embedded budget drivers, the federal government's spending floor was significantly raised again. As a result, federal spending was 9.6 percent of GDP in 1940. In 1950, it was 15.3 percent; in 1960, it was 17.3 percent; by 1964, it was 17.9 percent—and it had spiked higher still during the Korean War of the 1950s. So, while the federal government during the Cold War was substantially smaller than at its all-time World War II peak, its spending was still very high, nearing 1918's World War I peak of 16.6 percent of GDP. What had once been crisis-level spending was now commonplace.[57]

In addition to all of this, the federal government faced another less visible, but no less real, obstacle: providing entitlement benefits to an extremely large—and growing—population.

SECTION VI
The Great Society: The Great Entitlement Expansion

Approaching the 1964 election, the Democrats' dominance was already astounding: They had won six of the last eight presidential elections, losing only to Eisenhower, about whom presidential historian Leuchtenburg wrote: "No other man in the 20th century entered the White House with so lustrous a reputation as Dwight David Eisenhower ... Eisenhower was, as the historian Robert Burk has said, nothing less than 'America's most famous citizen.'"[58] Democrats' congressional dominance was greater still, holding majorities in the House and Senate every year since 1933 (except for 1947-1949 and 1953-1955). Then, in 1964 Lyndon B. Johnson won the third most lopsided victory up to that time (exceeded only in 1936 and 1864) with a 15.7 million popular-vote margin and a 486-52 electoral-vote advantage. Democrats won a 295-140 majority in the House (their biggest since 1937-1939) and a 68-32 majority in the Senate (their biggest since 1939-1941). The result was effectively one-party government.

Democrats used their dominance to pursue President Johnson's Great Society program, a combination of massively ambitious (and soon to be massively expensive) domestic federal programs for education, housing, health, and welfare that extended the US government's reach deep into the American society—and into the American economy: "Between 1965 and 1972 federal spending on these four social programs had multiplied almost six times."[59] At the center of the Great Society were its health care initiatives, and at the center of the health care initiatives was the concept of entitlement: a right granted by the government to defined individuals—i.e., those who are "entitled" to what has been granted. As regards the federal budget, these are generally benefit payments that can only be stopped or altered by a change in law—absent that, they continue. As such, they are mandatory expenditures that go on forever (unless changed by law), and they have become the federal government's biggest cost-driver.

Democrat President Harry Truman had campaigned for national health insurance in 1948 but failed to get it through Congress. The Kennedy administration also tried and failed. As economics professors Eli Ginzberg of Columbia University and Robert Solow of MIT observed, Lyndon Johnson saw his "electoral victory of 1964 as a mandate for social reform."[60] When Johnson's new administration picked the banner of government-provided healthcare back up, it did so with 32 more House seats and 16 more Senate seats than in 1949. They also had a president in Lyndon Johnson who was far more skilled in Congress's legislative process than Truman had been. The result of this preponderance of political power was "the beginning of a remarkable ten-year period of entitlement legislation that is unprecedented in all of U.S. history."[61] It began in a big way with the creation of Medicare and Medicaid, then by expanding Social Security's disability benefits and increasing its overall benefits and increasing benefits under the Aid to Families with Dependent Children program.

Enacted in 1965 under Title XVIII of the Social Security Act,[62] Medicare was created in two parts. Medicare Part A was rolled out on July 1, 1966, providing an entitlement to Social Security-eligible Americans for hospital and post-hospital services. To this same group, Medicare Part B provided an entitlement to a voluntary program offering doctor and other medical services. Part A was financed through the Social Security payroll tax (i.e., by employees and employers); while Part B, known as Supplementary Medical Insurance, "was financed by flat premiums charged to enrollees and half by general fund tax revenues" from the federal government.[63] The third part of the Democrats' healthcare entitlement legislation, Medicaid, "provided states with federal matching payments for medical care services delivered to recipients of federal-state public assistance programs and, at state option, to lower-income 'medically needy'[64] who were not receiving welfare assistance."[65]

As if creating two new expansive entitlement programs was not enough, Congress also included a major Social Security benefit increase, as well as expanding benefits coverage to temporarily disabled workers. The benefit increase amounted to an average 7 percent hike, was made retroactive to January 1965, and was paid in a lump sum in September. All told, it boosted beneficiaries' September payment by 56 percent. Additionally, the amount of earnings subject to the payroll tax was raised to $6,600 annually (this would be hiked four more times between 1966 and 1973). The benefit extension to temporarily disabled workers was funded by a diversion of 0.2 percent of payroll taxes from the retirement to disability program—breaking a promise that this would not be done when the disability program was created in 1956.[66]

When President Johnson signed the bill on July 30, 1965, at the Truman Library in Independence, Missouri, former president Truman said to him, "you have made me a very, very happy man."[67]

The story of the Great Society program is one of entitlement expansion, extension, and enrichment. It created a pattern that America's traditional Left would seek to follow repeatedly and all too often successfully over the next several decades. Its benefits would be expanded to include more individuals within a general area (as was done to bring temporarily disabled workers into Social Security's disability program) and extended to include entirely new types of beneficiaries, benefits, or both (as when healthcare became an entitlement for Social Security beneficiaries). And, of course, benefits would continue to be enriched.

All of these actions proved to be enormous accelerators for federal government growth, short-circuiting market principles that drive its participants toward equilibrium. Entitlement programs reverse the free-market dynamic; rather than moving toward that equilibrium, they foster disequilibrium. As Medicare and Medicaid would show quickly, neither the healthcare beneficiaries nor the providers have any incentive to reduce costs—as they would within competitive private-sector transactions. Instead, their incentive is to increase their benefits and thereby increase government spending . In such a dynamic where the government is paying, prices become meaningless for establishing market equilibrium between demand and supply. The effect was that entitlement benefit cost became effectively uncapped. Unlike Social Security, which applies a formula to determine benefits, there is little in Medicare and Medicaid's prevailing design that restricts costs on a per beneficiary basis. Within Social Security's benefit formula, the annual amount to the beneficiary is set; within Medicare and Medicaid, the annual amount to the beneficiary can vary greatly. Due to the lack of market incentives to reduce costs, the programmatic variability is almost always upward.

Even government has an incentive to increase expansion, extension, and enrichment of entitlement benefits. The proof (as will be shown shortly) is the long-term trajectory these programs have followed over the decades. Yet even in the short-term, this was clearly exhibited during the Great Society's beginnings.[68]

SECTION VII

1965-2000: Entitlements' Hidden Cost

Lit by Johnson in the mid-1960s, the entitlement-program powder keg exploded during the close of the 20th century, raising America's size of government to heretofore unimaginable levels.

Entitlement costs exploded in no small part because the federal government kept creating new entitlement programs, even under Republican president Richard Nixon. Federal budget scholar and senior fellow at the Hoover Institution, John F. Cogan, states that "President Nixon proposed a federal entitlement agenda that was even more ambitious than President Johnson's." And though it was Nixon who started the bidding, it was Congress that upped it each time.[69]

The progressive bidding began in Nixon's first year with a May 1969 proposal to "end hunger in America itself for all time,"[70] which aimed to turn the food-stamp program into an entitlement. He next proposed an additional thirteen weeks of federal unemployment benefits—on top of most states' twenty-six weeks—during economic downturns. Next, it was a welfare reform plan to provide "a basic income to those American families who cannot care for themselves."[71] Then it was a plan to transform discretionary grants into a "new revenue-sharing program that would permanently entitle states and municipalities to a portion of federal revenues."[72] Nixon finished his first year with a call for a 10 percent Social Security benefit hike, while also indexing benefits to inflation.

A case study in the Democrat Congress's ability to outbid President Nixon's reform measures was his 1969 proposed Family Assistance Plan (FAP). Designed to completely revamp America's welfare system, the plan centered on a negative income tax, and was developed by conservative economist and Nobel Laureate Milton Friedman. The proposed plan would "provide a federally guaranteed annual income floor to families with children in which the adult family head was unable to work," and would set an income guarantee at "about 40 percent of the poverty line." Recipients of the plan would retain some portion of this assistance until the family's income approached the poverty line.[73]

There were two keys to the Family Assistance Plan. First, replace existing welfare plans, such as Aid to Families with Dependent Children, with a grant program that allowed individual states to provide cash welfare disbursements to low-income families with children. Second, by replacing the existing welfare plans, FAP would also eliminate the disincentive to work inherent in those plans (which arose from the reduction of welfare benefits on a dollar-for-dollar basis—thereby creating a *de facto* high effective tax rate). What the traditional Left opposed in Nixon's proposal was not FAP itself, but that it would replace those existing welfare plans—the traditional Left intended FAP to supplement them instead. Simply: they wanted both. However, if the existing welfare plans weren't eliminated, then their disincentives also remained, thus resulting in the same problem—a disincentive to work due to a *de facto* high effective tax rate—but at a higher federal cost. The plan finally died in the Senate with Friedman writing its epitaph, calling the episode "a striking example of how to spoil a good idea."[74]

Nixon's FAP was a notable failure. So too was a 1974 attempt at a national health care plan. Regardless, the traditional Left was still quite successful in advancing entitlement expansion, extension, and enrichment. Cogan summarizes the traditional Left's success and Nixon's complicity in it:

> Richard Nixon's presidency constitutes the second phase of the most rapid expansionary period for entitlements in U.S. history. From 1969 to 1974, six new entitlements were created, and a seventh, the earned income tax credit, was well on its way to becoming law. Congress, often at President Nixon's request and invariably with his support, granted new entitlements for disabled workers, coal miners, school districts, state and local governments, and the long-term unemployed. Congress increased Social Security benefits for retired people and disabled workers by 69 percent and raised benefits sharply for newly entitled food stamp and Supplement Security Income programs.[75]

While hardly a member of the traditional Left himself, not only did Nixon not rein in its entitlement expansions—via veto—his actions spurred on the expansions.

The rise in the proportion of the federal budget allotted to entitlements is astounding both for its rapidity and its enormity. In 1965 when the Great Society was enacted, the federal government spent $118.2 billion. Of this, defense spending accounted for 43 percent ($51 billion), while Social Security

($17.1 billion), Medicaid ($0.3 billion), and other means-tested entitlements amounted to 18.8 percent collectively. Just ten years later, spending on federal entitlements eclipsed defense spending. A decade later, in 1975, when "the modern federal entitlement edifice was virtually complete,"[76] the federal government had tripled its spending to $332.3 billion. Of this, defense was now just 26.4 percent ($87.6 billion), while Social Security ($63.6 billion), Medicare ($12.2 billion), Medicaid ($6.8 billion), and other means-tested entitlements ($18.8 billion) amounted to 30.6 percent collectively.[77]

By 2000, even after the new Republican Congress enforced spending restraint and pushed for a balanced budget, federal entitlements were almost three times defense spending. Of the total $1.8 trillion spent, defense spending was just 16.5 percent ($295 billion). Social Security ($406 billion), Medicare ($194.1 billion), Medicaid ($117.9 billion), and other means-tested entitlements ($114.8 billion) collectively amounted to 46.6 percent of spending—almost half of the federal budget.[78]

With entitlement spending's enormous growth, the federal government grew as well; what is surprising is how little it actually did overall. In 1965, the federal government spent 16.7 percent of GDP; in 2000, it spent 17.7 percent.[79] What simultaneously limited the federal government's growth and masked entitlement spending's insidious budget impact was the "peace dividend" that resulted from the fall of the Soviet Union. Even with Reagan's buildup of defense in the 1980s, as a percentage of GDP military spending never approached its 1960s level. Then because of Reagan's success and the USSR's collapse, defense spending was able to plummet.[80]

Entitlement spending filled the entire fiscal vacuum caused by defense spending's decline—and then some. Despite some notable successes to restrain it, first in the early Reagan years and then under the new Republican Congress in the late 1990s, entitlements continued to grow. At most, success regarding entitlement spending meant slowing its rate of growth. As a result, in 1965, Social Security and other means-tested entitlement programs consumed 3.1 percent of GDP; in 2000, it was up to 8.2 percent. Ominously, the federal government's net interest spending grew from 1.2 percent to 2.2 percent of GDP over the same period.[81]

SECTION VIII
2000 to Present: Entitlements' Explosion Exposed

In contrast to the 1980s and 1990s, when efforts were made to reform entitlements and control their cost escalation, the most notable results in the 21st century have thus far been their continued expansion and extension. As in the Johnson and Nixon administrations, entitlements were increased under the George W. Bush and Obama presidencies. What has occurred since has been a stalemate. The Trump administration and Republican Congress proved unable to roll back Obamacare, while the Biden administration and the narrow-majority Democrat Congress proved unable to further increase entitlements legislatively—despite a desperate desire to do so. The result of incremental increase and status quo stalemate has been a further explosion of entitlement spending—one no longer masked by declining defense spending. As a percentage of federal outlays, in 2022 Social Security constituted 19.3 percent, Medicare 11.9 percent, Medicaid 9.4 percent, and other means-tested entitlements 10.1 percent. Combined, this amounts to 50.7 percent, just over half of the federal government's outlays.[82]

According to Congressional Budget Office estimates for fiscal year 2024, as percentages of GDP, Social Security spending will equal 5.2 percent; Medicare will hit 3.2 percent; Medicaid (combined with other mandatory health-program costs) will amount to 2.4 percent; and other mandatory programs will reach 3.1 percent. Combined, these mandatory entitlement spending groups will equal 13.9 percent—almost five times greater than estimated defense spending's 2.9 percent of GDP.[83] These entitlement spending groups will also constitute well over half the federal government's 2024 estimated spending of 23.1 percent of GDP. They are also more than total federal government spending as a percentage of GDP at the height of the Civil War and in any of the New Deal's pre-World War II years.

As an illustration, when OMB released its FY 2024 Historical Tables,[84] outside the crisis response to the COVID pandemic, 2022 spending as a percent of GDP was the highest since World War II.[85] It is safe to say that 2022 marked the largest non-crisis federal government in American history. This largeness of the federal government, which used to rise only temporarily, is now status quo.

SECTION IX
The Unsustainable Entitlement Future

As massive as the federal government has grown, it is just a warm-up for what is to come. As this book will later show in greater detail, mandatory spending is on autopilot, powered by entitlement programs, and it has federal spending on course to not just surpass any peacetime peak but to rival those of wartime. Instead of crisis being the thing that grows government, a growing government will be the crisis. And this crisis will not be temporary, as during wartime—it will be permanent until altered.

The mandatory spending autopilot is what drives—and will continue to drive—this unprecedented peacetime surge.

The US Government Accountability Office's May 2022 report entitled "The Nation's Fiscal Health" says it all: "The federal government faces an unsustainable fiscal future."[86] The report cites 2021's 33 percent increase in publicly held debt (to about 100 percent of GDP) from fiscal year 2019 to back up its projection.[87] It is an alarm that has been raised countless times in multiple official estimates over several decades—and yet just as often ignored.

The federal government has become so big that its mandatory spending autopilot now has its *own* autopilot: Debt. In its 2024 report, CBO showed, federal debt averaging 48.3 percent of GDP over the prior 50 years.[88] In 2019, just before the COVID-19 pandemic, it was 79 percent of GDP.[89] In 2021, the pandemic's second year, federal debt was just over 97 percent.[90] In its 2024 report, CBO projects that federal debt will hit 99 percent of GDP in 2024.[91]

The US Government Accountability Office (GAO) observes: "For most of the nation's history, the government's debt held by the public as a share of GDP ... decreased during peacetime ... "[92] If official estimates are correct, it will do just the opposite in the future, growing "faster than GDP in every year starting in 2024."[93] And it will continue to do so thereafter. According to CBO, it is estimated to reach 116 percent in 2034, which "would be the largest amount ever recorded in U.S. history." [94] The culprit? In its 2024 ten-year projection, CBO writes: "Outlays increase largely because of rising interest costs and growth in spending for the major health care programs. Revenues also rise over the period, but more slowly than outlays."[95]

In a vicious cycle, as interest spending increases it in turn drives higher federal debt levels. And with each turn in the cycle, the federal government grows larger. From a federal government that spent just under 3 percent of GDP in 1929, if current CBO long-term projections prove prophetic, it will have grown to one that spends more than that percentage (3.9 percent) just to service its net debt interest costs by 2034.

SECTION X
Conclusion: From Small to Enormous

Over nine decades, the federal government has grown from small to enormous. In 1929, compared to GDP, federal government outlays were just under 3 percent; its receipts amounted to 3.7 percent; it ran a surplus of 0.7 percent; and it lowered its debt to just 16.2 percent. According to CBO's estimates, federal government spending would amount to 23.1 percent of GDP in 2024; its revenues amount to 17.5 percent; it would run a deficit of 5.6 percent; with debt held by the public at 99 percent.[96] The quantitative size of government is already unprecedented for any sustained period of time, and certainly for peacetime. Official projections from every credible source show that the federal government's current trajectory is, in the words of GAO, "unsustainable." These warnings are decades old and are regularly repeated. They are also current; as Federal Reserve Chairman Jerome Powell stated on February 4, 2024: "The debt is growing faster than the economy, so it is unsustainable. It's time for us to get back to putting a priority on fiscal sustainability. And sooner's better than later."[97]

The federal government's qualitative changes are arguably even greater than its quantitative ones. The impact of the federal government on America's overall governance—at the state, local, and city government levels as well as federal—is incalculable. The amount of money the federal government spends and sends influences state and local governments at almost every juncture. What its money does not influence, its mandates increasingly dictate. Its impact is therefore no less on American society. The outcome is a nationalization and centralization of American government never seen before. Or envisioned. As a result, power and resources do not just flow from Washington, they flow to it as well, exerting a governmental gravitational pull, they draw in more of both.

The qualitative changes in spending have been profound. The clearest change has been entitlement spending. For decades it has undergone a process of expansion (adding benefits within designated categories of individuals), extension (including new classes of beneficiaries), and enrichment (increasing the benefits that designated individuals receive). The operation of these programs has undergone an equally dramatic change. Entitlements were at first extended to a relatively narrow and clearly defined group of individuals; as Cogan points out, for generations this meant veterans and their families. These veteran benefits were fixed and only changed by law. The class of beneficiaries was also limited by time—specifically lifetimes; they were not self-perpetuating. This original entitlement model was altered profoundly by Social Security in the 1930s, which created both a broad new beneficiary class (those who had worked in a covered occupation) and a self-perpetuating one: new beneficiaries were continually entering the workforce. The entitlement model was changed dramatically again with the Great Society programs of the 1960s when, thanks to Medicare and Medicaid, entitlements became effectively uncapped. Whereas benefits to a recipient once had been limited by—and could only be changed by—law, spending limits were now effectively removed, and the resultant spending increased without any changes in law. By bringing health care providers in to distribute the health care benefits of the new Medicare plan, providers joined beneficiaries in a system that effectively took the allocation of benefits beyond government control. The result was an effectively uncapped, and thereby uncontrolled, entitlement.

Simultaneously, new entitlements were created throughout the 1960s and 1970s. These too had a self-perpetuating aspect. Their beneficiary classes—the poor, the elderly, the sick, the disabled—would replicate over time and, as evidence showed, expand.

Beneficiaries' relationships to their programs also changed. In some cases, beneficiaries would be given by law—either through the legislative process, the judicial one, or both—an ownership stake in their benefits. (*Goldberg v. Kelly* in 1970 "ruled that welfare was akin to property and therefore was protected by the Constitution's due process provisions."[98]) In virtually every case, beneficiaries *felt* an ownership stake in their benefits and to increases in them. In response, Congress and presidents increased benefits and added changes to automatically raise them.

Washington had created a new element to the federal government: autopilot programs. These programs ran themselves and increased their spending without need for additional legislation and frequently without serious oversight. The federal government's role shifted from one of conducting these programs' oversight to handling their overdrafts. Unsurprisingly these entitlement programs grew rapidly; in so doing they have drawn yet more resources to Washington. They have grown so immense that they have now *de facto* created their own mandatory spending: federal debt. This debt has grown so fast that it has outpaced the economy, increased federal interest payments, and resulted in, yes, yet more federal debt. Left in their currently unchecked form, the entitlement programs will increasingly accelerate this trend.

The qualitative change in federal spending has led to a qualitative change in federal funding. At its inception, the federal government relied almost exclusively on tariffs for its revenues. To address its extreme need for revenue during the Civil War, an income tax was temporarily adopted, becoming permanent only with the Sixteenth Amendment in 1913. Then came Social Security's payroll tax introduced during the New Deal era. While income taxes before had been limited to a small group of wealthy taxpayers, the payroll tax imposed its burden on a substantial number of Americans across the income scale.

Yet even this powerful addition to the federal government's taxing power has proved insufficient to fund the rapid spending growth. In recent decades, the federal government has adopted two additional ways to fund its policies: imposing mandates that shift costs to others (Cogan cites the Affordable Care Act's mandates on individuals, employers, and states as notable recent examples, though the list is long[99]) and significantly increasing borrowing.

Today's major federal-funding change is the reliance on borrowing. Deficits have been the norm for the federal government throughout its transformation to a big-government model. Since 1930, the federal government has only had twelve annual budget surpluses, and none since 2001. Yet since 1993—with the exception of the years 2009-2013, which were dominated by the Financial Crisis—deficits sat below 4 percent of GDP. Starting in 2019, however, deficits rose above that threshold, and aren't projected to drop below it in any official CBO estimates. The federal government's funding needs have become so enormous that Americans—and their lawmakers—can no longer bear funding them strictly through taxes. The result is a reversion to two and a half centuries ago when the American Revolution was forced to rely on borrowing to meet its funding needs.

This shift to borrowing as an increasingly large means of funding should not be mistaken as a way to neutralize the impact of the federal government's growth on America. It will seriously dampen future economic growth. CBO states: "Large and growing federal debt would, over time, push up the cost of borrowing, reduce private investment, and slow the growth of GDP, all else being equal."[100] Consequently, CBO estimates real GDP growth will fall by roughly one third: dropping from an annual average of 2.5 percent per year from 1994 to 2023 to 1.7 percent from 2024 to 2054.[101] That is an enormous impact on future living standards.

Yet with all the qualitative changes that America's growth of government has wrought, those to its citizens are likely even greater. Over the last nine decades, Americans have become desensitized to big government and bigger entitlements. This is particularly true of the last fifty years. As Cogan writes: "By the end of the 1970s, the entitlement-program edifice that constitutes the modern American welfare state was essentially complete. Virtually all of today's major entitlements, with the exception of the Medicare coverage of prescription drugs and the Affordable Care Act's health-insurance subsidies, had been written into the statute books. The edifice was extensive, and it reached all segments of the population."[102]

This has profound implications. Many American children born in the 20th century did not grow up in an entitlement society. They would have had at least some sort of pre-entitlement foundation because their parents or other adults around them would have experienced a different, pre-entitlement environment. For children in the 21st century, their pre-entitlement foundation is small if not completely nonexistent. And it is diminishing. Of course, for entire segments of America—and increasing numbers and an increasing proportion of the population—the entitlement society is not just a fact of knowledge—a realization that it is there—it is a fact of life. It would be quite possible for a child of this century to grow up in an entitlement environment and surrounded by adults for whom entitlement programs have been their way of life. As early as 1980, nearly half of American households received benefits from a federal entitlement program; two-thirds of these received benefits from two or more programs.[103]

America is now living with an increasing population, and an increasing percentage of the population, for whom such a condition is not an anomaly but normality. Just as the qualitative changes of the last nine decades had profound impacts on the size of the federal government—its spending, its funding, and its debt—so too would those changes profoundly affect those distributing and receiving entitlement benefits. No group has benefited more from this change than America's socialist Left. The next chapter discusses what these changes have been, who has been affected, and how the socialist Left has benefited.

CHAPTER EIGHT

THE SOCIALIST LEFT FINDS A PATRON

SECTION I
Introduction

Having now charted the federal government's astronomical growth over the last ninety years, it starts to become evident how this, combined with concerted efforts to foster organizations across various segments of society, solved the socialist Left's existential conundrum in America. Enormous recurring federal expenditures have created a huge potential client base among both recipients and providers, as well as the interest groups (largely on the political spectrum's left) representing them. Even without a proactive government organizing effort, the Left as a whole would still have benefited from the increases in spending: the money *was* there and continues to be. However, the organizational support was there too. From the 1960s on, the federal government's efforts have been decidedly aimed at promoting the organization and mobilization of the Left. Money, means, and members—all were elements that the Left had lacked, particularly the socialist Left. As a result, the Left have flourished—the socialist Left, which had more to gain, in particular has. The socialist Left is now emerging for the first time in America's history as a serious and sustained political force, having taken advantage of the spending and organizing opportunities that the federal government has offered over the last six decades.

While this outcome may have been unprecedented for the American socialist Left specifically, there are both historical and theoretical precedents for the kind of rise they've experienced. What's unique about the socialist Left's experience in America is the rise of such a formerly fringe group. In the chicken-or-the-egg question of which must come first—a base of support to rally or an organization around which to rally—the socialist Left had neither. There was no lasting base from which a socialist Left organization could arise and be meaningfully sustained. Absent a sustained and meaningful socialist Left organization, the socialist Left thus could not take advantage of episodes—such as economic downturns—that could have advanced it and its policies.

Precedents existed for the federal government's intervention in the 1960s to encourage the organization of what has become America's traditional Left; only its scale was unequaled. The results from these conscious efforts also had precedents: recall the New Deal's FSA within the USDA under Secretary of Agriculture Henry Wallace. The efforts of the 1960s were successful compared to the failures thirty years earlier because of the amount, scope, and the duration of the resources committed. Once this conscious, concerted, and costly federal effort to organize the Left is understood, the massive organization of America's traditional Left—and the socialist Left's particular benefit from it—becomes predictable.

Decades and trillions of dollars later, the effect is clear: the traditional Left—particularly the socialist Left—has benefited to the detriment of America. This chapter traces exactly how this has occurred: From its early precedents, to the explosion of Left-backed interest groups, to the transformation of the Democrat Party from a center-left party into a party of the Left, to the socialist Left's rise to influence many of the Democrat Party's policy objectives.

Section Two shows how interest groups have been at the heart of politics throughout American history, becoming an important subject of study for political scientists. Examining both history and political science shows that the success of any interest group has always hinged on transactions between an organization and its members: specifically, that a successful organization must provide something to its members—most commonly, this meant tangible economic returns. It was the inability to enter into transactions with a meaningful number of Americans for a significant amount of time that historically doomed America's socialist Left.

Section Three describes how resources supplied to private groups by the federal government had encouraged their formation in the past—particularly in agriculture, such as with the previously discussed Grange and Farm Bureau. The New Deal would take this to a new level. The Democrat Party, through its control of the federal government, extended both money and authority on behalf of business, labor, and agriculture to address the Depression—and solidify its political coalition. Although the federal government had encouraged organizations before, its efforts during the New Deal era went far beyond those—including making changes in law, thereby permanently reshaping the policy and political landscape. It would be this same kind of support (starting in the 1960s through today), that for the first time supplied the basis for a transaction between the socialist Left and a significant—and growing—number of Americans.

Section Four shows how this organizing assistance developed a clear ideological bent in one particular effort: the USDA's Farm Security Administration, which unabashedly sought land redistribution and social reform in rural America. An increasingly ideological Henry Wallace and USDA staff devised and pursued—in opposition to agriculture's prevailing groups—the most redistributionist policy in America's history to that point. Although ultimately terminated by Congress, the FSA became a precedent for the Johnson administration's far more massive effort decades later: its War on Poverty and the Great Society. The Johnson administration's efforts would remain the federal government's prevailing approach thereafter.

Section Five examines how the Great Society allowed the traditional Left's organizing efforts to reach critical mass, thereby finally achieving vital structures. More than just quantitatively growing the federal government's size, the Great Society qualitatively changed the federal government, as exemplified by the 1964 Economic Opportunity Act's focus on creating organizations in the low-income communities it targeted. Federal government assistance in creating organizations (and providing dollars) allowed America's socialist Left the opportunity to enter into successful and sustained transactions with significant portions of American society for the first time.

Section Six documents the explosion of interest groups that resulted from the massive assistance given by the federal government. According to a 2021 Urban Institute study,[1] America "has roughly 1.8 million nonprofit organizations ... with expenditures of $1.94 trillion." This amounted to just under 10 percent of US GDP in 2020. Charity has become big business. Just how much of nonprofits' revenues come from government is indicated by the fact that their most commonly considered source—individual donations—make up just 18 percent of the revenue for those organizations with annual budgets over $500,000, and 30 percent for those with annual budgets under $500,000. From 1977 to 1997, the share of government funding for the Independent Sector's constituent institutions'[2] budgets grew from 26.6 percent to 31.3 percent, while private contributions fell from 26.3 percent to 19.9 percent.[3] That this enormous growth of government spending (a considerable amount of which goes directly to nonprofits) and federal actions aimed at creating nonprofits has led to their massive growth is hardly surprising. In fact, it is precisely what the history and political science study of interest groups in America would predict.

Section Seven examines how the Left have benefitted from the enormous growth of federal government spending and nurturing, and the resulting non-profit explosion. Unable to survive for a significant and meaningful time on its own, it stands to reason that the socialist Left and its organizations have benefitted the most from the federal government's efforts to redistribute money and authority: from a base of effectively zero, America's socialist Left had nowhere to go but up. This growth of the traditional Left and the socialist Left has had a profound effect on the Democrat Party. In just decades, it has gone from being a party significantly influenced by moderates and conservatives, to one dominated by the traditional Left with the socialist Left in the vanguard. No clearer evidence of the socialist Left's ascendancy in the Democrat Party could exist than the increasingly explicit embrace from party members of the "democratic socialist" label. A 2024 *Gallup* poll found 63 percent of Democrats said that if their party nominated a socialist for president, they would vote for that candidate.[4] The Democrat Party's policies, such as a tax on wealth, attest to the same willingness.

Section Eight concludes the chapter with a comparison of how far the socialist Left has progressed. In contrast to its efforts a century ago, as an independent party pursuing the traditional unified socialist agenda, today's socialist Left has gained more adherents and influence within the Democrat Party. Without a change in the federal policies that have nurtured the socialist Left, its influence on the traditional Left, the Democrat Party, and in America can only be expected to grow.

SECTION II
Interest Groups at the Heart of American Politics

Interest groups have always existed in America, under many names and forms. Anyone reading the proceedings of the Constitutional Convention will quickly recognize the many interests that contended there—large states versus small states, slave versus non-slave states. In his *Federalist* No. 10, James Madison argued that the Constitution's value was "to break and control the violence of faction" in American society.[5]

It's clear that Madison's view of interests, or as he says, "factions," was decidedly negative. In his words, the result of the pursuit of self-interest meant "our governments are too unstable, that the public good is disregarded." In recognizing "that the causes of faction cannot be removed," Madison stated that "relief is only to be sought in the means of controlling its effects." He also argued that "the federal Constitution forms a happy combination" by extending the number of contending interests. By taking in so many, he argued that "you make it less probable that a majority of the whole will have a common motive to invade the rights of other citizens; or if such a common motive exists, it will be more difficult for all who feel it to discover their own strength, and to act in unison with each other." Finally, "the same advantage which a republic has over a democracy, in controlling the effects of faction, is enjoyed by a large over a small republic." In short, the Constitution was America's best chance to control the unavoidable evil of faction.

Madison's appraisal of "factions" was hardly the last word. Turning interests into interest groups was far from automatic. Alexis de Tocqueville observed that to get large numbers of people to join together, the people must believe it serves their interests to do so. Over a hundred years later, the economist Mancur Olson made a seminal contribution to political science when he argued in his 1971 book, *The Logic of Collective Action*, that crossing the gulf between potential and realized potential was not a "given" for interest groups. Yet like Madison, Olson recognized the power interest groups could hold if and when they did realize their potential: organized interests could not only prevail over unorganized interests, but an organized minority could even prevail over an unorganized majority.

According to Olson, the key to organizing an interest (what he called a "latent group") into a successful group was the group's ability to provide an exclusive benefit, or "selective incentive," restricted to its members only. The reason for the selectivity, as Olson puts it was "so that those who do not join the organization working for the group's interest, or in other ways contribute to the attainment of the group's interest, can be treated differently from those who do."[6] In contrast to the successfully organized interest group with a selective incentive was the provision of a "public good" (a simple example of providing a "public good" would be creating a park open to everyone). The provision of "public goods" created a free-rider problem where nonmembers got access to a benefit without contributing to the cost of providing it: something for nothing that negated the need to join an organization. Political scientist Robert Salisbury, beginning in the late 1960s and over the next decades, would refine this into his exchange theory: members and organizations bonded by receiving something from the relationship.

These ideas have been firmly demonstrated by America's history of organized interests. Essentially, money had to change hands for groups to exist. It had to be worth money for members to join, while members had to have the money to pay dues or fees to sustain organizations. Some groups succeeded here, such as the farm organizations and labor unions discussed in the previous chapters—and it was at this elemental level that America's socialist Left failed. Repeatedly. The socialist Left never managed to enter into a sustained transaction with a significant number of Americans for a prolonged period of time.

America's successful organizations centered on occupations[7]—most notably agriculture and manufacturing—and looked to their members' financial interests.[8] In agriculture, the link to money was unmistakable, as America's focal agriculture protests frequently followed commodity prices: protests arising as prices fell, and then subsiding when prices rebounded. At the organizational level, American historian Richard Hofstadter observed that the Populists of the late 19th century failed in large part due to a lack of funds, while the roughly contemporaneous Nonpartisan League found success in large part because of their substantial dues.[9] In both agriculture and labor, organizations had to offer services for stability; for agriculture it was cooperatives, for labor it was collective bargaining.

That there were substantial examples of successful organizing of interests in America, but no significant socialist organizations, further underscores the socialist Left's failure to gain traction. Americans were simply not collectivists.[10] When the socialist Left tried to pursue utopian communes—as did Robert Owen in the 1820s—they were abject failures.[11] In labor, America's large unions pushed the socialist Left away, as with the AFL, and in some cases, the socialist Left itself even eschewed unions.[12] This is evident in the case of the IWW where the Wobblies dismissed the collective bargaining that unions sought for direct revolutionary action instead.[13]

Unable to enter into transactions, there were no socialist Left organizations to speak of; without organizations, there was no socialist Left. Combined with America's rapid upward mobility was rapid turnover in the marginalized population the socialist Left sought to organize—few stayed poor for long, but instead experienced upward mobility. Nor was this marginalized population inherently easy to organize, with the most marginalized regularly being the least organized. In short: distress does not automatically equal organization.[14] On its own therefore, America's socialist Left effectively amounted to nothing.

SECTION III
Government's Past Role as Patron

While it's often a chicken-or-the-egg question with successful organizations of which came first—a base to organize or an organization with which to organize— America's socialist Left effectively had neither. Locked out of significant and sustained transactions on their own, the socialist Left's only option was for outside support to help bridge the separation.

The study of interest groups focuses on patrons' instrumental role in the formation of said groups. This became particularly true in the mid-20th century as private foundations and unions took on the role of patron; however, before this, it was not unheard of for the federal government to take on this role. Often overlooked, the federal government regularly, if not frequently, supported private-sector organizations. During the Industrial Revolution, for example, both major canal companies and railroads benefited from government support. Admittedly not organized interests in today's conventional sense, both were assuredly organizations, and the federal assistance they received was also assuredly instrumental in their formation. Over time, federal government assistance would become more explicit and varied, while the recipients of that assistance became more recognizable as organized interests.

Changes in law were instrumental in the formation of the labor unions and cooperatives that farmers saw as the key benefits of their agricultural organizations.[15] Support for cooperatives extended further to the USDA, state agricultural colleges (which in turn had been helped by a series of federal laws enacted from the 1860s to 1914),[16] and state departments of agriculture.[17] Even President Theodore Roosevelt and his Country Life Commission embraced cooperatives in 1908—as did other prominent political leaders.[18] Eventually, the agricultural organizations that benefited from the cooperatives sought federal legislation to protect and promote them. In the 1920s, this pursuit of legislation would become more formalized still with the US Senate's Farm Bloc, which was led by the Farm Bureau,[19] and was a sizable bipartisan group of senators representing farm states[20] and collectively pursuing organized agriculture's interests. More proactive still was federal government assistance in the founding of organizations themselves. While the Grange was founded by a USDA employee,[21] the Farm Bureau, in the words of Olson, "was created by the government."[22] This is corroborated many times over as numerous writers describe its formation through the Chamber of Commerce and then its great expansion by the US Extension Service.

By the 1930s, then, government assistance to organizations already had ample precedent. Enter the New Deal, which took this to another level entirely. The Agricultural Adjustment Administration (AAA) is an example par excellence. The AAA's original purpose was to pay farmers to limit production, thereby reducing supply and driving up commodity prices. Needing to reach farmers directly to ensure its goals were being met, it relied on the USDA's Extension Service, a long-standing system of thousands of agents nationwide who worked with farmers to educate and advise on best agricultural practices. The relationship between the government's Extension Service and the Farm Bureau was so close that many farmers could not distinguish between the two.[23] The AAA greatly aided the Farm Bureau, tripling its membership,[24] and the program's direct payments to farmers gave them the means to pay organization dues.[25]

The value of such patronage in the formation of organized interests was thus well-established by the 1930s, but none of it was bestowed upon the socialist Left. In American agriculture they were effectively nonexistent; within American labor, they largely were ostracized. The federal government had been no more hospitable to the socialist Left than had been the rest of American society, especially after the post-World War I Red Scare. President Wilson had jailed Socialist Party President Eugene Debs, who ran the last of his presidential campaigns from behind bars (again, not winning a single electoral vote) and from late 1919 into early 1920, Wilson's attorney general, A. Mitchell Palmer, launched a series of raids that arrested thousands of suspected "reds."[26] And while the socialist Left embraced the New Deal as early as 1934,[27] the early Roosevelt administration as a whole did not reciprocate. It did not need to. The overwhelming New Deal coalition had no need for the moribund and insignificant socialist Left, which had been rejected not only within American society as a whole, but by two of the New Deal coalition's most important electoral groups: agriculture and organized labor.

SECTION IV
FSA: Federal Organizing Leans Left

Not until well into the 1930s was anything approaching a socialist Left policy attempted on a national scale. Fittingly, it did not come from any independent effort by the socialist Left itself. Nor did it come from a groundswell in overall society—as had the Populist movement of the 1890s—or even from the group targeted by the policy. Whereas the Farm Bloc of the 1920s originated within Congress and the farm organizations, this new policy—the Farm Security Administration—came from within the executive branch; precisely it came from a relatively small and isolated band of bureaucrats within the USDA who had succeeded in radicalizing their boss, Secretary Henry A. Wallace. Though the USDA had undergone an internal purge of leftists in February 1935, under Wallace it was becoming increasingly estranged from the farm organizations (particularly the Farm Bureau), as well as from key members of Congress. (This lack of widespread congressional support would doom the FSA in less than a decade—its fatal blow coming when Congress denied its appropriation in 1943; it was finally abolished shortly after World War II.)[28]

The FSA's intended objective was to redistribute farmland within rural America, but the only farm organizations that supported it—the Southern Tenant Farmers Union, whose members farmed land owned by others, and the minuscule Socialist Party—represented few and carried still less weight. Simply, there was no organized tenant movement to speak of.[29] On the other side, the FSA was opposed by agriculture's dominant organizations, and particularly its most powerful one: the Farm Bureau. When the policy was introduced in Congress, it was done purely as a courtesy to the administration as a whole—and even this was due to the widespread support of the New Deal's national farm-payment plan, not the policy in question. There, it encountered intense opposition too.

The whole FSA episode ran counter to the political science paradigm of policy development and maintenance known as the "iron triangle," which is discussed at length *vis-à-vis* military defense policy in Gordon Adams's 1981 book, *The Politics of Defense Contracting: The Iron Triangle*.[30] Adams describes military defense policy as being controlled by three groups: the relevant congressional committees, the executive branch bureaucrats who administered military programs, and organized defense interests. Although originally focused on the military, similar "triangles" can be identified in other policy areas and in other periods—US federal budget historian John Cogan[31] argues that a potent "triangle" formed as early as the late 19th century around the Civil War veteran pension program and included the Grand Army of the Republic, while agriculture's commodity programs formed many such triangles as well.[32]

Notably, the FSA had just one of an iron triangle's points: bureaucrats, and this only due to the enormous expansion of executive-branch authority that occurred during the New Deal era.[33] Much of this authority was provided by Congress, though some was claimed unilaterally. This new authority helped the USDA compensate for the other points that its redistributive land policy lacked.

Henry A. Wallace[34] became Franklin Roosevelt's Secretary of Agriculture in 1933, after working as an agricultural writer, editor, and successful entrepreneur. Wallace saw the AAA as giving farmers the same protection that businesses and labor had received from the National Industrial Recovery Act, which had given Roosevelt broad authority to oversee American industry in order to achieve the administration's wage and price objectives.[35] The AAA had not been intended to smooth differences in conditions between farmers,[36] only between agriculture in general and other economic sectors. Its goal had been to get relief into the sector as quickly as possible. For this reason, it had relied on the Extension Service for implementation, which proved a boon to the closely connected Farm Bureau. During the AAA's operation, Wallace came to believe that federal policy was responsible for worsening the farm tenants' plight, and further, that government had a responsibility to aid the unorganized.[37]

Thus was born a Special Committee on Farm Tenancy on November 17, 1936. Chaired by Wallace and including many liberal members, the Committee released its report on February 11, 1937, advising that the government should purchase land to resell to tenant farmers at favorable interest rates and to help establish small farmer cooperatives. Legislation embodying the Committee's recommendations was drafted in the USDA, which then asked Senator Bankhead of Alabama, a key sponsor of earlier New Deal economic legislation, to introduce it. With increased majorities after the 1936 election, Democrats easily passed it in July and the FSA came into being on September 1, 1937.[38]

Political scientists Fumiaki Kubo and Grant McConnell have both written about the FSA. According to Kubo, it was "extraordinarily redistributive" and "uniquely class-conscious,"[39] and McConnell saw it as the most significant anti-poverty legislation prior to the 1960s' Great Society programs.[40] Gunnar Myrdal, a Swedish economist and Nobel Prize winner, found it notable for Blacks' participation in it. Others, notably the Farm Bureau, labeled it "social-istic."[41] Unquestionably it was the most leftward leaning federal program up to that time, and would hold that title for the next three decades.

Not only did the FSA at least broadly share the socialist Left's policy goals, it shared the socialist Left's failure too. Even with the federal government playing an unprecedented role of patron, the socialist Left could not capitalize on it—no organization ever developed to back it, and despite having initially been introduced by prominent members in Congress, the FSA never garnered long-term congressional support. Its origin within the USDA, then, was not a source of strength, but indicative of weakness. Even at the bureaucratic level, the FSA both failed locally and ran afoul of the grassroots bureaucracy: the aforementioned Extension Service. Lacking two of an iron triangle's three points, the FSA wobbled along, eventually falling over like a one-legged stool.

Nonetheless, the course the FSA ran is important for understanding the socialist Left broadly in America. First, it showed the federal government taking an unprecedented role in American society, far beyond simply encouraging the formation of an organized interest or designing a policy. With the FSA, the federal government sought to implement its policy over an extended period, and by the time it was terminated, the FSA had been in operation longer than the New Deal's general farm policy had been at its start.

Second, it demonstrates the federal government taking its most decidedly ideological position to that point. The FSA was as leftist a policy as could conceivably be undertaken in America in its day. Throughout its history, American agriculture had never been collectivist; the furthest a socialist policy could go in America *was* with what the FSA did: the government buying land and redistributing it with restrictive conditions. It was the most redistributive policy in American history up to that point—far more even than the Social Security program (where lower income beneficiaries received proportionally larger benefits).

Finally, despite the federal government's aggressive and prolonged efforts on behalf of the FSA, this most "socialistic" of American policies failed. Even this concerted effort by the largest of patrons possessing both enormous political and economic power was not enough to save an essentially socialist Left policy, nor to spur the creation of a meaningful socialist Left organization. In order to compensate for the iron triangle's missing elements of organization and base, the third point—the bureaucracy—would have to contribute disproportionately more than it had with the FSA.

SECTION V
The Great Society Organizes the Left

After the defeat of the FSA in the 1940s, the socialist Left would continue its downward spiral over the course of the next two decades. First was the case of Henry A. Wallace himself. The FSA's largest champion, he became FDR's vice president from 1941 to 1945, but after following an increasingly leftward trajectory in Washington, Wallace was forced off Roosevelt's ticket by conservatives in 1944 (replaced by then-Senator Harry Truman of Missouri). He was subsequently fired as Secretary of Commerce by President Truman for being too favorably predisposed to the USSR. When Wallace ran as the Progressive Party's presidential candidate in 1948, he was soundly crushed—his most meaningful impact being the near defeat of his former administration by siphoning votes from President Harry Truman. Next came the USSR's alienation of America and the rest of its former World War II allies, thus forcing America's socialist Left (in the form of America's Communist Party) to adhere to Moscow's line at the cost of any legitimate domestic support.[42] The resulting Red Scare of the 1950s, just a generation removed from the one under President Wilson, ended any chance for the formation of a conventional independent political party capable of promoting a traditional unified socialist agenda. By the 1960s, the socialist Left's failure was unmistakable. In its wake, came the SDS's Port Huron statement, which signaled the surrender of the orthodox socialist approach in America, though it was merely formalizing the obvious.

Collectively authored by the Students for a Democratic Society, the Port Huron Statement was itself an example of what the contemporary socialist Left in America was and intended to become: patron-dependent. The FSA experience had proved that America's socialist Left could not stand on its own—even under the most favorable of circumstances—without someone else picking up its tab. In the case of the FSA, it was the federal government; in the case of the SDS, it was the United Auto Workers union. And just like the FSA after the federal government stopped funding it, the SDS shriveled when the UAW withdrew its patronage.[43] The lesson was clear. Patronage was essential to America's socialist Left; the deepest—if not the only—pockets from which it could hope to draw were the federal government's; and its only chance of doing so was by renouncing any explicit attachment to a traditionally socialist unified front. So, starting in the 1960s, it sought to adopt—and attract—patronage through a multiplicity of separate fronts.

At the same time as America's socialist Left was disintegrating into its myriad leftist causes, American political science was formulating the system of pluralism.[44] Through pluralism came a thorough reversal of James Madison's view of factions: instead of viewing factions as an evil to be controlled, pluralism sees interest groups as a positive good for society. This perceived beneficial effect resulted from the increased representation and strengthening of an individual's influence within society that organizations allowed.[45] The trend toward pluralism began in the early 1950s with David Truman's book *The Governmental Process*, which saw interest groups as important in the complex modern world.[46] It would reach its academic zenith in the early 1960s but would continue to be influential well into the 1980s.[47]

Pluralism meshed well with the constitutional framework that makes America especially susceptible to minority influence.[48] It also renewed the license of those in government for whom new interest groups would be favorable to the objectives they sought to promote. Under both the pluralist paradigm and the influence of bureaucrats with leftist agendas, the federal government became the chief sponsor of new interest groups in the 1960s. These groups in turn became advocates for increasing the number of federal government programs, even going as far as to sue for more benefits for recipients and for increasing the number of recipients. John Cogan describes the case of the Economic Opportunity Act's Legal Service Program as one such example. Created to establish legal offices to aid the poor, its first-year budget for legal services in 1965 "was nearly ten times the total amount spent by all civil legal aid offices in the United States in 1959."[49] Its funds "were a boon to activist legal services lawyers who stood ready to use federal funds to obtain greater legal rights for welfare recipients. The goal of the lawyers was to establish a welfare system that guaranteed poor people a legal right—an entitlement" to federal benefits.[50]

That America's socialist Left was at the same time dissolving itself into countless separate single-issue leftist movements, just as federal money was cascading in, made for a perfect storm of theory, bureaucracy, and advocacy.

That storm would break over America during the Johnson administration, with the Great Society program. Even before Johnson's landslide victory in 1964, an ideologically motivated administration operating under the pluralist model had produced the Economic Opportunity Act of 1964. The EOA's purpose was nothing less than "to eliminate the paradox of poverty in the midst of plenty in this Nation by opening to everyone the opportunity for education and training, the opportunity to work, and the opportunity to live in decency and dignity."

The EOA greatly expanded the government's scope for action. As Ginzberg and Solow in *The Great Society* write: "The Economic Opportunity Act of 1964 made poverty itself, and not only age or physical disability, an object of government policy."[51] The EOA, as the political scientist Jack Walker pointed out, followed a top-down path to enactment, as did much of the Johnson administration's anti-poverty legislation: such programs were not pursued by interest groups but by the administration itself.[52] It was the same model the FSA had followed a generation earlier, but on a vastly larger scale. It also added vastly more proactive means: "the Act encouraged the famous 'maximum feasible participation' of the poor in the design and operation of machinery aimed at assisting themselves."[53]

In January 1964, President Johnson tapped Peace Corps head Sargent Shriver to open a domestic front in the war on poverty by leading a Cabinet task force to develop legislation—again, just as had occurred with the FSA. In March, legislation was transmitted; in August, the EOA was enacted. The EOA established eleven new programs, the most prominent being its Section 202 "community action program." The official definition states that this program:

> mobilizes and utilizes resources, public or private, of any urban or rural … area … which provides services, assistance, and other activities of sufficient scope and size to give promise of progress toward elimination of poverty or a cause or causes of poverty through developing employment opportunities, improving human performance, motivation, and productivity, or bettering the conditions under which people live, learn, and work … [54]

Community action programs essentially gave a blank check to community organizers, ultimately resulting in the federal government providing up to 90 percent of their operating funds.[55] The programs these funds supported were to be developed, or at least coordinated, by a nonprofit agency—public or private—with the goal of harnessing "the maximum feasible participation of residents of the areas and members of the groups served" in their day-to-day running.[56] Once granted, due process was required before they could be terminated, making it hard to stop the funds from coming. This was a far cry from FDR three decades earlier, who, in the words of Black, was "concerned lest a permanent class of welfare recipients arise" when he ended the Civil Works Administration in 1934.[57]

The Director of the new Office of Economic Opportunity was given a budget of $800 million with effectively no strings attached, except the directive to spend it building up organizations within preferred communities—virtually anything would qualify for federal funding. The Director was also given far-reaching power to coordinate other federal agencies' anti-poverty programs—thus drawing in even more resources.

The parallel to the FSA of three decades earlier is striking. But while the FSA was largely an aberration within one agency, the EOA was a manifestation of an entire administration—the spirit of which would continue well beyond it. The EOA would not be dismantled until 1981 (meaning it lasted far longer than the FSA), and several of its programs would continue long after its dismantling—notably the Legal Services Corporation, which led the way for the traditional Left to pursue their agenda through the judiciary system.

Patronage is crucial to interest-group formation in general; it was even more important in the socialist Left's and the EOA's particular case. As Walker observed, patronage allows groups to arise where none existed,[58] and political scientist Robert Salisbury argues that money is so important that many interest groups had to wait until industrialization occurred for sufficient resources to be available. Patronage allows interest groups to survive even periods of public disinterest[59]—something America's socialist Left knew well. Not only could the federal government alone fill the role, only the federal government *would* do so with as moribund an entity as the socialist Left. Only the federal government's independence gave it the latitude to play the role no one else would.[60]

How important the federal government's patronage has been to the socialist Left is also crucial to understand. Most basically, it has given enormous sums of money over a prolonged period of time—six decades and counting. It has rehabilitated the socialist Left in America by simply being involved and allowing it to be involved, thus providing it with at least a patina of respectability in its various iterations—something the socialist Left had never obtained in its formal united front. The government also greatly expanded the socialist Left's potential client base; not only did the explosion of government programs spend enormous sums, but these programs have catered to tens of millions of people. Then, with the switch to in-kind aid, done on a most massive scale in Medicare (as described in detail by John Cogan in *The High Cost of Good Intentions*), the government expanded the socialist

Left's potential client base even further by bringing providers into the realm of potential supporters. Finally, the socialist Left was given new avenues of advancement for their agenda through the courts *vis-à-vis* the EOA's Legal Services Corporation, and then through direct action on a more massive scale than anything the socialist Left had been capable of before.

SECTION VI
The Left's Interest Group Explosion

The enormous increase in federal government spending and the deliberate intention to organize the unorganized—as exemplified by the Economic Opportunity Act—led to a dramatic rise in interest groups in the 1960s. This rise in organizations disproportionately benefited the traditional Left in general and the socialist Left in particular for two reasons. First, the enormous increase in spending created two new classes of potential clients to organize: recipients and providers. Second, because the Left collectively, and the socialist Left especially, had historically found it difficult to organize in America, the federal government's concerted effort to organize segments of society dramatically improved their situation: it was a bonanza to the organizers.

The 1960s saw the advent of the citizen group, which qualitatively changed the landscape of interest groups in America. Walker describes them as "a set of organizations claiming to represent broad collective interests."[61] Unlike business and occupational groups where the Left were almost nonexistent, the new citizen groups were dominated by the Left. Citizen groups also populated different policy areas (environmental, civil rights, anti-poverty), pursued a different type of policy (a redistributive one), and did so in a different way (confrontationally). Because their aims were what Olson termed "public goods," the benefits they sought could not be limited to just their members. This meant that in the absence of exclusive benefits (such as the higher wages that unions sought for their members alone), what citizen groups offered to their members was difficult to monetize in the form of dues, making them particularly dependent on patronage for survival.

As already shown, overall federal government spending exploded beginning in the 1960s. This is especially apparent in the area of social spending,
where payments to individuals rose from $343 billion from 1940 through 1964,
to $1.025 trillion from 1965 through 1980.[62] IRS data shows that 501I(3) and
501(c)(4) filings have risen, too, averaging just 4,875 from 1941 through 1960,
and growing to 9,642 from 1961 through 1981. And this has continued. Since
1982, we've seen an average of almost 30,000 nonprofit filings a year.[63] Driving
all of this was an increase in government funding to the independent sector,
which went from 26.6 percent in 1977 to 31.6 percent in 1997.[64]

This surge was especially evident in the Left-dominated area of social and
legal services, where federal government funding rose nearly eight times.[65]
Overall health and human services make up nearly half of America's nonprofits,[66]
and as 501(c)(3) organizations, have an enormous stake in policy.[67] From 1977
to 1997, the number of these groups went from 276,000 to 693,000—a rate 2.5
times that of business groups—with government providing 33 percent of their
funding. As the political scientists Jeffrey Berry and David Arons, who focus on
American interest groups, argue, a critical change occurred when the federal
government's approach to aid shifted from providing cash to rehabilitate the
poor toward focusing on in-kind assistance. Simultaneously, the amount spent
on undefined Department of Health Education and Welfare services (recall the
EOA's similar amorphousness) leapt from $353 million in 1969 to $1.7 billion
just three years later in 1972, while state spending on subcontracted services
(in-kind providers) went from 25 percent of their budgets to 49 percent in just
five years.[68] By 1996, the federal civilian workforce was 1.9 million; while the
government was employing 12.7 million subcontractors.[69]

This increase in government funding, while important in itself, also lent
a new credibility to organizations of the Left, which in turn, allowed them to
increase their nongovernmental funding too, thus qualifying for more government funding (such leveraging was open to rampant abuse[70]), and on and
on and on. These new organizations weren't limited to participating in just a
single federal program either. A single nonprofit could administer many federal
programs, thereby tapping multiple federal revenue streams: Berry and Arons
cite one nonprofit as operating thirty-five government programs.[71]

Political scientists believe generally that federal legislation was the genesis
of this interest-group rise, not the other way around. This, as per Walker, was

especially true for citizen groups.[72] As we've seen, historically, interest groups were privately funded, but after 1945, government largely eclipsed private patrons in the non-profit sector, funding both the formation and maintenance of said groups.[73]

The EOA, it would turn out, was the originator of citizen participation programs, and soon many laws included provisions requiring some citizen participation in the policymaking process.[74] The whole thing was and is cyclical and self-perpetuating. Participation that spurred interest groups and citizen groups in one area—such as the antiwar and civil rights movements—in turn prompted the formation of such groups in other policy areas.[75] Berry observes that liberals wanted just such citizen-group formation and that government provided it; both embraced pluralism's ethos that traditional politics alone was insufficient to achieve their desired reforms.[76]

Just as the new citizen groups of the 1960s and later were a deliberate effect of federal legislation, so too was the change in their approach to public participation. Berry notes that these citizen groups were "distinguished from earlier reform movements … by the breadth and durability of the lobbying organizations."[77] They also did not "cooperate" with other interest groups, instead opting for mass media and grassroots strategies to advance their agendas.[78] Favoring expansion of government and established on ideological bases, they were separate from traditional occupational interest groups, i.e., the organizations where the socialist Left had failed repeatedly. These new groups were, in a word, confrontational, and sought to expand the scope of conflicts. As cited by Walker in his book, *Mobilizing Interest Groups in America*, these new citizen groups "advocated proposals for the redistribution of resources and for increases in government regulation that would not lend themselves to resolution through logrolling, long-term agreements or through exclusive, face-to-face negotiations."[79] Walker attributes this confrontational, non-resolution style to the security these new citizen groups felt as a result of the funding they received from patrons—the most important of which was of course the federal government. Why be amenable when they would get their money anyway—when confrontation would not cost them their funding? And why be conciliatory when the funding implicitly, if not explicitly, encouraged confrontation?

More than this, there was a fundamental change in the actual policies being pursued. Gone were the distributional policies of the past where benefits were widely dispersed without a seeming cost to anyone (such as appropriations from Congress or agricultural-commodity payment programs). Now the policies aimed at a redistribution of society's resources—taking from one group to benefit another—as occurred with various regulatory policies that were directed at businesses' operations.[80] These were policies of the Great Society; these were the policies of the traditional Left—and the aims of the socialist Left in particular. And, as Walker points out, such policies were deliberately confrontational.

As Walker summarizes: the welfare state's growth "accentuated the ideological content of the public-policy debate and challenged the domination of established commercial interests in the policy-making process." This was no accident; this was intent. "Many of the new programs enacted during the postwar surge in the growth of government were intended either to constrain business or redistribute wealth."[81]

The areas into which the federal government inserted itself also favored a decidedly leftward direction, and over the 1960s and 1970s, hundreds of federally funded programs sprouted up in areas "that were once considered primarily matters of state or local concern," per Walker, such as "education, urban mass transportation, health care, and pollution control."[82] Thus, even the specific goals pursued were advances for the Left, things like: "expanding the welfare state, cleaning up the environment, advancing the rights of minorities, protecting unwary consumers, or promoting a greater emphasis upon occupational health and safety." As Walker notes, these "involved direct clashes between business interests on the one side, who preferred minimal government intervention, and citizen groups of the other, most of whom favored an expansionist state."[83] However, even if you add to these lists interest groups that came in droves following this,[84] they were still reinforced by the continued extension and expansion of the federal government since then—and the many additional movements and citizen groups that came later.

What has not changed is that a leftward direction dominates. This pattern of federal government expansion into new policy areas that favored the traditional Left's engagement on terrain favorable to their agendas matched perfectly the socialist Left's diaspora from a unified front into a multiplicity of policy areas, movements, and organizations. As James Gregory, historian of America's radical Left, writes of the period from the 1960s on:

The Left that mattered involved a constellation of social movements fighting for racial equality and Black Power, women's liberation and gay liberation, anti-imperialism and environmentalism ... While the sixties Left articulated grievances that were national or international in scope—notably resistance to war, racism, and sexism—its organizational forms and activism were almost entirely local. Apart from a handful of nationally coordinated antiwar marches in Washington DC, New York, and San Francisco, this movement constellation surged in hundreds of communities and campuses where local activists designed actions on their own or in loose coordination ... [85]

This dispersion of the socialist Left into a multiplicity of movements would only accelerate in the following decades and up into the present, coalescing as their increasing numbers and common goals—most notably the shared desire to obtain, enhance, and deploy increased state power on their causes' behalf—became clear. From there, it was a short step to seeking to obtain political power directly—not just as a client but as the entity wielding it.

SECTION VII
The Democrats' Capture by the Traditional Left

Over the last six decades, the concerted effort to organize and grow the traditional Left—with unmatched assistance from the federal government—has borne fruit. The traditional Left, and within them America's socialist Left, have attained heights previously beyond their reach. That this unparalleled growth in resources, numbers, organizations, and influence would be turned toward achieving political goals should only have been expected: the same progression has occurred in movements like those within the agriculture and labor organizations in earlier periods of American history.

The traditional Left, and increasingly the socialist Left, have been aiming their political aspirations at the Democrat Party for half a century. In the 1972 presidential election, Senator George McGovern forged a political base from the traditional Left and won the Party's nomination (though he ultimately lost the presidency). Two decades after the 1964 Economic Opportunity Act, Jesse Jackson would seek to lead his Rainbow-PUSH Coalition to the 1984 Democrat presidential nomination (although he fell short of even McGovern's ability to win the nomination). Although premature—and in the case of 1972, a debacle for Democrats—such efforts did not alter the traditional Left's migration to the Democrat Party, or the Democrat Party's migration to the left. As a result of these dual migrations, the Democrat Party has been captured by the traditional Left over the last two decades; and over the last six years, the traditional Left has seen the socialist Left in its vanguard.

The growing and unabashed socialist Left emergence from behind the cover of the myriad of movements into which they've ensconced themselves is an inescapable truth, as is the fact that the Democrat Party has moved significantly and rapidly left. One need only to look at the 2016 and 2020 presidential elections or to the policies recently pursued by the Biden administration and the Democrat Party (and called for with increasing stridence by growing numbers of its elected officials and its base supporters) to see the leftward movement, not to mention the numerous polls that document it.

While many polls have captured the Democrat Party's leftward movement (such as the earlier mentioned *Gallup* results showing over 60 percent of Democrats would support their party's nomination of a socialist for president), one stands starkly out for its extended examination of America's electorate and its depth of analysis: the Pew Research Center, which has since 1987 undertaken "an ambitious project to better understand the nature of American politics." According to *Pew*, they have "identified a broad range of beliefs and values that underlie common political labels and that ultimately drive political action. A voter typology emerged from this effort which classifies the electorate into distinct groupings, defined by their political, social, economic, and religious beliefs."[86] Reviewing five of these surveys (1999, 2005, 2014, 2017, and 2021), the Democrat Party's overall leftward movement and the emergence of the socialist Left within it becomes clear.

Pew's 1999 survey is an excellent starting point to show the beginning of Democrats' leftward march. This survey found "centrism" was the prevailing mood in the electorate as "party divisions and fault lines of the public are more traditional" than in previous years.[87] The survey identified "Socially Conservative

Democrats"[88] to be the largest of the Party's four groups. That year "Partisan Poor"[89] were second at 11 percent. Tied at third were "New Democrats"[90] and "Liberal Democrats,"[91] at 10 percent of registered voters apiece. As peculiar as "Socially Conservative Democrats" may sound to contemporary ears, they did not just exist, but were crucial to the Democrat Party's success. As *Pew* noted: "Democratic chances to retain control of the White House are once again threatened from within by social conservatives, who have rejected their party's standard-bearer to some extent in every Democratic defeat since 1968."[92]

Six years later, *Pew* found Republicans had "made some inroads among conservative Democrats" and that "Democrats [were] fractured by differences over social and personal values."[93] Conversely, by 2005 *Pew* noted that "Liberals"[94] were now Democrats' largest voting bloc, making up almost one-fifth (19 percent) of registered voters—almost double 1999's percentage.[95] Following behind "Liberals" were "Conservative Democrats"[96] at 15 percent, and "Disadvantaged Democrats"[97] at 10 percent. Commenting on Democrats' divide, *Pew* stated: "Most Liberals live in a world apart from Disadvantaged Democrats and Conservative Democrats."[98] Despite being the largest of the three groups, "Liberals" were the least loyal: Just 59 percent identified as Democrats (while 40 percent identified as Independents) versus 89 percent for "Conservative Democrats" and 84 percent for "Disadvantaged Democrats."[99]

Notable in 2005 was a pronounced division within the Democratic coalition on social and religious issues, which were "far more intense on the left than on the right."[100] This split was underscored by 33 percent of "Conservative Democrats" viewing the Republican Party favorably—compared to just 14 percent of "Liberals" who did.[101] In 2005, *Pew* described "Liberals" as the "most opposed to an assertive foreign policy, the most secular, and [those who] take the most liberal views on social issues such as homosexuality, abortion, and censorship. They differ from other Democratic groups in that they are strongly pro-environment and pro-immigration."[102]

In 2014, notable as the sixth year of Obama's presidency, *Pew* dropped "Conservative Democrats" entirely as a category in the Democratic coalition, and added political engagement as a variable in its typology analysis, which measured: "Those who regularly vote and routinely follow government and public affairs."[103] Among the three Democratic-leaning groups, "Solid Liberals"[104] were the largest as a percentage of registered voters (17 percent), then "Faith and Family Left" (16 percent) [105] and "Next Generation Left" (13 percent).[106] Registration numbers, however, are less important than the number of those who actually go out and vote. Based on political engagement, "Solid Liberals" far outstripped other Democrat groups in 2014, making up 21 percent of politically engaged voters—while "Faith and Family Left" (at 12 percent) and "Next Generation Left" (at 11 percent) showed up well below their share of registered voters. Thus, "Solid Liberals" were disproportionately stronger within the Democratic coalition.

"Solid Liberals" were also far more attached to the Democrat Party in 2014 than in previous years, with 89 percent claiming to be Democrat or to "Lean Democrat" (61 percent and 28 percent, respectively), 50 percent greater than in the previous survey. These "Solid Liberals" also said that they had "strongly backed Obama in 2012," while 84 percent approved of his job performance (51 percent strongly).[107]

Unlike the other two groups in the Democratic coalition (the "Faith and Family Left" and "Next Generation Left") who showed some divergence from leftist opinions,[108] "Solid Liberals" were left across the board. Most notable are the issues where this group diverged dramatically from a majority of the general public. On whether "government regulation of business is necessary to protect the public interest," 47 percent of the general public agreed, but 87 percent of "Solid Liberals" did. On government doing "more to help the needy even if it means going deeper into debt," 43 percent of the general public agreed, while 83 percent of "Solid Liberals" did. And on racial discrimination being "the main reason why many blacks can't get ahead these days," just 27 percent of the general public agreed, but 80 percent of "Solid Liberals" did.[109]

The liberal wing was not only the largest Democratic group by 2014, it was disproportionately dominant because of its high level of political engagement. It was also becoming more attached to the Democrat Party at the same time as the Obama administration, America's most left-leaning administration to that point, was making the Democrat Party more like them. Finally, Democrats' most leftward group was also moving more left themselves, and more divergent from the general public, as well as from other members in Democrats' coalition.

In 2017, a year after Trump's upset, "Solid Liberals" became both absolutely predominant in the Democrat Party, as well as more activist. *Pew* observed: "Trump's election has triggered a wave of political activism within the party's sizable liberal bloc, [although] the liberals' sky-high political energy is not nearly as evident among other segments in the Democratic base."[110]

Again, as the Democrats' most leftward bloc, those "Solid Liberals" pulled even further ahead of the rest of the Democratic coalition in voter registration numbers. At 19 percent, they were significantly larger than "Disaffected Democrats"[111] (the second largest at 14 percent), with "Opportunity Democrats"[112] third at 13 percent and "Devout and Diverse"[113] last at 9 percent.

And again, when measured by political engagement, the disparity between Democrats' most leftward group and the rest of the Democrat coalition continued to be pronounced. "Solid Liberals" were 25 percent of all politically engaged; "Disaffected Democrats" were 11 percent, "Opportunity Democrats" were 13 percent, and "Devout and Diverse" were 6 percent. When an attachment-engagement factor to the Democrat Party is calculated for each group (obtained from multiplying the political engagement percentage by the group's attachment to the Party), "Solid Liberals" outweighed all the other groups combined: 24.8 percent to 23.2 percent. This made "Solid Liberals" the Democrat Party's *de facto* majority based on political attachment and engagement.[114] Some metrics that show this: 59 percent say they have contacted an elected official, 49 percent say they have contributed money to a candidate, 39 percent say they have attended a political event or organized protest, and 19 percent say they worked or volunteered for a political candidate over the past year.[115]

In comparison to their earlier ambivalence about the Democrat Party, by 2017 "Solid Liberals" were almost totally attached to it—far and away the most loyal group of Democrats' coalition. *Pew* states: "Nearly two-thirds (64 percent) identity as Democrats, [while] another 35 percent lean toward the Democratic Party."[116] When comparing "Solid Liberals" to the other three groups measured that year ("Disaffected Democrats, "Opportunity Democrats," and "Devout and Diverse"), their unparalleled loyalty—and the Party's dependence on them—is evident. Consider percentage of separation from the Democrat Party. Only 1 percent of "Solid Liberals" were not in the Democrat column. The next lowest separation, that of "Disaffected Democrats," was 15 percent—not large in itself but comparatively huge. The other two groups' separation was greater still: "Opportunity Democrats" were 21 percent and "Devout and Diverse" were 41 percent.

"Solid Liberals" also were the most ideologically consistent. Seventy-one percent of those *Pew* categorized as "Solid Liberals" identified themselves as liberals. In comparison, 46 percent of "Opportunity Democrats" described themselves as moderates, as did 44 percent of "Disadvantaged Democrats," and 40 percent of "Devout and Diverse" described themselves as conservative. And "Solid Liberals" were almost unanimous in their opinions on government intervention in society: 96 percent thought government regulation of business necessary; 98 percent thought government benefits did not go far enough in allowing the poor to live decently; 100 percent thought stricter environmental laws were worth the cost; and 99 percent thought America's economic system "unfairly favors powerful interests."[117]

In just three years, "Solid Liberals" had become larger, more active, more Democratic, and more dominant within the party. They had also shifted further left—arguably no longer just liberal by historical standards. Their view of government made them almost unanimously statist.

Finally, *Pew*'s 2021 survey showed that Democrats' left has grown so large that it now exhibits divisions within itself: "In part because some issues that used to divide the Democratic Party—like same-sex marriage, abortion, and marijuana legalization—are no longer major fault lines, cleavages on the left flank of the party are now more evident. And, for the first time, this year's political typology identifies not just a single solid liberal group, but distinctions across several liberal groups."[118]

The most notable of the now three liberal groups are the "Progressive Left"[119] (7 percent of registered voters), included by *Pew* for the first time in 2021 and the furthest left. The other three primary Democrat voting blocs were categorized as the "Outsider Left"[120] (8 percent of registered voters), "Establishment Liberals"[121] (13 percent), and "Democratic Mainstays "[122] (17 percent). Over 60 percent of the Democrat coalition is now to the left. Additionally, Democrats' location of "left" is changing, with significant percentages in each of the coalition's three left blocs identifying as "very left." At least half of those responding in each of these groups self-identify as "very liberal" or "liberal."[123] Only "Democratic Mainstays" did not,[124] with 58 percent identifying as moderates. And of all four typology groups, over 75 percent were in favor of the government doing more to solve problems. According to *Pew*, widespread agreement exists "that the economic system unfairly favors powerful interests and that tax rates on large businesses and corporations—and on households with incomes over $400,000—should be raised, as should the federal minimum wage."[125]

As clear as this description may be, it still does not capture just *how* far left the Party has moved. Regarding the economic system unfairly favoring powerful interests, as cited above, the lowest level of agreement was 75 percent (by the "Outsider Left"), while the highest was 98 percent ("Progressive Left"). As to whether tax rates should be raised on businesses and corporations, the lowest level of agreement was 83 percent ("Establishment Liberals") and the highest 97 percent ("Progressive Left"). On raising the minimum wage, the lowest level of agreement was 85 percent ("Democratic Mainstays"); the highest was 98 percent ("Progressive Left"). There is essentially no longer any dispersion among Democrat groups on economic issues: all are very to the left.

Evidence of the Party's leftward movement is also clear when questions about America's fundamental institutions are raised. To the statement, "most U.S. laws and major institutions need to be completely rebuilt because they are fundamentally biased against some racial and ethnic groups," 71 percent of the "Progressive Left" and 63 percent of the "Outsider Left" agreed, though only 29 percent of "Establishment Liberals" and 38 percent of "Mainstay Democrats" did. Regarding the issue of Defund the Police and the statement: "Spending on police in your area should be decreased," 48 percent of the "Progressive Left" and 41 percent of the "Outsider Left" agreed.[126] Although the dispersion between the groups is greater here, all three are still decidedly to the left.

More evidence still: *Pew*'s analysis of their 2021 survey shows that 60 percent of those who identify as "Progressive Left" say they like political leaders who identify as democratic socialists, while just 4 percent say they do not. And, as *Pew* states, "[b]oth Establishment Liberals and Outsider Left are more likely to say they like this about a political candidate than to say they dislike it; still, about half of those in these groups say they neither like nor dislike candidates who use this self-description." Even 31 percent of "Establishment Liberals" and 23 percent of "Democratic Mainstays" say they liked a "democratic socialist" self-description.[127] The inescapable conclusion from *Pew*'s research is that a significant portion of the Democratic Party's coalition is now either socialist Left, or at least accepting of it.

To understand further how quickly and how far Democrats' leftward movement has gone, recall that "Progressive Left" was not even a category in previous years. It is also worth examining what "Progressive Left" is. James Gregory offers an insight into the meaning of "progressive" in his sympathetic work on "America's radical history." Faced with a myriad of leftist movements, Gregory asks, "What's left?" Answering his rhetorical question:

> In country after country, parties of the Left now fight to defend social spending, regulatory laws, and publicly owned enterprises, striving to ameliorate capitalism where once they fought to end it. Today, little distinguishes most electorally competitive socialist, social democratic, communist, labor, or green parties abroad from what in the US context has at various intervals been called progressivism or left liberalism … the "What's Left?" question is best answered with a fluid understanding that includes most who embrace the label "progressive."[128]

For all intents and purposes, the "progressive Left" *is* the socialist Left.

SECTION VIII
Conclusion

The federal government did for the Left, what the Left could not do for themselves. Through massive spending and patronage the traditional Left were invigorated, and within them, the socialist Left was resurrected. The previous chapter detailed the enormous and accelerating growth of the federal government over the last nine decades. Now, it is also worth putting these almost incomprehensibly massive sums into a more accessible context.

The Historical Tables by the Office of Management and Budget includes a compilation of payments to individuals since 1940, when said payments amounted to $2.1 billion. In 2023, these annual payments amounted to $4.3 trillion and a whopping lifetime total of $73.6 trillion. To understand the explosion: From 1940 to 1964, payments amounted to $342.9 billion; from 1965 to 1980—a decade less in duration— they leapt to $2 trillion. And *since* 1980, federal payments have totaled $71.3 trillion, with $59 trillion of that total (over 80 percent) being paid out from 2000 to 2023. In 2023 and the pandemic's aftermath, just over 16 percent of everything America produced was allotted to these individual payments.[129]

These enormous sums, and the even greater ones of overall federal spending (according to CBO, $6.1 trillion in 2023[130]) were bound to affect many Americans' behavior, at least indirectly. John Cogan in his study of federal entitlement programs, details the impact federal pension payments have had on veterans throughout America's history. Historically, these veteran pension payments were comparatively fixed in amount (Congress's payment changes being relatively small) and effectively limited in duration (capped by the lifetimes of the veterans and their spouses). However, today's federal payments dwarf those, not just in dollar amount, but in who is eligible to receive them. Rather than paying a fixed amount to a diminishing number of individuals (as with payments to US veterans throughout the nation's prior history), these new payouts are perpetually growing in cost and number of recipients. Inevitably, their impact grows with them; in the words of Shakespeare: The "increase of appetite had grown by what it fed on."[131] Such a massive supply of spending was bound to create its own demand.

Yet the traditional Left did not have to rely just on the indirect effect of such massive federal spending to surge ahead. The federal government also directly sought to create an organized client base with the Johnson administration's declaration of an "unconditional war on poverty in America."[132] This signaled the start of the effort to organize in the 1960s, which to this day has not stopped, as the growth of spending and interest groups show. It has now been entrenched, and self-reinforcing, for decades.

Unlike the massive federal spending increases, the federal government's involvement as a participant in organizational efforts had precedents—even if far less ambitious. They also had a theoretical underpinning: pluralism. The federal government had provided resources to specific groups in the past. For almost two centuries, it had provided pension benefits to veterans on a recurring basis; since the 1930s it had done so too for the elderly and the disabled through the New Deal's Social Security program. It also provided assistance for organizing—the Grange and the Farm Bureau are great examples in agriculture, as are the federal government's widespread endorsement of cooperatives and the New Deal's AAA. In industry, labor unions owed their growth to 1930s federal legislation that allowed them to compensate for their lack of unity and financial strength.[133] The federal government had even combined the extension of resources and organizational assistance in support of a leftward ideological end: the FSA was essentially a redistributionist Great Society program three decades before the Great Society itself.

What was unprecedented in this new effort was its expansion in the level of resources committed and its extension into new policy areas and sectors of society. These dwarfed previous efforts, stretching far beyond anything previously attempted (consider that even the FSA had a singularly rural focus—and targeted just a subset within this group), and its duration can be better measured in decades than years. That this was deliberate is unmistakable. As Cogan writes: "A novel feature … was that the poor themselves would be actively involved in designing many of the new local programs."[134]

With the Economic Opportunity Act of 1964 came an embodiment of the larger effort to organize the unorganized in an obvious leftward slant. The importance of organization was a learned lesson from the FSA's failure. As the radical organizer Saul Alinsky pointed out in his primer *Rules for Radicals*: "Change comes from power, and power comes from organization. In order to act, people must get together."[135] Three decades after the FSA, the federal government took aim again with a far bigger arsenal of resources and scored a bullseye. Many have made the connection between the EOA and the rise of citizen groups since.[136] Walker directly called out the importance of the federal government's role as interest-group patron.[137]

The result was a new creation. Rather than the "iron triangle" of 20th century political science literature, which implicitly assumed that a base of support needed to exist for interest groups to represent, the new model was a "left quadrangle"—bureaucrats, base supporters, organizations, *and* champions in Congress. Starting from within the federal government, programs created group and base, organizations and organized, alike and simultaneously. Unlike America's historical bottom-up movements, which were overwhelmingly conservative in their goals, the new pattern was a top-down one and overwhelmingly leftist in its goals.

The combination of enormous overall spending and targeted, massive organizing had its intended effect. Conservative author Daniel Flynn writes in *A Conservative History of the American Left* how the EOA torrent unleashed a self-reinforcing cycle through the Office of Economic Opportunity of giving government dollars to local organizers, outside agitators and to protests for more money.[138] Advocated and administered by the executive branch and funded by the legislative branch, the effort spilled into the judicial branch. Immediately after the EOA's enactment, federally funded legal advocates began suing the federal government for greater federal benefits.[139] They would often prove successful; three major Court decisions (*King v. Smith, Thompson v. Shapiro,* and *Goldberg v. Kelly*) expanded benefit eligibility and essentially made federal benefits a right for those who qualified.[140] These led to further legal battles and lower court rulings.[141] The result was greatly increased entitlement costs, far exceeding earlier estimates.[142]

A process of self-reinforcement extended back into government itself, and the level of staff in Congress who could support the spiral increased dramatically. Congressional staff leapt from 1491 staffers in 1966 to 4804 in 1978.[143] House Democrat newcomers in the Watergate class of 1975 (the largest since 1948) "thought reform had not gone far enough, by 60 percent to 38 percent."[144] In the 1970s, Congress became "by far the fastest growing branch of government"[145] at a time when Democrats, who were moving decidedly leftward, dominated it.

Each corner of the left quadrangle reinforced the others. New programs added new clients (both recipients, and in many cases providers); swelling numbers of clients bolstered the organizations representing them; rising client numbers required more bureaucrats to administer the programs and gave increased power to the administrators. The new clients, organizations, and bureaucrats testified to how well the programs worked—and how much better still they could work with additional funds—and pressed Congress for more money. As early as 1981, when the Reagan administration sought to scale back the entitlement onslaught, an entrenched opposition among the traditional Left resisted any reform or curtailment.[146]

The new base of millions of recipients and service providers and countless organizations representing them soon sought political power in their own right. While the process by which they had come about it and its leftward direction were unique, the desire for direct political power was not. The Farmers' Alliance, the Populists, the Nonpartisan League, and the Farm Bloc had all done likewise. Even had this new political power not been conceived with that intent—and it undoubtedly was—a surge from the left would have occurred. The federal government's outpouring of resources and opportunities meshed perfectly in the 1960s with the socialist Left's abandonment of its historical unified approach for a dispersion into the multiplicity of causes of the traditional Left. There, the socialist Left enhanced the traditional Left's stridency while the federal government's spending and patronage increased the traditional Left's power.

That the traditional Left's attempts at direct political power would come through the Democrat Party was also not surprising. After all, that was where the money and programs organizing them had originated. These traditional Left attempts have occurred at regular intervals over the last six decades. In 1972, they succeeded—albeit with ultimately disastrous results—at winning McGovern the Democrat nomination. In the 1980s, there was another attempt with Jesse Jackson's PUSH campaign. In 2008, the traditional Left would see the most thoroughly Left administration up to that point in American history hold office for eight years, greatly deepening the traditional Left's penetration of the Democrat Party. In 2016, Senator Bernie Sanders, the democratic socialist from Vermont, would take Hillary Clinton, the establishment liberal, the distance in the fight for the Democrat Party's nomination. In the aftermath of Clinton and the establishment Left's upset defeat, the radicalization of the Democrat Party accelerated over the next four years. The winnowing out of the Democrat Party's non-Left groups is clearly shown by polling over these decades. This polling evidence is reinforced by the Party's policy evidence: the policies embraced and pursued have become far more Left. What is considered Left now is much further to the left than what it had been before. And it is becoming increasingly so.

The decades since the 1960s have proven the old observation "there's money in poverty."[147] For America's socialist Left there has been a lot more than just money there. Beneath poverty's veil there has been an ascent, a flowering beyond anything it had ever been able to achieve on its own and power to an unimagined degree. At Eugene Debs' highwater mark in 1920, America's Socialist Party won almost 900,000 votes, just over 3 percent of the total. In 2021, using the Pew Research Center's voter typology categories, the *de facto* socialist Left group in America, "Progressive Left," comprised 7 percent of registered voters. Even 32 percent of the "Outsider Left," 31 percent of "Establishment Liberals," and 23 percent of "Democratic Mainstays" also said they liked "elected officials who identify as democratic socialists." Weighting each group according to their acceptance of democratic socialists, each group of the Democrat Party's coalition (except "Outsider Left") surpasses Debs' 1920 share of the electorate. Combined, they account for 14.7 percent of all registered voters. In 1920, Debs did not win a single electoral vote; combined in 2020, the Democrat Coalition—with over one in seven registered American voters saying they accepted democratic socialists—elected Joe Biden president. The forces that have produced the current cresting of America's socialist Left have been increasing over the last six decades. Unchecked, they will continue to grow within the country and particularly within the Democrat Party. In addition to its spurring of the encroachment of government into people's lives, the COVID pandemic was an enormous fillip to government spending in general and social spending especially. The difficulty large portions of our society would have in weaning themselves from what were supposed to be temporary emergency benefits is further evidence that once provided by the federal government, these benefits become expected by segments of the population. Demand only grows and migrates to those promising to continue them. In this respect, it is not unlike the New Deal's political model—only on a far, far larger scale.

Within the Democrat Party, the dynamic is even more powerful because the socialist Left, the mis-named "progressives," have more ways to exert their influence than through voting alone. They are a far bigger share of the Democrat base than they are of society as a whole. Beyond voting, they can—and do—contribute money, volunteer, and protest in disproportionately greater numbers than the rest of that base.

As a result, despite being a minority of a minority in American society, the socialist Left is increasingly the vanguard of the majority—the traditional Left—within the Democrat Party. There is now also nowhere for the Democrat Party to go but left. The obvious reason is that Left is increasingly all there *is* within the Democrat Party. Conservatives departed long ago; the moderates are decreasing rapidly. Simultaneously the Democrats are attracting the traditional Left that used to stand outside the two-party system. As a result, the traditional Left are increasing absolutely within the Democrat Party and increasing relatively at an even more rapid pace. Growing in numbers absolutely and relatively, while participating disproportionately, it is no wonder that the socialist Left has made, and will continue to make, strides within the Democrat Party.

CHAPTER NINE

THE REALITY OF AN AMERICAN SOCIALIST LEFT FUTURE

SECTION I
Introduction

What will a socialist Left future actually look like for America? Politically, it will mean vastly increased government power. Economically, it will mean greatly reduced performance. Combined, this will produce a dynamic of decline perpetuated by greater and greater government interference—more centralized control, more limitations, and fewer individual freedoms—while yielding diminishing economic returns and a lower standard of living. This is evidenced in three places: America's own failed socialist experiments of the past; the current unsustainable fiscal condition created by the traditional Left's entitlement edifice—an edifice that the socialist Left will vastly expand if given the opportunity; and the failed socialist states abroad.

Economically, the socialist Left's plans are unsustainable. As shown in previous chapters, socialism's promise has always exceeded its performance. Running counter to capitalism, any plan of the socialist Left is forever falling short of free-market performance. By detaching itself from the free markets that balance unlimited demand with limited supply, a socialist Left economy will always run headlong into misallocations of society's resources. If given sufficient latitude—and particularly if not subsidized by capitalism—it collapses.

Politically, Americans—including most who naively say they would support one—would find a socialist Left government unendurable (as have people the world over throughout history). Whatever limits appear to constrain its power would be eventually overturned, giving the government a monopoly over meaningful decisions, which would mean an utter repudiation of America's founding principles and Constitution. In any serious conflict between the individual and the state, the state would always win. At the same time, the state would keep growing larger as its failing policies would then require increasing state interference to remain in place.

There is historical precedence that shows the predictors of failure for government-run systems, and many of those are showing up today. Many current federal government programs are already fiscally unsustainable anti-free market ventures. As federal government expenditures approach one-quarter of the US economy's production[1] and beyond (though certainly influencing even more when its regulatory mandates are included), it's clear the US economy will not be able to support this burden in the foreseeable future. And this is without the massive additional burdens that today's socialist Left seeks to impose.

Looking back at the federal entitlement programs that have been erected (primarily by America's traditional Left) over the last decades, a pattern of failure appears. It is first manifested fiscally, in an individual program's overspending. This is due to an inherent conceptual flaw by which the program initially diverges from a free-market approach, and then effectively precludes the free market altogether. Having excised competition, the individual program then falls short of its original goals, requiring additional government support (higher operating subsidies, greater impediments to limit competition, etc.). Amazingly, a single program's failures often spur the creation of new programs (or the addition of new activities to the existing program). As programs multiply, their singular failures become collectively systemic. Finally, as they continue operating, this systemic failure becomes cyclical—spiraling further into both fiscal and program failure.[2] The socialist Left would, at the outset, both accelerate and expand this five-stage process—separation from market competition, overspending and underperforming, the application of further government support, the accretion of further government programs, and the generation of systemic failure—by extending government control over the economy far beyond what currently exists.

And the flaws *are* inherent. Any effort by the socialist Left to address its fiscal failure will further accelerate the economy's descent. Nowhere is this clearer than in the prospect of a wealth tax. Desperation from insufficient revenues generates a welter of policies to compensate: more mandates (such as dictates that completely shift costs to the private sector), higher taxes in existing areas (such as increased income and payroll taxes), and entirely new revenue grabs, such as an unprecedented wealth tax. Superficially, a wealth tax might seem like an easy solution: money is needed; others' money exists; take others' money. However, this overlooks two crucial elements of such a confiscatory policy: its inevitable progression and debilitating ramifications.

To understand a wealth tax's inevitable progression, Americans need only look back at the rapid progress of the income tax. Remember, in just seventy years, the income tax went from being a temporary levy that targeted only top earners in the Civil War era, to a permanent and universal payroll tax in the 1930s. A wealth tax's debilitating ramifications are twofold: it eliminates the incentive of individuals to create and keep wealth, and the state's use of the wealth it confiscates is less productive than that of the private individuals who earned it.

Thus, the result of a wealth tax levied purely to fund the socialist Left's additional demands would be a consumption by the federal government of private savings and capital beyond the massive revenue increases *already needed* to meet the federal government's current unsustainable demands. The cost of these existing programs combined with what would be required to carry out the socialist Left's new programs would consume the very resources needed for investment necessary to increase future productivity and living standards. The result would be long-term economic decline.

If economically, the failure of a socialist Left in America is inherent, what about looking at it politically? It is difficult to find historical examples of the socialist Left gaining power anywhere—let alone in the US—by being a political majority. Rather, it usually has either seized power internally from within a parliamentary coalition, imposed itself militarily, or been imposed by external forces. Regardless of how power was attained, however, the common element of socialist Left regimes is that they never relinquish that power willingly. The result is that a society must endure the socialist Left's failures until the people wrest power from it. The recovery from said regimes—such as in the former USSR and its satellite socialist states—has historically resembled a battle against inflation: the longer the duration, the greater the damage and more painful and prolonged the recovery.[3]

With the understanding that a rise of the socialist Left in America would lead to its inevitable—and ultimately catastrophic—fall, this chapter will first take a look at the socialist Left's past and present failures to put its ideology into practice in America. From the 19th century through to the 21st, socialist Left polices have failed, from America's rural communes of the 1820s to the inner cities of today. Disparate in motive, era, and participants, these attempts are similar in their renunciation of free-market capitalism and the dynamic of decline this creates. Today, many cities—and even whole states, such as California—are already exhibiting the ill-effects of a rise in socialist Left policy and are suffering the resulting loss of population and businesses. Sadly, many Americans are already living the prologue of what a socialist Left's rise and failure in America would resemble.

Section Two explains *that* the socialist Left has repeatedly failed in America. Section Three explains *why* the socialist Left is inherently doomed to failure. By eschewing capitalism and the free market, socialism diverges from the most productive economic system in human history. At the crux of this failure is socialism's insistence on ignoring free-market allocation of resources. By doing so, resources are increasingly squandered as they yield decreasing returns. The result is an impoverished society.

Section Four shows how even the existing—and less extensive—programs of the traditional Left are already unsustainable. Following their current trajectory, sufficient revenue cannot be raised without inflicting dire economic costs on the country. This unsustainability, however, does not concern the socialist Left. The redistribution of resources, which are then increasingly controlled by the state, is its goal. But this certainly *should* concern the vast majority of Americans.

Section Five describes how the traditional Left is seeking new sources of revenue, with the socialist Left urging the country toward increasingly drastic measures. Nowhere is this clearer than in the rising calls for a wealth tax. This section discusses a wealth tax's inherent dangers—the two greatest being the precedent it would set and the economic decline it would trigger.

Section Six considers what a socialist Left state would mean (or not mean) in America by using and debunking the "Nordic model," often cited as a socialist Left success.

Section Seven concludes the chapter with a summation—and a caution.

SECTION II
The Socialist Left's Historical Failures in America

European proponents of communal systems first made their way to America in the early 19th century. Two such advocates were Étienne Cabet, a French socialist who in his utopian work, *Voyage in Icaria*, first used the term "communism" in print in 1839, and Wilhelm Weitling, a German tailor and prominent communist. Both failed when they came to America. Cabet failed first in Texas and then was run out of his own commune in Nauvoo, Illinois, while Weitling gave up the socialist cause completely, getting a job with the US immigration service and spending his spare time working on various inventions.[4]

Robert Owen, the most famous international proponent of the communal experiment during the first quarter of the 1800s, and the most prominent person to attempt planting it in America, has already made an appearance in this book, alongside his failures. Coming from Britain, Owen was a very successful capitalist who then invested his fortune in trying to supplant the system that had made him rich. He brought his socialist experiment and penchant for self-promotion to America in 1824, and was, in fact, the first person to use the term "socialism" in print in 1827.[5] Owen tried to graft his socialist effort on to an existing communal settlement in Indiana called Harmony, paying over $100,000 for 20,000 acres and the opportunity to transform theory into practice.[6] Owen's "New Harmony" barely survived two years, due to its participants' habitual refusal to do productive work. Still, drafting on Owen's socialist publicity tour, several other Owenite communes were attempted. These too failed, none of them lasting longer than four years.[7]

New Harmony, "the most famous experiment in communal living in American history,"[8] started with a host of advantages—primarily that the leading socialist theorist of the day was bankrolling it. Thus, participants at New Harmony did not have to "pay to play"—they just had to show up. They were also free to leave at any time (eventually all did), making them willing participants while they were there (unlike most later citizens of socialist states). Finally, it was not isolated. The capitalist system remained in place all around New Harmony, which gave the settlement access to markets that allowed it to determine prices for its production.

The general problem that doomed New Harmony, then, was the problem that would continue to doom socialist efforts everywhere: socialism is dependent on subsidies. Because New Harmony's residents refused to work, thus preventing it from being self-sustaining, when Owen's money ran out so did its residents, and New Harmony folded. Its essential problem was that Americans were overwhelmingly uninterested in a socialist system—too uninterested, at least, to put their own money and effort into it.

The socialist Left's history of political failure in America reverberates still, in the dabbling of today's dilettante adherents. Thus far there have been only scattered legislative successes. Despite high profiles and fawning establishment media coverage, even the most prominent champions of the socialist Left, like Senator Bernie Sanders of Vermont and Rep. Alexandria Ocasio-Cortez (D, NY-14), have been unable to put their policies into wide-scale practice. Scattered attempts which can be linked to the socialist Left—like the Defund the Police Movement, Seattle's short-lived autonomous zone (known by the acronyms CHOP and CHAZ),[9] and "sanctuary cities," which are now seeing their utopian principles of an open-door promise for illegal immigrants collapsing under the pressure of President Biden's open-border policy—have been rapid failures akin to New Harmony almost two centuries ago.

On a larger scale, not so-scattered cases of socialist Left political failure show up across many American cities. Almost all are heavily Democrat, and their governments are not moderate ones. Crime and homelessness, fleeing populations and businesses, are all stark testaments to this failure. The only difference between today's policies and projects, and the socialist Left's failures of yesteryear, is that today, the socialist Left ventures benefit from heavy subsidization by the larger political jurisdictions—both state and federal—around them. While these subsidies sustain the programs and ameliorate their impact on the population, ultimately, they only slow the descent without changing its direction.

The failure of America's socialist Left is not simply past history but present tragedy—eloquent eulogies spanning centuries. As the next chapter will show, it is also a supreme political liability. "What's past is prologue" indeed. So too, what is present.

SECTION III
The Liability of Government Monopoly

There is a reason why socialism has failed economically everywhere, and why even the traditional Left's programs fail fiscally in America. It is not simply a failure of execution, either, as the apologists of the traditional Left and socialist Left continually argue when they claim that more dollars, a more expansive program, or more time would have yielded success. It is one of fundamental economic practice. As the preeminent Austrian economist Ludwig von Mises argues in his opus, *Socialism*, it is the negation of economic principles by the rejection of free markets that is the root cause of failure here.[10] Succinctly, von Mises states that because the socialist Left's vision is one of government monopoly, it can never succeed.

Socialism's increasing underperformance is stark when compared to capitalism. There's a reason the members of America's early communal efforts quickly walked away: because better opportunity awaited just beyond the commune's gates. When there was still an East Germany, West Germany was the destination for those who could escape; today, South Korea plays the same role for North Korea. If capitalism is allowed to exist within the socialist system in any form, it is usually severely limited and often increasingly curtailed; this can be done *de jure* by laws or *de facto* by constraining choices and actions by regulations, mandates, and subsidies so that only the government's preferred option can prevail.

As von Mises argues, the socialist Left's fatal misconception is that it believes that the competition that drives free market capitalism is inefficient—and that careful planning can eliminate that inefficiency. But competition is the driver—and the enforcer—of efficiency. Eliminating competition—by mandated government monopoly or by insulating specific government programs from it—is the reason why the traditional Left's particular programs and the socialist Left's economies are always inefficient or, as von Mises argues, ultimately cannot function. Thus, the socialist Left's economies fall ever further behind capitalism and, absent government support, fail. Following this, less societal wealth is produced than would otherwise exist. Only by increasing social wealth can a society's standard of living increase. Under socialism, the reverse happens. It is impossible to make more from less. The best the socialist Left can do is to allocate around its lack of wealth production—creating select winners amidst a losing majority. Over time, as wealth creation continues to falter, even these "winners" grow fewer and fewer.

If the socialist Left achieves its ultimate goal of full control of society's means of production, the inherent inefficiency will be institutionalized and maximized. Its impact will expand and, no longer merely limited to individual programs, will be applied statewide. Its effects will accelerate. Its central planning and its exclusion of free markets will mean there can be no pricing mechanism. As von Mises points out, without freely determined prices there can be no objective economic benchmarks. There can also be no objective prioritization of the economic opportunities to pursue, and thus no objective determination for the investment of resources among those opportunities or for the resources produced.

Where the traditional Left often seeks a divergence from capitalism, the socialist Left's goal is the elimination of capitalism altogether. The result is a self re-inforcing spiral of socialist impoverishment that is at first relative but soon becomes absolute. Its increase of government yields a decrease of its economy, a dynamic of decline where both drive the other in turn. Those afflicted by the cycle can endure only so long, and soon there comes opposition and eventually rebellion, just as occurred in America's earliest socialist communes, in its applications abroad, and in the increasing exodus from American cities pursuing socialist Left policies today.

Ultimately the socialist Left is economically doomed to fail. This increasing failure produces a steep political slope for the socialist Left, especially in America. Yet despite its ultimate, inevitable failure, the pain it inflicts between inception and demise is incalculable. Estimates of the death toll that has resulted from the application of communist and socialist ideology abroad range upwards of 100 million people.[11] As the British economist John Maynard Keynes famously wrote in *A Tract on Monetary Reform* in 1923, "[the] long run is a misleading guide to current affairs. *In the long run* we are all dead."[12] Being vindicated by the future is cold comfort for being victimized in the present.

SECTION IV
The Evidence of America's Fiscal Trajectory

One need only look to America's current fiscal trajectory to see where a socialist Left supremacy will lead. As briefly discussed in Chapter Seven, entitlement spending has already put the federal government on an unsustainable fiscal path. Yet even this enormous and growing spending burden—approaching one quarter of America's GDP, plus an imposed regulatory burden—is just a fraction of what the socialist Left wants to see under government control. Von Mises defines socialism as "the socialization of the means of production with its corollary, the centralized control of the whole of production by one social or, more accurately, state organ."[13] Simply, regardless of the means the socialist Left uses to achieve it, the ultimate aim is nothing less than full control over the economy: the allocation, use, and distribution of all resources.

And make no mistake—control of the means of production is still the goal of socialism and the socialist Left. The 2021 platform of the Democratic Socialists of America (which claims several Members of the US House of Representatives as members) states: **"We propose a program of transformative regulation, nationalization, social ownership, and internationalism that builds the solidarity and democratic power necessary for us to succeed.** We call for the nationalization of businesses like utilities and critical manufacturing and technology companies, alongside regulation of corporate, communications, data, and financial sectors. We seek to ensure social and worker control over these businesses."[14]

What fails to work on the individual program level will only multiply with each new subsidized program—again evidenced by the fiscal deficits brought on by mandatory entitlement spending. Official projections estimate that on its current trajectory, America will have to devote a massive future share of its economy for federal government spending. Already at 24.8 percent of GDP in 2022 and 22.7 percent in FY 2023, CBO projects federal spending to reach 23.1

percent in 2024, 24.1 percent in 2034, 25.7 percent in 2044, and 27.3 percent by 2054.[15] This is a level that, according to CBO, has [been] exceeded only twice, "for a three-year span during World War II and for two years amid the coronavirus pandemic."[16]

As a result of this spending surge, deficits, debt, and net federal interest payments on that debt will surge as well. According to CBO, the deficit will be 5.6 percent of GDP in 2024, 6.1 percent in 2034, 7.3 percent in 2044, and 8.5 percent in 2054—a percentage again exceeded in the past century only during World War II and the pandemic.[17] Debt is predicted to rise from 99 percent of GDP in 2024 to 116 percent in 2034, 139 percent in 2044, and 166 percent in 2054. CBO states that federal debt will set a record early in its climb "surpass[ing] its highest level in history in 2029," when it hits 107 percent of GDP. Ominously, federal debt is projected to grow "in every year of the 2024-2054 period … in 2054, such debt reaches 166 percent of GDP and is on course to grow larger still." CBO estimates that just servicing this debt, in the form of net interest payments, will go from 3.1 percent of GDP in 2024 to 3.9 percent in 2034, 5 percent in 2044, and 6.3 percent in 2054.

If the current federal trajectory continues, even today's high spending level will be surpassed—and not due to war or some exogenous event brought on by crisis, but an endogenous crisis of government creation. Nor will it be a temporary one, if left unchecked. Instead of an interruption to normalcy, it will be a new enduring and enervating normal.

This shift to borrowing as an increasingly large means of funding should not be mistaken as a means of neutralizing the impact of the federal government's growth on America. It hardly needs to be stated that such resulting debt levels would have seriously negative economic effects. This growing level of debt would "push up the cost of borrowing, reduce private investment, and slow the growth of GDP, all else being equal."[18] The effect is captured in CBO's estimate that real GDP growth would drop by one-third, from its average of 2.5 percent over the last 30 years to just 1.8 percent in 2034 and 1.6 percent in 2044 and the following ten years.

Despite all of this clearly on the horizon, the socialist Left would take America beyond even this catastrophic trajectory of deleterious social, economic, and fiscal effects by implementing its far more expansive and expensive vision—the Green New Deal or Sanders' prodigal promises.

While America has continued to succeed despite mismanagement and profligacy from its traditional Left, state after state abroad has collapsed under the rule of the socialist Left. In addition to fiscal failure at the programmatic and systemic levels, there is abundant evidence that outright federal program failure also occurs—failure in the day-to-day operations, not just overall. As Americans are continually reminded from their own experience with the traditional Left's policies, these programs over-promise, under-perform, and over-spend. Americans already know this—as well as the debilitating negative spiral these programs trigger, both singularly and collectively. When possible, Americans often seek to avoid these programs—despite the programs' heavy incentives to attract participants and onerous prohibitions to bar outside competition.

It is the rare government program that out-performs its private-sector competition. Even with heavy subsidization and enforced monopolies, they frequently do not. And, over a prolonged period and absent strict federal prohibition of competition, they *will* not. Despite systematic subsidization, it is striking how often Americans eschew these subsidized federal services, such as public schools (through private, charter, or home schooling, and, tragically, absenteeism—a heightened occurrence following the widespread and prolonged school closures during the pandemic) or Obamacare (known as the Affordable Care Act, or ACA, is dependent on enormous government subsidies).[19] If private sector alternatives were allowed to compete on a level playing field, we would see this even more. And virtually all would eschew the program itself if a cash equivalent of their government subsidy was offered for use at their discretion.

One might point to America's national parks as an example of a successful entity of government monopoly. And it's true, they are wonderful—but these parks are wonderful because of the unique wonders that they alone have. Not because of what the government has done for them. In fact, their entrances are crowded with amenities—just across the border on the private-sector side. And despite their subsidized and monopolized wonders, the parks themselves are all too often relatively under-used and their amenities outdated.

Similarly, and even more conspicuously, while the US Postal Service has a monopoly on mail delivery, where the private sector is allowed to compete—in parcel delivery—it dominates, even though USPS is heavily subsidized and can deliver packages too.

Nothing, however, has brought home federal program failure like America's public school system. Despite heavy government spending and their own tax payments, millions of parents regularly opt to pay for private school for their children—essentially paying twice for education. If offered the cash amount for what the government spends on their child—and what they contribute with their taxes—to pay for the school of their choice (public, private, or otherwise), most parents would undoubtedly accept it. The surge in school choice initiatives since COVID's forced school closures is evidence of parents' growing demand that they be allowed to have such a choice for their children's education.[20] It is also the reason why teachers' unions so adamantly oppose parents' choices— American Federation of Teachers President Randi Weingarten going so far as to say it "undermines democracy."[21] As Mancur Olson in his *Logic of Collective Action* showed decades ago, unions thrive only in the absence of competition.

Again, the reason for such program failure—in spite of heavy subsidies and often legislated monopoly status—is the absence of competition. Without the fillip of competition, government programs quickly become inefficient providers of their products and services. And consumers react. In short order, their products and services become undesirable and then avoided—usually in direct relation to the proximity of competition: the closer competition is allowed to creep, the quicker the federal program is deserted.

Yet America's socialist Left does not just seek to control every aspect of a single federal program, or even to control every aspect of every federal program, but for *everything to be* a federal program under their control. As the next chapter shows, when Americans realize this reality, it will be another huge liability for the socialist Left.

These failures—conceptual failure, fiscal failure at the program level, out-right operating failure at the individual program level, fiscal failure at the systemic level, and a cyclical pattern of increasing failure—create a dynamic of decline that has doomed the socialist Left's efforts throughout history.

It is virtually impossible to name a federal program that became subsidy-free and self-sustaining; it is all too easy to identify programs that lost customers, despite increasing subsidies and a legal prohibition against direct competition. If this is what occurs to virtually everything the federal government does, what will happen when America's socialist Left would have government do virtually everything? Depending on Americans' individual perspectives—of one program, one sector, or economy-wide—none would support the socialist Left's plan except its most deluded adherents or most heavily subsidized participants.

The issue here is that all too often socialism's fundamental problems do not become evident until after they are adopted. Like the Sirens' song of Homer's *Odyssey*, the sailors who harkened to its seductive call did not see the rocks until they were upon them. And all too many all too often are so lured. Ludwig von Mises writes "the incomparable success of Marxism is due to the prospect it offers of fulfilling those dream-aspirations ... which have been so deeply embedded in the human soul from time immemorial."[22]

SECTION V
The Socialist Left's Insatiable Demand for More Revenue

A socialist Left future in America will, naturally, need and demand more revenue for its planned enormous government. This will spur new taxes—and undoubtedly higher deficits and debt, despite it all. Once all these socialist Left dominoes have fallen, that is when Americans will really bear the brunt, subjected to lower economic growth and a lower standard of living.

There are three reasons for the acceleration of the current spending, tax, and debt binge under the socialist Left: necessity, proclivity, and ideology. As outlined in the previous section, the traditional Left's subsidized spending spiral begets more of the same. As noncompetitive federal programs fall further behind the private-sector benchmark, they require increased subsidies to keep pace—both to operate and to retain clients. This also fits with the traditional Left's proclivity to increase their programs' benefits and beneficiaries. The history of these programs has been one of enlargement. By offering more and more to more and more, they become ever more expansive and expensive. Thus, even without necessity, proclivity would suffice; even without proclivity, necessity would suffice. Together, they fuel today's unsustainable federal spending surge.

To these reasons the socialist Left adds its ideology, which hinges on wealth confiscation and state control. To the socialist Left, the private sector's allocation of resources is "unjust." It therefore wants to redistribute resources according to criteria it deems "just." So even without the fiscal necessity arising from its programs' failures or its own proclivity to increase said programs, its ideology demands wealth redistribution. Higher taxes are therefore inevitable under the socialist Left.

Of all the socialist Left's falsehoods, none is greater than its vow that only the rich will pay its new taxes. According to Congress's official revenue estimator, the Joint Committee on Taxation, the top 0.5 percent of tax return filers (those making over $1 million annually) would pay $942 billion in combined income, payroll, and excise taxes in 2023, with a combined average marginal rate of 41.6 percent. According to the Congressional Budget Office, the 2023 federal budget deficit was $1.695 trillion—even after the top earners' $942 billion tax payment. Thus, even if the amount of tax taken from these top earners were doubled and another $942 billion extracted, it would still leave over a $700 billion deficit:[23] not only would it *not* eliminate today's deficits, it would also fail to offset the future deficits from the traditional Left's existing programs, much less the expense of the socialist Left's far greater demands. For the socialist Left, more government revenue is not a necessary evil, but a positive good. More than a means, a funding mechanism, it is also an income-redistribution mechanism.

Thus, a wealth tax is the socialist Left's greatest goal and its quintessential policy. When asked for his motive, infamous bank robber Willie Sutton famously replied, "Because that's where the money is." Today, democratic socialist Senator Bernie Sanders has his eyes on the same prize, claiming " … people understand that there is something profoundly wrong when the three wealthiest people in this country own more wealth than the bottom half of America."[24]

What level of wealth Sanders feels would be "profoundly" right he never says. And for good reason. Access to the ultimate prize of America's saved wealth will not be granted by providing specifics. Just how lucrative is the prize is clear. Those making over $1 million annually were estimated to earn $3.2 trillion in income in 2023; in contrast, the total household wealth of America's top 1 percent is estimated at $24.6 trillion in the fourth fiscal quarter of 2023. Nationally, America's 2023 income is estimated to be $19.9 trillion, while total household wealth in the fourth fiscal quarter of 2023 was estimated to be $147 trillion.[25] The huge discrepancy between earnings and wealth is an obvious attraction for the socialist Left. But it is not the only one.

For simplicity of explanation, we will say that "income" means annual earnings (technically, not all earnings are classified as income under the Internal Revenue Code) and that "wealth" means all retained assets (which could come from a variety of sources—inheritance, income, investment, etc.). Income is therefore just a subset of wealth: one component and earned over a single year rather than accumulated over many years. Wealth is therefore a far larger target than income alone.

Wealth is also far less flexible. Taxing income at the confiscatory levels needed by the socialist Left would invariably trigger the phenomenon described by Reagan economist Arthur Laffer and known as the Laffer Curve: Once taxed at a sufficiently high level, individuals will alter their work to avoid the tax (reducing work, shifting earnings to lower-taxed types of activity, getting paid "under the table," etc.), and revenue growth would begin to slow. Eventually it will fall absolutely. However, it would be far harder for those targeted to avoid a wealth tax. Further, a wealth tax also would go directly at the wealth (the whole) redistribution—not just the more limited income (the subset) redistribution—that the socialist Left craves.

The danger here should not be lost on Americans. Its threat is demonstrated by the history of income tax in the United States. Recall that income tax went from a temporary emergency measure aimed only at the rich during the Civil War, to a constitutional amendment a half century later. In so doing, an entirely new taxing opportunity was created across the entire income scale. It was soon seized. Roughly two decades after the Sixteenth Amendment was ratified, its new income taxing ability allowed creation of the payroll tax—simply a tax on income by another name.... and on a vastly expanded scale.

Nor would the new taxes be sufficient to offset the rise in spending. To understand why, simply examine the lessons learned from the big-government model over the last nine decades. Spending exceeds revenues in politics, just as wants exceed resources in economics. The reason is straightforward and goes back to economics: an incentive mismatch exists between paying for and doling out and receiving benefits.

Individuals at all income levels have an incentive to find ways to reduce the taxes they pay—witness again the Laffer Curve. Individuals also have an incentive to obtain as great a share of federal spending as possible; at the same time, federal politicians and bureaucrats have great incentive to increase that spending—as shown by the federal government's history with entitlement programs. That government program spending then increases to compensate for its uncompetitive nature. Finally, the further diversion of resources from the private sector, via increased taxes and spending, reduces the productivity of the private sector, which in turn accelerates the dynamic of lower than anticipated revenues and higher than anticipated spending. The mismatch of these incentives—one which serves to push revenues lower, the other to push spending higher—will only be greatly increased under a socialist Left government.

The socialist Left's historical failure has been rooted in economic failure—one such example being the previously discussed entitlement edifice of the traditional Left, which requires increased subsidies to keep operating, new programs to compensate for earlier failures, and new revenues to fund both. If allowed, the socialist Left would pursue a far greater number of these programs on a far more massive scale, aiming to ultimately reach every aspect of society.

Yet despite this cycle of objective failure, the socialist Left is spurred on by its ideology. There is simply no room for objective evaluation in its subjective view of the world. To the socialist Left (Marxists, several House Members, Senator Bernie Sanders, the Democratic Socialists of America, and more), the results of a free market's operation are inherently unjust—despite their beneficial return to society. To the socialist Left, any outcome arising from a system that has implemented its own priorities is preferable. So bad results from a socialist system are better than the good results from what it deems to be a bad system: a capitalist free market.

As a result, the socialist Left's cycle of decline is inevitable: government intrudes increasingly in the private sector; the economy increasingly begins to underperform; economic underperformance prompts more government intrusion, and the economy's underperformance accelerates. Even if the socialist Left does not want to instigate this process (and who would?) and promises not to (and who wouldn't?), it will. But to cap the problem, the socialist Left does want to instigate the process of greater government intrusion into the economy. The burden of additional taxes, and debt—plus the resulting decrease in the economy's performance—are all part of the drag that a socialist Left government would impose on America.

At their roots, the socialist Left's programs are theoretically unworkable because they seek to replace the workings of the free market. As von Mises observes: "Under Capitalism, capital and labor move until marginal utility are everywhere equal."[26] Under government programs—particularly those championed by the socialist Left—this movement does not occur, whether by legislation or political decision. Therefore, capital does not flow to where it is most productive, except by coincidence. The outcome is that the return on capital is therefore less than it otherwise would be.

As the socialist Left's policies seek to replace capitalism, they fall ever further behind it. As von Mises observes, once capitalism is replaced entirely, the free market's pricing mechanism is lost, and with it goes the socialist Left's ability to objectively identify the proper opportunities to pursue, the ability to allocate resources properly to the opportunities it chooses, and the ability to properly distribute the diminishing resources that are produced. What occurs is a self-reinforcing cycle of impoverishment, first relative to capitalism and then absolutely. It was this cycle that collapsed America's voluntary socialist communes in a matter of years; and it was this cycle that collapsed the repressive USSR in a matter of three generations. Ironically, the USSR could, with substantial assistance from its capitalist allies, fight and win a total war against Nazi Germany; yet once that capitalist aid was ended, it could not manage the peace that followed.

SECTION VI
A Socialist Left State's Implications for America

On one hand, it is hard to describe a socialist Left government in America because there is no successful one to point to. It therefore must be largely a hypothetical exercise. On the other hand, the countless failed examples and the policies of the socialist Left make such a government's description depressingly easy. For these reasons, the socialist Left's proponents are elusive when it comes to their promises' particulars.

Despite myriad examples of failed socialist states, apologists like Bernie Sanders will forever seek another for validation. It has always been thus—including for American apologists like John Reed who a century ago in *Ten Days that Shook the World* waxed poetic about the founding of the Soviet

Union. Sanders's attempt is the "Nordic model," which looks at countries like Denmark and Sweden—and conveniently not at the socialist examples of places like Venezuela or Cuba.[27] In common parlance this is known as "cherry-picking," and it is small wonder that Sanders would seek to do so.

However, there are several problems with Sanders's cherry-picking attempt. The largest is that cherries actually exist. Sanders' Nordic model" does not: the Scandinavian countries are not socialist. The misconception that they were spread so wide that Denmark's Prime Minister Lars Rasmussen felt the need to debunk it: "I know that some people in the U.S. associate the Nordic model with some sort of socialism. Therefore, I would like to make one thing clear. Denmark is far from a socialist planned economy. Denmark is a *market* economy."[28] Lawrence Reed, president emeritus of the Foundation for Economic Education, further cites the Heritage Foundation's 2023 annual Index of Economic Freedom (a report that measures "the impact of liberty and free markets around the globe and ... confirms the formidable positive relationship between economic freedom and progress"[29]) to prove his point. In it, all the Scandinavian countries— Denmark (9), Sweden (10), Norway (11), Finland (12)—score higher than the US (25). Reed concludes: "while Nordic nations dabbled in welfare-state socialism a half-century ago, they learned some lessons from the resulting stagnation. They reversed course. They are now among the freest, most capitalist countries on the planet ... "[30]

Even doctrinaire socialists like Jordan Shilton have identified a "dramatic swing to the right in Scandinavia"[31] since at least the 1990s. As James Pethokoukis of the American Enterprise Institute writes: "One gets the sense that [Sanders] last examined the Nordic model decades ago and has missed all the many pro-market changes since the 1970s and 1980s ... The vision of Scandinavia that's apparently in his head is the version that was failing."[32]

Many aspects of the Scandinavian countries are anathema to Sanders. As the Committee to Unleash Prosperity points out in "Sweden and Other Scandinavian Countries are Rejecting Socialism": there are no minimum-wage laws in Scandinavia (Sanders wants America's higher); they allow school choice nationwide (something America's leftist-dominated teachers unions vehemently oppose), and they have lower corporate tax rates than the US (Sanders feels America's rate is already too low).[33] What the Scandinavian countries do have is the rather unique situation of being comparatively small with homogenous populations that have offset large social spending with high tax rates and an external defense subsidy provided by NATO. The idea that America can afford the first is preposterous; that America would tolerate the second is dubious. And that America could replicate the last is ludicrous—after all, America has been the chief provider of the free world's defense since World War II.

The second refutation of Sanders's point comes from America's own eye test. Simply: even if it were true that the US should model Scandinavia, does anything in America's left-most cities in any way resemble the Scandinavian countries?

That America's current social spending is unsustainable has already been discussed; to see why that is, one need only look to the rate of Scandinavian taxation. According to World Population Review's 2024 compilation of highest marginal income tax rates, Scandinavia's are staggering. The lowest are found in Iceland at 46 percent and Norway at 46.4 percent. Next is Sweden at 52 percent, Denmark at 57.11 percent, and at the top is Finland at 66.75 percent. Additionally, each nation adds an enormous sales tax. Again according to World Population Review, in 2023, Iceland and Finland's sales tax sat at 24 percent, while Denmark, Sweden, and Norway were all at 25 percent.[34] How Americans would react to such taxation levels is not hard to fathom in light of the ongoing migration from high-tax blue states to low- or no-tax red states.[35]

Low defense spending also helps pay for social spending's freight. According to World Bank estimates for 2022, Iceland spends roughly zero percent of its GDP on defense.[36] Sweden spends 1.3 percent, Denmark 1.4 percent, Norway 1.6 percent, and Finland 1.7 percent. In contrast, US defense spending averaged 4.2 percent of GDP from 1974-2023.[37] However, this low defense spending is likely coming to an end in Scandinavia (and throughout the world), as Russian and Chinese aggression have prompted a global rethinking of the advisability of appearing defenseless today. Finland joined NATO in April 2023 and Sweden in March 2024.

So why do Sanders and others in the socialist Left keep extolling Nordic socialism? Because despite it being far from actual socialism, this bait-and-switch is as close to a socialist success story as they can get. Real stories of socialism's success do not exist, so the socialist Left must package and propound fictions in a vain attempt to make itself appear palatable.

Sanders's promises of utopian paradises, like those of all the socialist Left, degenerate into dystopian disasters. Sanders offers up Medicare for All, making "public colleges and universities tuition-free," "meaningful and decent-paying jobs," "affordable housing," "combatting climate change," "criminal justice reform," "comprehensive immigration reform," and that we "can and should have a full-employment economy."[38] Superficially, that sounds nice—until it becomes a reality. The socialist Left has never fulfilled anything approaching these promises—yet Sanders and the socialist Left never cease making them.

Take one example of failure via government intrusion into our economy: America's health care system. The federal government has been deeply involved in America's $4.5 trillion health care system since the creation of Medicare and Medicaid—in fact, there are few areas of America's economy where the federal government is *more* involved. Yet Medicare's Hospital Insurance Trust Fund will begin running deficits in 2030 and exhaustion in 2035, while Medicaid is helping to drive the federal government's increasing spending, deficits, and debt.[39] In the private sector, the federal government regulates health care as extensively as any area of private endeavor, so here too costs are exploding faster than virtually any other area of our economy. Despite enormous federal government intrusion in the public (as a direct participant) and private (as an intrusive regulator) sectors over the last six decades, nothing in our health care system argues for more government control. The point: even with enormous government control in both the public and private health care markets, not only has the federal government been unable to restrain cost explosions, but it has also been a major factor in—and reason for— America's high health care costs and inefficiency.

Consider the federal government's track record when it spends directly on health care. Prior to the Great Society programs of Medicare and Medicaid, its spending on health care was negligible. Over the 1994-2023 period, it spent on average 4.3 percent of GDP per year on its major health care programs. In 2024, CBO estimates it will be 5.6 percent; in 2034, 6.7 percent; in 2044, 7.8 percent; and in 2054, 8.3 percent. And this is all net spending—"which does not account for premiums or other offsetting receipts"—its gross spending is higher still: 9.8 percent of GDP in 2054 according to CBO.[40] Against this tide of federal spending for just a portion of America's health care costs, Bernie Sanders and the socialist Left nevertheless argue for complete government control through Medicare for All.

Up to this point, America has only seen the socialist Left act in its barest form: government by negation, largely reactive. Even with the Biden administration providing America's socialist Left its greatest access to power yet, and even in its deepest blue environs, the socialist Left is constrained. Therefore, the most common manifestation of its policies so far has come in preventing government from acting conventionally. Defund the Police, Open Borders, sanctuary cities, the nonenforcement of laws on the books, executive orders, and regulatory and bureaucratic actions—all are hallmarks of the socialist Left's current limits. Although powerful and devastating to the areas they affect, these actions still testify to the socialist Left's inability to muster majorities to proactively implement its policies.

But what if the socialist Left had the power to be proactive? Its actions would be far more expansive and their effects, through which America is already suffering, would be far worse. The Biden administration's proposals on climate policy offer a hint of how pervasive and invasive the socialist Left's reach would be on Americans' lives. Already, regulations that would ban gas stoves and furnaces, constrain the number of offshore oil-drilling leases over the next five years, and restrict power plants' operations are being discussed. And in late January 2024, the Biden administration announced a pause on approving new LNG (liquified natural gas) export-terminal building permits—reversing a policy Obama and it too, in its first three years, followed.[41] As the liberal Center for American Policy gushed in March 2024: "And still, the Biden administration is only just getting started. The administration is preparing to finalize pollution standards on power plants and vehicles, energy standards on furnaces ... and more. The work of reaching the nation's new and ambitious climate, justice, and conservation goals has begun."[42]

Thus far this administration has only slowed new fossil-fuel development. What if the socialist Left had the means to not simply slow, but stop fossil-fuel production? The result would be devastating to America's economic and energy security and Americans' wallets—and these regulations would certainly not be ones our chief global adversary, China, would follow. How much more effectively could the socialist Left achieve its ends if it could legislate its intentions, rather than relying on questionable administrative actions and hoping that Congress and the courts do not swat them down? At the highest level, a socialist Left government would mean the subordination of individual rights and an elevation of the state's. In any meaningful contest between the two, the state would win—a complete reversal of America's foundational principles (starting with the Constitution's Ninth and Tenth Amendments) and the Constitution that embodies them.

SECTION VII
Conclusion

Government programs are inherently anti-free market. Either they do what the private sector is not doing (with the justification that the undertaking is too expensive, too sensitive, too important, or too complex for the private sector) or they subsidize it (with the claim that the private sector is too expensive or too callous). In both instances, the government program at its inception is divorced from market operations and competition. From this initial separation, the divergence from the workings of the marketplace only widens over time.

At the micro level, a government program starts out new and shiny, but soon becomes old and rusty, corroded without the burnishing of competition. At the macro level, as programs pile upon each other, you get the same result, but sector-wide. The dynamic of decline really sets in with the severance from competition and occurs regardless of the intentions of the originators. It happens all the faster if the originators are entirely opposed to free-market operations. The difference between the two is the difference between the traditional Left and the socialist Left.

As the program, and then the sector, falters in its performance and expands in its purview, more government intrusion follows. Mandates are increased, competition is more effectively barred, rationing occurs. Americans do not know the realities of rationing, except in times of exceptional duress (and, as in the case of gas rationing in the 1970s, even then they balked), because private options always have remained. But under a socialist Left government how long would private options remain? As evidence, look again at the Left's stringent opposition to school choice. The point is that a system based on government control will inevitably devolve into a dynamic of decline—whether it is intended (or admitted to) or not. And it will do so all the quicker when it is not just an economic system of government control but one of government monopoly.

An American socialist Left state would bring about a gradual economic collapse. Inevitably it would confiscate capitalism's savings, while its state control would take time to produce its effects. This continued subsidization by capitalism would serve to temporarily ameliorate socialism's worst effects. (Politically, the socialist Left does provide subsidies to some, which of course buy the socialist state public support and time.) As its economic system increasingly underperformed—and the resources of capitalism were consumed—the ratio of subsidized in the population would fall, and what political support it had would wane. What would be immediately evident would be the socialist Left's elevation of the state over the individual, and its total refutation of America's Constitution and traditions. While a prediction of what would occur under a socialist Left government in the US, it is also a synopsis of what has happened with socialist governments abroad and across time.

As has been made clear, the increase of government control under the socialist Left is inevitable—and hardly surprising. After all, the socialist Left comes into power because of an increase in government power. Its rise is the very reverse of Marxist doctrine's economic determinism. Rather than the economy producing the socialist Left state as Marx's doctrine predicted, it is a socialist Left government that produces a socialist economy. Nowhere has this state-centered dynamic been truer than in the case of America's socialist Left, which owes its current rise to the growth of the federal government.

Instead of economic determinism, the socialist Left exists due to government determinism. And to quote Justine Medina, former staffer to Rep. Alexandria Ocasio-Cortez and now a top leader in the New York State Communist Party: "It is true the path there will be unkind to those who block progress, but Communism is good and should not scare you."[43] With such a dark warning, it is not surprising that the socialist Left state survives only so long as it retains the power to enforce its stay.

CHAPTER TEN

THE AMERICAN SOCIALIST LEFT'S INHERENT POLITICAL LIMITATIONS

SECTION I
Introduction

That political failure is inevitable for America's socialist Left has been made clear. *Why* this is the case is inherent to the very ideals of the socialist Left— particularly when found in America.

As the last chapter showed, the socialist Left is economically unsustainable; its promise always exceeds its performance. Running counter to capitalism, it is forever falling short of it. By detaching itself from the free markets that balance unlimited demand with limited supply, a socialist Left economy will always run itself headlong into misallocations of society's resources. Given sufficient time and reach—and if not sustained by subsidies—it collapses.

The economic expropriation by, and subsidization of, the socialist Left then triggers political problems. In fact, these problems occur even before the economy's performance starts its spiraling descent. The socialist Left economy's subsidization is a zero-sum game: what benefits one comes at the expense of another. Expropriated wealth and subsidized services must be taken from someone in the first instance and paid by someone in the second. There is no other way for these seemingly "free resources" to be provided; as the Nobel economist Milton Friedman was fond of referencing: TANSTAAFL—there ain't no such thing as a free lunch.[1]

When the political implications of the socialist Left's declining economic performance are considered, we see that zero-sum game compound: resulting in decreasing winners and increasing losers politically. While this happens for the socialist Left across the globe, in America, it faces additional political problems, both related and unrelated to its economic ones. Still, its legacy of economic failure is a huge dual handicap in America, where economic failure means political failure. Founded on capitalist ideals and dreams of prosperity, America has heightened economic expectations, making Americans particularly unforgiving politically of any party's poor economic performance—even if that failure is temporary. And of course, for the socialist Left, poor economic performance is anything but temporary; instead, it is inherent and accelerating.

Economic performance was premised by Marx to be the core of the socialist Left's message and validation. Because Marxism rests on its assertion of economic determinism—that economic systems determine societies' political systems, and thus the course of history—the repeated failure of the socialist Lefts' economies destroys any assertion that socialism is inevitably destined to replace capitalism. Poor economic performance therefore actually exposes Marxism's ideological vulnerability. If socialism cannot replicate itself—if its own economic system continually fails, thus invalidating its own ideology, and with it, its political claims—how is it to replace capitalism? If economic development does not produce socialism—and more important, if socialism cannot produce an economy capable of sustaining itself, without relying on subsidies (primarily capitalist resources)—how can Marxist ideology be valid? Simply, it cannot. Marxism and the socialist Left's ideology both fall with their economic failure.

In more standard electoral terms, America's socialist Left is also weak. Despite its increasing visibility in the vanguard of the Democrats' traditional Left majority, in terms of actual numbers of members, the socialist Left is itself still a minority within the Democrat Party. The Democratic Socialists of America claim, and are claimed by, just a handful of Democrat members in Congress. And while many more Democrats claim to be comfortable with the democratic socialist label, by no means do all and few of those dare explicitly adopt the label themselves. Yet even if all Democrats did, 2020 exit polling showed Democrats to account for 37 percent of the American electorate, or just over one-third of voters. America's socialist Left, even at its current heightened level, is still only a minority within a minority. Is it consequential? Yes. Is it disproportionately so? Yes. But is it an outright majority? Thankfully, no ... for now.

Put simply, the socialist Left has no historical legacy of economic success or political support. Economically, its efforts to implement the socialist system—from its communes in the early 19th century to its nascent chaotic efforts today—have all been met with rapid failure. This contributed to there never being a meaningful socialist Left party that attracted meaningful support for a meaningful duration. Party membership is key in American politics, instilling loyalty—votes, participation, and contributions—that induces people to "stick" through adversity. The efficacy of this is clear from the socialist Left's current ability to leverage this loyalty legacy within the Democrat Party: millions of Democrats remain loyal to a party that increasingly does not represent them. Thus, the socialist Left is also a profound threat to the party that hosts it, driving out moderates just as the traditional Left earlier drove conservatives from Democrats' ranks. While such exoduses increase the socialist Left's control, they also threaten the Democrat Party.

Because there is and has been no formal socialist Left party to a meaningful degree in America, there is also no political coherence. America's socialist Left is a multiplicity of separate movements, a result of its disintegration and dispersion in the 1960s. Without a party to forge them into cohesion, they remain a political cacophony. Everything cannot be achieved at once; and if everything is a priority, then nothing is. But without a formal party structure to determine priorities and enforce discipline, none of these disparate movements will willingly yield to another. So, then: what of its myriad "justice movements" comes first? For most Americans, even if not alienated by the socialist Left's increasing extremism within particular movements, they are still left out in the cold by the entirety's overall confusion.

Nor is the political threat to the socialist Left only internal. Foreign proponents of its ideology have enormous power to undermine it. Historically, this was the USSR undermining the American Communist Party and socialism at home and serving as an alienating liability abroad. Today, China is rapidly assuming this same role, with North Korea, Venezuela, and Cuba doing so to lesser extents.

If failure is inevitable for the socialist Left in America, why, then, should Americans be concerned? History shows that once in power, the socialist Left's path to failure is rarely quick and never painless. Ultimate failure does not mean immediate failure. As its own proponents profess, it is not simply a political party but a revolutionary one. It is therefore prepared to fight, not just to attain power but to retain it too. It will go down, but it won't go down easily, quickly, or painlessly.

Mapping how we get there, Section Two of this chapter outlines the socialist Left's historical failures, both economic and political, before noting the burgeoning failures already visible in its inability to implement its policies in ultra-Left enclaves today. While the historical absence of a formal socialist Left in America is unusual relative to the world, the failure of socialist policies in America is not. After all, its policies fail everywhere. And all these historical failures equate to American liabilities.

Section Three describes the socialist Left's zero-sum economic practice of subsidization and the political problems that arise from its initial expropriation of wealth from some and its ongoing subsidization by others—which naturally means creating political enemies. As noted already, both problems only increase over time and are particularly acute in the US. Americans have both high economic expectations, and low tolerance for the abridgement of their political freedoms. While socialist Left propagandists like Senator Bernie Sanders claim that only the ultra-rich will pay, socialism's insatiable ideological and fiscal demands mean that its expropriation will extend down the wealth ladder; soon it is not simply the large capitalists who are the only enemy, but the "bourgeoisie" (middle class). Before long, it is the so-called "petty bourgeoisie" (small entrepreneurs) too. The same phenomenon of progression—or rather, regression—applies to paying subsidies; soon the more productive are footing the costs for the less productive.

Section Four examines the socialist Left's particularly American political liabilities, due to its historic lack of a permanent political presence here. The lack of a socialist Left legacy translates into a lack of loyalty across the broad population. In other words, its current flowering lacks roots. As political seasons change, the socialist Left will again be threatened by the historical withering that has continually afflicted it here—that it is no more than an annual, not a perennial able to weather the inevitable vicissitudes of politics.

The aforementioned lack of coherence that makes up the socialist Left further necessitates that it attach itself to a stronger, more established party—in this case, the Democrat Party—to which it transfers parasitically all its issues. Just as the socialist Left is afflicted by a self-reinforcing cycle of economic underperformance, so it is inflicting a similar cycle of political debilitation on the Democrat Party. The further the socialist Left moves in, the other elements on which political competitiveness depend—compromise, accommodating issues beyond its ideological purview, working in alliance with other coalition partners—are pushed out. This is, to return to an earlier discussion, the sacrifice of the middle.

Section Five shows that the socialist Left's political threats in America have origins both domestically and abroad. Since the advent of the USSR, what socialism does in practice abroad has been relevant to the socialist Left in America—its posture, its promises, and its prospects. For over a century, this contrast between practice and theory has been decidedly negative for every socialist party in the world, including America's socialist Left. The USSR's practices regarding the things that America's socialist Left professes to be a priority today (e.g., human rights, environmental policy, economic justice, foreign policy, minority rights) were unmitigated disasters by every standard. As China's communist government increasingly matches, if not surpasses, these failures in practice, the appeal of the American socialist Left at home is undermined. Its basic premise, that free market capitalism is the root of all evil and state planned socialism is the source of all salvation, is utterly refuted by socialism's reality.

In its recap of the socialist Left's liabilities in America, Section Six issues a warning to America. While preordained, the socialist Left's fall from power is never painless; nor is it quick. There is currently a buffer between socialist Left policies and political consequences as the Democrat Party's legacy supporters remain loyal—for now. At present, the socialist Left can attribute the failure of its policies to partisan politics (Republican opposition and Democrat implementation) rather than the programs themselves. So, while America can take solace in the socialist Left's ultimate failure, no one who wants America to succeed can recuse themselves from opposing the socialist Left. Ignoring the socialist Left's rise and its consequences will only extend the duration of its influence and raise the cost of rectifying its damage.

SECTION II
The Socialist Left's Legacy of Political Failure in America

American Socialism Before Marx

American socialism—just as socialism itself—predated Karl Marx, though he unquestionably became socialism's leading theorist. So too, its lack of success. Notably no socialist movements took hold during the American revolution, a direct contrast with what occurred during the English Revolution (when the fringe groups—the Diggers, the Ranters, and the Fifth Monarchy Men tried and failed) or later during the French Revolution (most notably Francois-Noel Babeuf's secret society, the Conspiracy of the Equals, which ended with Babeuf's execution in 1797).[2] As the last chapter described, later efforts in America fared little better. Although a few were attempted, they died almost immediately. As mentioned earlier, both Étienne Cabet and Wilhelm Weitling brought their communal ideas from Europe; neither left any notable trace. Even the more prominent Robert Owen's "New Harmony" barely survived two years before collapsing.

Marxist Socialism and the Refuge of Politics

It cannot be overstated that the socialist Left's failures in America revealed a consistent truth: its economic theories do not work. As Ludwig von Mises in his opus *Socialism* points out, socialism's economic failure led it into politics which made evident the gulf that yawns between socialism in practice and socialism in theory. This in turn led to a divide between practitioners and theoreticians. Marx, the quintessential example of the latter, despised and dismissed the former (e.g., he deemed utopian socialists like Owen hopelessly naïve). This is not to say that Marx did not want socialism to exist in practice; he did and went to his grave anticipating its inevitability. But Marx expected that practice to arise from what he deemed to be sound socialist theory—i.e., his theory (at the core of which was economic determinism: that capitalist economic development would produce the conditions for socialism). However,

Marx's dismissal and disregard would begin a pattern persistently followed over socialism's course—from Lenin to Stalin, to Mao, to today—with the size of the leader's power determining how harsh the treatment of adherents who were judged to deviate from socialism's "proper course" (i.e., whatever paths the socialists who actually held power followed: Lenin, Stalin, Mao, *ad infinitum*).

Ludwig von Mises observes that before Marx could cross over to the comparative simplicity of subjective theorizing, he was confronted by the objective reality of economic failure. Had socialist communes worked in practice, people would have flocked to them rather than from them. As von Mises writes, rather than refuting the obvious, Marx simply avoided it—by literally claiming the foundation of his theory upon it, despite there being no evidence that his theory worked. Instead of contradicting the economic evidence, Marx simply claimed that it validated his theory. Marx rested his socialist theory on economic determinism, which argued that the prevailing mode of production determined human history, with human history arising as the superstructure atop an economic foundation. With each new mode of production, another chapter of history began. Once capitalism, the penultimate mode of production, reached its full level of development, Marx theorized that socialism would replace it and the state would control the means of production. According to Marxism, the socialist outcome is inevitable.

Von Mises declares that Marx's dodge was particularly shrewd: He used economics, which refuted socialism in practice, as the theoretical explanation for how socialism would be realized. Instead of taking the blame, the socialist Left's economic failures were explained away as being due to a lack of necessary economic development. In short, Marx simply ignored the failures and assumed the result instead.

Marxist Socialism in America

It is true that socialism fared far better politically abroad, even as it struggled economically. Yet socialism's political failures in America rivaled its economic ones (see Chapter Six). Echoing Werner Sombart's earlier question as to why there was no socialism in America, von Mises asks: "Why are conditions much more propitious in the United States which—although foremost in capitalist production—is most backward in awakening class-consciousness in the proletarians?"[3]

As argued in Chapter Six, American socialists could never sustain socialist organizations, let alone a functioning independent political party, for a meaningful number of people for a meaningful period of time. The reason was a fundamental disconnection between the goals of potential members and potential organizers. America's farmers and workers, for example, sought a greater share in the capitalist system, not its overthrow. America's socialist agitators, following Marxist orthodoxy, rejected the incremental gains American farmers and workers sought, dismissing these as nothing more than bourgeois reforms; they wanted to overturn the capitalist system completely, not improve it.

Thus, the potential audience and aspiring agitators never connected, meaning America's socialist and communist parties won very few adherents and fewer still elections. In the seven presidential elections from 1896 through 1920, the socialist ticket (headed five times by Eugene Debs) won a cumulative 3,352,623 votes and zero electoral votes. This cumulative total is less than the worst performing major party candidate in any *single* election over that same period: in 1912, the Republican nominee and incumbent president, Taft, won 3,483,922 despite finishing third behind Wilson and Roosevelt. Later, America's Communist Party fared even worse.

While America's socialist Left has won a few local elections over the years, it has never come close to implementing its policies in a significant way for a substantial number over a sustained duration. The result is that America's socialist Left has no legacy of success, either economic or political. Nor does it have any organization to speak of here.

America's Socialist Left Looks Abroad

When America's socialist Left looked abroad for examples of socialism's successes to validate its ideology in America, it found just the opposite. The two most prominent socialist systems of the 20th century—the Communist Party of the USSR (the Union of Soviet Socialist Republics) in Russia and its imperial dependents, and the Nazi Party (the National Socialist German Workers' Party) in Germany—are arguably the most horrendous states in human history. Both existed only by force—brutally oppressive in their internal relations and brutally aggressive in their foreign relations.

Not that America's socialist Left did not try to embrace socialism's first state. It did so relentlessly from 1917 right up until the economic and political collapse of the USSR in 1991. Yet even the most ardent *apparatchik* could not sell to America—at least with the exception of America's intelligentsia—the USSR's abysmal record in every conceivable area. Thus, the USSR's poor record became yet another millstone around the neck of America's socialist Left, adding to the socialist Left's domestic economic and political failures.

SECTION III
Dependence on Subsidies Is an Unsolvable Problem

Ludwig von Mises identifies the root cause of socialist economies' failure as a lack of " … above all one quality which is indispensable for every economic system which does not live from hand to mouth but works with indirect and roundabout methods of production: that is the ability to calculate, and therefore to proceed rationally."[4] The ability to calculate only comes from markets freely balancing supply and demand.[5] Absent free markets, as in socialist economies, central planning must attempt to fill the calculation void. Inevitably, these calculations fail, and the prices that result from central planning rarely match the actual supply and demand. Even when they do, briefly, conditions are continually changing—and are doing so across a plethora of products and services. The resulting mismatch means prices are too high or too low on one side of the supply and demand scale, throwing it out of kilter. Simply, the result of the mismatch is a subsidy to one side that over-stimulates either supply or demand: in one case supply would exceed demand, in the other case demand would exceed supply.

As rational economic maximizers, people seek a higher return on every transaction and migrate to the one that delivers the greatest—especially Americans. Nothing offers a greater return than a subsidy—the higher, the better for the recipient. While price is subsidies' most common form, it's not its only form. Government can provide a tax credit, for example, to a recipient, or a provider, or both. A subsidy can also be a restriction on a provider's competitors (as in the case of the US Postal Service) or imposed mandates on a provider's competitors that increase the competitors' costs (as occurs when health care insurers are required to include prescribed benefits in their coverage plans). It is possible, even, to conceive a version of a socialist system that effectively takes ownership of production by offering subsidies that essentially dictate producers' actions. Von Mises states that "private property exists only where the individual can deal with his private ownership in the means of production in the way he considers most advantageous."[6] To subvert this, sufficiently excessive government subsidization (with tangible benefits too good to turn down) can preclude an individual from choosing any other course. A small example of this would be so-called green energy subsidies that are so generous that they essentially mandate production or adoption of heavily subsidized products.

Regardless, once a subsidy is provided, either to the producer or the recipient, supply and demand ceases to be able to reach proper equilibrium: again, either supply exceeds demand or demand exceeds supply. America's traditional Left, through their expansive and ever-expanding welfare state, have unleashed an unsustainable fiscal burden (e.g., the trillions of dollars moving throughout the American health care system) while leaving clients and providers often unsatisfied. America's socialist Left would follow this path, adding even more programs in which all are required to participate. Ultimately, this would mean inefficiency and eventually collapse or rationing, if pursued widely and long enough.

While economically subsidies occur under socialism because its economy is divorced from the balancing effect of a free market, politically subsidies can occur because the ideology demands expropriation of the capitalist class—a pure taking to be redistributed. Under socialism, the state can enforce that confiscation of wealth—at least until the confiscated wealth runs out.

To envision the dilemma of socialism and the socialist Left's operation of it, consider the production and sale of bread. As basic as bread appears, its production and sale require a multitude of complex transactions. Imagine every element being decided by central planning: from payment to farmer, to payment for transportation, to payment for baking, to payment for distribution, to price to consumer. Within each of these steps are countless components that must also be priced. Under capitalism, markets are constantly changing these prices based on demand and supply. Under socialism, all these prices are subject to central planning. The result? For anyone old enough to have visited the Soviet Union of decades ago, or unfortunate enough to live in the Venezuela of Nicolás Maduro today: empty shelves in state stores.

Initially, a socialist Left government would bridge the gap between its rhetoric and reality by taking from capitalism in general (its savings, infrastructure, technology, and more) and specifically from individuals with resources (those Senator Bernie Sanders calls "the rich"). These takings would then be used to finance the shortfall between its promise and performance, and to redistribute throughout society via its programs. This gives the socialist Left the means to finance its grandiose schemes initially, but separated from market forces, again, supply and demand cannot be balanced. In comes subsidization and goods are mispriced, and thereby misallocated.

Naturally, this expropriation and redistribution creates winners and losers. Supporters of the socialist Left are upfront about the disparate treatment. As Marx stated in *Critique of the Gotha Program*: "From each according to his means, to each according to his needs!"[7] But who determines "means" and "needs?" Under socialism, it is the state. Therefore, at the core of Marx's statement lies a subsidy flowing from means to needs. Clearly there is also a disconnect in this redistribution: those with the "means" have every incentive to supply less (and will), while those with the "needs" have every incentive to demand more (and will). The result will be a shortfall on the supply side and rationing on the demand side. What the socialist Left is *not* upfront about is how quickly this disparity extends throughout society and the size of its enervating impact. There was truth in the Soviet workers' sardonic sarcasm: they pretend to pay us, and we pretend to work.

In contrast to capitalism, where both parties benefit in a free exchange and society prospers (described by Adam Smith's "invisible hand" and explained by Milton Friedman in the making a of pencil),[8] under the socialist Left's subsidization, what one group loses another group gains and society is impoverished. Were America to subsidize in accordance with a socialist Left government, it would create a zero-sum situation, where someone's gain is the result of another's loss. In turn, this zero-sum situation would create a zero-sum politics. The socialist Left's subsidies would also encounter the TANSTAAFL trap: there ain't no such thing as a free lunch. Subsidies cannot be delivered unless someone pays for them. They can only be permanently delivered on a wide scale by government fiat (because unless compelled, no one willingly pays the cost of subsidizing others). Such subsidization creates political opposition from the very beginning. Divorced from a balancing of supply and demand, a socialist Left economy underperforms, and its perpetual need to compensate demands additional resources. The expropriation then moves further down the income scale and the opposition to it grows apace. To keep people in line, and eventually to hold them in place—lest they leave like the residents of America's early 19th century communes—the socialist Left's political repression would grow, meaning opposition to the socialist Left would increase further still.

Such zero-sum economic situations and zero-sum politics are general conditions for the socialist Left and are hardly unexpected. The socialist Left is a revolutionary party for a reason: they anticipate opposition. However, the socialist Left's general problems are particularly acute in America. Here the economic system (capitalism) and the political system (Constitution) are more deeply embedded than they are elsewhere.

SECTION IV
The Socialist Left's Distinctly American
Political Weaknesses

In addition to its economic liability, which both creates, and is itself a political weakness, America's socialist Left has several weaknesses which are purely political. Its aforementioned extreme lack of coherence is one, and its lack of an independent political organization (and thus, a significant number of long-standing supporters) is another major impediment to its political fortunes in America. Further, even as it stands today at the height of its political influence historically, America's socialist Left remains a distinct minority, even within the Democrat Party it increasingly influences. Further, despite desperately needing the Democrat Party to advance its agenda, the socialist Left is itself the largest threat to the Democrat Party.

Economic Failure as a Political Liability

Economic failure is a political loser in most places, but nowhere more than in America. And no political movement in world history has a greater record of economic failure than socialism.

America has only known prosperity. This is because it has only known capitalism, and it has embraced capitalism like no other nation in history. With the world's largest economy, Americans both expect and demand positive performance from their economy. As has been discussed, even pre-dating our nation's founding, prosperity is more than the norm in the United States; it is only rarely interrupted. And those interruptions are poorly tolerated. Economic downturns, even mild and temporary ones, elicit immediate political response. For the socialist Left, to which economic failure is inherent, this is an acute limitation in America. Not only does it warn Americans away from the socialist Left before the fact, but any adherents will abandon it in droves when its economy begins to underperform.

No American politician campaigns on *less* prosperity (recall again Sombart's observation that "All Socialist utopias came to nothing on roast beef and apple pie").[9] The corollary is that prosperity is a prerequisite for American political success. Even transient economic failure during a single administration has been sufficient to defeat presidents of both parties—Hoover in 1932, Carter in 1980, and George H. W. Bush in 1992.[10] Every American incumbent president who has lost reelection in the last century has been plagued by economic difficulties (almost all have had an economic contraction within a year of running for reelection).

Socialism has no economic successes to point to, either in America or abroad. Nor are its failures merely transitory; they are permanent and systemic. With this history, America's socialist Left can only promise that, through radical change, it will somehow diverge from all similar attempts that have gone before it and yield not simply a radical transformation of society, but a dramatic improvement in America's already world-leading economic performance.

Economic Failure as Ideological Underminer

Ideologically, socialism's systemic economic failure also undermines the Marxist premise on which it rests. If, as Marx's economic determinism argues, socialism is the culmination of capitalism's development, how can socialism underperform the capitalism it is destined to replace? Going backward is not going forward; anyone except the most politically purblind can see that. And as soon as the economy starts to falter, all historical precedence indicates that the political party causing it is rejected. However, that rejection will be even deeper for the socialist Left. For an ideology built on economic determinism, economic regression is a fatal flaw to its own reasoning. The problem facing the socialist Left is akin to that of the myriad doomsday cults throughout history: what happens when doomsday does not come? The cult passes into oblivion. How much faster will this occur when the cult produces its own doomsday? If the pivotal part of Marxism is invalidated by its practice, then the theory that rests on it is invalidated as well. So too, the political movement that espouses that theory.

A Lack of Legacy Supporters

America's socialist Left lacks both significant supporters to rally and a single standard to rally around. Both are enormous liabilities in American politics where the greatest indicator of how an American will vote is their political-party affiliation. In 2020, exit polling showed that 94 percent of both Republicans and Democrats supported their party's candidate: that is greater than the breakdown by ideology, gender, race, age, or any other sampled variable.[11]

Party organizations are crucial for success in American politics. As discussed earlier, there is a reason why America is a two-party system. Third parties have little impact beyond playing the role of occasional spoiler: none have won an election since the Republicans in 1860. Nor has one emerged to replace either party since that period, when the Whigs were dispatched. No third party has even placed second in a presidential contest since 1912 when Theodore Roosevelt and his Progressive Party ("Bull Moose Party") did so, of course doing so only *because* it was Theodore Roosevelt angling for another term; and the party never approached that height again. With third parties having such limited hope of political impact in America, the "no party" movement of today's socialist Left is even more hamstrung over the long-term.

A formal independent political organization and its members create a floor for a party in American politics. Even in their worst moments, these floors hold they sustain a party. Despite their 1964 presidential debacle, for example, when Republicans won 38.5 percent of the popular vote, in 1968 they won the presidency. Despite their 1972 presidential disaster, when Democrats won 37.5 percent of the popular vote, in 1976 they won the presidency.

Legacy equals resiliency. Lacking supporters or party, America's socialist Left will be hard pressed to survive the inevitable downturns that regularly befall the country's two established major parties. And, without such a legacy, its adherents remain a small minority among Americans. Despite their currently outsized role in the vanguard of the traditional Left, which makes up the majority within the Democrat Party, the socialist Left remains itself a minority within a minority. It's true that those who consider themselves part of the socialist Left have enjoyed successful political leveraging, but the lack of significant membership dictates their strategy as a matter of necessity, not choice. The socialist Left was forced to abandon an independent party approach in the early 1960s, and that holds true today. It therefore must find a host through which to pursue its agenda indirectly: the Democrat Party.

Facing this reality, and to paraphrase Walt Kelly's *Pogo*: America's socialist Left has met its greatest enemy, and it is itself.[12] As the socialist Left rises in the Democrat Party, it is driving out moderates now and will likely drive out establishment liberals later, following the already departed conservative Democrats of the past. In America, this sacrifice of the middle is fatal to national electoral success—witness again the presidential elections of 1964 and 1972, when Republicans and Democrats, respectively (and inadvertently), made that sacrifice. In sum, America's socialist Left is a political parasite that will eventually kill its host.

The socialist Left's retreat six decades ago into the multiplicity of movements that constitute today's traditional Left came at a cost: control and coherence. Its abandonment of a traditional Marxist approach was also an abdication of its ability to determine its own priorities and articulate a unified message. Wrong as Marxism is in theory and practice, as von Mises notes, its unified message has proven powerful and persuasive abroad. America's socialist Left lacks even this kind of unity. Instead, it speaks through the myriad of voices into which its diaspora found homes. Americans can easily discern the difference between a party that *represents* a variety of causes and a movement that is no more than a variety of causes. It is this chaotic cacophony that the socialist Left broadcasts to America and that will ultimately drive Americans away.

Both the political and economic liabilities of America's socialist Left reinforce the other. While socialist Left parties worldwide share similar economic liabilities, the political liabilities that arise from the socialist Left's unique situation in America remain unmatched. Nowhere is economic failure a bigger political liability than in America. As a result, it has no legacy on which to build a party or to retain long-term supporters, so it must remain dependent on other, more established parties, to the endangerment of its host. As a multiplicity of movements with at least as many voices and priorities, the socialist Left is political schizophrenia.

SECTION V
The Socialist Left's External Political Liabilities

While its domestic political problems are naturally dominant, America's socialist Left has international liabilities as well. Currently, China and a handful of socialist states offer egregious negative examples of the socialist Left's agenda. Historically, from the creation of the USSR in 1922, to its demise in 1991, America's socialist Left had to answer for—and largely answer to—the USSR. The Soviet Union was a negative in virtually every aspect of its existence: Political rights (gulags), human rights (Soviet Jews and ethnic minorities), the environment (Chernobyl), its economy (backward), the restriction of its entire population ("Mr. Gorbachev, tear down this wall"), and a belligerent foreign policy (holding half of Europe under its thumb for decades and actively threatening the other half). Such problems became inescapable when Khrushchev delivered his denunciation of Stalin and "government-by-fear and Stalinist terror"[13] in his "cult of personality" speech before the USSR's Twentieth Party Congress in February 1956.[14]

For all who cared to look, and eventually even for those who sought to deliberately look away, the USSR was a negative example for human rights, economic policy and performance, aggressive foreign policy, and more. Practically, no one wanted to go there, and everyone wanted to leave. Having only the hammer (and sickle) of force, every challenge became a nail, every opponent someone to be mowed down.

Only its most deluded apologists saw the USSR as anything other than a universal failure that utterly undermined the socialist Left's appeal. How big a liability this was is evidenced by the collapse of its fawning American appendage, the CPUSA, and the dispersion of America's socialist Left into the various movements of the traditional Left.[15] Nor did any other socialist state present a better picture to Americans. Tens of thousands of Americans would die fighting the aggression of North Korea and North Vietnam, while in between Americans faced the threat of nuclear missiles from Cuba.

After the USSR's collapse, state-run socialism was, if not effectively defunct, at least in wholesale retreat. Certainly, some states that professed its failed ideology remained. But these were either backward basket cases—such as Cuba and North Korea—or like China, which was seemingly moving rapidly away from socialism's traditional central planning, as encouraged by the West.

The result of socialism's total reversal abroad was that it was no longer a drag on America's socialist Left at home: its theory was freed from the oppression of its practice. Out of sight, it became out of mind for most Americans—to the socialist Left's great advantage. Socialism did not have any negative contemporary examples because it did not meaningfully exist at home *or* abroad. Therefore, absence made the heart grow fonder—and the mind grow weaker—in America's traditional Left.

This luxury is coming to an end—if not already over. America's socialist Left is not only producing its own disturbing domestic examples, as policies are randomly pursued in ultra-Left enclaves (e.g., the anti-Semitism of so-called "progressives" and the debasement of America's so-called elite colleges' academic credibility through their application of radical DEI programs).[16] Its failures are daily splashed across headlines and television screens. Its external liability is rising, too, as North Korea and Cuba continue to play their historical roles as repressive regimes, while Venezuela's descent into chaos under President Nicolás Maduro, whose socialist policies took that nation's GDP from $373 billion in 2013 to just $45 billion in 2018, provides an updated version of what socialism does to those subjected to it.[17]

However, it is China that is on track to replace the USSR as the world's *bête noire*. China is increasingly replicating the USSR's aggressive and oppressive legacy as its provocation across its borders continues to mount—especially regarding Taiwan. Its domestic oppression (from political dissidents to its one-child policy, which existed from 1980 to 2016), so habitual and so long overlooked, continues apace. Its oppression of minorities is on a scale even the Soviet Union scarcely attempted—especially of its Uyghur minority—in what is now regularly labeled genocide by Republicans and Democrats alike.

Because of its far more outward orientation and its larger economy, China is arguably a greater threat than the Soviet Union was. In pursuit of economic competition, and an aspiration to eventually surpass the West, China regularly practices intellectual-property theft on a gargantuan scale, while its economic relations with developing nations approach economic colonialism through its Belt and Road Initiative.[18] These practices and their resulting liabilities have mounted under China's current leader. President Xi Jinping is accruing personal power on a scale unseen since Chairman Mao Zedong, and he seeks to use it in an increasingly authoritarian manner. As China becomes more oppressive and aggressive, an increasingly negative reality of socialism is juxtaposed beside its promises. And as the Soviet Union did decades ago, it's becoming a growing liability for America's socialist Left.

SECTION VI
Conclusion

The socialist Left has distinct liabilities the world over; in America, its liabilities are distinctly greater. Historically, the socialist Left has failed those it has sought to govern. Abroad, it has had to resort to force to pursue its agenda—and eventually to prevent its citizens' escape. In early 19th-century America, it saw voluntary participants leave its communes after just a few years. Today in the cities and states where its policies are pursued, its failures are again driving an exodus.

This historical failure is rooted in economic failure. As Chapter Nine showed, when pursued as isolated programs, the socialist Left's economic flaws are evident individually. When the socialist Left has imposed its programs on whole societies, their inherent economic flaws have been evident systemically. Even in their more limited form, the programs espoused by America's traditional

Left have proven to be unsustainable fiscally. The federal government's fiscal condition is already approaching crisis levels, despite the crisis faced being one of internal creation: the traditional Left's entitlement edifice.

The socialist Left's political problems run parallel to its economic failures. Simply: as its economy fails, the opposition to it grows. However, its political failure runs deeper than this. Like its zero-sum economic practice of subsidization, the socialist Left faces zero-sum politics: fomented by its political repression, it has political opponents even before its failing economy can produce more. If it takes hold in America, the result of the socialist Left's zero-sum politics will be heightened by Americans' deep embrace of entrepreneurship, small businesses, and strong attachment to constitutionally-guaranteed freedoms (freedoms that have not just existed since the United States' founding, but, as this book has shown, have in many cases predated it)—all things that the socialist Left cannot accept and still fully pursue its ideological agenda.

Thus, the political liabilities that the socialist Left faces in America are even greater than those it confronts abroad. Economic failure is a political liability everywhere, but it is especially lethal in America. In America, prosperity is not simply expected; it is demanded. It is hard to hold on to adherents by promising prosperity but delivering penury. Of course, economic failure is doubly damning for the socialist Left, whose ideology rests on the Marxist belief in economic determinism. Unable to even economically replicate itself under its own rule over an extended duration, socialism is in no position to permanently replace capitalism. This contradiction between ideological promise and practical results is clear to a demanding and discerning American audience.

Compared to conventional American political parties, the socialist Left fares even worse. Unlike the two major parties, it has no legacy supporters on which it can count for core support. Lacking a formal party, it has no organization to which prospective supporters could rally. As a result, America's socialist Left remains just a small fraction of America's electorate—despite its outsized influence within the Democrat Party via the traditional Left. Additionally, the socialist Left poses a long-term threat to its Democrat Party host by driving out that party's more moderate members—as well as alienating swing voters in general elections.

Without a party to give it structure or present a formal agenda of priorities, the socialist Left remains a mass of separate movements each pursuing individual goals, which are often at odds with each other. What emerges is an incoherent cacophony, daily delivered in ultra-Left enclaves such as Seattle, San Francisco, New York, and other sanctuary cities whose policies' free benefits attract recipients but threaten to drive out the tax base needed to finance them.

Nor are the socialist Left's political liabilities purely of American origin. Historically, the USSR's negative examples of socialism undermined America's socialist Left, and today China increasingly does likewise (alongside North Korea, Cuba, and Venezuela). Together these living examples of actual socialism invalidate the promises of America's socialist Left.

Thus, the failure of America's socialist Left is not simply a tale of the past; it is a present reality. Its dynamic of descent remains the same, making for a supreme liability. The historical legacy of the socialist Left undercuts America's socialist Left of today at every juncture, and the vast majority of Americans are repelled by both past and present failures. And once those who say they would welcome a socialist Left government actually experience living under one, most would also be similarly repelled.

While past and present, domestic and foreign, examples confirm the socialist Left's inevitable failure in America, they also serve as a caution. Once in power, the socialist Left's demise is always painful and rarely quick. The USSR lasted seven decades. The cost it inflicted stretched even further—both before it came into being and arguably to this day.

Any time a socialist state collapses, it is gradual because it is rarely imposed in its entirety immediately; so long as capitalism persists, socialism will confiscate and live off its surpluses. Because crime—when successful—does pay. And when it is perpetrated on a societal level, the payoff is huge. The plunder from its expropriations can buy the socialist Left time to entrench itself, making the relinquishment of political power protracted and painful. Once in power, the socialist Left makes its state the ultimate monopoly.[19] Like all monopolists, the socialist Left never cedes power willingly. Confrontation is endemic to it, both in theory and practice. The socialist Left is, after all, a revolutionary party, not simply a political one. So, with the rationalization that it is the agent of historical change, the socialist Left takes a confrontational stance in order to divide opponents. The socialist Left is prepared to fight: to grasp power, to confront the opposition it knows will come, and to retain power as opposition to it mounts. Its violent language, a universal through the socialist Left's history, is not mere rhetoric; it is prophetic. As Mao said: "Political power grows out of the barrel of a gun."

Additionally, there are beneficiaries of the socialist Left's policies who will support its efforts to retain power, like the recipients of its redistributive policies. Marx and Lenin learned, well before Lennon and McCartney, that money can indeed buy love—or at least mercenary loyalty. Temporarily, until the money runs out.

In America, the socialist Left's leverage within the Democrat Party gives it invaluable cover. If socialism's policies were being pursued through an independent socialist Left party, their failures would be directly linked to it. Because they are being advanced within the Democrat Party, the socialist Left is buffered from their consequences. The socialist Left can dismiss criticism of its policies as simple partisan political opposition aimed at the Democrat Party, rather than to socialist Left policies. Failure of those policies can also be blamed on their political execution by the Democrats, rather than on the policies' fundamental flaws. And, because of the Democrat Party's substantial number of legacy supporters, socialist Left policies that it adopts receive support from Democrats that these policies would be unable to achieve on their own.[20] In short, the socialist Left benefits each way: They are insulated from attacks on their policies and their policies' failures, while they also get to leverage substantial Democrat Party support for them.

Combatting America's socialist Left is akin to fighting a guerrilla war. As an opponent, the socialist Left is amorphous, existing in a multiplicity of movements within the broader traditional Left, and through them, in the Democrat Party. It is difficult to engage America's socialist Left directly as it lurks among these larger groups. Even alone, it adopts the title of "progressive" and seeks to cloak itself. It should be remembered though: guerrilla warfare is a sign of weakness, not of strength. It is adopted because its combatants are unable to wage a traditional campaign. Still, its weakness does not make it any less necessary to defeat—and to do so as quickly as possible. The same is true of America's socialist Left.

CHAPTER ELEVEN

CONCLUSION

To put things bluntly: a socialist Left uprising is occurring in America. It is real, and it is unprecedented. And it is making inroads into American society. This has, hopefully, been made abundantly clear. It is not an illusion, nor is it the rhetorical conjuring of conservatives bent on making America's traditional Left appear extremist. The evidence is all around us in a myriad of causes, each of which the socialist Left seeks to use as a vehicle for its agenda. Americans are right to be worried: a recent *Gallup* poll found 42 percent of Americans saying they would vote for a socialist for president if nominated by their political party.[1] Never mind that the United States has never before seen a significant socialist Left leader exert meaningful influence for a sustained period. There is evidence all around the world as to what happens when the socialist Left gains power. From every angle viewed, the socialist Left is decidedly un-American, both historically and compared to our founding principles.

America's socialist Left defies easy answers. That is partly by design: after all, America remains as it has been since before its founding: a people oriented to the right and center of the ideological spectrum. It's also partly by default of the socialist Left's historical futility in America. But, for the purposes of this book, here are some answers.

Who is the socialist Left? They run the gamut: from those who claim to be members of the Democratic Socialists of America (as do a handful of Members of Congress), to those who adopt the democratic socialist label (as has

Vermont's Senator Bernie Sanders for years), to those who are not repelled by the democratic socialist label (as are an increasing number on the far left of the Democrat Party), to those who oppose denouncing socialism (as did 86 House Democrats in a vote in the House of Representatives in February 2023), to the 63 percent of Democrats who told *Gallup* recently that they would support a socialist candidate for president if their party nominated one,[2] to those who cloak their socialist predilections under the term "progressive" and their agenda under "justice" movements.

What are the socialist Left's policies? Overarchingly, they are those that promote the concentration of power in a central state and away from individuals. In America, the Constitution's Ninth and Tenth Amendments reserve powers not explicitly given to the federal government to both individuals and to the states. The socialist Left's agenda seeks to move in the opposite direction: to place more power in the central government and leave an ever-decreasing portion to individuals and the states. Such efforts can take many forms. From opposing school-choice programs that give parents and students freedom to take government money to the schools that best serve their needs, to resisting increased flexibility for patients to make individual choices in health care, to taking more money from the private sector by increasing existing taxes and by seeking entirely new ways of taxing—such as insidious wealth-tax proposals that aim to vastly enlarge the resources that the federal government can tax.

Where is the socialist Left? Look first at the bluest environments. Following the October 7, 2023, terrorist attacks on Israel, the socialist Left's pro-Palestine and anti-Semitic demonstrations erupted on self-styled elite college campuses and in major cities. Its open-borders policies have spawned sanctuary cities across the country.[3] Its Defund the Police policies are also pervasive and similarly situated in blue cities.[4] Its policies that can be best categorized as environmental extremism are being pursued nationally by the Biden administration, and its Diversity, Equity, and Inclusion (DEI) policies have penetrated academic and corporate America.

When did the socialist Left begin? Again, it's a tricky question. As this book has covered, experiments in socialist communal living date back to the Mayflower pilgrims and then later in the early 19th century. There were also socialist presidential tickets in the early 20th century (five headed by Eugene Debs). All ended in failure. Or you could point to the 1960s, when the Students for a Democratic Society released their Port Huron Statement ushering in a new Left, a few years before the Johnson administration's Great Society programs essentially kick-started the traditional Left—and within it, the socialist Left. Then there was the Obama administration's crucial rehabilitation of the traditional Left, into which the socialist Left had immersed itself decades earlier. And there was of course 2016, when self-proclaimed democratic socialist Senator Bernie Sanders revealed the socialist Left's resurrection by challenging Hillary Clinton in the Democratic primaries, and Clinton's subsequent defeat unhinged the traditional Left. This was followed in rapid succession by the 2018 takeover of Congress by a radicalized Democrat majority, and the Biden administration in 2021, which has legitimized the socialist Left and given it more political influence than at any time in American history.

Out of all of these questions, the "why" and the "how" of the socialist Left are even more perplexing. In contrast to the abundant possible answers for the socialist Left's who, what, where, and when, there have been a paucity of answers as to why and how the socialist Left has now unleashed its unprecedented assault on America. Those are the questions on which this book has primarily focused.

Why is America's socialist Left rising in a meaningful way *now* for the first time? It is because for the first time, it has the resources to do so. These resources—economic, political, legal, organizational, and in the number of supporters—are things America's socialist Left could never muster on its own. The only reason it has them now is due to the way the federal government has, over the last six decades, compensated for the socialist Left's inability. From this sustaining governmental foundation has come the socialist Left's ascendancy within the traditional Left and—through the traditional Left's control of today's Democrat Party—the socialist Left's first significant political influence in American history.

The socialist Left's drive for power is not simply an ideological desire dictated by Marxist doctrine to take control of the state. The socialist Left *needs* state power, not just to sustain itself, but because without it, its agenda will fail again, just as it has throughout its history. None of the aforementioned examples could exist without government authority advancing or abetting it—at the local, state, or federal levels. None. The socialist Left cannot exist in a state of competition. And it cannot exist without state protection. Its economic policies fail in competition with free markets and capitalism. Its political policies fail if not imposed by the state: given a choice, people will flee them—as evidenced by those Americans who fled from the forgotten socialist communities of the 1820s, and as have people abroad throughout history. Therefore, unable to win through conventional political means, America's socialist Left needs an ideological coup, lest today's unique opportunity vanish. As a result, the near-term goal of those who consider themselves part of the socialist Left is to topple America's past and recast it, in order to write America's future in its own image. And it must do so aggressively.

The rise of America's socialist Left appears to have been rapid. From the 1960s to 2000, it was as dormant as it has ever been, more dispersed and marginalized than at any other point in its history of failure in America. Even the traditional Left was marginalized at the national level of presidential politics. For four decades, being labeled "leftist" meant being identified as a political loser. Rather than running to the Left's standard, Americans almost universally ran from it. Yet from this nadir, the traditional Left rebounded under Obama's presidency, when it was rehabilitated and embraced, if not explicitly, at least implicitly, by Democrats. In short: Obama brought the traditional Left into America's political mainstream. This was a boon for the socialist Left, which needed the traditional Left's rehabilitation for its more extreme ideology to have any chance at emergence. Too, the traditional Left was where the socialist Left had been incubating since the 1960s.

The traditional Left's rehabilitation stuck, working wonders for the socialist Left. From 2008 to 2016, through Obama, the traditional Left returned to American politics and captured the Democrat Party. As the traditional Left rose, the socialist Left rose within it.

In the 2016 Democrat primaries, the socialist Left went public via the campaign of Vermont's democratic socialist Senator Bernie Sanders. With establishment liberal Hillary Clinton's defeat in the general election later that year, outrage within the traditional Left spurred the socialist Left to make further headway via the Democrats' midterm win of the House of Representatives in 2018. By 2020, the socialist Left was ascendant in the Democrat Party—so much so that its very popularity began to undermine it: the multiplicity of candidates espousing socialist Left proposals split Democrat support, allowing holdover establishmentarian Joe Biden to advance over the infighting. But despite the socialist Left's failure to capture the Democrat standard, it nonetheless has succeeded in frequently capturing the Democrats' standard bearer.

However, it would be a serious mistake to equate the socialist Left's rise solely to the confluence of fairly recent political coincidences. It is the long-term growth of the federal government—both quantitatively and qualitatively—that made the socialist Left's short-term success not just possible, but potentially, and ominously, permanent. To make the point transparently clear: this potential for the socialist Left would still exist without the confluence of short-term political coincidence, but today's opportunity could never have been so realized without the long-term growth of government.

As has already been illustrated, the socialist Left's rise is every bit the profound break it appears to be. It begins with the socialist Left's need to discredit and destroy the idea of American exceptionalism. One need only look at the founding of the United States to see that American exceptionalism is real, and so if the principles that make this true continue to be embraced, the socialist Left will continue to be rejected, just as it has been throughout American history. But let's consider for a moment that the idea of American exceptionalism does seem discordant with the 21st century's ethos—as the *New York Times'* "1619 Project" would have us believe. If this is the case, it is merely indicative of how influential the socialist Left rhetoric has lately been—not proof that America is not exceptional. America was exceptional before it was America. There is evidence to prove that is neither braggadocious nor subjective; it is fact, stemming from the American colonists' transformation of the already unique English government tradition from which they came. In addition to its unique political heritage, America had a unique economic foundation in English capitalism. Capitalism was unfettered to an unparalleled degree that was accelerated by the colonies' separation from their mother country.

While it gestated over generations, America was born in a single one. From 1776, to 1789, separate colonies became the United States of America. Even counting all the events that led up to the push for independence, the time was incredibly short. Significantly, thirteen colonies governed by England's largely unwritten constitution transformed first into independent states, each with their own constitutions, then again to join together as one, by a single constitution of its own creation.

It was the Constitution that enshrined America's existing exceptionalism.

In hindsight, it was the logical conclusion to the colonies' formation under capitalism and republicanism: the Constitution became the capstone that held its two overarching principles in place. Thus, America's newly created system of governance was self-reinforcing and self-perpetuating. The product of America's exceptionalism, the Constitution also ensured its continuance.

Reviewing America's creation, its Constitution, and the history that followed, it is easy to understand why the socialist Left is so intent to overturn it all entirely. In contrast to every other Western nation, America has excluded the socialist Left throughout its history. If the current system—principles, history, and Constitution—are allowed to stand, America will continue to do so: there simply is no place for it under America's prevailing system.

Premised on competition, where individual liberty and free markets go hand in hand, the prevailing system in America is antithetical to the socialist Left. The political system where a socialist Left would thrive—and what it would impose—is premised not on the individual's freedom of action, but on the state's. Its economic system is premised not on free markets, but on the state's control of them. Each in their true form, America and the socialist Left, cannot coexist together for long. Something must give, and throughout America's history, it has always been the socialist Left.

Of course, the socialist Left has made its attempts, but where it existed it was never serious nor sustained; it existed primarily on paper, and even then, only in the footnotes of American history. Where it has appeared, the history of the socialist Left in America can be summed up as: separation, agitation, organization, marginalization, alienation, and dispersion. The pre-Civil War separate socialist communities failed in short order. In the post-Civil War era, it agitated to drive other large organizations to radical ends. These efforts also failed. Around the early 20th century, it sought to organize Americans under its own political banners. Despite repeated runs for the presidency, these never received a single electoral vote. During the Great Depression, a period of turmoil and upheaval seemingly most conducive to its call, the socialist Left was thoroughly marginalized—including in the New Deal: in the 1932 presidential election, Norman Thomas, the Socialist candidate, received fewer votes than Socialist Eugene Debs received in 1920 (885,000 versus 898,000). Following World War II, America's socialist Left chose the USSR's interests over America's, which led it to alienate the Americans it professed to want to represent.

Finally, in acceptance of its failure by conventional Marxist standards, America's socialist Left ceased to exist as a separate political entity altogether, dispersing into the causes and movements of America's traditional Left. Defeated and unable to succeed following Marxist orthodoxy, where a single party led the class struggle under which all else must be subsumed, America's socialist Left went in the opposite direction. It subsumed the class struggle under a myriad of causes. True adherents of the socialist Left would have dismissed this as a benighted bourgeois attempt—at worst, side-tracking the revolution, and certainly not leading one.

And with that, America's socialist Left was gone. Or so it seemed.

Historically, what had stymied the socialist Left was America's small-government model, which had prevailed both theoretically and practically. The federal government was not expected to do much and behaved accordingly. The model was rocked only when crises occurred, usually wars, and in these eras, spending and borrowing surged and the existing bureaucracy swelled. Yet when the crises ended, the federal government retrenched back into its small-government mode, even in the wake of crises as large as the Civil War and World War I. Despite an enlarged government's proven efficacy in surmounting the crisis at hand, and even increasing revenue (such as the income tax instituted during the Civil War), these were still insufficient to overturn the prevailing small-government model.

What qualitatively broke the small government model was the rapid succession of crises of the Great Depression, World War II, and the Cold War. In just sixteen years, three of America's most transformative crises effectively overlapped. Ironically, this was roughly the same span of time it took Americans to go from colonists to citizens of the United States. Over these sixteen years, the federal government grew, and even during periods of shrinking, it never returned to its former size, because by then, its larger size was deemed necessary.

For example: the payroll tax, which extended the existing income tax across the entire working population, embodies this qualitative transformation. What had started as a tax for the rich during the Civil War became a tax for all and for all time—not just through a crisis or the working lives of those who were immediately hit with it, but for all future generations. Suddenly, the government could collect significantly more revenue, which greatly expanded what it could pay for, allowing the federal government to become much more expansive and expensive.

While the payroll tax was the first blow to the small-government model, the *coup de grâce* was the Johnson administration's Great Society programs. In the sixty years since, the federal government has exploded in size, extent, and cost. The federal government's impact is hard to measure. Its spending numbers alone are staggering, but these do not begin to capture the impact of rules, regulations, and mandates. But, as Critical Race Theory and the various "justice movements" championed by "progressives" have made clear, nothing is seemingly outside its scope today.

To finish our recap, it's important to consider how, over the last sixty years, the federal government could not have created more perfect conditions for the socialist Left if it had tried (it is therefore hard to argue against the idea that at least some were trying). Looking at America through a political science lens, its rich history of organized groups gave rise to interest-group theory that sought to explain their formation and maintenance. Groups organized to advance defined interests went from an unavoidable evil at the nation's founding to a perceived good in the second half of the 20th century. But interest groups do not simply arise; they must connect with potential members to form an organization based on a mutual exchange of benefits. America's socialist Left never made this connection because it could never make an exchange—it had nothing to offer Americans beyond platitudes and promises. It needed, as had other groups before it, a patron. Because the socialist Left's problems were so insurmountable in America, it needed a patron of the highest order: the federal government.

Historically, the federal government had extended its patronage to groups before (recall the Farm Bureau in the early 20th century, the labor unions of the 1930s, and the ideologically leftist Farm Security Administration in the late 1930s). What the federal government had not done before the 1960s, however, was play the role of patron so explicitly and with such great resources. The pluralist school of political thought, which saw interest groups as positive and necessary, provided theoretical cover. The Economic Opportunity Act of 1964 afforded it the legislative means, while the Great Society programs provided the resources.

Thus, the 1960s turned out to be a perfect confluence. As the socialist Left abandoned the historic, single-party approach of Marxist orthodoxy for a dispersion into the multiplicity of causes of the traditional Left, the federal government was adopting the unorthodox approach of organizing the unorganized—the very areas into which the socialist Left was moving.

The legitimacy of the Democrat Party helped augment the traditional Left, and in the intervening decades, like Frankenstein's monster, the traditional Left subjugated its creator. Now, having incubated within the traditional Left, the socialist Left is their vanguard. Through the long-term effect of enormous federal resources, and its successive leveraging of the traditional Left—and through it the Democrat Party—the socialist Left has achieved a level of political power it could never have attained on its own.

But still, the socialist Left's inherent limitations cannot be easily overcome in the short-term and not at all over the long-term. At the heart of these limitations lies economics. Marxism puts the economy at the core of its ideology, just as the social ownership of the means of production is at the core of Marx's socialism. The two are inextricably linked, and both are doomed to fail. Failure is at the heart of the socialist economy: a Ponzi scheme relying on subsidies—frequently capitalism's resources—until it goes bankrupt. Socialism means the absence of competition: an end of capitalism and free markets for state monopoly ownership. The absence of marketplace competition (and, as the economist Ludwig von Mises would specify, the inability to calculate value) leads the undertaking to quickly unravel. It is the reason why socialist economies have failed abroad, and the reason why they did here in the 1820s. It is why these policies will fail again in the US if attempted by today's socialist Left. For proof, Americans need only to look at the federal entitlement programs—from health care to welfare—that the traditional Left have assembled over the last six decades. These programs are already fiscally unsustainable—a nonpartisan verdict shared by the Congressional Budget Office and the Government Accountability Office—and the current level of spending is just a fraction of what the socialist Left is seeking. For proof, just look at the Green New Deal, the expensive and expansive manifesto calling for a ten-year mobilization that would sweep the country, discussed in Chapter One. This proposal could cost up to $93 trillion and was embraced by several Democrat presidential candidates in 2020.

The six decades of program failure we've already seen from the traditional Left is just a microcosm of what the socialist Left intends. A process of failure is exhibited in these programs across the board. Generally, the programs are uncompetitive at the outset—in fact, their expunging of competition is frequently claimed as evidence for their need—and grow more so until eventually the programs fail even in their government-assisted versions (subsidies, limitations on private sector competition, forcing beneficiaries to only use the government program), as their goods or services are rejected by those they were ostensibly designed to help. More government programs are often added to bolster the failing ones. Finally, the accretion of anti-competitive programs becomes systemic: the entire edifice begins to teeter under monopolistic maladministration. If this sounds far-fetched, look no further than the Obamacare fiasco as an example of programmatic degeneration and the systemic failure of the federal government's involvement in America's health care system.

The socialist Left's mammoth economic failures are a political liability. For those who care to debate the socialist Left about its own ideology, economic failure is a fatal flaw for Marxism—by its own admission. Marxists believe that socialism is the economically inevitable replacement to capitalism. Yet, as shown throughout history, capitalism has never once produced socialism. As posed earlier in this book, if socialism cannot even replicate itself economically, how can it possibly replace the more productive capitalist system? What's more, wherever socialism has been overturned, capitalism has sought to take root, and former socialist Left countries have been reborn, as in the former Warsaw Pact nations of Eastern Europe.

In America, the socialist Left's economic weakness is lethal. The two major political parties are routinely rejected for bad economic performances that are but fractions of the systemic collapses the socialist Left have inflicted abroad. It is not surprising then that with economic failure at its core, the socialist Left could never maintain an organization in America. Without either, there is no legacy support for America's socialist Left today. As a result, the socialist Left will be unable to politically withstand its inevitable economic failures.

This is why the socialist Left has sought a home in the Democrat Party—it's the only way for it to have any impact on American politics. Yet, as we know, its parasitic presence there endangers its host, driving away the moderates on whom political majorities depend. Further, because it has no party organization to develop and enforce it, America's socialist Left has no coherent agenda; it is strictly comprised of extremist versions of the causes of the traditional Left. Finally, America's socialist Left must live down the actions of its ideological compatriots abroad. Throughout its existence, the USSR was fatal to America's socialist Left, and though it's had a thirty-year respite since the Soviet Union's demise, lately communist China's rise and its increasingly heavy-handed practices at home and abroad portend to be a new and growing drag on America's socialist Left.

Still, despite all of this, Americans must be concerned about the rise of the socialist Left in their country. Inevitable failure does not equate to immediate failure. Once the socialist Left attains political power, it never willingly relinquishes it, making its descent as painful as its hold on power was complete.

To complete the recap, America's socialist Left has three distinct advantages because of its insulation within the Democrat Party. Opposition to its policies can be deflected as simple partisan opposition to the Democrats—and not to the socialist Left specifically. Failure of its policies can be deflected as flaws in Democrats' implementation of them—and not to the policies themselves. And between these two scenarios, America's socialist Left can use the Democrat Party's legacy supporters to advance their policies—even when these Democrats might otherwise oppose those policies.

SECTION I
How Can America Respond?

America is confronted with the conundrum of how to oppose a flawed but amorphous and dangerous enemy. To understand what must be done, we must first remember what has been done: how America's socialist Left got to where it is today through both direct and indirect support from the federal government. Directly, the federal government has assisted it through programs that support the socialist Left's ideological agenda or funnel assistance toward it. The federal government has indirectly assisted it by massive spending that has created a mammoth foundation of potential adherents for the socialist Left in the form of tens of millions of subsidized recipients and providers. To start, we must seek to directly and indirectly reverse the factors that sustain America's socialist Left.

Identify

Before any real action can be taken, we must first identify what the socialist Left means: state control and, ultimately, state monopoly. While this may seem trivial, it is not. Many in America's traditional Left are embracing the title of socialist Left or democratic socialist because this is fashionably *avant-garde*. "Socialist" is still a derogatory term to the overwhelming majority and so the title should be readily attached to those who willingly embrace it—and America's establishment media should not be allowed to sanitize it by ignoring it. Equally, the title needs to be affixed to those policies which embody socialist Left principles and likewise to those politicians who advance such policies. In sum: if the shoe fits, the socialist Left should have to wear it.

Americans should also be cognizant of the code words that the establishment media and the traditional Left use to tentatively advance the socialist Left; those opposed to the socialist Left must strive to not use them and thereby avoid adding legitimacy to them. Despite the insistence of both groups, there is nothing "progressive" about the socialist Left's policies. The socialist Left is "progressive" only in the subjective Marxist claim that socialism is a "progression" in humanity's inevitable development. In any objective sense, the socialist Left is regressive in the extreme.

Economically, the socialist Left admits that it wants to dismantle capitalism, despite capitalism yielding the highest living standard in history by far. To go back is not "progressive," all claims to the contrary notwithstanding. The socialist Left is equally regressive when it comes to liberty. To realize its goals, the socialist Left elevates the state over the individual. Under the socialist Left there is no rule of law in which the individual's rights are secure in relation to the state's; in its place is Marxism's "dictatorship of the proletariat." By thus reducing individual liberty, the socialist Left would effectively take Americans back beyond not just their constitutional rights, but beyond those that prevailed in the original thirteen colonies. In order to curtail the socialist Left's ability to push for these regressive changes, the channels by which the socialist Left receives funds from the federal government also need to be identified and severed.

Oversight

Once these have been identified, the federal government's spending programs should be thoroughly audited. According to the Congressional Budget Office, the federal government spent $6.1 trillion in fiscal year 2023 and amassed a $1.7 trillion deficit—6.2 percent of US GDP.[5] If ever there existed justification for a complete audit of where all this spending and overspending is going, this is it. For fiscal year 2024, the IRS's funding request was $14.1 billion.[6] In the Democrats' 2022 Inflation Reduction Act, an additional $80 billion was provided to the IRS, with the claim that it would result in $400 billion in additional receipts. If this much can be allocated for the oversight of tax revenue, why not toward resources for the oversight of far greater amounts of federal spending? There are certainly ample examples of abuse to go along with the federal government's enormous spending. Consider that the Department of Labor's Office of Inspector General reported that "at least $191 billion in pandemic unemployment benefits could have been improperly paid, with a 'significant portion' attributable to fraud."[7] Or that the EITC program has a fraudulent payment rate of 25 percent.[8] David Ditch of the Heritage Foundation calls the US Department of Housing and Urban Development's Community Development Fund "a *de facto* slush fund for local projects" that directs "taxpayer funds toward strongly ideological causes." (In 2023 these included "thinly disguised training in critical race theory for Rhode Island teachers, millions of dollars for LGBTQ activist organizations in the New York City area, and a trio of earmarks to highlight ethnic groups in Seattle."[9]) The list goes on and on.

At the same time, if the federal government is auditing where all this money is going, it should also be taking note of *whom* it is going to. It should not be too much to ask of the federal programs that dole out cash in buckets to present an accounting of where it is ending up—not just the initial grants, but those organizations to whom the recipients are passing it. It is increasingly demanded that private-sector supply chains be scrutinized; why not the federal government's funding chains that channel taxpayers' money? How, following Uri Berliner's revelations of bias—a "distilled worldview of a very small segment of the U.S. population"—is federal money still going to NPR?[10] Yet it is, both directly and even more, indirectly.

There should also be prohibitions as to what sorts of organizations can even receive federal money. Such stipulations were included six decades ago in the

Economic Opportunity Act of 1964,[11] and restrictions are routinely placed on what sort of activities federal money can be used for. Why should admittedly socialist Left organizations be permitted to receive federal funds—even indirectly? Federal programs that fail to exercise proper oversight across the board, no matter their political affiliation, should see their funding cut. If organizations find such stipulations restrictive, they can always forego taking federal money. This in no way limits what they can do with money received another way, only what they can do if they are receiving taxpayer money.

Of course, some federal programs are inherently socialist Left in their aims and have no need to back-channel their money to the socialist Left; they do it upfront. As happened with the FSA in the 1940s, such programs should be eliminated as quickly as possible. There is no shortage of private organizations capable of identifying such programs, but the federal government should also be doing this.

These limitations should not be confined just to federal funding either. Federal legislation has often made it easier for the socialist Left to organize and to lobby for that increased funding, but seeing the writing on the wall, there is no longer any justification for the federal government to organize groups. And there is even less for such groups to turn around and use federal funds to lobby the federal government for more funds.

Of course, the socialist Left's current political success rests upon the enormous spending edifice that the federal government has constructed over the last sixty years. All the federal efforts that have directly aided the socialist Left's organization, and even the federal funds channeled directly to sustaining it, would be far less consequential without this spending edifice's massive potential group of supporters comprised of benefit recipients and providers.

Count

To be uncounted is to be unknown. The federal government's spending level is already known, and though its astronomical amount is almost incomprehensible, it is still just a portion of the federal government's overall economic impact on America. Americans should demand that the cost of the federal government's regulations and mandates be added to this number and made public. This heretofore unknown amount would be both a more accurate economic measure and a powerful tool for convincing Americans of the federal government's impact on society.

With this new knowledge, the next item on the agenda should be to contain the size of the federal government at its current level of impact on America's economy. As a percentage of GDP, it should grow no bigger. If there is a desire or need to increase it in one area, then this increase should be offset elsewhere. While not the reduction truly needed, even this curtailment of government increase would be a major breakthrough. More beneficial still would be to allow the economy to grow at a swifter pace than the government's impact, thereby *de facto* reducing its adverse economic effect—at least proportionally. Finally, the development of new regulations should be overseen by Congress, not unelected bureaucrats. Robert Moffit of the Heritage Foundation argues that Congress should return to applying the Administrative Procedures Act of 1946 and "restore the formal rulemaking process that was the norm until the 1970s," thereby ending "the excessive delegation of vast lawmaking authority to unelected federal officials."[12]

The ultimate goal should of course be to cut the size of the federal government absolutely. There are many federal policies and programs that are ripe for elimination or at least drastic reduction—such as the Department of Energy's Office of Energy Efficiency and Renewable Energy (EERE), which has been waging a consumer-costly war on home appliances. The EERE is headed by Jeff Marootian, a Biden appointee whose nomination has since been withdrawn, but who was nonetheless allowed to stay on. As Senator John Barrasso (WY-R), stated, "Jeff Marootian is an unelected, unaccountable, and unconfirmed bureaucrat who is carrying out President Biden's orders to attack affordable household appliances."[13] Another target for elimination: the approximately $300 million the Department of Justice gives out under various auspices to sanctuary cities with policies blocking cooperation with US Immigration and Customs Enforcement.[14]

The Congressional Budget Office routinely publishes lists of these possible reductions. In December 2022, it put out two volumes of large (over $300 billion) and small (under $300 billion) spending savings over ten years. Together, these amounted to trillions in possible spending reductions.[15] If the issue is that there aren't *enough* people urging for cuts in spending, then think tanks—nonpartisan, moderate, and conservative—could offer their own versions of these lists. Even the Committee for a Responsible Federal Budget, which endorsed the Biden administration program with the eerily Orwellian name the Inflation Reduction Act, released a document containing $3.6 trillion in proposed spending reductions. With $6.1 trillion in federal spending in fiscal year 2023, even a small reduction of 10 percent would yield well over $600 billion in annual savings, while leaving federal spending still substantially above its pre-pandemic 2019 baseline level of $4.4 trillion. The point is that oversight is being done outside of government. Why not on the inside? Oversight is a legitimate and historical role of Congress; with spending, deficits, and debt at today's levels, oversight should be a priority of the executive branch as well. And, in the inevitable discussions and negotiations that must take place over the federal government's unsustainable spending growth, programs that advance the socialist Left's agenda (such as the Biden administration's Equity Action Plan for education, which "calls for steering funding and contracts based on identity characteristics of the recipients or institution"[16]) should be at the top of the chopping list.

Simultaneously, a budget should be instituted to replicate spending account-ability on the federal government's regulatory dictates. To those who say it cannot or should not be done: the same was said of the Congressional Budget Office fifty years ago. The problem is not that it *cannot* be done; the problem is that it *has not* been done—at least by the government: it's estimated that the cost of federal regulations in 2022 was $3.1 trillion, an amount equal to 50 percent of the federal government's $6.3 trillion spending that year.[17] The same process of reduction should be applied to the regulatory arena; undoubtedly there are untold numbers of outmoded and inefficient regulations still inflicting their "invisible taxes" on the nation. It is high time for a thorough audit of federal regulations by the relevant federal agencies, the Government Accountability Office, and the congressional committees with oversight jurisdiction.

Original Purpose

The proposed efforts can be instituted with a simple roadmap: returning federal government programs to their original intents. Almost all federal social programs began with the ostensible purpose of helping the truly needy until those individuals could take care of themselves. And, almost all long ago burst beyond their original purpose: there are now 97 million Americans on Medicaid—that is 29 percent of the population in a program "designed for the poor and most vulnerable."[18] No one disputes that the truly needy should have a safety net, but also no one (other than the socialist Left) can dispute that federal assistance was not intended to become permanent—sadly, a way of life for too many. Instead of aiding those who truly need it through a crisis, many federal programs have themselves become a fiscal and societal crisis.

As John Cogan observes in his book, *The High Cost of Good Intentions*, virtually all federal programs exploded beyond their originally stated purposes. To correct this, we must transition back to those original purposes: removing those who should not be in the program; then, where applicable, setting time limits and work requirements on others. Furthermore, these policies work. As Ron Haskins wrote for the Brookings Institution: "Clearly, federal social policy requiring work backed by sanctions and time limits while granting states the flexibility to design their own work programs produced better results than the previous policy of providing welfare benefits while expecting little in return."[19]

Competition

The socialist Left's fundamental economic flaw—state monopoly and its exclusion of competition—will be its downfall in the end, so it's important to head this off before it brings America down with it. Americans should thus demand that the private sector be brought into the public sector as much as possible and seek ways to bring free-market dynamics into federal programs—especially in entitlement programs, where the bulk of America's fiscal threat lies. This means removing barriers that block the private sector from competing on a level playing field with federal programs, and eliminating barriers that trap beneficiaries.

The federal government effectively bars competition in several basic ways. For one, it can simply block it. Such prohibitions should be immediately removed; the federal government has no business—and should have no interest in—eliminating competition which will benefit the consumers of its goods and services. Another way the federal government can effectively stifle competition without legally prohibiting it is to provide subsidies at uncompetitively high levels for the service provided—thereby pushing out private-sector competitors on the supply side. As an example, Americans who get their health care through the Obamacare exchanges receive a federal subsidy that equals about 80 percent of their premium cost.[20] The effect is obvious: " ... the public option would drive out private competition by providing government privileges to the public option over other private options that would not be able to compete."[21] This excessive subsidization is costly to the taxpayer who foots the bill; ultimately it is also detrimental to those who will see the quality of the good or service deteriorate over time with increasing lack of competition—and likely find the subsidy failing to fully compensate for the diminished quality. If the federal government is going to *de jure* compete with the private sector, it should do so *de facto*—by only subsidizing at a competitive level and allowing individuals to enter into the marketplace; otherwise, it should not undertake the endeavor in question.

Another way the federal government blocks competition is by forcing its program recipients to use their assistance *only* within a federal program. For example, the federal government offers student loans for higher education in a wide variety of forms that recipients can use at a wide range of institutions and for a wide variety of purposes. In a word: choice. Why not other federal assistance? Recipients should be able to use their assistance where they see fit—thereby bringing in competition from the demand side. This can be done by providing recipients assistance with as much flexibility as possible in its use. As much as feasibly possible, states should receive what federal entitlement assistance they receive in the form of block grants, lump sums with freedom in program design that make states active participants in aiding their own populations—populations that they know far better than Washington does. Block grants are hardly new; they have been used for almost six decades.[22] So there is no reason they should not be implemented more broadly. Individuals should also receive their federal assistance in a form as close to personal accounts as possible—just as Health Savings Accounts (HSAs) work for millions' health care expenses today. Such accounts could be drawn on through a debit card (just as HSAs currently operate); this would allow both recipient flexibility and government oversight to ensure the card was used for the purpose intended.

Among the federal government's panoply of assistance, no two areas are more in need of innovation from competition than federal health care and public-school education.

In health care, federal government entitlement programs are bleeding money, driving deficits and debt. Obviously, reform is needed. In its 2024 long-term budget outlook, the Congressional Budget Office estimated federal health care mandatory programs' net spending will be 5.6 percent of GDP in 2024; it will increase almost 50 percent to 8.3 percent in 2054.[23] Despite these astronomical costs, none of these programs are giving their recipients the care they deserve as they limit the services and providers included. It would be far better for the government to make deposits to individual accounts and allow recipients to use them the way HSA owners use their deposits. It would give recipients the flexibility to choose the services they want, when they want, and from whom they want. It would also give them an incentive to be value-conscious consumers: savings would stay in their account, finally giving federal health care recipients a reason to comparatively shop for services.

This kind of competitive reform shouldn't be limited to the traditional federal-entitlement programs of Medicare and Medicaid. Obamacare and the federal regulation of health care are also prime targets. An insightful 2020 paper by leading health care experts at the Health Policy Consensus Group presents a comprehensive reform plan that would stretch across the individual health care arena. As one of the authors, Doug Badger, summarizes, its recommendations for individual-coverage reform focus on three basic actions: ending individual entitlements to ACA premiums and Medicaid expansion; giving states broad flexibility to design their own assistance plans; and allowing recipients to spend subsidies on plans they choose. The result would "lower premiums by up to 24 percent, cover nearly four million more people through private coverage, and improve access to medical providers by 8 percent."[24] This would be a far better approach than the current one that is based on excluding competition, and should also appeal to all but those committed to a big-government monopoly approach.

Moving on to education, America's public K-12 system woefully underperforms because of federal policy that does everything short of explicitly prohibiting competition.[25] In comparison to America's higher-education system, which is the envy of the world precisely because of its foundation on competition, the K-12 schools fall far behind. And, in contrast to federal college assistance, which can be used at virtually any higher-education institution in any region of the country, federal K-12 assistance is effectively limited to a family's local public school. Absent a school choice option, parents who wish to send their children to better public schools in other neighborhoods have essentially one choice: move. And parents wishing to send their children to private schools must foot the bill themselves—despite the funds for public schools also ultimately coming from their tax dollars. In much of America's K-12 school system there is almost no freedom of choice for parents or students, and hence almost no competition within the overall system.

If earlier evidence of underperformance was not enough, the COVID pandemic, which shut down schools in early 2020 through much of 2021, highlighted the terrible cost of the K-12 system having limited competition. In addition to being locked into neighborhood schools, during COVID, millions of students were locked out of even these. Lacking choice, they were forced for extended periods into "remote learning" online—where learning was all too often just a remote possibility. Even when schools would not open, children could not leave. The terrible cost of remote learning is only now showing itself. There's also data to show that the lockdowns had little effect on the COVID-19 mortality rate[26]—but the costs on the schoolchildren were enormous. As the *New York Times* wrote: "Research has documented the profound effect school closures had on low-income students and on Black and Hispanic students, in part because their schools were more likely to continue remote learning for longer periods of time."[27] A Harvard University 2022 report laid the blame for loss of learning squarely on closures, calling them the "primary driver of widening achievement gaps ... Within school districts that were remote for most of 2020-21, high-poverty schools experienced 50 percent more achievement loss than low-poverty schools ... In contrast, math achievement gaps did not widen in areas that remained in-person."[28] These school lockdowns—or more accurately, "lockouts"—were pushed by national teachers' unions, which only grudgingly acceded to school reopening in many areas.[29]

Americans must ask how, despite spending more, are they getting less from their schools? One answer is obvious: increasing emphasis on non-academic instruction—time spent there is time taken away from learning. America's public-school parents and children have had to endure added insult to their injury as many public schools—usually in the bluest jurisdictions—have increasingly swapped an emphasis on indoctrination for the desired one of education. Any number of leftist causes have elbowed their way into public-school curricula at the expense of teaching basic educational skills, again with the backing of leftist teacher unions. According to a 2023 Manhattan Institute paper, 93 percent of 18- to 20-year-olds "had heard about at least one of eight CSJ [Critical Social Justice] concepts from a teacher or other adult at school."[30]

The reason that the unions can pursue these lockouts and teach-ins is simple: public-school parents and children have no alternative but to accept the unions' dictates. The solution to this detrimental monopoly is equally straightforward: all parents should be able to take the money the federal government spends on their children's education and use it at any school—public or private—that their children qualify to enter. Further, if parents want to supplement this money out of their own pocket, that additional K-12 spending should receive favorable tax treatment akin to that for higher-education spending.

The overall goal here should be to broadly apply oversight to the federal government's operations—especially its spending and regulatory programs—and to inject competition everywhere it is feasible on both the supply and demand sides. There is no greater antidote to America's socialist Left than its antithesis: competition and free markets. These also happen to be the only ways to make the federal government smaller, function better, and reduce its uncontrolled costs. Injecting competition into federal programs will accomplish so much more than just their reform; while this is vitally important, changing their entire dynamic—in both how their goods and services are produced, but also in how these are received—is even more so.

Do not be mistaken: simply changing how much the federal government spends is not enough; changing *how* it spends what it spends is equally important. All too often in its past, instead of reforming the federal government's programs through the application of competition and the injection of free market principles, America has acquiesced in allowing roughly a quarter of the nation's economy to become a vast governmental black hole into which money by the trillions flows but no light escapes. The sooner this changes, the better.

SECTION II
Opposition Arguments

Inevitably there will be those—and not just from the socialist Left—who will dispute these assertions. It is therefore useful to anticipate and overturn some of their likely claims.

Argument: The Federal Government Cannot Get Smaller

The basis of this argument is that modern society demands so much from the federal government that it cannot get any smaller, only larger. Viewed historically, this would appear to be irrefutable: for almost the last century, the federal government has grown immodestly and immensely—not always at the same pace, but always on the same trajectory: upward.

However, looked at fiscally and economically, we arrive at a very different conclusion. Economically, demands always exceed resources; economics is the discipline of determining how limited resources can best be allocated. Fiscally, the federal government is on an unsustainable path that will effectively devour the nation's resources in the foreseeable future. This is neither a novel conclusion, nor an ideological one.

For decades, arguably since the creation of pay-as-you-go entitlement programs, it has been clear that the declining ratio of workers to beneficiaries (barring huge compensating productivity increases) could not service the spending demands of an increasing entitlement-beneficiary population. This obvious scenario has been attested to over decades by an array of budget estimators, including the nonpartisan Congressional Budget Office, the Government Accountability Office, and the trustees of the Social Security and Medicare programs. Nongovernmental think tanks have similarly echoed these official warnings.

The real question is not whether the federal government *should* get smaller—it undoubtedly must. But how to accomplish it? Having seen America's traditional Left create an unsustainable fiscal problem over the last six decades, it is clear that solving this one requires an ideological shift in direction, away from the left and to the right.

Argument: The Rich and Corporations Can and Must Pay More in Taxes

This argument springs from a willful ignorance of how much the so-called rich pay in taxes currently, and who actually pays the taxes the government levies. If most Americans were asked, the rate of taxation they would describe as "fair" would undoubtedly be well less than the 41.6 percent top marginal-income and employment-tax rate that those making over $1 million already pay. If queried again about how that "fair" rate should be administered, few would likely describe the progressive tax rates that currently exist; most would likely imagine that wealthier individuals pay more in taxes because the same tax rate applied to larger incomes accordingly yields greater tax revenues proportional to the greater income. However, this is **not** how the federal government's progressive income-tax rates work: moving to progressively higher rates of taxation (not just higher tax payments) as income rises. Fewest of all could describe the so-called economic justification (it is claimed that additional dollars yield diminishing returns to individuals—despite the obvious fact that a dollar yields the same absolute utility to whoever holds it) for such a progressive tax system.

The point is: the criticism that those with money should pay more in taxes because they could pay more in taxes—and theoretically will simply agree to do so—rests on a series of unexamined assertions. What instead should be examined is where the socialist Left really seeks to tax. Their support of a wealth tax is a good starting place, as is the rapid extension of the income tax in the last century. Both are great indicators of where the socialist Left's aspiration for vast new taxing power would lead: draining resources from America's more productive private sector. It should be noted, too, where the comparatively less-taxed income targets lie: in the middle and lower-middle classes. With the income tax's history as a guide, this is who would eventually be hit by a wealth tax too. The introduction of the payroll tax (simply an income tax by another name) is a case study in how it was accomplished—and could be again if the authority to tax wealth is granted to the socialist Left. There should be no mistake: the federal government cannot tax its way out of the spending hole dug by programs of the traditional Left—let alone the expansive promises of the socialist Left. As David Burton of the Heritage Foundation writes: "Even using the lower cost estimates, confiscating every dollar earned by every taxpayer with incomes of $200,000 or more would only pay for about half of the progressive agenda ... The reality is that progressive promises can only be funded by increasing taxes on the middle class from three to ten times their current level ... "[31]

Above all, Americans should be repeatedly reminded that the socialist Left seeks a government monopoly. Period. This monopoly extends throughout the economy, and through it, throughout society; it is not simply limited to specific sectors as the socialist Left falsely claims. Finally, it should be remembered who pays government taxes: society. Regardless of who is taxed directly, it is society that pays the taxes indirectly. Taxes redirect resources away from where they would otherwise be—the more productive private sector, where they are allocated by a free market—to the government, which overrides the most productive use of resources in favor of its subjective priorities. The result is a comparatively diminished return on society's resources: a cost that society bears. Just as TANSTAAFL (there ain't no such thing as a free lunch), so too TANSTAAFT (there ain't no such thing as a free tax).

The real question, then, is not whether the wealthy and corporations pay too little in taxes, but whether American society on the whole can afford the cost of more taxes—especially at the essentially unlimited level the socialist Left seeks. When properly posed, the answer is clearly "no."

Argument: Conservatives Will Not Address Health Care

To this assertion, the first question should be: where has the absence of conservative principles in health care gotten us? Last year, Phillip Swagel, director of the Congressional Budget Office wrote to Senator Whitehouse (D-RI): "The United States spends a larger share of its ... GDP on health care than other advanced economies and performs worse on various measures of health outcomes than many of those same countries. In 2019, U.S. health expenditures were 17.6 percent of GDP, nearly 7 percentage points higher than the average of other comparably wealthy countries."[32] America lives under a patchwork of health care options: government-, employer-, or individual-provided, as well as unprovided health care coverage—all crippled by government mandates and regulations. The federal government dictates what benefits must be included in its policies; the same applies to employers (unless they operate self-funded plans—"large group plans"), and even who can provide what types of care in areas where federal spending and tax policy do not directly touch. A 2016 Wharton School study found that 80 percent of health care spending was "government-affected."[33] It is no wonder families bounce back and forth between government and employer coverage—and often out of coverage altogether. Few areas of America's economy work worse, and none does so on such a vast scale. In 2020, health care spending equated to one-fifth[34] of our GDP; even outside the pandemic, the US spends over $4.5 trillion on health care.[35] All this has arisen under the direction of America's traditional Left and the malign neglect of America's conservatives.

Not just a huge part of America's economy, health care is also the largest area of federal-government spending, and the primary driver of the federal government's fiscal woes. If health care were absent from the federal budget, the budget would essentially be balanced: According to CBO, in 2024 net federal spending on health care (i.e., spending on Medicare, Medicaid, and the Children's Health Insurance Program, minus Medicare revenues and offsetting receipts) will be 5.6 percent of GDP; the deficit will also be 5.6 percent.[36] And health care's net spending burden on the budget (minus Medicare revenues) is projected to only get worse: net Medicare spending will grow to 5.4 percent (from 3.2 percent in 2024), while Medicaid and CHIP (plus premium tax credits and related spending) will grow to 2.8 percent (from 2.4 percent in 2024) in 2054.[37]

On top of this, health care is a burden on a family's budget too. Even if provided by an employer, the cost of health coverage is borne by employees through lower wages. Government exchanges are often little better: "the deductible in the [Obamacare] exchanges can be as high as $8,700 for an individual and $17,400 for a family. If you combine the average premium that people without subsidies paid last year with the average deductible they faced, a family of four potentially had to pay $25,000 for their health insurance plan before receiving any benefits."[38] With the government flooding the market with increasing subsidies, it is no surprise that insurance premiums increased 143 percent from 2013 to 2019.[39]

Where a family will land in this coverage mishmash can be its biggest worry, as well as one of its biggest expenses. Health coverage often also offers one of the least efficient returns. Because the federal government has mandates on what kind of coverage policies must provide, it also can direct who provides what services. As a result, families often wind up paying for coverage options they neither need nor want, while at the same time they may be foreclosed from choosing lower-cost quality provider options. It took the COVID pandemic to open wide the telemedicine door; hundreds of rules were waived on a bipartisan basis at the federal and state level.[40] But even that is only temporary; it is anyone's guess how long it will remain now that the pandemic is deemed to be over.[41] Similarly, high-skilled nurse practitioners could easily handle many routine health issues for a family if allowed—and at a fraction of the cost.

The federal government-constructed system serves neither taxpayers nor beneficiaries—nor even providers—well. Our health care is a testament to the resilience of American ingenuity in the face of government interference. But ingenuity is not infinity. This is the reason that the preferred employer-based system is continually under siege and why more and more people are pushed from it—or out of coverage altogether. The system can only endure so much interference and so many mandates for so long.

Sadly, this threatened collapse from government mandates has become the socialist Left's prime argument for having the federal government take over America's entire health care system. And the socialist Left has one big idea as to how this should happen. Sanders's latest Medicare for All proposal is proof.[42] After all, a national health care system is among the traditional Left's oldest policy quests, extending all the way back to the Truman administration,[43] while Medicare for All and "single-payer" are the socialist Left's mantras today.

It is not hard to see what the future of a socialist Left government-run system would look like. We only need look abroad to where government-run systems do prevail—along with lengthy wait lists and rationed care. Recently, the UK's National Health Service set a new record with over seven million wait-listed for routine procedures—with almost 400,000 of those waiting over a year to begin health treatment.[44] Simply: government-run equals government rationing; and rationing equals waiting. And of course, in health care, waiting can be fatal.

In light of the many negative impacts of America's current health care system—on the federal budget, the nation's families, the economy—as well as the necessity of foreclosing America's largest policy area to the socialist Left, the real response to conservatives' reluctance to enter the health care fray is that someone besides the socialist Left must address the issue, whether they want to or not. Additionally, conservative reforms are already out there. In print, *Modernizing Medicare* by Robert Moffit and Marie Fishpaw offers a blueprint for injecting competition into this enormous entitlement program.[45] In Congress, the Coronavirus Aid, Relief, and Economic Security Act[46] waived many Medicare rules, such as lifting restrictions on telehealth and allowing greater use of non-physician practitioners, that should serve as a blueprint for future—and permanent—reform.[47] And in December 2023, the US House of Representatives passed the Lower Cost, More Transparency Act, promoting price transparency across a wide array of health care services and more health care coverage options for small businesses (the CHOICE Arrangements Act).[48]

Argument: Conservatives Cannot Overcome the Establishment Media's Influence

Unquestionably our establishment media—outlets like the three traditional television networks (*ABC, NBC, CBS*), the historic print media of newspapers like the *New York Times* and *Los Angeles Times*, and most legacy magazines have a great deal of influence—especially on themselves. They also are some of the most subjective and leftward-slanted voices in America. While the establishment media's liberal bias has been noted for decades, *The Economist* in 2023 released a story based on its analysis of hundreds of phrases that indicate political leanings used in publications over the course of 2009 to 2022. It found that American journalism used terms more traditionally associated with Democrats far more than with Republicans.[49] Certainly, this bias helps the Democrat Party, the traditional Left, and the socialist Left, even as it sacrifices objectivity, accuracy, and ultimately audience—as increasing numbers of Americans abandon it altogether.[50] To appreciate, simply consider: where would the Biden administration be without the establishment media's selectively favorable coverage? Had there been objective reporting early on America's southern-border crisis or the Biden administration's failed domestic policies, it's hard to believe that Biden would have sought reelection. However, it is also important that the reverse is appreciated: that even despite this slant—from fawning praise to blind-eye neglect—a growing majority of Americans look upon the Biden administration unfavorably.[51] Americans are increasingly becoming more demanding and discerning consumers, trusting what they see with their own eyes, rather than what they are told to think.

America's establishment media, then, is not the great obstacle that it once was, and in fact has probably never had *less* influence on American society than they do today. *Gallup* 2022 polling found America's confidence in the media to be at an all-time low (with the lowest point reached in 2016). Only 7 percent of Americans have a "great deal" of trust in the media and just 27 percent have a "fair amount" of confidence: together, only about one-third have some confidence in the media. This is not just a collapse in credibility, it is a collapse in audience, too. A 2023 Pew Research Center article described how US daily newspaper circulation declined from roughly 60 million in 2000 to just over 20 million in 2022.[52] Conversely, conservative media outlets are doing very well: *Fox News* regularly bests its liberal competition. Additionally, there have never been more alternatives to the establishment media for news and entertainment than currently. In sum, the establishment media's effective monopoly is gone.

Argument: Conservatives Are Too Extreme

This has long been a line of attack by America's Left against conservatives. When Republican presidential nominee Senator Barry Goldwater said in 1964, "I would remind you that extremism in the defense of liberty is no vice! And let me remind you also that moderation in the pursuit of justice is no virtue!" Democrats responded with the infamous "Daisy Girl" ad, basically implying Armageddon if Goldwater won. And it worked. So much so that six decades later, America's traditional Left continue to level this same charge against conservatives at every opportunity. Lately, however, that charge is weakening. Because, as shown, Americans can see the socialist Left's extremism on almost a daily basis. Conservatism is generally the status quo, following America's founding principles inherently, while also consciously seeking to do so. In contrast, the traditional Left has routinely sought to recast America's founding principles to their liking in order to advance their agenda. Today, with the socialist Left in their vanguard, the traditional Left is being pulled even further and further from the mainstream. As a result, the traditional Left's ongoing struggle has been to hide their increasing extremism while charging mainstream America with the Left's own sin. A case in point is the traditional Left's adoption of the socialist Left's extreme DEI initiatives, charging the mainstream with inherent racism even as these initiatives call for their own blatant racism.[53]

There are, of course, extremists on both the left and right. Yet only on the left are the leaders themselves the extremists seeking to move their camp, and the country as a whole, away from America's principles. Because, again, the socialist Left *must* do these things if it is to have any hope of instilling its principles; but that doesn't make it any less extreme. As a result, those seeking to uphold America's founding principles look anything but extreme when juxtaposed to the socialist Left.

Argument: Reducing the Size of Government Will Hurt the Poor

No charge against applying conservative principles to the federal government is less accurate than that it will hurt the most vulnerable. No one seeks to remove the federal safety net for those truly in need. This was the safety net's original intent and remains its proper mission. If the federal government had kept to its original dimensions and intentions, it would not be in the fiscal crisis, nor American society in the social crisis, that both are now in. It is not conservatives who will renege on the original intent of these programs—in fact, the traditional Left already have by vastly expanding them beyond it. And it is the socialist Left that wants to expand this government net across all society. This is the proper baseline that needs to be set for discussion to be in any way productive. When entitlement programs are expanded beyond their original intent, it is often the poor who suffer. A case in point: "states that expanded Medicaid under the ACA are providing *fewer* services to children (and other vulnerable populations) than states that didn't expand."[54]

Second, not only does the edifice created by the traditional Left not work, it works worst for those most dependent on it. In its first half century, the federal government had spent well over $22 trillion on the War on Poverty. Currently, it is spending over $1 trillion per year and is projected to spend over $12 trillion over the next decade.[55] As a point of comparison, in February 2024, CBO reported federal debt held by the public to be $26.2 trillion and 97.3 percent of GDP in fiscal year 2023. It is time to admit the obvious: poverty won. The money spent and the programs designed have created a dependency for recipients (and in many cases, providers) which has then become an incubator for the socialist Left. Rather than moving people to independence, these programs have made millions of Americans thoroughly dependent on government for almost every aspect of their existence. The self-interest of the entire operating system—providers, bureaucrats, advocates, and politicians—is centered on keeping tens of millions dependent. These dependents have no idea how a free-market economy works because their economic world is entirely government-run. They know no way other than government programs.

The proper order of things has been entirely reversed: instead of acting as public servants, the government has made the public subservient. Scaling back the federal government is to return it to its proper role, generally, and in people's lives. Programs should be targeted only at those truly in need and designed with independence as their goal, not dependence.

SECTION III
Conclusion

Any discussion of ending the cycle of dependence for millions of Americans, and ending the continuing expansion of the federal government, will bring us back to America's origins. It returns us to the Lockean sense of property, the protection of which motivated colonists to come to America, and then motivated the designers of the Constitution. For John Locke, government was instituted to protect property, where "property" is broadly defined as an individual's entire ownership of their possessions—including, and most important, the ownership they have over themselves. Over the last six decades, the Lockean view that motivated the Constitution's framers has been abandoned by many of the Left. In their hands, government is the biggest threat to Americans' property. Not just external property, though this is surely true, but property in the broad Lockean sense: individuals' ownership of themselves. Through their use of state-distributed benefits, the traditional Left have created a group of recipients who live in a subsistence economy.

Never receiving enough to generate real wealth and the advancement through opportunity this entails, they are held in a perpetual serfdom of government dependency from which all too few escape.

By so becoming serfs of the state, this ever-growing population of Americans is unconsciously stripped of their property, their Lockean ownership of themselves—as well as tangible external property. They lose both because their dependency on government subsidies will never allow them to free themselves or allow them the means to accumulate meaningful property and wealth. While such an outcome was arguably unintended by the traditional Left, the socialist Left absolutely seeks it. The fundamental difference between the traditional Left and the socialist Left is one of scope *and* intent: the socialist Left wants to extend the state's monopoly throughout society. The socialist Left desires this limitation on property because allowing individuals to accumulate wealth on their own would also mean denying a socialist Left government the ability to distribute resources directly.

Through a socialist Left's statewide subsistence economy, individuals will ultimately lose the property they have in themselves, too dependent to pursue their own course by their own initiative. This is the most insidious outcome of the socialist Left's subsistence economy: not just its citizens' perpetual impoverishment, but their being chained to the system that imposes it. Far from "progressive," the socialist Left essentially offers a return to a feudal society. The American constitution, borne of Locke and what the colonists took from the English government tradition, was written with the aim of wresting rights from the government and embedding them in individuals. The socialist Left's goal is the reverse: reclaiming those rights from individuals and returning them to the state—a state it controls and one which controls all society.

Let there be no mistake: the socialist Left is the aggressor in America's current ideological conflict. It is because it must be. Because it cannot prevail conventionally. After all, conventional American politics locked out the socialist Left for over two centuries.

At its broadest level, this book is one about the dynamics wrought by various forms of government. These broad movements work like tides on the shore, and the current rise of the socialist Left is due to a diversion from the original limited federal-government model. At its core, capitalism, republicanism, and Constitution created a positive, self-reinforcing, and self-perpetuating dynamic in society. This has worked amazingly well for over two hundred years, and despite being adulterated, it still does for America's vast majority. However, over the last six decades, this intended dynamic has been subverted by an ever more expansive, extensive, and expensive federal government for a growing segment of American society. This subversion was started by the traditional Left, but it's the socialist Left that intends to overturn America's original dynamic completely and recreate the whole of society according to its ideological goal of a socialist Left state as the ultimate owner of everything. It intends to achieve this by instilling a dynamic that continually drives individuals to dependency on the state.

To stop this, Americans must strive to reinstitute America's original dynamic: to restore individuals' ownership of themselves. The idea of reversing the welfare state's encroachment may sound fanciful—it is difficult to imagine mass migration away from statist solutions when the prevailing dynamic drives ever more people toward government programs. Yet, reverse the statist dynamic to one focused on the individual, and the seemingly inexorable statist trajectory will reverse too: liberated individuals will become free actors extending free markets and demanding reforms that seem unimaginable today. Only by restoring America's original dynamic can the costly damage of the traditional Left be reversed—and the ultimate damage of the socialist Left prevented.

What does reversing today's dynamic look like? Instead of creating programs, the government should be seeking markets. This means giving beneficiaries access to existing markets because the keys to reform are choice on the demand side and competition on the supply side. Each will reinforce the other, reducing cost and increasing performance.[56] In capitalism, consumers rule. Ludwig von Mises termed it "economic democracy" as consumers dictate production,[57] rather than the state monopoly that the socialist Left seeks.

The government program that ignores markets plays to the socialist Left's predilection and purposes. In contrast, if given a choice, people will demand more. Their demand will foment change. Can conditions arise where markets can be improved? Of course. As the Nobel Prize-winning economist Alvin Roth writes: "If there's one thing we've learned about flawed markets, it's that people flee from them, either physically or by resorting to back channels and black markets. Either way, flawed markets can undermine not just communities but whole nations. The Berlin Wall was a monument to that fact."[58]

How soon will people flee from the absence of a market toward one? Starting from the premise of a market is far superior to starting from the premise of another government program, because the democracy of the market is superior to the autocracy of a one-size-fits-none government-designed and -run program that leaves all meaningful choices in the hands of legislators, administrators, and bureaucrats and none in the hands of the citizens it is supposed to serve. So how do we get to a point where we can begin to roll back the underpinnings of America's socialist Left? How do those who would fight back win the electoral victories needed to implement reform of the federal government? I suggest that we are closer than we think. The evidence for this goes back to a similar political juncture half a century ago, as the traditional Left took hold of the Democrat Party. Describing Democrats walking off the pier hand in hand with the traditional Left in 1972, Theodore White wrote of their Miami convention's culmination:

> Beyond the convention hall, watching, was a third party of national Democrats—which could be described only as a state of mind among voters who for decades had thought of the Democrats simply as the party of the common man.... No matter how few or many people were tuned in at the wee hours of the morning to hear the endless talk, no matter how loyal were the Democrats who stayed watching to the end, the convention gave the sense of a movement rushing through and beyond the political and cultural limits all politicians had up to now accepted.[59]

The comparison with the impact of the socialist Left on today's Democrat Party is joltingly unmistakable. Americans then were aghast at what they were seeing. So are Americans today. Only today's stakes with the socialist Left are far, far higher. So too will be America's counterreaction when it comes.[60]

Speaking then of the programs of the traditional Left, White said: "Somehow, by the end of the sixties these programs had themselves become values. However much the real world might fear liberal programs, it must submit because programs were morality, even after programs had gone wrong in visible practice."[61]

How much more does this apply to the socialist Left's failed programs that have "gone wrong in visible practice" today? What the traditional Left did largely unintentionally in 1972, the socialist Left intends to do—and do more extensively and aggressively—now. In comparison to the Miami convention floor of 1972—a time when television cameras brought only a smattering of news into America's homes for a half hour a night—the socialist Left's toxicity is being constantly pumped into America's consciousness in virtually unlimited quantities and through every means imaginable. America's establishment media cannot stop the flow any more than King Canute could turn the tide. Americans who see the writing on the wall must ride this wave and turn it against the socialist Left. All not under the socialist Left banner are potential recruits for our own. If we but have the courage to pursue them.

ENDNOTES

Introduction

1   On February 2, 2023, 86 Democrats (with another 14 voting "present") refused to support a resolution denouncing socialism in the House of Representatives. This is almost half of all House Democrats. Mychael Schnell, "House Passes Resolution Denouncing Socialism, Vote Splits Democrats," *The Hill*, February 2, 2023.

2   Michael Gonzalez's *BLM: The Making of a New Marxist Revolution* documents this, while numerous socialist organizations support BLM's agenda. Michael Gonzalez, *BLM: The Making a New Marxist Revolution* (New York: Encounter Books), 2021.

3   Alexis de Tocqueville, *Democracy in America,* trans. George Lawrence (Garden City: Anchor Books, 1969), 238.

4   Ludwig von Mises, *Socialism: An Economic and Sociological Analysis*, trans. J. Kahane (Mansfield Centre: Martino Publishing, 2012).

5   Werner Sombart, *Why is There No Socialism in the United States?*, trans. Patricia M. Hocking and C.T. Husbands (London: The MacMillan Press, Ltd., 1976), 106.

6   Congressional Budget Office, Historical Budget Data, February 2024.

7   Lydia Saad, "Democrats' Identification as Liberal Now 54%, A New High," *Gallup*, January 12, 2023.

8   Saad, "Democrats' Identification as Liberal Now 54%, A New High."

9   The export of liquified natural gas (LNG) was heavily promoted during the Obama administration, backed by the Trump administration, and supported by the Biden administration initially. Despite the US jobs it creates, the dirtier fossil fuels it replaces, and the security it brings to the country and our allies, these are not sufficient for the climate leftists. Saul Elbein, "Biden Bucks Obama's Legacy on Climate and Gas with LNG Export Pause," *The Hill*, January 27, 2024.

10   Matthew Daly, "In Rift with Biden, Manchin Vows to Block Oil, Gas Nominee," *AP News*, March 10, 2023.

11   Jon Levine, "Powerful Teachers Union Influenced CDC on School Reopenings, Emails Show," *New York Post*, May 1, 2021, and "Investigation Reveals Biden's CDC Bypassed Scientific Norms to Allow Teachers Union to Re-Write Official Guidance," House Committee on Oversight and Accountability, March 30, 2022.

12   Doug Badger, "Biden's Bid to Expand Obamacare via IRS is Illegal," The Heritage Foundation, June 17, 2022.

13   House Ways & Means Committee, "The Biden Tax Hike Will Likely Exceed $7 Trillion," March 14, 2024.

14   Mao Zedong, "Report on an Investigation of the Peasant Movement in Hunan," in *Selected Works of Mao Tse-tung, Volume I* (Peking: Foreign Languages Press, 1967), 28.

15   The departure tax is included in Assembly Bill 259 by California state Assembly member Alex Lee, introduced on January 19, 2023. Michael Nathanson, "California Wealth and Exit Tax Shows a Window Into the Future," *Bloomberg Tax*, March 17, 2023.

16   Even those self-identifying as liberal made up only 24 percent of America's voters according to 2020 presidential exit polling.

17   Rep. Andy Barr, "Rep. Barr Questions Chair Powell on Inflation, Monetary Policy, and Fed Bank Capital Requirements," Press release, March 8, 2023.

18   Barack Obama, *Dreams from My Father: A Story of Race and Inheritance* (New York: Three Rivers Publishing Group, 2004), 168.

19   A recent *Gallup* poll found 42 percent of respondents would support a socialist for president if their party nominated one. Saad, "Democrats' Identification as Liberal Now 54%, A New High."

20   Legislators in California, Connecticut, Hawaii, Illinois, Maryland, Minnesota, New York, and Washington announced plans to "tax stocks, bonds and other assets that can appreciate in value yet currently do not trigger a tax payment until they are sold." The proposals vary greatly, with some resembling Elizabeth Warren-style wealth taxes, while others increase their current income taxes. Additional states have since tried similar approaches. Aimee Picchi, "A National Wealth Tax Has Gone Nowhere. Now Some States Want to Tax the Ultra-Rich," *CBS News,* January 20, 2023.

21   As Citizens Against Government Waste observed in a May 10, 2021, article: "In 1990, there were 12 European countries that had imposed a wealth tax on their citizens, but only three still have such a tax. In France, the wealth tax led to an 'exodus of an estimated 42,000 millionaires between 2002 and 2012.'" In addition to being expensive to administer, distorting investment and savings decisions, "it didn't raise much revenue." Frances Floresca, "A Wealth Tax Will Slow Down Economic Growth," *Citizens Against Government Waste,* May 10, 2021.

22   Megan Kuhfeld, et al., "The Pandemic Has Had Devastating Impacts on Learning. What Will It Take to Help Students Catch Up?" Brookings Institution, March 3, 2022.

23   Phil Kerpen, Stephen Moore, and Casey B. Mulligan, "A Final Report Card on the States' Response to COVID-19," *National Bureau of Economic Research,* Working Paper 29928, April 2022.

24   Joseph Zeballos-Roig, "Bernie Sanders Seeks $6 Trillion Infrastructure Package, Which Senate Democrats are Considering Passing Without the GOP," *Business Insider,* June 17, 2021.

25   Edmund Burke's *Thoughts on the Cause of the Present Discontents and Speeches* was a pamphlet originally published in 1770. Edmund Burke, *Thoughts on the Cause of the Present Discontents and Speeches* (London: Cassell and Co., Ltd., 1886).

26   Joe Manchin, "Manchin Responds to Sanders Op-ed in *West Virginia Gazette-Mail*," Press release, October 15, 2021.

27   Rebecca Shabad, "Tulsi Gabbard Announces She's Leaving the Democratic Party," *NBC News,* October 11, 2022.

28 *New York Post* editorial: "Democratic Socialists of America Cheer Murder and Kidnapping of Israelis at Hands of Hamas Terrorists," October 8, 2023. "The DSA is the party of Ilhan Omar, Cori Bush, Rashida Talib—and oh yes, New York's very own Alexandria Ocasio-Cortez and Jamaal 'Fire Alarm' Bowman."

29 Kabir Khanna and Jennifer De Pinto, "CBS News Poll Finds Fewer Americans Expecting Economic Slowdown Now," *CBS News,* January 7, 2024. Poll taken January 3-5, 2024.

30 Robert Moffit and Doug Badger, "Forging a Post-Pandemic Policy Agenda: A Road Map for COVID-19 Congressional Oversight," The Heritage Foundation, January 19, 2023.

31 Grace-Marie Turner, "Build on Success," *American Healthcare Choices Newsletter,* Galen Institute, January 13, 2023.

Chapter I

1 Bernie Sanders, *Where We Go from Here: Two Years in the Resistance* (New York: Thomas Dunne Books, 2018), 9.

2 Sanders, p. 10

3 Michael D. Shear and Matthew Rosenberg, "Released Emails Suggest the DNC Derided the Sanders Campaign," *New York Times,* July 22, 2016.

4 Sanders, p. 20.

5 *CNN,* "Election 2016 Democratic Party Primary Delegate Estimate," 2016.

6 The tendency for a binary political system to form under such circumstances was noted by Maurice Duverger decades ago. Maurice Duverger, *Political Parties: Their Organization and Activity in the Modern State* (London: Methuen, 1964).

7 Leigh Ann Caldwell, "Despite Objections, Congress Certifies Donald Trump's Election," *NBC News,* January 6, 2017.

8 Darren Samuelsohn, "Could Trump Be Impeached Shortly After He Takes Office?" *Politico,* April 17, 2016.

9 Matea Gold, "The Campaign to Impeach President Trump Has Begun," *Washington Post,* January 20, 2017.

10 Melissa Chan, "There's Already a Campaign to Impeach President Donald Trump," *Time Magazine,* January 20, 2017.

11   Jacob Taylor, "Rep. Waters Calls for Harassing Admin Officials in Public, Trump Calls Her 'Low IQ,'" *NBC News*, June 25, 2018.

12   Jane Timm, "Democrats Gain 40 House Seats, as NBC Projects TJ Cox Wins California's 21st District," *NBC News*, December 6, 2018.

13   Barbara Ransby, "'The Squad' Is the Future of Politics," *New York Times*, August 8, 2019.

14   Jon Levine, "Former AOC Aide Justine Medina Now Working as New York Communist Party Boss," *New York Post*, May 13, 2023.

15   Salvador Rizzo, "What's Actually in the 'Green New Deal' from Democrats?" *Washington Post*, February 11, 2019.

16   Doug Holtz-Eakin, "How Much Will the Green New Deal Cost?" Aspen Institute, June 11, 2019.

17   Bureau of Economic Analysis, "Gross Domestic Product (Second Estimate) … Third Quarter 2021," November 24, 2021.

18   As will be discussed later in the book, once in operation, actual government program costs almost always exceed estimates.

19   Michael Bopp, et. al., "Investigations in the 116th Congress: A New Landscape and How to Prepare," Gibson, Dunn and Crutcher, LLP, January 29, 2019.

20   Alex Moe, "House Investigations of Trump and His Administration: The Full List," *NBC News*, May 27, 2019.

21   According to the US Centers for Disease Control and Prevention (CDC), the first lab-confirmed COVID case in America occurred on January 20, 2020.

22   Bureau of Economic Analysis, "Gross Domestic Product, First Quarter 2024 (Advance Estimate)," April 25, 2024.

23   Congressional Research Service, "Unemployment Rates During the COVID-19 Pandemic: In Brief," March 12, 2021. US Bureau of Labor Statistics, "Monthly Labor Review," June 2021.

24   Congressional Research Service, "Federal Reserve: Tapering of Asset Purchases," January 27, 2022.

25   Committee to Unleash Prosperity, *Unleash Prosperity Hotline*, February 6, 2024.

26   Mike Gonzalez and Andrew Olivastro, "The Agenda of Black Lives Matter Is Far Different From the Slogan," The Heritage Foundation, July 3, 2020.

27   Major Cities Chiefs Association, Intelligence Commanders Group, "Report on the 2020 Protests and Civil Unrest," October 2020. The details in this discussion of the protests come from this report.

28   "Report on the 2020 Protests and Civil Unrest."

29   "Report on the 2020 Protests and Civil Unrest."

30   Yael Halon, "Ben Carson Defends Terry Crews' Black Lives Matter Critique: 'We Are Putting Everything in the Context of Color,'" *Fox News*, July 1, 2020.

31   Adina Campbell, "What Is Black Lives Matter and What are the Aims?" *BBC*, June 12, 2021.

32   David Weigel, "Hickenlooper Denounced Socialism—and Then Got Booed in San Francisco," *Washington Post*, June 2, 2019.

33   Jeremia Kimelman, "Full Transcript: 2019 Democratic Debate Night Two," *NBC News*, June 28, 2019.

34   Catherine Lucey, "Biden Leads Democratic Push to Block New Abortion Restrictions After Shifting Stance in Campaign," *Wall Street Journal*, November 28, 2021.

35   Biden announced in March 2020 that he would pick a woman as his vice president if elected. Kate Sullivan, "Biden Says He Will Pick Woman to Be His Vice President," *CNN*, March 15, 2020.

36   Edward-Issac Dovere, *Battle for the Soul: Inside the Democrats' Campaign to Defeat Trump* (New York: Penguin Random House, 2021).

37   *RealClearPolitics*, "2020 Democrat Nomination," Historical Archive, 2020.

38   The White House, "Fact Sheet: The American Jobs Plan," March 31, 2021.

39   Committee for a Responsible Budget, "What's in President Biden's American Jobs Plan?" April 2, 2021.

40   The White House, "Fact Sheet: The American Families Plan," April 28, 2021.

41   Committee for a Responsible Budget, "What's in President Biden's American Families Plan?" April 28, 2021.

42   Emily Cochrane, "Democrats Float $6 Trillion Plan Amid Talks on Narrower Infrastructure Deal," *New York Times*, June 20, 2021.

43   Budget authority refers to spending allowance, the money that will be spent over time.

44   Phillip Swagel, "Letter to Senator Lindsey Graham Re: Economic Analysis of Budget Reconciliation Legislation," Congressional Budget Office, August 4, 2022.

45   Penn Wharton Budget Model, "Update: Budgetary Cost of Climate and Energy Provisions in the Inflation Reduction Act," University of Pennsylvania, April 27, 2023.

46   Congressional Budget Office, 10-Year Budget Projections, February 2024 and Congressional Budget Office, Historical Budget Data, February 2024.

47   Eli Ginzberg and Robert M. Solow, *The Great Society: Lessons for the Future* (New York: Basic Books, 1974), 9.

48   One that saw defense spending rise from $53.4 billion in 1963 to $82.5 billion in 1969, cost $399 billion over those years, and require an income and corporate surtax—in addition to forever scaring Democrats, and ultimately forcing Johnson to not seek reelection in 1968. Budget data is from Office of Management and Budget, Historical Tables, Table 3.1.

49   On January 19, 2024: 45 strong disapproval and 25 percent strong approval. *Rasmussen Reports*, Biden Approval Index History.

50   Hanna Trudo, "Restless Progressives Eye 2024," *The Hill*, November 28, 2021.

Chapter 2

1   Maurice Duverger, *Political Parties: Their Organization and Activity in the Modern State* (London: Methuen, 1964).

2   The preeminent economist Ludwig von Mises states: "My own definition of Socialism, as a policy which aims at constructing a society in which the means of production are socialized, is in agreement with all that scientists have written on the subject." Ludwig von Mises, *Socialism: An Economic and Sociological Analysis*, trans. J. Kahane (Mansfield Centre: Martino Publishing, 2012), 20.

3   Daniel Flynn, *A Conservative History of the American Left* (New York: Crown Forum, 2008), 211.

4   Flynn, p. 241.

5   Flynn, p. 263.

6   Tom Hayden, "Port Huron Statement" (Students for a Democratic Society, 1962), pp. 5-6.

7   Hayden, p. 10.

8   Flynn, p. 263.

9   Flynn, p. 266.

10 Saul Alinsky, *Rules for Radicals: A Pragmatic Primer for Realistic Radicals* (New York: Vintage Books, 1989), 37.

11 Barry Goldwater, "1964 Republican National Convention Presidential Nomination Acceptance Speech," July 17, 1964.

12 Democrats won two Senate seats, which brought their majority to 68 seats, their largest total since their 69 seats in the 76th Congress of 1939-1941. With the addition of those 37 seats in the House, Democrats brought their majority to 295, their largest total since their 334 seats in the 75th Congress of 1937-1939.

13 Robert A. Caro, *The Years of Lyndon Johnson: Master of the Senate* (New York: Vintage Books, 2003), xxi.

14 John Cogan, *The High Cost of Good Intentions: A History of U.S. Federal Entitlement Programs* (Stanford: Stanford University Press, 2017), 191.

15 Flynn, p. 278.

16 Theodore White, *The Making of the President 1972* (New York: Atheneum Publishers, 1973), 161.

17 Ron Elving, "George McGovern, An Improbable Icon of Anti-War Movement," *It's All Politics: Political News from NPR,* October 22, 2013.

18 To achieve this, Carter won every southern state except Virginia and Oklahoma, and no state west of the Mississippi except Texas.

19 Todd S. Purdum, "Clinton Angers Friend and Foe in Tax Remark," *New York Times,* October 19, 1995.

20 Bill Clinton, "Address Before a Joint Session of the Congress on the State of the Union," January 23, 1996.

21 Robert Dole, "Republican Party Response to President Clinton's 'Address Before a Joint Session of the Congress on the State of the Union,'" January 23, 1996.

22 Lydia Saad, "Americans' Political Ideology Held Steady in 2020," *Gallup,* January 11, 2021.

23 Liz Halloran, "Obama Humbled by Election 'Shellacking,'" *NPR,* November 3, 2010.

24 Charles P. Blahous, "Spending Growth, Not Tax Policy, Is the Main Driver of Federal Debt," Testimony before the US Senate Budget Committee, May 18, 2023.

25 Bernie Sanders, *Where We Go from Here: Two Years in the Resistance* (New York: Thomas Dunne Books, 2018), 83.

26 Editorial Board, "Democratic Socialists of America Cheer Murder and Kidnapping of Israelis at Hands of Hamas Terrorists," *New York Post,* October 8, 2023.

Chapter 3

1 Regardless of origin, by the time of the American Revolution, most of the colonies had become royal colonies.

2 Isaiah Berlin, "Chapter 1: John Locke" in *The Age of Enlightenment: The Eighteenth Century Philosophers* (New York: New American Library, 1984), 30.

3 Books have been written over the origins and evolution of the terms "Whig" and "Tory." For simplicity's sake, from the time of the "Glorious Revolution" of 1688, the Whigs politically supported greater limits on monarchical influence and power in England's government.

4 Adam Smith, *An Inquiry into the Nature and Causes of the Wealth of Nations* (New York: The Modern Library, 1994), 633.

5 The combined population of England and Wales in 1700 is generally estimated at about 5.5 million and Scotland's at just over 1 million.

6 Estimates vary for America's population from 1700 to 1780, but there is general consensus that it grew roughly tenfold: from approximately 250,000 to 2.7 million.

7 Peggy M. Baker, "The Plymouth Colony Patent: Setting the Stage" (Pilgrim Society & Pilgrim Hall Museum, 2007).

8 Nathaniel Philbrick and Thomas Philbrick, eds., *The Mayflower Papers: Selected Writings of Colonial New England* (New York: Penguin Books, 2007), 14.

9 Daniel J. Boorstin, ed., *An American Primer* (Chicago: University of Chicago Press, 1966), 22.

10 Boorstin, p. 20.

11 All quotations of the Magna Carta are from: G.R.C. Davis, *Magna Carta* (London: British Museum, 1963), 23-33.

12 i.e. revenue

13 Nicholas Vincent, "Consequences of Magna Carta" (British Library, March 12, 2015).

14 Vincent, "Consequences of Magna Carta."

15 Vincent, "Consequences of Magna Carta."

16 Chronicle of Melrose Abbey, quoted in Vincent, "Consequences of Magna Carta."

17 It is estimated that even more were killed in Ireland. "British Civil Wars," National Army Museum, Website.

18 "English Bill of Rights 1689" (Yale University, Lillian Goldman Law Library, 2008).

19 Alvin Rabushka, *Taxation in Colonial America* (Princeton: Princeton University Press, 2008), 326.

20 At their establishment: Pennsylvania, North Carolina, South Carolina, Maryland, Delaware, New Hampshire, New York, and Georgia were all proprietary colonies.

21 Samuel Eliot Morison, *The Oxford History of the American People, Volume One, Prehistory to 1789* (New York: New American Library, 1972), 243.

22 Morison, *Volume One,* p. 243.

23 Rabushka, p. 573.

24 Morison, *Volume One,* p. 247.

25 Bernard Bailyn, *The Ideological Origins of the American Revolution* (Cambridge: The Belknap Press, 1992), 28-29.

26 Thomas Hobbes, *Leviathan,* ed. C.B. MacPherson (New York: Penguin Books, 1982), 186.

27 Hobbes, p. 44. C.B. MacPherson's full quote reads: "And it would have to be left to the sovereign to decide how much of men's powers the sovereign would need to have . . ."

28 Hobbes, p. 229.

29 Bailyn, p. 27.

30 John Locke, *The Second Treatise of Government,* ed. Thomas Peardon, (Indianapolis: Bobbs-Merrill Educational Publishing, 1981), xix.

31 Locke, p. 29.

32   Locke, p. 32.

33   Locke, p. 54.

34   Locke, p. 73.

35   Locke, p. 75.

36   Locke, p. 85.

37   Bailyn, pp. 34-35.

38   Sir Robert Walpole is recognized as being Britain's first Prime Minister from 1721-1742.

39   Bailyn, p. 39.

40   Bailyn, p. 43.

41   Bailyn, pp. 45-46.

42   Oliver Goldsmith, "The Deserted Village," in *Immortal Poems of the English Language*, ed. Oscar Williams (New York: Washington Square Press, 1952), 211-222.

43   Goldsmith, p. 212.

44   Murray N. Rothbard, *Economic Thought Before Adam Smith: An Austrian Perspective on the History of Economic Thought, Volume I* (Auburn: Ludwig von Mises Institute, 2012), 213.

45   Rothbard, *Volume I*, p. 299.

46   Rothbard, *Volume I*, p. 226.

47   As would later be the consequence of the tariff wars of the 1930s (Smoot-Hawley in the US), such an approach of favoring exports and discouraging imports set off reciprocal actions in other nations.

48   Rothbard, *Volume I*, p. 218.

49   Rothbard, *Volume I*, p. 246.

50   Smith, p. 475.

51   Smith, p. 482.

52   Smith, p. 484.

53   Smith's quote on the topic: "He generally, indeed, neither intends to promote the public interest, nor knows how much he is promoting it … By pursuing his own interest he frequently promotes that of the society more effectually than when he really intends to promote it." Smith, pp. 484-485.

54   Smith, p. 631.

55   Smith, p. 632.

56   Edwin Perkins, *The Economy of Colonial America* (New York: Columbia University Press, 1988), 195.

57   Richard Hofstadter, *America at 1750: A Social Portrait* (New York: Vintage Books, 1973), 134.

58   Hofstadter, p. 139.

59   Perkins, p. 234.

60   Perkins, p. 11.

61   Perkins p. 12.

62   Perkins, p. 212.

63   Perkins, p. 213.

64   Perkins, p. 213.

65   Hofstadter, p. 140.

Chapter 4

1   In Chapter 3, the colonies' mother country was synonymous with England alone. Following the Acts of Union of 1707, England and Scotland joined into a united kingdom to be called Great Britain, or, more simply, Britain.

2   Howard H. Peckham, *The Colonial Wars: 1689-1762* (Chicago: The University of Chicago Press, 1964), 2.

3   Peckham, p. 1.

4   Peckham, p. 56.

5   Peckham, p. 38.

6   Peckham, p. 55.

7   Peckham, p. 155.

8   Colin Bonwick, *The American Revolution* (Charlottesville: The University Press of Virginia, 1991), 70.

9   To reiterate Smith's quote on the subject: "In every thing (sic) except foreign trade, the liberty of the English colonists to manage their own affairs their own way is almost complete." Smith, p. 631.

10 Edwin Perkins, *The Economy of Colonial America* (New York: Columbia University Press, 1988), 187, 195.

11 Bonwick, p. 71.

12 Bonwick, p. 71.

13 Bonwick, p. 73.

14 Bonwick, p. 73.

15 The parallel but contrasting language in the Declaration of Independence ten years later is striking: "that these United Colonies are, and of Right ought to be Free and Independent States."

16 Bonwick, p. 75.

17 Bonwick, p. 75.

18 For a readily accessible text of the Suffolk Resolves see: Joseph Warren, The Suffolk Resolves (Suffolk: *Essex Gazette*, September 20, 1774).

19 As penned by Ralph Waldo Emerson.

20 David McCullough, *John Adams* (New York: Simon and Schuster, 2001), 118.

21 McCullough, p. 129.

22 McCullough, p. 119.

23 McCullough, p. 121.

24 John Locke, *The Second Treatise of Government*, ed. Thomas Peardon (Indianapolis: Bobbs-Merrill Educational Publishing, 1981), vii.

25 Locke, p. 126.

26 Locke, p. 32.

27 Emphasis in the original. Samuel Eliot Morison, *The Oxford History of the American People: Volume One, Prehistory to 1789* (New York: New American Library, 1972), 248.

28 Perkins here was citing a paper by Lance Davis and Robert Huttenback of the California Institute of Technology that compared tax rates in the American colonies and Britain. Perkins, p. 195.

29 Alvin Rabushka, *Taxation in Colonial America* (Princeton: Princeton University Press, 2008), 756.

30 Only John Hancock, president of the Continental Congress, and Charles Thomson, the Congress's Secretary, signed the Declaration of Independence on July 4; most signed on August 2.

31 Gordon S. Wood, *The Radicalism of the American Revolution* (New York: Vintage Books, 1991), 5.

32 Smith, p. 666.

33 Bruce Lancaster, *The American Revolution* (Boston: Houghton Mifflin Company, 2001), 4.

34   James Thomas Flexner, *Washington: The Indispensable Man* (New York: New American Library, 1984), 183.

35   Robert Leckie, *George Washington's War: The Sage of the American Revolution* (New York: HarperCollins, 1993), 659.

36   McCullough, p. 130.

37   Morison, *Volume One*, p. 362.

38   Morison, *Volume One*, p. 365.

39   The rebellion lasted only a few months during 1786-1787 and was put down with minimum bloodshed; it was the Confederation that suffered the real harm. Unquestionably, those pushing for a stronger central government leveraged the uprising for their purposes. As will be seen later in this book, the Shays uprising bears striking resemblance to the Farmers' Holiday Association movement of the 1930s. David P. Szatmary, *Shays' Rebellion: The Making of an Agrarian Insurrection* (Amherst: University of Massachusetts Press, 1980).

40   Morison, *Volume One*, p. 366.

41   This and the following two quotations are all included in Morison, *Volume One*, p. 394.

42   Max Farrand, *The Records of the Federal Convention of 1778*, Volumes I-III (New Haven: Yale University Press, 1966), xvi.

43   Alfred Kelly, Winfred Harbison, and Herman Belz, *The American Constitution: Its Origins and Developments* (New York: W.W. Norton and Co., 1983), 74.

44   Kelly, Harbison, and Belz, p. 69.

45   Kelly, Harbison, and Belz, p. 71.

46   Farrand, *Volume I*, p. xi.

47   Ralph Ketcham, ed., *The Anti-Federalist Papers and the Constitutional Convention Debates* (New York: New American Library, 1986), 199.

Chapter 5

1   Alvin Rabushka, *Taxation in Colonial America* (Princeton: Princeton University Press, 2008), 15.

2   Their governments' small sizes also gave American colonies the latitude of relying on some unusual methods for funding. In addition to taxes,

fees played a role far larger than they do today. Some were particularly unusual, such as public loan office revenues (by which colonial governments charged interest on loans collateralized by land). That fees and loan office receipts could play such a comparatively large revenue role attests to colonial governments' small size. Rabushka, p. 17.

3   The pilgrims of Plymouth were seeking freedom to practice their religion. For those immigrating after the prolonged English Civil War, governmental chaos was all too real; the same would be true for many emigrating from continental Europe who had witnessed widespread warfare there.

4   Rabushka, p. 270.

5   Rabushka, p. 437.

6   Rabushka, p. 558.

7   The most notable conflicts in these periods were: King William's War (1689-97), Queen Anne's War (1702-13), King George's War (1744-48), and of course the climactic French and Indian War (1756-63).

8   For a breakdown of comparative costs: In 1775, civil government in America cost about £66,000 and was offset by colonial revenue (Rabushka, p. 756 and p. 765). The British army in colonial America cost about £200,000 per year and Britain's infamous Navigation Acts raised approximately £33,000 from the American colonies (Rabushka, p. 756). Where the American colonies' cost of government was £266,000, Britain's was £10.4 million (Rabushka, p. 725); in comparison to the American colonies' revenue cost of roughly £100,000, Britain's was £11.1 million (Rabushka, p. 725). The American colonies' cost of government was just 2.6 percent of Britain's, while its revenues were just 0.9 percent of Britain's. As a further comparison, according to the American Battlefield Trust, the American colonies' population in 1775 was 2.5 million and Britain's was approximately 8 million. American Battlefield Trust, "American Revolution Facts," November 16, 2023.

9   Calvin D. Linton, ed., *The Bicentennial Almanac: 200 Years of America* (Nashville: Thomas Nelson. Inc., 1975), 44.

10   Alexis de Tocqueville, *Democracy in America*, trans. George Lawrence, ed. J.P. Mayer (Garden City: Anchor Books, 1969), 113.

11   Tocqueville, pp. 114-115.

12   Morison, Samuel E. *The Oxford History of the American People, 1789 through Reconstruction, Volume Two* (New York: New American Library, 1972), 34.

13   Morison, *Volume Two*, p. 34.

14   Morison, *Volume Two*, p. 34.

15   Additionally, when the new Congress finally did form in 1789, not all the states had ratified the Constitution (North Carolina would not until November 21, 1789, and Rhode Island would not until May 29, 1790).

16   Timetable is from Linton, *Bicentennial Almanac*. The description of Hamilton's efforts is from Forrest MacDonald, *Alexander Hamilton: A Biography* (New York: W.W. Norton & Co., 1979), 187.

17   US Census Bureau, "Bicentennial Edition: Historical Statistics of the United States, Colonial Times to 1970, Parts 1 and 2," 1975), Series Y 335-338 (Washington, DC: Department of Commerce, 1975). Unless otherwise noted, historical figures in this category for other years also comes from this data series.

18   Debt fell to just $38,000 in 1834 and 1835.

19   The war with Mexico, 1847-1849, caused surging spending and deficits, although receipts did rise in two of the three years, much like the pattern during and following the War of 1812.

20   In 1816, customs were $36.3 million of its $47.7 million total; in 1851, they were $49 million of its $52.6 million (US Census Bureau, Historical Statistics ... Series Y 352-357). Out of $30.6 million in total spending, $16 million went for the army, $3.9 million for the navy, $7.2 million for interest payments on the public debt, and $3.5 million for "interest payments by Government corporations and other business-type activities on securities issued by the Treasury." (US Census Bureau, Historical Statistics ... Series Y 457-465, p. 1115, footnote #2.) In 1851, out of $47.7 million in total spending, $11.8 million went for the army, $9 million for the navy, $3.7 million for interest payments on the public debt, and $23.2 million for "interest payments by government corporations and other business-type activities on securities issued by the Treasury." (US Census Bureau, U.S Historical Statistics ... Series Y 457-465.) Unless otherwise noted, historical figures in this category for other years also comes from these data series.

21 In 1816, out of 4,837 civilian employees, 3,341 were in the Post Office; in 1851, out of 26,274 total employees, 21,391 were in the Post Office. (US Census Bureau, U.S Historical Statistics ... Series Y 308-317.) Unless otherwise noted, historical figures in this category for other years also comes from this data series.

22 Tocqueville, p. 125.

23 Morison, *Volume Two*, p. 441.

24 Federal fiscal data relative to GDP in this section and the following sections in this chapter were calculated from the US Census Bureau's Bicentennial Statistics and measures of US GDP obtained from MeasuringWorth's comparators at www.measuringworth.com. The MeasuringWorth comparators are an invaluable tool for gauging monetary values across times in comparable terms. All estimates of US fiscal data in relation to GDP, prior to the compilation of this data for years 1930 and later by the Office of Management and Budget's Historical Tables, relies upon the MeasuringWorth comparators for the periods being examined.

25 Cynthia G. Fox, "Income Tax Records of the Civil War Years," *Prologue Magazine* 18, no. 4 (1986).

26 Fox, p. 2.

27 Fox, pp. 3-4.

28 Tocqueville, p. 219.

29 Tocqueville, p. 177.

30 Morison, Samuel E. *The Oxford History of the American People, Volume Three, 1869-1963* (New York: New American Library, 1972), 75.

31 Steven R. Weisman, *The Great Tax Wars* (New York: Simon and Schuster, 2002), 94.

32 Weisman, pp. 98-99.

33 Fox, p.1.

34 Weisman, p. 101.

35 Weisman, p. 132.

36 Weisman, p. 145.

37 Alfred Kelly, Winfred Harbison, and Herman Belz, *The American Constitution: Its Origins and Development, Volume II* (New York: W.W. Norton & Co. 1991), 401.

38 Senator La Follette of Wisconsin, whose state had an income tax, said: "The success of any given amendment is very improbable." Weisman, p. 234.

39 Weisman, p. 202.

40 Weisman, p. 234.

41 Linton, p. 283.

42 Weisman, p. 279.

43 Woodrow Wilson, "Message to Congress," 63rd Cong., 2nd Sess., Senate Doc. No. 566 (1914): pp. 3-4.

44 The Zimmerman telegram, sent from Germany to Mexico, promised a return of territory to Mexico in exchange for their participation against America in the event of war.

45 Gary Mead, *The Doughboys: America and the First World War* (Woodstock: Overlook Press, 2002), 13.

46 Linton, p. 290.

47 Mead, p. ix.

48 Discussing the Americans' participation in the Second Battle of the Marne, German General Erich Ludendorff stated in 1927: "With more than a million fresh, young, ardent Americans pressing forward into the battle, the result was inevitable ... It was assuredly the Americans who bore the heaviest brunt of the fighting on the whole battlefront during the last few months of the war." Quoted in Mead, p. 189.

49 Source for the legislative timetable: Linton, pp. 290-297.

50 Quoted in Weisman, p. 320.

51 Weisman, p. 324.

52 Weisman, p. 324.

53 Weisman, p. 321.

54 The first on September 8, 1916 (Weisman, p. 307); the second on October 3, 1917 (Weisman, p. 327); and the third, the Revenue Act of 1918, which was signed by Wilson on February 24, 1919 (Weisman, p. 337).

55 Weisman, p. 337.

56 Weisman, p. 319.

57 Kendrick Clements, *Woodrow Wilson: World Statesman* (Chicago: Ivan R. Dee, 1999), 122.

58 Clements, p. 172.

59   Clements, p. 174.

60   Clements, p. 181. Wilson tapped Herbert Hoover to run the Food Administration, despite Hoover being a Republican. Hoover would elevate his reputation into the stratosphere through his leadership acumen on food—from production to conservation to feeding millions—at home and abroad during WWI and its aftermath.

61   Quoted in Clements, p. 183.

62   Morison, *Volume Three*, pp. 215-17.

63   Weisman, p. 341.

64   John W. Dean, *Warren G. Harding* (New York: Times Books, 2004), 57.

65   Dean, pp. 32-41.

66   Dean, p. 97.

67   Weisman, p. 343.

68   Morison, *Volume Three*, p. 278.

69   Morison, *Volume Three*, p. 277.

70   Quoted in Robert Sobel. *Coolidge: An American Enigma* (Washington, DC: Regnery Publishing, 1998), 4-5.

71   Sobel, p. 75.

72   Quoted in Sobel, p. 9; President Coolidge's Sixth Annual Message, December 4, 1928.

73   Will Rogers quoted in Morison, *Volume Three*, p. 281.

74   In this section, US economic statistics are from MeasuringWorth comparators and US fiscal information is from the US Census Bureau, "Bicentennial Edition, Historical Statistics of the United States, Colonial Times to 1970" (Washington, DC: Department of Commerce, 1975).

75   In exact amounts: in 1920, spending fell by two-thirds to $6.4 billion. In 1921, it fell another 20 percent to $5.1 billion. In 1922, it fell 35 percent to $3.3 billion.

Chapter 6

1   Samuel E. Morison, *The Oxford History of the American People, Volume One* (New York: Mentor Books, 1972), 85.

2   Morison, *Volume One*, p. 109.

3 Ludwig von Mises, *Socialism: An Economic and Sociological Analysis*, trans. J. Kahane (Mansfield Centre: Martino Publishing, 2012), 15.

4 Mises, p. 15.

5 Mises cogently shows how the terms were used interchangeably by Marx and by the early Marxist parties. He also explains the later differentiating between the two as being part of the infighting between factions in the early USSR. See: Mises, pp. 543-549.

6 Marx identified the industrial working class, or proletariat, of capitalism as being the revolutionary driver; while Lenin and Mao both led revolutions in countries where agriculture dominated their economies.

7 Morison, *Volume One*, p. 85.

8 Daniel J. Flynn, *A Conservative History of the American Left* (New York: Crown Forum, 2008), 11-12.

9 Flynn, p. 12

10 MeasuringWorth is an unequaled tool for calculating relative values over time. Its relative worth comparators are used extensively in this chapter to calculate nominal, real GDP, and real GDP per capita over time. According to its website, it "evolved as a spinoff from the EH.Net website that was created in the 1990s by Samuel H. Williamson (with the help of a grant from the NSF) to be a source of useful tools for economic historians...The MeasuringWorth Foundation is a non-profit corporation. The Foundation is the owner and operator of the MeasuringWorth website." Unless otherwise noted, all citations of US GDP (nominal and real), real GDP per capita, and population were obtained from https://measuringworth.com.

11 Department of Commerce, "Bicentennial Edition: Historical Statistics of the United States, Colonial Times to 1970" (Washington, DC: Department of Commerce, 1975).

12 Alexis de Tocqueville, *Democracy in America*, trans. George Lawrence, ed. J.P. Mayer (Garden City: Anchor Books, 1969), xiv.

13 Tocqueville, p. 9.

14 J. Hector St. John de Crèvecoeur, *Letters from an American Farmer* (New York: Penguin Books, 1986), 67.

15 Tocqueville, pp. 60-64.

16 Tocqueville, p. 177.

17 Tocqueville, p. 177.

342 Endnotes

18   Tocqueville, p. 248.

19   Tocqueville, p. 238.

20   For example, obviously, de Tocqueville's remarks here did not encompass or consider those enslaved, though de Tocqueville does write of them elsewhere in his work.

21   Among the many leaders with whom Owen met were presidents Monroe and John Quincy Adams.

22   Flynn, p. 20.

23   Flynn, p. 32.

24   Flynn, p. 73.

25   MeasuringWorth comparator for this period.

26   Rochdale cooperatives operated on a set of principles that centered on how a cooperative should function, its membership, and its aims.

27   Andrew McKay and Martin Abrahamsen, "Helping Farmers Build Cooperatives: The Evolution of Farmer Cooperative Service" (Washington, DC: Farmer Cooperative Service, USDA, 1962), 6.

28   Benjamin Hibbard, *Marketing Agricultural Products* (New York: Appleton and Co., 1921), p. 34 and Martin Abrahamsen and Claud Scroggs, eds., *Agricultural Cooperation* (Minneapolis: University of Minnesota Press, 1957), 73.

29   Joseph Knapp, *The Rise of American Cooperative Enterprise: 1620-1920* (Danville: Interstate Publishers, 1969), 437.

30   Abrahamsen and Scroggs, p. 58.

31   David Montgomery, "Chapter 3: Labor in the Industrial Era," in *Bicentennial History of the American Worker* (Washington, DC: US Department of Labor, 1976), 6.

32   Montgomery, p. 1.

33   Among the many examples: The Greenback Party, The Wheel, The Brothers of Freedom. Carl Taylor, *The Farmers' Movement: 1620-1920* (Westpoint: Greenwood Press 1953), 205.

34   Donald Talbot and Ross Hadwiger, *The Policy Process in American Agriculture* (San Francisco: Chandler Publishing, 1968), 1, 90.

35   Robert McMath, *Populist Vanguard: A History of the Farmers' Alliance* (Chapel Hill: University of North Carolina: Press, 1975), 3.

36   Hibbard, p. 223 and McMath, pp. 30 and 151.

37 McMath, p. 151.

38 Flynn, p. 91.

39 Montgomery, p. 8.

40 Flynn, p. 95. The following description of the Haymarket riot is also from Flynn, p. 95.

41 Such as the six-month Homestead strike in Pennsylvania aimed at Andrew Carnegie. Montgomery, p. 8.

42 Montgomery, p. 9.

43 Morison, Samuel E. *The Oxford History of the American People, 1789 through Reconstruction, Volume Two* (New York: New American Library, 1972), 106.

44 McMath, p. 156.

45 Norman Pollock, ed. *The Populist Mind* (Indianapolis: Bobbs-Merrill Co., 1967), xxii.

46 Pollock, p. xliv and Richard Hofstadter, *The Age of Reform* (New York: Alfred Knopf, 1955), 34.

47 Hofstadter, p. 58.

48 Flynn, p. 81.

49 Flynn, p. 90.

50 Flynn, p. 114.

51 Flynn, pp. 146-8.

52 MeasuringWorth comparator for the period.

53 Thomas Greer, *American Social Reform Movements Since 1865* (Port Washington: Kennikat Press, 1965), 213.

54 Knapp, p. 100.

55 Knapp, p. 308.

56 One holdover was the Nonpartisan League, which was formed around World War I in North Dakota from Alliance and Populist Party remnants. The NPL had some electoral success but effectively ended within a few years.

57 As one example, the American Society of Equity sought to reduce crop production to drive up crop prices in 1908 and used vigilante action to enforce it in Kentucky. Abrahamsen and Scroggs, p. 23.

58 Knapp, p. 113.

59 Cooperative activist Aaron Sapiro's approach envisioned that farmers one day could use cooperatives to gain monopoly power and set prices, not merely take them. The Sapiro approach was pursued well into the 1920s before it was ultimately replaced by the Nourse approach, which valued promoting economic efficiency. Randall Torgerson, *Producer Power at the Bargaining Table* (Columbia: University of Missouri Press, 1970), 95.

60 David Truman, *The Governmental Process* (New York: Knopf, 1951), 107.

61 McKay and Abrahamsen, p. 78.

62 Abrahamsen and Scroggs, p. 245.

63 McKay and Abrahamsen, p. 79.

64 Philip Taft, "Chapter 4: Workers of a New Century," in *Bicentennial History of the American Worker* (Washington, DC: US Department of Labor, 1976), 2.

65 Taft, p. 3.

66 Taft, p. 2.

67 Taft, p. 7.

68 Taft, p. 9.

69 Flynn, pp. 164-168.

70 Flynn, pp. 156-7.

71 Flynn, p. 187.

72 For those interested in a thorough discourse on the differentiation's origins with the Soviet Union's infighting, von Mises gives an excellent description in the Epilogue to his book *Socialism.*

73 Twelve years later, in 1924, headed by Senator Robert La Follette, the Progressive Party won only La Follette's home state of Wisconsin, 13 electoral votes, and just 4.8 million votes overall—16.6 percent of the total.

74 Hofstadter, p. 3.

75 Hofstadter, pp. 5 and 144.

76 Hofstadter, pp. 232-236.

77 1924 Progressive Platform.

78 MeasuringWorth comparator for the period.

79 Flynn, p. 193.

80 MeasuringWorth comparator for the period.

81 John Shover, *Cornbelt Rebellion: The Farmers' Holiday Association* (Urbana: University of Illinois, Press, 1965), 16. Similar conditions of indebtedness had prompted Shays' Rebellion a century and a half earlier.

82 Shover, p. 37.

83 Grant McConnell, *The Decline of Agrarian Democracy* (Berkeley: University of California Press, 1953), 100.

84 McConnell, p. 84.

85 Irving Bernstein, "Chapter 5: Americans in Depression and War," in *Bicentennial History of the American Worker* (Washington, DC: US Department of Labor, 1976), 1.

86 Named after Senator Robert Wagner, NY-D.

87 For a contemporary comparison, during the COVID-19 lockdowns the monthly unemployment rate peaked at 14.8 percent in April 2020; a year later in April 2021, while still above the pre-lockdown level, the rate was just 6.1 percent.

88 Hofstadter, p. 302.

89 Conrad Black, *Franklin Delano Roosevelt: Champion of Freedom* (New York: PublicAffairs, 2003), 272, 341. As Black also notes, FDR ignored the Left's call to nationalize the banks, and when Senator Robert La Follette Jr. and other reformers called for more aggressive reforms, Roosevelt refused (pp. 275 and 283). Black also quotes FDR as complaining to the propertied class "that I am the best friend the profit system ever had" (p. 409).

90 Bernstein, p. 2.

91 Bernstein, p. 5.

92 Bernstein, p. 7.

93 Flynn, p. 212.

94 Another example to underscore the administration and its party's adversarial stance to the already unpopular socialist Left is the 1938 creation of the House Un-American Activities Committee under Rep. Martin Dies, a Texas Democrat. HUAC was responsible for investigating subversive activities of individuals and organizations—particularly those associated with communism. This was hardly contrary to FDR's own feelings. Black

quotes Roosevelt's June 24, 1938, fireside chat: "Communism ... is just as dangerous as Fascism." Black, p. 455.

95 Werner Sombart, *Why is There No Socialism in the United States?* (London: The McMillan Press, 1976), 106.

96 Saul Alinsky, *Rules for Radicals* (New York: Vintage Books, 1989), xviii-xix.

97 Department of Commerce, *Bicentennial Edition: Historical Statistics of the United States, Colonial Times to 1970* (Washington, DC: Department of Commerce, 1975).

98 D.H. Oliver, "Antitrust, Bargaining, and Cooperatives: ABCs of the National Agricultural Marketing and Bargaining Act of 1971," *Harvard Journal on Legislation* 9 (1971-72): 514.

99 Such as had existed earlier with the Greenback Party and the Populist Party.

100 Wesley McCune, *Who's Behind Our Farm Policy?* (New York: Frederick Praeger Inc., 1956), 59.

101 William Block, *The Separation of the Farm Bureau and the Extension Service* (Urbana: University of Illinois Press, 1960), 120.

102 Leo Troy, "Trade Union Membership: 1897-1962" (Washington, DC: National Bureau of Economic Research, 1965), 1.

103 To address work stoppages both Roosevelt and Truman resorted to facility seizures seventy-one times from 1941 to 1952. Peter Kihss, "Seizure of Mines," *New York Times*, March 6, 1978.

104 Jack Barbash, "Chapter 6: Unions and Rights in the Space Age" in *Bicentennial History of the American Worker* (Washington, DC: US Department of Labor, 1976), 1.

105 Melvin W. Reder, "The Rise and Fall of Unions: The Public Sector and the Private," *Journal of Economics* 2, no. 2 (1988): 106. The Bureau of Labor Statistics reported that in 2023 union membership among public-sector workers was 32.5 percent versus 6 percent for private sector workers. BLS also states that total union membership rate in 1983 was 20.1 percent. Bureau of Labor Statistics, "Economic News Release: Union Members Survey," January 23, 2024.

106 Barbash, p. 5.

107 Reder, p. 106.

108 Wallace came in far behind even La Follette's 1924 Progressive run, when he won 4.8 million popular votes and 13 electoral votes.

109 Calvin D. Linton, ed., *The Bicentennial Almanac: 200 Years of America* (Nashville: Thomas Nelson. Inc., 1975).

110 Flynn, p. 303.

111 Tom Hayden, "Port Huron Statement" (Students for a Democratic Society, 1962).

112 Recently this most notably occurred in 2000 when Ralph Nader's presidential bid drew away enough votes from Democrat Al Gore to swing Florida, and thereby the nation, to Republican George W. Bush. Overlooked too is the impact that Libertarian candidate Jo Jorgenson (1.9 million votes and 1.18 percent of the popular vote total) had in the 2020 election: had Jorgenson's popular votes gone to Trump, this would have flipped the states of Arizona, Georgia, and Wisconsin. Federal Elections 2020, Federal Election Commission, Washington, DC, 2022.

113 Some specific examples: the Muckrakers of the early 20th century and the counterculture of the 1960s.

114 Richard Cyert and James March, *A Behavioral Theory of the Firm* (Engelwood Cliffs: Prentice-Hall, 1963), 52.

Chapter 7

1 In 2021, total government spending was 29.7 percent of GDP. In 2022, it was 24.8 percent, and in 2023 it was 22.7 percent. Congressional Budget Office, Historical Budget Data, February 2024, Table 1a.

2 MeasuringWorth comparators are used for these periods in this paragraph.

3 Office of Management and Budget, Historical Tables, Table 1.2.

4 Department of Commerce, *Bicentennial Edition: Historical Statistics of the United States, Colonial Times to 1970* (Washington, DC: Department of Commerce, 1975). and MeasuringWorth comparators.

5 Federal spending would surpass 10 percent of GDP four times between 1933 and 1941 (when it topped out at 11.7 percent); it would not fall below 7.6 percent (1938) during those years. OMB Historical Tables, Table 1.2.

6 Entitlement spending is defined as: "Authority to make payments (including loans and grants) for which budget authority is not provided in advance

by appropriation acts to any person or government if, under the provisions of the law containing such authority, the US government is legally required to make the payments to persons or governments that meet the requirements established by law (2 USC § 622(9))." US Government Accountability Office, "A Glossary of Budget Terms Used in the Federal Budget Process," Washington, DC, September 2005.

7   Ron Chernow, *The House of Morgan: An American Banking Dynasty and the Rise of Modern Finance* (New York: Grove Press, 2010), 312-313.

8   Calvin Linton, ed. *The Bicentennial Almanac: 200 Years of America* (Nashville: Thomas Nelson, Inc., 1975), 318.

9   Department of Commerce, *Bicentennial Edition: Historical Statistics of the United States, Colonial Times to 1970.*

10 MeasuringWorth comparator for this period.

11 "The Federal Revenue Act of 1932 almost doubled tax rates—again, the perfect medicine to kill the patient." Chernow, p. 347.

12 Milton Friedman and Anna Schwartz, *A Monetary History of the United States: 1867-1960* (Princeton: Princeton University Press, 1993), 693.

13 Friedman and Schwartz, p. 693.

14 Friedman and Schwartz, pp. 10-11.

15 Friedman and Schwartz, pp. 688-89.

16 Glen Jeansonne, *Herbert Hoover: A Life* (New York: New American Library. 2016), 287.

17 America's nominal GDP fell 12 percent in 1930, 16 percent in 1931, 23 percent in 1932, and 4 percent in 1933. Nominal and real GDP data in this paragraph are from MeasuringWorth comparators for the period.

18 Even in real terms, the economy did not do so until 1936.

19 In 1937, the economy dropped again, 6 percent in nominal terms and 3.3 percent in real terms.

20 Jeansonne, p. 312.

21 Historical fiscal data from the Department of Commerce, "Bicentennial Edition: Historical Statistics of the United States, Colonial Times to 1970."

22 Conrad Black, *Franklin Delano Roosevelt: Champion of Freedom* (New York: Public Affairs, 2003), 233.

23 As OMB's Historical Tables show, in 1931, outlays increased to 4.2 percent, and 6.8 percent in 1932—proportionately large but insufficient. Table 1.2.

24   FDR is quoted as saying "[It] has accentuated the stagnation of the eco-
     nomic life of the people. It has added to the ranks of the unemployed." John
     F. Cogan, *The High Cost of Good Intentions: A History of U.S. Entitlement
     Programs* (Stanford: Stanford University Press, 2017), 70.

25   Cogan, p. 73.

26   William E. Leuchtenburg, *The American President: From Teddy Roosevelt
     to Bill Clinton* (New York: Oxford University Press, 2015), 132.

27   Leuchtenburg, p. 132.

28   Leuchtenburg, p. 134.

29   Leuchtenburg, p. 135.

30   By the time he signed the bill, which amounted to $116 million, the number
     of unemployed Americans had leapt to 7 million. Linton, p. 322.

31   Leuchtenburg, p. 138.

32   Jeansonne, p. 256.

33   Linton, p. 328.

34   OMB Historical Tables 1.1 and 1.2.

35   Linton, p. 330.

36   Linton, p. 330.

37   OMB Historical Table 1.2.

38   Black, pp. 342-343.

39   Black, p. 342.

40   Geoffrey Kollmann, "Social Security: Summary of Major Changes in the
     Cash Benefits Program," in *CRS Legislative Histories 2* (Congressional
     Research Service, Library of Congress, 2000), 4-5.

41   Kollmann, p. 4.

42   Spending leapt to a high of 10.6 percent of GDP in 1934; it did not fall
     below 1938's 7.6 percent of GDP. OMB Historical Tables 1.1 and 1.2.

43   OMB Historical Table 1.1.

44   The US did not regain its 1929 GDP in nominal terms until 1941 and not in
     real terms until 1936. In between the two junctures, the economy shrunk
     in nominal and real terms in 1938. Source: MeasuringWorth comparators
     for this period.

45   Linton, pp. 347-352.

46   OMB Historical Table 1.1.

47   Library of Congress, Digital Collections, "Today in History—October 23, The Lend Lease Act."

48   Linton, p. 348.

49   Linton, p. 351.

50   OMB Historical Table 1.2.

51   In 1943, deficit spending hit 29.6 percent of GDP; in 1944, 22.2 percent; and in 1945, 21 percent. The deficit spending in 1943 surpassed the previous record for total federal government spending and 1944's and 1945's did not miss the mark by much. Source: Historical Tables 1.1 and 1.2. For earlier comparisons relative to GDP, MeasuringWorth comparators are used together with the Department of Commerce, *Bicentennial Edition: Historical Statistics of the United States, Colonial Times to 1970*.

52   Winston Churchill's Sinews of Peace speech at Westminster College in Fulton, Missouri, March 5, 1946.

53   On June 26, 1948, the US launched Operation Vittles, which the UK later joined. The airlift lasted until September 30. During this time, US and UK planes made over 278,000 airdrops with American crews flying over 189,000 flights over 600,000 flying hours and 92 million miles. Katie Lange, "The Berlin Airlift: What It Was, Its Importance in the Cold War," US Department of Defense, June 24, 2022.

54   Samuel E. Morison, *The Oxford History of the American People: Volume Three, 1869-1963* (New York: Mentor Books, 1972), 426.

55   Federal spending peaked at 42.7 percent of GDP during World War II, but it never fell below 11.4 percent (in 1948)—roughly what it was in 1941—as compared to 3.4 percent in 1930. OMB Historical Tables 1.2.

56   Defense spending is from OMB Historical Table 6.1; international affairs spending is from OMB Historical Table 3.1; and Social Security and retirement spending is from OMB Historical Table 11.1.

57   OMB Historical Table 1.2 for federal spending 1940-1964; MeasuringWorth comparator and the Department of Commerce, *Bicentennial Edition: Historical Statistics of the United States, Colonial Times to 1970* for prior years.

58   Leuchtenburg, pp. 327-328.

59   "In real terms, spending in 1972 was between four and five times what it had been in 1965." Eli Ginzberg and Robert M. Solow, *The Great Society: Lessons for the Future* (New York: Basic Books, 1974), 11.

60   Ginzberg and Solow, p. 8.

61   Cogan, p. 195.

62   P.L., pp. 89-97.

63   Cogan, p. 200.

64   The term "medically needy" includes "members of single-parent households, disabled people, and elderly people"; states could also "cover medically needy people who were not living in poverty and would otherwise qualify for public assistance." Cogan, p. 202.

65   Cogan, p. 200.

66   Cogan, p. 206.

67   David McCullough, *Truman* (New York: Simon and Schuster, 1992), 984.

68   Social Security, which was three decades old when Medicare and Medicaid began, saw policymakers follow the pattern of increasing revenues to meet accelerating costs, and then using any surpluses to justify increasing benefits. Benefit increases would follow, as occurred in 1967. As Cogan writes: "Again, surplus Social Security revenues provided the fuel for a benefit hike." With a surplus available, President Johnson called benefits "grossly inadequate"; after back-and-forth with Congress, legislation was passed increasing benefits: retirees who had earned lower wages received a 25 percent boost, while retirees who earned higher wages received an 11 percent increase. Cogan, p. 205.

69   Cogan, p. 232.

70   Cogan, p. 232.

71   Cogan, p. 232.

72   Cogan, p. 232.

73   Cogan, pp. 239-240.

74   Cogan, p. 244.

75   Cogan, p. 262.

76   Cogan, p. 263.

77   OMB Historical Tables, Tables 8.1 and 8.3.

78   OMB Historical Tables, Tables 8.1 and 8.3.

79   OMB Historical Tables, Table 8.4.

80 In 1965, defense spending equaled 7.2 percent of GDP; in 2000, it had dropped to 2.9 percent. OMB Historical Table 8.4.

81 OMB Historical Tables, Table 8.4.

82 OMB Historical Tables, Table 8.3.

83 Congressional Budget Office, "The Budget and Economic Outlook: 2024 to 2034," Washington, DC, February 2024. Also, MeasuringWorth comparators and the Department of Commerce, *Bicentennial Edition: Historical Statistics of the United States, Colonial Times to 1970* for Civil War spending as a percentage of GDP and OMB Historical Tables, Table 1.2 for New Deal's pre-World War II years.

84 OMB Historical Tables, Table 1.2.

85 According to CBO's Historical Budget Data, February 2024, federal government spending reached a high of 30.8 percent of GDP in 2020, 29.7 percent in 2021, and 24.8 percent in 2022. In 2024, spending as a percent of GDP is projected to reach 23.1 percent. These levels are comparable to the wartime year of 1942 (23.8 percent) and 1946's post-war spending (24.2 percent), OMB Table 1.2.

86 The full quote, which showcases the unanimity of this prediction, reads: "The federal government faces an unsustainable fiscal future. At the end of fiscal year 2021, debt held by the public was about 100 percent of gross domestic product (GDP), a 33 percent increase from fiscal year 2019. Projections from the Office of Management and Budget and the Department of the Treasury, the Congressional Budget Office, and GAO all show that current fiscal policy is unsustainable over the long term." US Government Accountability Office, "The Nation's Fiscal Health: Federal Action Critical to Pivot toward Fiscal Sustainability," Washington, DC: Annual Report to Congress, May 2022.

87 US Government Accountability Office, "The Nation's Fiscal Health . . ." p. 1.

88 Congressional Budget Office, "The Budget and Economic Outlook."

89 Congressional Budget Office, Historical Budget Data, February 2024.

90 US Government Accountability Office, "The Nation's Fiscal Health . . ." p. 8.

91 Congressional Budget Office, "The Budget and Economic Outlook."

92 US Government Accountability Office, "The Nation's Fiscal Health . . ." p. 4.

93 US Government Accountability Office, "The Nation's Fiscal Health . . ." p. 1.

94 Congressional Budget Office, "The Budget and Economic Outlook," 9.

95 Congressional Budget Office, "The Budget and Economic Outlook," 9.

96 Congressional Budget Office, "The Budget and Economic Outlook."

97 Victoria Guida, "Fed's Powell: 'Urgent' for US to Focus on Debt Sustainability," *Politico*, February 4, 2024.

98 Cogan, p. 223.

99 Cogan, p. 372.

100 Congressional Budget Office, "The Long-Term Budget Outlook," March 2024, p. 11.

101 Congressional Budget Office, "The Long-Term Budget Outlook," 34. The consequences of such a macro-level outcome flows down to individuals. As CBO states in the same report: "Consequently, they would be less productive, their compensation would be lower, and they would therefore be less inclined to work. Those effects would increase over time as federal borrowing grew" (p. 11).

102 Cogan, p. 287.

103 Actual percentage of households who received benefits from a federal entitlement program was 49 percent. Cogan, pp. 287-288.

Chapter 8

1 Lewis Faulk, et al., "Nonprofit Trends and Impacts 2021," Center on Nonprofits and Philanthropy, Urban Institute, 2021.

2 Institutions categorized as (501 (c) (3) and 501 (c) (4).

3 Murray Weitzman, et. al., *The New Nonprofit Almanac: The Essential Facts and Figures for Managers, Researchers, and Volunteers* (New York: John Wiley and Sons Inc., 2002), 94.

4 Full question from *Gallup*: "If your party nominated a generally well-qualified person for president who happened to be a socialist would you vote for that person?" Lydia Saad, "Felonies, Old Age Heavily Count Against Candidates," *Gallup*, January 26, 2024.

5 This and all quotations in the following paragraph are from James Madison, "Federalist Paper Number Ten" in *The Federalist Papers* (New York: Mentor Books, 1961).

6 Mancur Olson, *The Logic of Collective Action: Public Goods and the Theory of Groups* (Cambridge: Harvard University Press, 1965), 51.

7   Jack L. Walker, "The Origin and Maintenance of Interest Groups in America," *American Political Science Review* 77 (1983), p. 392.

8   Jack L. Walker, "Pathways to Influence in American Politics," in *Mobilizing Interest Groups in America: Patrons, Professions, and Social Movements* (Ann Arbor: University of Michigan, 1991), 10.

9   By 1919, the NPL had 250,000 dues-paying members and was organized in 13 states: Charles Russell, *The Story of the Non-Partisan League* (New York: Harper & Brothers Publishers, 1920), 323.

10 Trudy Peterson, ed. *Farmers, Bureaucrats, and Middlemen: Historical Perspectives on American Agriculture* (Washington, DC: Howard University Press, 1980), 81-95.

11 Daniel J. Flynn, *A Conservative History of the American Left* (New York: Crown Forum, 2008) and Ivan Emelianoff, *Economic Theory of Cooperation* (Ann Arbor: Edwards Brothers Inc., 1942), 7.

12 James Gregory, "Remapping the American Left: A History of Radical Discontinuity," in *Labor: Studies in Working Class History* 17, no. 2 (2020): 11-45, 17.

13 Gregory, p. 18.

14 Jack L. Walker, "The Mobilization of Political Interests in America," in *Mobilizing Interest Groups in America: Patrons, Professions, and Social Movements* (Ann Arbor: University of Michigan, 1991), 27.

15 George W. Ladd, *Agricultural Bargaining Power* (Ames: Iowa State Press, 1964), 102-103.

16 Jim Hightower, *Hard Tomatoes, Hard Times* (Cambridge: Schenkman Publishing Co., 1973), 102.

17 Joseph Knapp, *The Rise of the American Cooperative Enterprise: 1620-1920* (Danville: Interstate Publishers, 1969), 3.

18 Andrew McKay and Martin Abrahamsen, "Helping Farmers Build Cooperatives: The Evolution of the Farmer Cooperative Service" (Washington, DC: Farmer Cooperative Service, USDA, 1962), 3.

19 Donald Talbot and Ross Hadwiger, *The Policy Process in American Agriculture* (San Francisco: Chandler Publishing, 1968), 8.

20 O.M. Kile, *The Farm Bureau Through Three Decades* (Baltimore: Waverly Press, 1948), 100.

21   Martin Abrahamsen, *Cooperative Business Enterprise* (New York: McGraw-Hill, 1976), 90. The first large national agricultural organization, founded by O.H. Kelly on December 4, 1867, in Washington, DC. A simply inscribed stone marks the spot on the National Mall.

22   Olson, p. 149.

23   Hightower, p. 236.

24   Fumiaki Kubo, "Henry A. Wallace and Radical Politics in the New Deal: Farm Programs and a Vision of the New American Political Economy," *The Japanese Journal of American Studies*, no. 4 (1991), p. 42.

25   In regard to labor unions, the federal government's Wagner Act solved their free-rider problem.

26   Palmer's largest raid occurred on January 2, 1920, and resulted in the arrest of 3,000 suspects. According to a January 3 frontpage *New York Tribune* article: Palmer "personally directed the raids made tonight in radical centers throughout the country ... in nearly 50 cities in all parts of the country ... All of those arrested were aliens, and all were members of the Communist party ... They will be turned over to the immigration officials of the Department of Labor for deportation."

27   Gregory, p. 34.

28   William Block, *The Separation of the Farm Bureau and the Extension Service* (Urbana: University of Illinois Press, 1960) and E.P. Roy, *Cooperatives: Development, Principles, and Management* (Danville: Interstate Publishers, 1976), 57. President Truman signed The Farmers Home Administration Act of 1946 that formally abolished the FSA.

29   As the previous chapter's discussion of the Farmers' Holiday Association noted, an agricultural movement *had* arisen during the Depression, but it had existed in a different section of the country, had been comprised of relatively wealthy farmers—not tenants (Shover, p. 6)—and had vanished after the AAA payment program began. John Shover, *Cornbelt Rebellion: The Farmers' Holiday Association* (Urbana: University of Illinois Press, 1965).

30   Gordon Adams, *The Politics of Defense Contracting: The Iron Triangle* (New York: Routledge, 2019).

31   John F. Cogan, *The High Cost of Good Intentions: A History of U.S. Federal Entitlement Programs* (Stanford: Stanford University Press, 2017), 39.

32   William Browne, "Farm Organizations and Agribusiness," in *Food Policy and Farm Program,* ed. Donald Talbot and Ross Hadwiger (New York: Academy of Political Science, 1982), 201.

33   Both the NIRA and the AAA extended executive branch authority a great deal and had broad objectives. Theda Skocpol and Kenneth Finegold, "State Capacity and Economic Intervention in the Early New Deal," *Political Science Quarterly* 97, no. 2 (1982): 255-278.

34   Henry A. Wallace's father, Henry C. Wallace, was himself a former Secretary of Agriculture (1921-1924).

35   Kubo, pp. 51-67.

36   Edwin Nourse, Joseph Davis, and John Black, "Three Years of the Agricultural Adjustment Administration," Brookings Institution, 1937.

37   Kubo, pp. 51-67.

38   Research for this paragraph relied on Kubo pp. 49-55.

39   Kubo, p. 56.

40   Grant McConnell, *The Decline of Agrarian Democracy* (Berkeley: University of California Press, 1953), 100.

41   Talbot and Hadwiger, p. 12 and Kile, p. 100.

42   Flynn, p. 239 and Ludwig von Mises, *Socialism: An Economic and Sociological Analysis*, trans. J. Kahane (Mansfield Centre: Martino Publishing, 2012), 551.

43   Walker, "The Origin and Maintenance of Interest Groups in America," p. 404. Allan Cigler and Burdette Loomis, eds., *Interest Group Politics*, Third Edition (Washington DC: Congressional Quarterly Press, 1991), 22.

44   Olson, pp. 111-131, provides an excellent short summary of pluralism's origins and development.

45   Cigler and Loomis, p. 4.

46   Jeffrey Berry, *The Interest Group Society* (Boston: Little, Brown and Co., 1984), 9.

47   Berry, p. 9.

48   Cigler and Loomis, p. 28.

49   Cogan, p. 221.

50   Cogan, p. 221.

51   Eli Ginzberg and Robert M. Solow, eds., *The Great Society: Lessons for the Future* (New York: Basic Books, 1974), 9.

52　Walker, "The Mobilization of Political Interests in America," p. 23.

53　Ginzberg and Solow, p. 9

54　EOA, p. 1.

55　EOA, p. 515.

56　EOA, p. 516.

57　EOA, p. 521. As Black observes, "This was a glimpse of the true Roosevelt. He was never a bleeding heart." Three decades later, Johnson's entire administration would be. Conrad Black, *Franklin Delano Roosevelt: Champion of Freedom* (New York: PublicAffairs, 2003), 316.

58　Walker, "The Mobilization of Political Interests in America," p. 31.

59　Thomas Gais, Mark Peterson, and Jack Walker, "Interest Groups, Iron Triangles, and Representative Institutions," *British Journal of Politics* 14 (1984): 161-185, p. 183.

60　Theda Skocpol and Kenneth Finegold, "State Capacity and Economic Intervention in the Early New Deal," p. 269.

61　Walker, *Mobilizing Interest Groups in America: Patrons, Professions, and Social Movements*, p. 139.

62　OMB Historical Tables, Table 11.1.

63　The actual number is 29,997: National Center for Charitable Statistics and IRS. The Nonprofit Almanac provides a multidimensional picture of what occurred in the nonprofit sector. By any metric, the nonprofit sector surged: Overall (nonprofit operating expenses on a per capita basis almost tripled from 1959-1998); in employee growth, in volunteer increase, relative to the business sector, and relative to the overall economy (as a percentage of GDP, nonprofit operating expenses went from 3.5 percent in 1959 to 8.5 percent in 1999). Murray Weitzman, et. al., *The New Nonprofit Almanac: The Essential Facts and Figures for Managers, Researchers, and Volunteers* (New York: John Wiley and Sons Inc., 2002), 26.

64　In dollar amounts: from $29.5 billion in 1977 to a staggering $207.8 billion in 1997. with an annual rate of change over the period of 6 percent. Weitzman, pp. 94, 100, and 102.

65　Going from $5.6 billion in 1977 to $40.1 billion in 1998. Weitzman, p. 96.

66　Jeffrey M. Berry and David F. Arons, *A Voice for Nonprofits*, Brookings Institution, 2005, 5.

67　Berry and Arons, p. 23.

68   HEW oversaw a broad range of federal social services from 1953-1979, then later became the Department of Health and Human Services. Spending figures are from Berry and Arons, p. 13.

69   Berry and Arons, p. 19.

70   Berry and Arons, p. 13 and Cogan.

71   Berry and Arons, pp. 20-21.

72   Berry, p. 88 also underscores patronage's particular importance for citizen groups, citing the role of private foundations such as the Ford Foundation.

73   Walker, "The Origin and Maintenance of Interest Groups in America," pp. 398-404.

74   Berry, p. 31.

75   Berry, p. 26.

76   Berry, p. 30.

77   Berry, p. 29.

78   Gaius, Peterson, Walker, p. 173.

79   Walker, "Mobilizing Interest Groups in America," pp. 139-140.

80   Walker, "Mobilizing Interest Groups in America," p. 127.

81   Walker, "Mobilizing Interest Groups in America," p. 126.

82   Walker, "Mobilizing Interest Groups in America," p. 126.

83   Walker, "Mobilizing Interest Groups in America," p. 130.

84   e.g., "group mobilization based on causes ranging from civil rights to women's issues to the environment to consumer protection." Cigler and Loomis, p. 21.

85   Gregory, p. 14 and p. 30.

86   Pew Research Center, "Retro-Politics: The Political Typology: Version 3.0" (Washington, DC, November 11, 1999), 1.

87   *Pew*, 1999, p. 2.

88   Defined by *Pew* as the 14 percent of registered voters with "mixed ideological values" and "much stronger ties to unions," "more financially satisfied" and with "a penchant for partisan defection." *Pew*, 1999, p. 3.

89   Defined by *Pew* as "social welfare loyalists." *Pew*, 1999, p. 3.

90   Defined by *Pew*, 1999, as "Clintonites," as this survey notably coincided with the conclusion of Clinton's eight-year presidency. *Pew*, 1999, p. 3.

91   Defined by *Pew* as "Secular progressives." *Pew*, 1999, p. 3.

92   *Pew*, 1999, p. 2.

93   Pew Research Center, "Beyond Red vs. Blue" (Washington, DC, May 10, 2005), part 1, p. 1.

94   Defined by *Pew* as the most secular, and who take the most liberal views on social issues. *Pew*, 2005, part 1, p. 7.

95   *Pew*, 2005, part 1, p. 5.

96   *Pew* notes that "religious orientation and conservative views set this group apart." *Pew*, 2005, part 1, p. 8.

97   Defined by *Pew* as: "Least financially secure of all the groups, these voters are very anti-business, and strong supporters of government efforts to help the needy." *Pew*, 2005, part 1, p. 8.

98   *Pew*, 2005, part 1, p. 8.

99   *Pew*, 2005, part 2, p. 3.

100 *Pew*, 2005, part 4, p. 5.

101 *Pew*, 2005, part 5, p. 5.

102 *Pew*, 2005, part 5, p. 7.

103 Pew Research Center, "Beyond Red vs. Blue: The Political Typology" (Washington, DC, June 26, 2014), 3.

104 Defined by *Pew* as "Highly educated and affluent, Solid Liberals strongly support the social safety net and take very liberal positions on virtually all issues." *Pew*, 2014, p. 10.

105 Defined by *Pew* as those who "combine strong support for activist government with conservative attitudes on many social issues." *Pew*, 2014, p. 9.

106 Defined by *Pew* as "Young, well-educated and financially comfortable, [they] have very liberal attitudes on many issues ... are supportive of an activist government, but wary of expanding the social safety net." *Pew*, 2014, p. 7.

107 *Pew*, 2014, appendix 1, pp. 10-11.

108 37 percent of "Faith and Family Left" were self-described conservatives and 56 percent of "Next Generation Left" said the "government cannot afford to do much more to help the needy." *Pew*, 2014, appendix 1, p. 7.

109 *Pew*, 2014, appendix 1, p. 11.

110 Pew Research Center, "Political Typology Reveals Deep Fissures on the Right and Left" (Washington, DC, October 24, 2017), p. 2.

111 Defined by *Pew* as those who "strongly believe the economic system unfairly favors powerful interests and that business corporations make too much profit." *Pew*, 2017, p. 6.

112 Defined by *Pew* as those who "have liberal attitudes on most issues ... They stand out from other Democratic groups in their strong belief that hard work is enough for most people to get ahead." *Pew*, 2017, p. 7.

113 Defined by *Pew* as those who are "racially and ethnically diverse," they "voice strong support for the social safety net and further action on racial equality" but "take more conservative views ... on a number of issues." *Pew*, 2017, p. 5.

114 *Pew*, 2017, p. 5.

115 *Pew*, 2017, p. 5.

116 *Pew*, 2017, appendix 1, p. 8.

117 *Pew*, 2017, appendix 1, p. 9.

118 Pew Research Center, "Beyond Red vs. Blue: The Political Typology" (Washington, DC, November 9, 2021), part 2, p. 3.

119 Defined by *Pew* as those who hold "very liberal views across a range of issues" and "are more liberal than the other three Democratic-oriented groups on many issues." *Pew*, 2021, part 11, pp. 1-2.

120 Defined by *Pew* as those who hold "liberal views on most issues and over-whelmingly" vote Democratic but "aren't particularly enamored with the Democratic Party." *Pew*, 2021, part 8, p. 1.

121 Defined as "deeply liberal ... are the typology group most likely to see value in political compromise and tend to be more inclined toward more measured approaches to societal change." *Pew*, 2021, part 10, p. 1.

122 Defined by *Pew* as those who "generally favor policies that expand the social safety net and support higher taxes on corporations but ... are somewhat more hawkish ... on foreign policy and less liberal on immigration policy and some social issues." *Pew*, 2021, part 2, p. 4.

123 Broken down: 42% of the "Progressive Left" identified as "Very Liberal," while 37% identified as "Liberal." For the "Outsider Left," the breakdown was 20% and 27%, while "Establishment Liberals" identified as 12% "Very Liberal," 41% "Liberal." *Pew*, 2021, part 2, p. 3.

124 Of "Mainstay Democrats," 5% identified as "Very Liberal" and 35% as "Liberal." *Pew*, 2021, part 2, p. 3.

125 *Pew*, 2021, part 2, pp. 5-6.

126 *Pew*, 2021, part 2, p. 7.

127 *Pew*, 2021, part 2, p. 13.

128 Gregory, p. 14

129 Figures are from OMB Historical Tables, Table 6.1. Actual percentage: 16.1 percent.

130 CBO, Historical Budget Data, February 2024.

131 *Hamlet*, Act 1, Scene 2.

132 Cogan, p. 190.

133 Ladd, pp. 102-103.

134 Cogan, p. 190.

135 Saul Alinsky, *Rules for Radicals* (New York: Vintage Books, 1989), 113.

136 Berry, p. 31.

137 Walker, *Mobilizing Interest Groups in America.*

138 Flynn writes on the topic: "Most egregious of the OEO programs was the political skullduggery of the Community Action Program (CAP), which spread money to urban political machines and left-wing non-profits it designated as Community Action Agencies (CAA). In Syracuse, New York … The unelected radicals to whom they dispersed the money enlisted the services of Saul Alinsky, the professional disrupter … Alinsky received $10,000 in federal money to travel to Syracuse for a series of lectures in which he taught activists how to raise hell on the public's dime. When the police arrested the protesting welfare mothers whom the tax-funded activists had organized, the radicals used federal tax dollars to bail them out." Flynn, p. 278.

139 Cogan, p. 221.

140 Cogan, p. 217.

141 Cogan, p. 29.

142 Cogan, p. 230.

143 James L. Sundquist, *The Decline and Resurgence of Congress* (Washington, DC: Brookings Institution, 1981), 408.

144 Sundquist, p. 397.

145 Sundquist, p. 414.

146 Cogan, p. 301.

147 Cogan, p. 242

Chapter 9

1   In fiscal year 2023, expenditures were $6.1 trillion, 22.7 percent of GDP. Congressional Budget Office, "The Budget and Economic Outlook: 2024 to 2034" (Washington, DC: Congressional Budget Office, February 2024).

2   Obviously, not every government program generates a systemic failure. Many programs simply exist singly.

3   While an analogy, inflation is frequently a byproduct of socialist Left governments: as the economy craters, the official currency depreciates in value—often to the point of approaching worthlessness and being replaced by a black-market economy.

4   Murray Rothbard, *Classical Economics: An Austrian Perspective on the History of Economic Thought, Volume II* (Auburn: Ludwig von Mises Institute, 2012), 308-311.

5   Rothbard, *Volume II*, p. 308.

6   Daniel Flynn, *A Conservative History of the American Left* (New York: Crown Publishing, 2008), 22.

7   Flynn p. 31.

8   Flynn, p. 18.

9   Capitol Hill Organized Protest and Capitol Hill Autonomous Zone, respectively.

10   Ludwig von Mises, *Socialism: An Economic and Sociological Analysis*, trans. J. Kahane (Mansfield Centre: Martino Publishing, 2012).

11   See David Satter, "100 Years of Communism—and 100 Million Dead," *Wall Street Journal*, November 6, 2017. Numerous other publications arrive at similarly enormous totals—totals which are sadly continuously climbing. These deaths are the result of both deliberate actions (e.g., killing and imprisonments of political opponents), misguided ones (e.g., collectivization, such as occurred in the USSR in the 1930s, and forced industrialization, such as occurred with China's Great Leap Forward from 1958 into 1960), and of course, there is Communism's naked aggression via wars against other nations.

12   John Maynard Keynes, *A Tract on Monetary Reform* (Hawthorne: BN Publishing, 2008), 80.

13   Mises, p. 15.

14 The bolded text was intentionally stylized by the DSA. Democratic Socialists of America, "Democratic Socialists of America 2021 Platform," 2021.

15 CBO, Historical Budget Data, February 2024 and Congressional Budget Office, "The Budget and Economic Outlook: 2024 to 2034," Washington, DC: Congressional Budget Office, February 2024, and Congressional Budget Office. "The Long-Term Budget Outlook: 2024 to 2054." Washington, DC: Congressional Budget Office, March 2024.

16 CBO, "The Long-Term Budget Outlook," 17.

17 CBO, "The Long-Term Budget Outlook." Looking just at the decade 2025-2034, deficits will amount to $20 trillion; and deficits will "equal or exceed 5.2 percent of GDP in every year … Since at least 1930, deficits have not remained that large for more than five years in a row." CBO, "The Budget and Economic Outlook: 2024 to 2034," February 2024, p. 12. The following quotation is also from CBO, "The Long-Term Budget Outlook," March 2024. p. 9; and the figures also from this CBO source.

18 CBO, "The Long-Term Budget Outlook," March 2024, p. 11 and the following figures are also from this CBO source.

19 In their September 2023 report on Obamacare, health care actuaries Daniel Cruz and Greg Fann wrote in a paper for the conservative Paragon Health Institute: "The ACA individual market policies have produced far less enrollment at a much higher unit cost than projected. Federal spending on the ACA exchanges, totaling $60 billion in 2021, resulted in an increase of 1.6 million Americans covered under private insurance" while "non-group coverage increased by 2.9 million enrollees. The cost to taxpayers has been $36,798 per additional private insurance enrollee and $20,739 per additional non-group enrollee, which is more than triple CBO's original projections of $10,538 and $6,850, respectively." Daniel Cruz and Greg Fann, "The Shortcomings of the ACA Exchanges: Far Less Enrollment at a Much Higher Cost," Paragon Health Institute, September 2023.

20 School choice legislation allows parents flexibility to use state funds to educate their children. According to the Committee to Unleash Prosperity, over a dozen states adopted or expanded school choice programs in 2023; another fifteen could be on the way in 2024 and 2025. Nor are private

schools the only option: charter and home schooling also qualify for state funds under many states' school choice programs. Committee to Unleash Prosperity, *Unleash Prosperity Hotline*, Issue #924, December 28, 2023.

21 Joshua Q. Nelson, "Teachers Union Boss Randi Weingarten Claims School Choice 'Undermines Democracy,'" *Fox News*, December 19, 2023.

22 Mises, p. 17.

23 Joint Committee on Taxation, "Overview of the Federal Tax System as in Effect for 2023," Joint Committee of Taxation, May 11, 2023, JCX-9R-23, Tables A-6 and A-8 and Congressional Budget Office Historical Budget Data, February 2024.

24 Bernie Sanders, *Where We Go From Here: Two Years in the Resistance* (New York: Thomas Dunne, 2018), 242.

25 JCT, "Overview of the Federal Tax System as in Effect for 2023, Table A-6, p. 39 and Board of the Governors of the Federal Reserve System, "Distribution of the Household Wealth in the U.S. Since 1989," Federal Reserve, 2023.

26 Mises, p. 229.

27 Jordan Shilton, "Bernie Sanders and the 'Scandinavian Model,'" *World Socialist Website*, February 26, 2016.

28 Quoted in Lawrence Reed, "Don't Call Scandinavian Countries 'Socialist,'" Foundation for Economic Education, April 18, 2023, p. 1.

29 "2023 Index of Economic Freedom," The Heritage Foundation, 2023.

30 Reed, p. 2.

31 Shilton, p. 2

32 James Pethokoukis, "What Bernie Sanders and the Socialists Keep Getting Wrong About Scandinavia," American Enterprise Institute, February 3, 2020, 1.

33 Committee to Unleash Prosperity, *Unleash Prosperity Hotline*, Issue #760, April 27, 2023.

34 World Population Review, "Highest Taxed Countries: 2024," World Population Review website, 2024.

35 Megan Henney, "High-Tax Exodus Accelerates as More Americans Flee to Florida, Texas," *Fox News*, February 7, 2023.

36 World Bank Group Data, "Military Expenditure (% of GDP)," World Bank Group, 2022.

37   Congressional Budget Office, "The Budget and Economic Outlook."

38   Sanders, 2018, pp. 254-260.

39   Congressional Budget Office, "The Long-Term Budget Outlook," 20.

40   Congressional Budget Office, "The Long-Term Budget Outlook," 24.

41   Saul Elbein, "Biden Bucks Obama's Legacy on Climate and Gas with LNG Export Pause," *The Hill*, January 27, 2024.

42   Trevor Higgins, Rachel Chang, and Devon Lespier, "The Biden Administration Has Taken More Climate Action Than Any Other in History," The Center for American Progress, March 6, 2024.

43   Jon Levine, "Former AOC Aide Justine Medina Now Working as New York Communist Party Boss," *Fox News*, May 13, 2023.

Chapter 10

1   Milton Friedman is commonly associated with this acronym and discussed his use of it and its origins in a Hoover Institution essay published in 1993. Milton Friedman, "Why Government Is the Problem" (Stanford: Hoover Institution, Stanford University, 1993), 17.

2   Murray Rothbard, *Classical Economics: An Austrian Perspective on the History of Economic Thought, Volume II* (Auburn: Ludwig von Mises Institute, 2006), 299-307.

3   Ludwig von Mises, *Socialism: An Economic and Sociological Analysis*, trans. J. Kahane (Mansfield Centre: Martino Publishing, 2012), 560.

4   Mises, p. 510.

5   Mises, pp. 131-137.

6   Mises, p. 276.

7   Karl Marx and Frederick Engels, *Selected Works* (New York: International Publishers, 1977), 325.

8   In a famous two-and-a-half-minute *tour de force* video clip, Milton Friedman famously demonstrated how capitalism efficiently pulls together from around the world the resources necessary to make a pencil.

9   Werner Sombart, *Why is There No Socialism in the United States?* (London: The Macmillan Press, LTD, 1976), 106.

10   In 2020, Trump, too, faced a severe economic downturn as a result of the COVID pandemic and particularly the shutdowns that accompanied it.

And, while not an elected incumbent, ahead of the 1976 election Ford saw the economy shrink in 1974 and 1975 (according to Macrotrends' use of World Bank data: U.S. GDP Growth Rate, 1960-2024) and was plagued by high inflation throughout his short presidency—leading to his ill-advised WIN (Whip Inflation Now) campaign in 1974.

11   *CNN*, "2020 Exit Polls National Results," 2020.

12   It is worth noting that this has occurred even within the radical DSA following its pro-Palestinian stance in the wake of Hamas' terrorist attack on Israel on October 7, 2023.

13   Roy A. Medvedev and Zhores A. Medvedev, *Khrushchev: The Years in Power* (New York: W. W. Norton and Co., 1978), 66.

14   At the first Party Congress following Stalin's death, Nikita Khrushchev delivered a secret speech that discussed Stalin's excesses. Khrushchev said, "Later...Stalin, abusing his power more and more, began to fight eminent Party and Government leaders and to use terroristic methods against honest Soviet people." (Quoted in Frankland, p. 124.) Frankland writes regarding the confession: "The immediate effect of the speech was to throw the whole country into—as Khrushchev put it—a 'fever.'" Mark Frankland, *Khrushchev* (New York: Stein and Day, 1967), 126.

15   See Daniel Flynn, *A Conservative History of the American Left* (New York: Crown Publishing, 2008) for a thorough description of CPUSA's servile relationship to the USSR.

16   As called out by Pershing Square Capital Management CEO Bill Ackman in a January 3, 2024 post on *X* that details his investigation and experience with these at Harvard.

17   Michael Stott, Joe Daniels, and Vanessa Silva, "How Venezuela's Nicolás Maduro Outfoxed the West," *Financial Times*, March 4, 2023.

18   China's Belt and Road Initiative, a massive global infrastructure-development plan begun in 2013 under President Xi Jinping that has spent $1 trillion thus far and could total up to $8 trillion eventually. James McBride, Noah Berman, and Andrew Chatzky, "Backgrounder: China's Massive Belt and Road Initiative," (New York: Council on Foreign Relations, February 2, 2023).

19   As von Mises writes: "In a socialist community the State as organized society would form such a monopoly." Mises, p. 385.

20　As an example, how many of the 63 percent of Democrats who told *Gallup* they would support a democratic socialist as their party's presidential nominee would do so without the party's nomination? Lydia Saad, "Felonies, Old Age Heavily Count Against Candidates," *Gallup*, January 26, 2024.

Chapter 11

1　Lydia Saad, "Felonies, Old Age Heavily Count Against Candidates," *Gallup*, January 26, 2024.

2　Saad, "Felonies, Old Age Heavily Count Against Candidates."

3　"Today, more than 10 states and 180 cities and counties across the country have sanctuary policies," writes Domenic Vitiello in "As Red States Send Migrants to Blue States, Sanctuary Cities are Crucial," *Washington Post*, September 15, 2022. Numerous other estimates put the number in the hundreds.

4　Sam Levin, "These US Cities Defunded Police: 'We're Transferring Money to the Community,'" *The Guardian*, March 11, 2021.

5　Congressional Budget Office, "The Long-Term Budget Outlook: 2024 to 2054," March 2024.

6　IRS, "Fiscal Year 2024 Budget in Brief" (Washington, DC: Department of the Treasury, Publication 5530, 2023).

7　Tami Luhby, "At Least $191 Billion in Pandemic Jobless Benefits Improperly Paid, Watchdog Tells Congress," *CNN*, February 8, 2023.

8　Rep. Kevin Brady, "Earned Income Tax Credit," Press release from Rep. Kevin Brady, May 18, 2022.

9　David Ditch, "Defunding the Left, Reducing Handouts to States, Eliminating Waste: Priority Appropriations Savings for Congress," The Heritage Foundation, May 18, 2023.

10　Uri Berliner, "I've Been at NPR for 25 Years. Here's How We Lost America's Trust," *The Free Press*, April 9, 2024. Regarding NPR funding: "The Truth about NPR's Funding—and Its Possible Future," Howard Husock, *The Hill*, April 17, 2023.

11　The Economic Opportunity Act of 1964 states: "No part of any funds appropriated or otherwise made available for expenditure under authority of this

Act shall be used to make payments to any individual unless such individual has executed and filed with the Director an affidavit that he does not believe in, and is not a member of and does not support any organization that believes in or teaches, the overthrow of the United States Government by force or violence or by any illegal or unconstitutional methods." "Economic Opportunity Act of 1964." Public Law 88-452—August 20, 1964. Washington, DC, Government Publishing Office, 1964, pp. 533-534.

12   Robert Moffit, "How to Roll Back the Administrative State," The Heritage Foundation, February 17, 2011.

13   Thomas Catenacci, "Failed Biden Nominee Quietly Appointed to Top Role Overseeing War on Household Appliances," *Fox News,* September 19, 2023.

14   Jessica Vaughn and Nathan Desautels, "Still Subsidizing Sanctuaries," Center for Immigration Studies, July 13, 2023.

15   Congressional Budget Office, "Options for Reducing the Deficit, 2023 to 2032—Volume I: Larger Reductions," 2022 and Congressional Budget Office, "Options for Reducing the Deficit, 2023 to 2032—Volume II: Smaller Reductions," 2022.

16   Ditch, p. 5.

17   Nicole Crain and W. Mark Crain, "The Cost of Federal Regulation to the U.S. Economy, Manufacturing and Small Business," National Association of Manufacturers, October 2023.

18   Grace-Marie Turner, "Looking Forward," *American Healthcare Choices Newsletter,* Galen Institute, December 16, 2022.

19   Ron Haskins, "Welfare Reform, Success or Failure? It Worked," Brookings Institution, March 15, 2006.

20   John Goodman, "Is There a Republican Alternative to the Democrats' New Health Reform?" Brief Analysis No. 148, Goodman Institute, August 10, 2022, p. 2.

21   Health Policy Consensus Group, "Health Care Choices 20/20: A Vision for the Future," Galen Institute, November 18, 2020, p. 11.

22   Congressional Research Service, "Block Grants: Perspectives and Controversies," November 4, 2022.

23   Congressional Budget Office, "The Long-Term Budget Outlook."

24   Health Policy Consensus Group, p. 1.

25 Using 2022 data from the Program for International Student Assessment (PISA), which measures "the performance of 15-year-old students in reading, mathematics, and science literacy every 3 years" in 81 countries and education systems, including 37 OECD countries, the National Center for Education Statistics found that "there were 5 education systems with higher average reading literacy scores for 15-year-olds than the United States, 25 with higher mathematics literacy scores, and 9 with higher science literacy scores." These findings are hardly outliers, nor are they limited to only older students: similar results have been found routinely through the years and across age categories. For students in grade five, the Progress in International Reading Literacy Study (PIRLS) international assessment found that he average US score was "lower than the scores of their peers in 3 education systems," while a similar international assessment of students in grade four showed "fourteen education systems had higher average mathematics scores than the United States" and that "seven education systems had higher average science scores than the United States." Source: National Center for Education Statistics, "International Comparisons: Mathematics and Science Achievement at Grades 4 and 8," US Department of Education, Institute of Education Sciences, 2021.

26 "Lockdowns in Europe and the US decreased COVID-19 mortality by a measly 0.2% on average, while the economic costs of the lockdowns were enormous." Grace-Marie Turner, "Quick Takes," *American Healthcare Choices Newsletter,* Galen Institute, February 4, 2022.

27 Sarah Mervosh, "The Pandemic Erased Two Decades of Progress in Math and Reading," *New York Times*, September 1, 2022.

28 Dan Goldhaber, et al. "The Consequences of Remote and Hybrid Instruction During the Pandemic," Center for Education and Policy Research, Harvard University, May 2022.

29 House Republicans investigating the role played by the Centers for Disease Control and Prevention, and the American Federation of Teachers and National Education Association, the nations' two biggest teacher unions, found: " ... CDC allowed AFT to insert language into the Operational Guidance that made it more likely schools across the country would remain closed after February 2021." Jessica Chasmer, "Republicans Expose

'Uncommon' CDC, Teachers' Union Ties on COVID School Reopening Guidance in Report," *Fox News*, March 30, 2022.

30   "Critical Race Theory (CRT) and radical gender ideology, together known as Critical Social Justice (CSJ), is widespread in American schools," Zach Goldberg and Eric Kaufman, *School Choice Is Not Enough: The Impact of Critical Social Justice Ideology in American Education* (New York: Manhattan Institute, February 23, 2023).

31   David Burton, "It Is Arithmetically Impossible to Fund the Progressive Agenda by Taxing the Rich," The Heritage Foundation, August 14, 2019, p. 1.

32   CBO Director Phillip Swagel, "Letter to the Honorable Sheldon Whitehouse," Congressional Budget Office, March 17, 2023.

33   Health Policy Consensus Group, "Health Care Choices 20/20: A Vision for the Future," Galen Institute, p. 8.

34   Actual: 19.7 percent. Preeti Vankar, "U.S. National Health Expenditure as Percent of GDP from 1960 to 2022," *Statista*, February 16, 2024.

35   Grace-Marie Turner, "What It's All About," *American Healthcare Choices Newsletter*, Galen Institute, January 26, 2024.

36   Congressional Budget Office, "The Long-Term Budget Outlook: 2024 to 2054."

37   Congressional Budget Office, "The Long-Term Budget Outlook: 2024 to 2054."

38   Goodman, "Is There a Republican Alternative to the Democrats' New Health Reform?"

39   Grace-Marie Turner, "Marching Toward Socialism," *American Healthcare Choices Newsletter*, Galen Institute, August 12, 2022.

40   Health Policy Consensus Group, "Health Care Choices 20/20: A Vision for the Future," p. 4.

41   They were set to expire five months after the health emergency ends with Congress only extending them on a short-term basis.

42   Conservative health care expert Grace-Marie Turner of the Galen Institute criticizes Sanders's "new and improved Medicare-for-All 2023 bill" as "an even more aggressive government takeover of U.S. health care." Grace-Marie Turner, "Epic Errors," *American Healthcare Choices Newsletter*, Galen Institute, July 14, 2023.

43 Even in Truman's time, his proposed system was wildly expensive. Cogan writes, "It would require a 4 percent payroll tax on the first $3,600 of earnings, double the Social Security payroll tax at that time. Similarly, the proposal's outlays would more than double those of Social Security." John F. Cogan, *The High Cost of Good Intentions: A History of U.S. Federal Entitlement Programs* (Stanford: Stanford University Press, 2017), 146.

44 Anders Hagstrom, "UK Hits Record 7M Citizens Waitlisted for 'Routine' Health Care Under State-Run System," *Fox News,* October 13, 2022.

45 Robert Moffit and Marie Fishpaw, *Modernizing Medicare: Harnessing the Power of Consumer Choice and Market Competition* (Baltimore: Johns Hopkins University Press, 2023).

46 Public Law 116-136.

47 Robert Moffit and Doug Badger, "Forging a Post-Pandemic Policy Agenda: A Road Map for COVID-19 Congressional Oversight," The Heritage Foundation, January 19, 2023.

48 Grace-Marie Turner, *American Healthcare Choices Newsletter,* Galen Institute, December 15, 2023.

49 "American Journalism Sounds Much More Democratic Than Republican," *The Economist,* December 14, 2023.

50 Conservatives have long dominated radio, but newer upstart conservative outlets like *Fox News* and myriad conservative print outlets are now rapidly gaining audience.

51 According to a February 2024 *Gallup* poll, only 38 percent of registered voters thought President Biden deserved to be reelected. Jeffrey Jones, "U.S. Voters: Biden, Most in House Don't Deserve Another Term," *Gallup,* February 2, 2024.

52 Michael Lipka and Elisa Shearer, "Audiences are Declining for Traditional News Media in the U.S.—with Some Exceptions," Pew Research Center, November 28, 2023.

53 A January Johns Hopkins Medicine's Office of Diversity, Inclusion, and Health Equity (DEI) newsletter called out "privilege": "Privilege is an unearned benefit given to people who are in a specific social group. Privilege operates on personal, interpersonal, cultural and institutional levels, and it provides advantages and favors to members of dominant groups at the expense of members of other groups." Among those with such

"privilege"? "In the United States, privilege is granted to people who have membership in one or more of these social identity groups: White people, able-bodied people, heterosexuals, cisgender people, males, Christians, middle or owning class people, middle-aged people, and English-speaking people." *Fox News* Staff, "Top Hospital Triggers Backlash with Diversity Officer's 'Privilege' List: 'Pisses Me Off,'" *Fox News,* January 12, 2024.

54   Grace-Marie Turner, "Looking Forward," *American Healthcare Choices Newsletter,* Galen Institute, December 16, 2022.

55   Rachel Sheffield and Robert Rector, "The War on Poverty After 50 Years," The Heritage Foundation, September 15, 2014. For current and future spending see: House Budget Committee, "60-Year Anniversary of the War on Poverty—Are We Winning or Losing?" January 24, 2024.

56   Choice and competition are also popular amongst Americans. Grace-Marie Turner of the Galen Institute points out that the competition between private health care plans in Medicare Advantage has attracted 28 million Americans. Grace-Marie Turner, "Build on Success," *American Healthcare Choices Newsletter,* Galen Institute, January 13, 2023. In education, meanwhile, 2023 was a banner year for the expansion of school choice programs. *Rasmussen* polling reported that 56 percent of voters said that "generally speaking, school choice programs offer better educational opportunities for students," versus just 15 percent who said they do not. "Scott Rasmussen's Number of the Day for March 7, 2023," *Ballotpedia.*

57   Ludwig von Mises, *Socialism: An Economic and Sociological Analysis,* trans. J. Kahane (Mansfield Centre: Martino Publishing, 2012), 21, 41, 444.

58   Alvin Roth, *Who Gets What—and Why?* (Boston: Mariner Books, 2015), 167.

59   Theodore H. White, *The Making of the President 1972* (New York: Atheneum Publishers, 1973), 179-180.

60   As an example, in June 2023, *Gallup* polling found conservatism on social issues in America at its highest (at 38 percent, up from 33 percent in 2022) in almost a decade. Jeffrey M. Jones, "Social Conservatism in U.S. Highest in About a Decade," *Gallup,* June 8, 2023.

61   White, pp. 33-34.

BIBLIOGRAPHY

Abrahamsen, Martin and Claud Scroggs, eds. *Agricultural Cooperation.* Minneapolis: University of Minnesota Press, 1957.

Adams, Gordon. *The Politics of Defense Contracting: The Iron Triangle.* New York: Council on Economic Priorities, 1981.

Alinsky, Saul. *Rules for Radicals.* New York: Vintage Books, 1989.

"American Revolution Facts." Washington, DC: American Battlefield Trust. November 16, 2023.

Appleby, Joyce. *Inheriting the Revolution: The First Generation of Americans.* Cambridge: The Belknap Press, 2000.

Ashton, Robert. *The English Civil War.* London: Orion Books, 1997.

Backus, Fred. "Americans Increasingly See Border as Crisis, Call for Tougher Measures, CBS News Poll Finds." *CBS News.* January 7, 2024.

Badger, Doug. "Biden's Bid to Expand Obamacare via IRS Is Illegal." Washington, DC: The Heritage Foundation. June 17, 2022.

Bailyn, Bernard. *The Ideological Origins of the American Revolution.* Cambridge: The Belknap Press, 1992.

Baker, Peggy M. "The Plymouth Colony Patent: Setting the Stage." Plymouth: Pilgrim Society & Pilgrim Hall Museum, 2007.

Barr, Andy. "Barr Officially Reintroduces the TABS Act, Calling for a Makeover of the CFPB." Press release from Rep. Andy Barr. Washington, DC: US Congress, March 8, 2023.

Benedict, Murray and Oscar Stine. *The Agricultural Community Programs.* New York: Twentieth Century Fund, 1956.

Berlin, Isaiah. "Locke." In *The Age of Enlightenment: The Eighteenth Century Philosophers*. New York: New American Library, 1984.

Berliner, Uri. "I've Been at NPR for 25 Years. Here's How We Lost America's Trust." *The Free Press*. April 9, 2024.

Berry, Jeffrey M. and David F. Arons. *A Voice for Nonprofits*. Washington, DC: Brookings Institution. 2005.

Berry, Jeffrey. *Lobbying for the People*. Princeton: Princeton University Press, 1977.

Abrahamsen, Martin. *Cooperative Business Enterprise*. New York: McGraw-Hill, 1976.

Berry, Jeffrey. *The Interest Group Society*. Boston: Little, Brown and Co., 1984.

Black, Conrad. *Franklin Delano Roosevelt: Champion of Freedom*. New York: PublicAffairs, 2003.

Blahous, Charles and Liam Sigaud. "The Affordable Care Act's Medicaid Expansion Is Shifting Resources Away from Low-Income Children." Arlington: Mercatus Center, George Mason University, December 13, 2022.

Block, William. *The Separation of the Farm Bureau and the Extension Service*. Urbana: University of Illinois Press, 1960.

Board of the Governors of the Federal Reserve System. "Distribution of the Household Wealth in the U.S. Since 1989." Washington, DC: Federal Reserve, 2023.

Boards of Trustees of the Federal Hospital Insurance and Federal Supplementary Medical Insurance Trust Funds. "Annual Report of the Boards of Trustees of the Federal Hospital Insurance and Federal Supplementary Medical Insurance Trust Funds." Washington, DC: March 31, 2023.

Boorstin, Daniel J., ed. *An American Primer*. Chicago: University of Chicago Press, 1966.

Bopp, Michael, et. al. "Investigations in the 116th Congress: A New Landscape and How to Prepare." Washington, DC: Gibson, Dunn and Crutcher, LLP, January 29, 2019.

Breay, Claire and Julian Harrison. *Magna Carta in Context*. London: British Museum, July 28, 2014.

Brenan, Megan. "Americans' Trust in the Media Remains Near Record Low." *Gallup*. October 18, 2022.

Browne, William. "Farm Organizations and Agribusiness." In *Food Policy and Farm Programs*. New York: Academy of Political Science, 1982.

Bruce, Andrew. *The Non-Partisan League*. New York: MacMillan Co., 1921.

Bureau of Economic Analysis. "Gross Domestic Product, Third Quarter (Second Estimate); Corporate Profits, Third Quarter 2021 (Preliminary Estimate)." Washington, DC: Bureau of Economic Analysis, 2021.

Bonwick, Colin. *The American Revolution*. Charlottesville: The University Press of Virginia. 1991

Burke, Edmund. *Thoughts on the Cause of the Present Discontents and Speeches*. London: Cassell and Co., Ltd., 1886.

Byrne, Kerry. "On This Day in History, Jan. 2, 1920, Thousands Detained By the DOJ in Nationwide 'Palmer Raids.'" *Fox News*. January 2, 2022.

Burton, David. "It Is Arithmetically Impossible to Fund the Progressive Agenda by Taxing the Rich." Washington, DC: The Heritage Foundation. August 14, 2019.

Caldwell, Leigh Ann. "Despite Objections, Congress Certifies Donald Trump's Election." *NBC News*. January 6, 2017.

Catenacci, Thomas. "Biden Admin Is Preparing to Target Americans' Gas Furnaces Amid Stove Crackdown." *Fox News*. June 7, 2023.

Catenacci, Thomas. "Failed Biden Nominee Quietly Appointed to Top Role Overseeing War on Household Appliances." *Fox News*. September 19, 2023.

Chan, Melissa. "There's Already a Campaign to Impeach President Donald Trump." *Time Magazine*. January 20, 2017.

Chasmer, Jessica. "Republicans Expose 'Uncommon' CDC, Teachers' Union Ties on COVID School Reopening Guidance in Report." *Fox News*. March 30, 2022.

Campbell, Adina. "What Is Black Lives Matter and What Are the Aims?" *BBC*. June 12, 2021.

Churchill, Winston. "Sinews of Peace." London: U.K. Archives, March 5, 1946.

Chernow, Ron. *The House of Morgan: An American Banking Dynasty and the Rise of Modern Finance*. New York: Grove Press, 2010.

Clements, Kendrick. *Woodrow Wilson: World Statesman*. Chicago: Ivan R. Dee, 1999.

Clinton, William J. "State of the Union Address." Washington, DC: US Congress, January 23, 1996.

CNN. "2020 Exit Polls National Results." *CNN*. 2020.

CNN. "Election 2016 Democratic Party Primary Delegate Estimate." *CNN*. 2016.

Cochrane, Emily. "Democrats Float $6 Trillion Plan Amid Talks on Narrower Infrastructure Deal." *The New York Times*. June 20, 2021.

Cochrane, Willard. *The Development of American Agriculture*. Minneapolis: University of Minnesota Press, 1979.

Cogan, John F. *The High Cost of Good Intentions: A History of U.S. Entitlement Programs*. Stanford: Stanford University Press, 2017.

Committee for a Responsible Budget. "What's in President Biden's American Families Plan?" Washington, DC: Committee for a Responsible Budget, April 28, 2021.

Committee for a Responsible Budget. "What's in President Biden's American Jobs Plan?" Washington, DC: Committee for a Responsible Budget, April 2, 2021.

Committee to Unleash Prosperity. *Unleash Prosperity Hotline*. Issue #760. Washington, DC: Committee to Unleash Prosperity, April 27, 2023.

Committee to Unleash Prosperity. *Unleash Prosperity Hotline*. Issue #924. Washington, DC: Committee to Unleash Prosperity, December 28, 2023.

Congressional Budget Office. "Historical Budget Data." Washington, DC: Congressional Budget Office, February 2023.

Congressional Budget Office. "Historical Budget Data." Washington, DC: Congressional Budget Office, February 2024.

Congressional Budget Office. "Monthly Budget Review: Summary for Fiscal Year 2023." Washington, DC: Congressional Budget Office, 2023.

Congressional Budget Office. "Options for Reducing the Deficit 2021 to 2030." Washington, DC: Congressional Budget Office, 2021.

Congressional Budget Office. "Options for Reducing the Deficit, 2023 to 2032— Volume I: Larger Reductions." Washington, DC: Congressional Budget Office, 2022.

Congressional Budget Office. "Options for Reducing the Deficit, 2023 to 2032— Volume II: Smaller Reductions." Washington, DC: Congressional Budget Office, 2022.

Congressional Budget Office. "The Budget and Economic Outlook: 2022 to 2032." Washington, DC: Congressional Budget Office, 2022.

Congressional Budget Office. "The Budget and Economic Outlook: 2023 to 2033." Washington, DC: Congressional Budget Office, 2023.

Congressional Budget Office. "The Budget and Economic Outlook: 2024 to 2034." Washington, DC: Congressional Budget Office, February 2024.

Congressional Budget Office. "The Long-Term Budget Outlook: 2024 to 2054."
Washington, DC: Congressional Budget Office, March 2024.

Congressional Research Service. "Block Grants: Perspectives and Controversies."
Washington, DC: Library of Congress, November 4, 2022.

Congressional Research Service. "Federal Reserve: Tapering of Asset Purchases."
Washington, DC: Library of Congress, January 27, 2022.

Congressional Research Service. "Medicaid: An Overview." Washington, DC:
Library of Congress, February 22, 2021.

Congressional Research Service. "Medicare Primer." Washington, DC: Library
of Congress, May 21, 2020.

Coolidge, Calvin. "Sixth Annual Message." Charlottesville: Miller Center,
University of Virginia, December 4, 1928.

Cox, Jeff. "Inflation Surged 6.8% in November, Even More Than Expected, to
Fastest Rate Since 1982." *CNBC*. December 10, 2021.

Crain, Nicole and W. Mark Crain. "The Cost of Federal Regulation to the U.S.
Economy, Manufacturing and Small Business." Washington, DC: National
Association of Manufacturers, October 2023.

Crèvecœur, Jean de. *Letters from an American Farmer*. New York: Penguin
Books, 1986.

Cruz, Daniel and Greg Fann. "The Shortcomings of the ACA Exchanges: Far
Less Enrollment at a Much Higher Cost." Plano: Paragon Health Institute,
September 2023.

Cyert, Richard and James March. *A Behavioral Theory of the Firm*. Engelwood
Cliffs: Prentice-Hall, 1963.

Daly, Matthew. "In Rift with Biden, Manchin Vows to Block Oil, Gas Nominee."
AP News. March 10, 2023.

Davis, G.R.C. *Magna Carta*. London: British Museum, 1963.

Dean, John W. *Warren G. Harding*. New York: Times Books, 2004.

Democratic Socialists of America. "Democratic Socialists of America 2021
Platform." 2021.

Desilver, Drew. "U.S. Students' Academic Achievement Still Lags That of Their
Peers in Many Other Countries." Washington, DC: Pew Research Center,
February 15, 2017.

Ditch, David. "Defunding the Left, Reducing Handouts to States, Eliminating
Waste: Priority Appropriations Savings for Congress." Washington, DC:
The Heritage Foundation. May 18, 2023.

Dole, Robert. "Republican Party Response to President Clinton's 'Address Before a Joint Session of the Congress on the State of the Union.'" January 23, 1996.

Dovere, Edward-Isaac. *Battle for the Soul: Inside the Democrats' Campaign to Defeat Trump*. New York: Penguin Random House, 2021.

Duverger, Maurice. *Political Parties: Their Organization and Activity in the Modern State*. London: Methuen, 1964.

"Economic Opportunity Act of 1964." Public Law 88-452—August 20, 1964. Washington, DC: Government Publishing Office, 1964.

Edgar, Walter. *Partisans and Redcoats: The Southern Conflict That Turned the Tide of the American Revolution*. New York: HarperCollins, 2001.

Editorial Board. "Democratic Socialists of America Cheer Murder and Kidnapping of Israelis at Hands of Hamas Terrorists." *New York Post*. October 8, 2023.

Elbein, Saul. "Biden Bucks Obama's Legacy on Climate and Gas with LNG Export Pause." *The Hill*. January 27, 2024.

Emelianoff, Ivan. *Economic Theory of Cooperation*. Ann Arbor: Edwards Brothers Inc., 1942.

"English Bill of Rights 1689." New Haven: Yale University, Lillian Goldman Law Library, 2008.

Farrand, Max. *The Records of the Federal Convention of 1778*. Volumes 1-3. New Haven: Yale University Press, 1966.

Fawk, Lewis, Mirae Kim, et. al. "Nonprofit Trends and Impacts 2021." Washington, DC: Urban Institute, October 26, 2021.

Federal Election Commission. "Federal Elections 2020: Election Results for the U.S. President, the U.S. Senate and the U.S. House of Representatives." Washington, DC, October 2022.

Feingold, Kenneth. "From Agrarianism to Adjustment: The Political Origins of New Deal Agricultural Policy." *Politics and Society* 11 (1981): 1-27.

Flexner, James Thomas. *Washington: The Indispensable Man*. New York: New American Library, 1984.

Floresca, Florence. "A Wealth Tax Will Slow Down Economic Growth." Washington, DC: Citizens Against Government Waste, May 10, 2021.

Flynn, Daniel J. *A Conservative History of the American Left*. New York: Crown Forum, 2008.

Fox, Cynthia G. "Income Tax Records of the Civil War Years." *Prologue Magazine* 18, no. 4 (1986).

Frankland, Mark. *Khrushchev*. New York: Stein and Day, 1967.

Friedman, Milton and Anna Schwartz. *A Monetary History of the United States: 1867-1960*. Princeton: Princeton University Press, 1993.

Friedman, Milton. *Why Government Is the Problem*. Stanford: Hoover Institution, Stanford University, 1993.

Gais, Thomas and Jack Walker. "Pathways to Influence in American Politics." In *Mobilizing Interest Groups in America: Patrons, Professions, and Social Movements*. Ann Arbor: University of Michigan, 1991.

Gais, Thomas, Mark Peterson, and Jack Walker. "Interest Groups, Iron Triangles, and Representative Institutions." *British Journal of Politics* 14 (1984): 161-185.

Galston, William. "The Liberal Faction of the Democratic Party Is Growing, New Polling Shows." Washington, DC: Brookings Institution, January 11, 2019.

Gaventa, John. *Power and Powerlessness*. Urbana: University of Illinois Press, 1980.

Ginzberg, Eli and Robert M. Solow. *The Great Society: Lessons for the Future*. New York: Basic Books, 1974.

Gold, Matea. "The Campaign to Impeach President Trump Has Begun." *The Washington Post*. January 20, 2017.

Goldberg, Zach and Eric Kaufman. *School Choice Is Not Enough: The Impact of Critical Social Justice Ideology in American Education*. New York: Manhattan Institute, 2023.

Goldhaber, Dan, et al. "The Consequences of Remote and Hybrid Instruction During the Pandemic." Cambridge: Center for Education and Policy Research, Harvard University, May 2022.

Goldsmith, Oliver. "The Deserted Village." In *Immortal Poems of the English Language*. Edited by Oscar Williams. New York: Washington Square Press, 1952.

Goldwater, Barry. "1964 Republican National Convention Presidential Nomination Acceptance Speech." San Francisco, July 17, 1964.

Gonzalez, Mike and Andrew Olivastro. "The Agenda of Black Lives Matter Is Far Different From the Slogan." Washington, DC: The Heritage Foundation. July 3, 2020.

Gonzalez, Mike. *BLM: The Making of a New Marxist Revolution*. New York: Encounter Books, 2021.

Goodman, John. "Is There a Republican Alternative to the Democrats' New Health Reform?" Dallas: Goodman Institute. Brief Analysis No. 148. August 10, 2022.

Greer, Thomas. *American Social Reform Movements Since 1865*. Port Washington: Kennikat Press, 1965.

Gregory, James. "Remapping the American Left: A History of Radical Discontinuity." *Labor: Studies in Working Class History* 17, no. 2 (2020): 11-45.

Gruenberg, Mark. "Michigan Makes History, First State to Repeal Right-to-Work (for Less) in 60 Years." *People's World*. March 16, 2023.

Guida, Victoria. "Fed's Powell: 'Urgent' for US to Focus on Debt Sustainability." *Politico*. February 4, 2024.

Hagstrom, Anders. "UK Hits Record 7M Citizens Waitlisted for 'Routine' Health Care Under State-Run System." *Fox News*. October 13, 2022.

Halon, Yael. "Ben Carson Defends Terry Crews' Black Lives Matter Critique: 'We Are Putting Everything in Context of Color.'" *Fox News*. July 1, 2020.

Hardin, Charles. *The Politics of Agriculture*. Glencoe: Free Press, 1952.

Haskins, Ron. "Welfare Reform, Success or Failure? It Worked." Washington, DC: Brookings Institution, March 15, 2006.

Hayden, Tom. "Port Huron Statement." New York: Students for a Democratic Society, 1962.

Cigler, Allan and Burdette Loomis, eds. *Interest Group Politics*. Third Edition. Washington, DC: Congressional Quarterly Press, 1991.

Henney, Megan. "'Great Migration' Continues as More Americans Flee to Florida, Texas." *Fox News*. June 6, 2023.

Henney, Megan. "High-Tax Exodus Accelerates as More Americans Flee to Florida, Texas." *Fox News*. February 7, 2023.

Hibbard, Benjamin. *Marketing Agricultural Products*. New York: Appleton and Co., 1921.

Hicks, John. *The Populist Revolt*. Lincoln: University of Nebraska Press, 1961.

Higgins, Trevor, Rachel Change, and Devon Lespier. "The Biden Administration Has Taken More Climate Action Than Any Other in History." Washington, DC: The Center for American Progress, March 6, 2024.

Hightower, Jim. *Hard Tomatoes, Hard Times*. Cambridge: Schenkman Publishing Co., 1973.

Hobbes, Thomas. *Leviathan.* Edited by C.B. MacPherson. New York: Penguin Books, 1982.

Hofstadter, Richard. *America at 1750: A Social Portrait.* New York: Vintage Books, 1973.

Hofstadter, Richard. *The Age of Reform.* New York: Alfred Knopf, 1955.

Holtz-Eakin, Doug. "How Much Will the Green New Deal Cost?" Washington, DC: The Aspen Institute, June 11, 2019.

House Budget Committee. "60-Year Anniversary of the War on Poverty—Are We Winning or Losing?" Washington, DC: US Congress, January 24, 2024.

House Committee on Oversight and Accountability. "Investigation Reveals Biden's CDC Bypassed Scientific Norms to Allow Teachers Union to Re-Write Official Guidance." Washington, DC: US Congress, March 30, 2022.

House Ways & Means Committee. "Republican Press Release: Remarks of Rep. Tom Rice (R-SC)." Washington, DC: US Congress, May 18, 2022.

House Ways & Means Committee. "The Biden Tax Hike Will Likely Exceed $7 Trillion." Washington, DC: US Congress, March 14, 2024.

Husock, Howard. "The Truth about NPR's Funding—and Its Possible Future." *The Hill.* April 17, 2023.

Index of Economic Freedom. "2023 Index of Economic Freedom." Washington, DC: The Heritage Foundation. 2023.

Internal Revenue Service. "Financial Report: Fiscal Year 2021." Washington, DC: Department of the Treasury, November 8, 2021.

Internal Revenue Service. "Fiscal Year 2024 Budget in Brief." Washington, DC: Department of the Treasury. Publication 5530. 2023.

Isaacson, Walter. *Benjamin Franklin: An American Life.* New York: Simon & Schuster, 2003.

Health Policy Consensus Group. "Health Care Choices 20/20: A Vision for the Future." Paeonian Springs: Galen Institute, November 18, 2020.

Jeansonne, Glen. *Herbert Hoover: A Life.* New York: New American Library, 2016.

Johnson, Lyndon B. "Annual Message to Congress on the State of the Union." Washington, DC: US Congress, January 8, 1964.

Joint Committee on Taxation. "Overview of the Federal Tax System as in Effect for 2022." Washington, DC: Joint Committee on Taxation, June 28, 2022.

Joint Committee on Taxation. "Overview of the Federal Tax System as in Effect for 2023." Washington, DC: Joint Committee on Taxation, May 11, 2023.

Jones, Jeffrey. "Social Conservatism in U.S. Highest in About a Decade." *Gallup*. June 6, 2023.

Jones, Jeffrey. "U.S. Voters: Biden, Most in House Don't Deserve Another Term." *Gallup*. February 2, 2024.

Kasperowicz, Peter. "Rand Paul's 'Festivus Report' Airs $482 billion Worth of Federal Waste Grievances." *Fox News*. December 23, 2022.

Keegan, John. *The First World War*. New York: Vantage Books, 2000.

Kelly, Alfred, Winfred Harbison, and Herman Belz. *The American Constitution: Its Origins and Developments*. New York: W.W. Norton and Co., 1983.

Kerpen, Phil, Stephen Moore, and Casey B. Mulligan. "A Final Report Card on the States' Response to COVID-19." Cambridge: National Bureau of Economic Research. Working Paper 29928. April 2022.

Ketcham, Ralph. *The Anti-Federalist Papers and the Constitutional Convention Debates*. New York: New American Library, 1986.

Keynes, John Maynard. *A Tract on Monetary Reform*. Hawthorne: BN Publishing, 2008.

Khrushchev, Nikita. "On the Cult of Personality and Its Consequences." Washington, DC: Wilson Center Digital Archive.

Kihss, Peter. "Seizure of Mines." *The New York Times*. March 6, 1978.

Kile, O.M. *The Farm Bureau Through Three Decades*. Baltimore: Waverly Press, 1948.

Kimber, Richard. "Collective Action and the Fallacy of the Liberal Fallacy." *World Politics* 33 (October 1980): 178-196.

Kimelman, Jeremia. "Full Transcript: 2019 Democratic Debate Night Two." *NBC News*. June 28, 2019.

Knapp, Joseph. *The Rise of American Cooperative Enterprise: 1620-1920*. Danville: Interstate Publishers, 1969.

Kollmann, Geoffrey. "Social Security: Summary of Major Changes in the Cash Benefits Program." In *CRS Legislative Histories 2*. Washington, DC: Congressional Research Service, Library of Congress. 2000.

Kubo, Fumiaki. "Henry A. Wallace and Radical Politics in the New Deal: Farm Programs and a Vision of the New American Political Economy." *The Japanese Journal of American Studies*, no. 4 (1991).

Kuhfeld, Megan, et. al. "The Pandemic Has Had Devastating Impacts on Learning. What Will It Take to Help Students Catch Up?" Washington, DC: Brookings Institution, March 3, 2022.

Ladd, George W. *Agricultural Bargaining Power*. Ames: Iowa State Press, 1964.

Lancaster, Bruce. *The American Revolution*. Boston: Houghton Mifflin Company, 2001.

Lange, Katie. "The Berlin Airlift: What It Was, Its Importance in the Cold War." Washington, DC: US Department of Defense, June 24, 2022.

Latham, Earl. *The Group Basis of Politics*. Ithaca: Cornell University Press, 1963.

Leckie, Robert. *George Washington's War: The Sage of the American Revolution*. New York: HarperCollins, 1993.

Leonard, Ben. "Telehealth Rules Could Hitch a Ride on Year-End Omnibus." *Politico*. November 11, 2022.

Leuchtenburg, William E. *The American President: From Teddy Roosevelt to Bill Clinton*. New York: Oxford University Press, 2015.

Levin, Sam. "These US Cities Defunded Police: 'We're Transferring Money to the Community.'" *The Guardian*. March 11, 2021.

Levine, Jon. "Former AOC Aide Justine Medina Now Working as New York Communist Party Boss." *New York Post*. May 13, 2023.

Levine, Jon. "Powerful Teachers Union Influenced CDC on School Reopenings, Emails Show." *New York Post*. May 1, 2021.

Library of Congress, Digital Collections. "Today in History – October 23, The Lend Lease Act." Washington, DC: Library of Congress.

Linton, Calvin D. *The Bicentennial Almanac: 200 Years of America*. Nashville: Thomas Nelson Inc., 1975.

Lipka, Michael and Elisa Shearer. "Audiences are Declining for Traditional News Media in the U.S.—with Some Exceptions." Washington, DC: Pew Research Center, November 28, 2023.

Lipset, Seymour M. *Agrarian Socialism*. Berkeley: University of California Press, 1950.

Locke, John. *The Second Treatise of Government*. Edited by Thomas Peardon. Indianapolis: Bobbs-Merrill Educational Publishing, 1981.

Lowi, Theodore J. *The Politics of Disorder*. New York: Morton, 1974.

Lucey, Catherine. "Biden Leads Democratic Push to Block New Abortion Restrictions After Shifting Stance in Campaign." *Wall Street Journal*. November 28, 2021.

MacDonald, Forrest. *Alexander Hamilton: A Biography*. New York: W.W. Norton & Co., 1979.

Madison, James. "Federalist Paper Number Ten." In *The Federalist Papers*. New York: Mentor Books, 1961.

Major Cities Chiefs Association Intelligence Commanders Group. "Report on the 2020 Protests and Civil Unrest." Salt Lake City, October 2020.

Manchin, Joe. "Manchin Responds to Sanders Op-ed in West Virginia Gazette-Mail." Statement from Senator Joe Manchin. Washington, DC: US Congress, October 15, 2021.

Martin, James Kirby, ed. *Ordinary Courage: The Revolutionary War Adventures of Joseph Plumb Martin*. St. James: Brandywine Press. 1993.

Marx, Karl and Friedrich Engels. *Selected Works*. New York: International Publishers, 1977.

Marx, Karl and Friedrich Engels. *The Communist Manifesto*. New York: Penguin Books, 1979.

McBride, James, Noah Berman, and Andrew Chatzky. "Backgrounder: China's Massive Belt and Road Initiative." New York: Council on Foreign Relations, February 2, 2023.

McConnell, Grant. *The Decline of Agrarian Democracy*. Berkeley: University of California Press, 1953.

McCullough, David. *John Adams*. New York: Simon and Schuster, 2001.

McCullough, David. *Truman*. New York: Simon and Schuster, 1992.

McCune, Wesley. *Who's Behind Our Farm Policy?* New York: Frederick Praeger Inc., 1956.

McKay, Andrew and Martin Abrahamsen. "Helping Farmers Build Cooperatives: The Evolution of Farmer Cooperative Service." Washington, DC: Farmer Cooperative Service, USDA, 1962.

McMath, Robert. *Populist Vanguard: A History of the Farmers' Alliance*. Chapel Hill: University of North Carolina Press, 1975.

Mead, Gary. *The Doughboys: America and the First World War*. Woodstock: Overlook Press, 2002.

The MeasuringWorth Foundation. "MeasuringWorth—Relative Worth Comparators and Data Sets." *MeasuringWorth—Relative Worth Comparators and Data Sets*. 2024.

Medvedev, Roy A. and Zhores A. Medvedev. *Khrushchev: The Years in Power*. New York: W. W. Norton and Co., 1978.

Mervosh, Sarah. "The Pandemic Erased Two Decades of Progress in Math and Reading." *The New York Times*. September 1, 2022.

Mises, Ludwig von. *Socialism: An Economic and Sociological Analysis.* Translated by J. Kahane. Mansfield Centre: Martino Publishing, 2012.

Moe, Alex. "House Investigations of Trump and His Administration: The Full List." *NBC News.* May 27, 2019.

Moffit, Robert and Doug Badger. "Forging a Post-Pandemic Policy Agenda: A Road Map for COVID-19 Congressional Oversight." Washington, DC: The Heritage Foundation. January 19, 2023.

Moffit, Robert and Marie Fishpaw. *Modernizing Medicare: Harnessing the Power of Consumer Choice and Market Competition.* Baltimore: John Hopkins University Press, 2023.

Moffit, Robert. "How to Roll Back the Administrative State." Washington, DC: The Heritage Foundation. February 17, 2011.

Morison, Samuel E. *The Oxford History of the American People.* Volumes I-III. New York: Mentor Books, 1972.

Morris, Richard B., ed. *Bicentennial History of the American Worker.* Washington, DC: US Department of Labor, 1976.

Mueller, Eleanor. "Labor Watchdog Finds Nearly $46 Billion in Potentially Stolen Jobless Benefits." *Politico Pro.* September 22, 2022.

Nathanson, Michael. "California Wealth and Exit Tax Shows a Window Into the Future." *Bloomberg Tax.* March 17, 2023.

National Center for Education Statistics. "International Comparisons: Mathematics and Science Achievement at Grades 4 and 8." Washington, DC: US Department of Education, Institute of Education Sciences. 2021.

Nelson, Joshua Q. "Teachers Union Boss Randi Weingarten Claims School Choice 'Undermines Democracy.'" *Fox News.* December 19, 2023.

Norman, Greg. "New York Lowering Minimum Test Scores for Student Proficiency in Math, English: The 'New Normal.'" *Fox News.* March 17, 2023.

Nourse, Edwin, Joseph Davis, and John Black. "Three Years of the Agricultural Adjustment Administration." Washington, DC: Brookings Institution. 1937.

Obama, Barack. *Dreams from My Father: A Story of Race and Inheritance.* New York: Three Rivers Publishing Group, 2004.

Office of Management and Budget. "Historical Tables." Washington, DC: The White House, 2024.

Oliver, D.H. "Antitrust, Bargaining, and Cooperatives: ABCs of the National Agricultural Marketing and Bargaining Act of 1971." *Harvard Journal on Legislation* 9 (1971-72).

Olson, Mancur. *The Logic of Collective Action: Public Goods and the Theory of Groups*. Cambridge: Harvard University Press, 1965.

Paarlberg, Donald. *Farm and Food Policy*. Lincoln: University of Nebraska Press, 1980.

Peckham, Howard H. *The Colonial Wars: 1689-1762*. Chicago: The University of Chicago Press, 1964.

Penley, Taylor. "Seattle Reverses Course on Defunding Police as Crime Ravages Locals; 'A Huge Crisis.'" *Fox News*. March 22, 2023.

Penn Wharton Budget Model. "Update: Budgetary Cost of Climate and Energy Provisions in the Inflation Reduction Act." Philadelphia: University of Pennsylvania, April 27, 2023.

Perkins, Edwin. *The Economy of Colonial America*. New York: Columbia University Press, 1988.

Perret, Geoffrey. *Eisenhower*. Holbrook: Adams Media Corporation, 1999.

Peter G. Peterson Foundation. "Here's Everything the Federal Government Has Done to Respond to Coronavirus So Far." New York, March 15, 2021.

Peterson, Trudy, ed. *Farmers, Bureaucrats, and Middlemen: Historical Perspectives on American Agriculture*. Washington, DC: Howard University Press, 1980.

Pethokoukis, James. "What Bernie Sanders and the Socialists Keep Getting Wrong About Scandinavia." Washington, DC: American Enterprise Institute, February 3, 2020.

Pew Research Center. "Beyond Red vs. Blue: The Political Typology." Washington, DC: June 26, 2014.

Pew Research Center. "Beyond Red vs. Blue: The Political Typology." Washington, DC: November 9, 2021.

Pew Research Center. "Beyond Red vs. Blue." Washington, DC: May 10, 2005.

Pew Research Center. "Political Typology Reveals Deep Fissures on the Right and Left." Washington, DC: October 24, 2017.

Pew Research Center. "Retro-Politics, The Political Typology: Version 3.0." Washington, DC: November 11, 1999.

Philbrick, Nathaniel and Thomas Philbrick, eds. *The Mayflower Papers: Selected Writings of Colonial New England*. New York: Penguin Books, 2007.

Picchi, Aimee. "A National Wealth Tax Has Gone Nowhere. Now Some States Want to Tax the Ultra-Rich." *CBS News*. January 20, 2023.

Pollock, Norman, ed. *The Populist Mind*. Indianapolis: Bobbs-Merrill Co., 1967.

Rabushka, Alvin. *Taxation in Colonial America.* Princeton, NJ: Princeton University Press, 2008.

Ransby, Barbara. "'The Squad' is the Future of Politics." *New York Times.* August 8, 2019

Rasmussen Reports. "Daily Presidential Tracking Poll." Asbury Park: *Rasmussen Reports.*

RealClearPolitics. "Historical Archive: 2020 Democratic Nomination."

RealClearPolitics. "RCP Poll Average: Democratic Presidential Nomination 2020."

Reder, Melvin W. "The Rise and Fall of Unions: The Public Sector and the Private." *Journal of Economics* 2, no. 2 (1988).

Reed, Lawrence. "Don't Call Scandinavian Countries 'Socialist.'" Atlanta: Foundation for Economic Education, April 18, 2023.

Reed, Lawrence. "The Mayflower Compact: As an Idea, America Began in 1620, Not 1776." Atlanta: Foundation for Economic Education, November 11, 2020.

Rizzo, Salvador. "What's Actually in the 'Green New Deal' from Democrats?" *The Washington Post.* February 11, 2019.

Roosevelt, Franklin Delano. "Presidential Inaugural Address." Washington, DC, March 4, 1933.

Ross, Jean and Seth Hanlon. "The Build Back Better Act's Investments in the IRS Will Substantially Reduce the Tax Gap." Washington, DC: Center for American Progress, November 17, 2021.

Rossiter, Clinton, ed. *The Federalist Papers.* New York: New American Library, 1961.

Roth, Alvin. *Who Gets What—and Why?* Boston: Mariner Books, 2015.

Rothbard, Murray N. *Economic Thought Before Adam Smith: An Austrian Perspective on the History of Economic Thought, Volume I.* Auburn: Ludwig von Mises Institute, 2012.

Rothbard, Murray N. *Classical Economics: An Austrian Perspective on the History of Economic Thought, Volume II.* Auburn: Ludwig von Mises Institute, 2012.

Roudabeh, Kishi and Sam Jones. "Demonstrations and Political Violence in America: New Data for Summer 2020." Princeton: Princeton University, September 3, 2020.

Roy, E.P. *Cooperatives: Development, Principles, and Management.* Danville: Interstate Publishers, 1976.

Royster, Charles. *A Revolutionary People at War: The Continental Army and American Character, 1775-1783*. Chapel Hill: The University of North Carolina Press, 1979.

Russell, Charles. *The Story of the Non-Partisan League*. New York: Harper & Brothers Publishers, 1920.

Saad, Lydia. "Democrats' Identification as Liberal Now 54%, A New High." *Gallup*. January 12, 2023.

Saad, Lydia. "Felonies, Old Age Heavily Count Against Candidates." *Gallup*. January 26, 2024.

Salisbury, Robert. "An Exchange Theory of Interest Groups." *Midwest Journal of Political Science* 13, no. 1 (February 1969): 1-32.

Samuelsohn, Darren. "Could Trump Be Impeached Shortly After He Takes Office?" *Politico*. April 17, 2016.

Sanders, Bernie. *Where We Go from Here: Two Years in the Resistance*. New York: Thomas Dunne Books, 2018.

Satter, David. "100 Years of Communism—and 100 Million Dead." *Wall Street Journal*. November 6, 2017.

Shabad, Rebecca. "Tulsi Gabbard Announces She's Leaving the Democratic Party." *NBC News*. October 11, 2022.

Shear, Michael D. and Matthew Rosenberg. "Released Emails Suggest the D.N.C. Derided the Sanders Campaign." *The New York Times*. July 22, 2016

Sheffield, Rachel and Robert Rector. "The War on Poverty After 50 Years." Washington, DC: The Heritage Foundation. September 15, 2014.

Shilton, Jordan. "Bernie Sanders and the 'Scandinavian Model.'" World Socialist website. February 26, 2016.

Shover, John. *Cornbelt Rebellion: The Farmers' Holiday Association*. Urbana: University of Illinois Press, 1965.

Skocpol, Theda and Kenneth Finegold. "State Capacity and Economic Intervention in the Early New Deal." *Political Science Quarterly* 97, no. 2 (1982): 255-278.

Smialek, Jeanna. "Jumping Prices and the Ghost of 2013's Market Meltdown Loom Over the Fed." *The New York Times*. November 3, 2021.

Smith, Adam. *An Inquiry into the Nature and Causes of the Wealth of Nations*. New York: The Modern Library, 1994.

Sobel, Robert. *Coolidge: An American Enigma*. Washington, DC: Regnery Publishing, 1998.

Social Security and Medicare Trustees. "The Trustees Summary of the 2021 Social Security and Medicare Trustees Reports." Washington, DC: Social Security Administration, 2021.

Sombart, Werner. *Why is There No Socialism in the United States?* Translated by Patricia M. Hocking and C.T. Husbands. London: The MacMillan Press, Ltd., 1976.

Stott, Michael, Joe Daniels, and Vanessa Silva. "How Venezuela's Nicolás Maduro Outfoxed the West." *Financial Times*. March 4, 2023.

Sullivan, Kate. "Biden Says He Will Pick Woman to Be His Vice President." *CNN*. March 15, 2020.

Sundquist, James L. *The Decline and Resurgence of Congress.* Washington, DC: Brookings Institution, 1981.

Swagel, Phillip. "Letter to Senator Lindsey Graham Re: Economic Analysis of Budget Reconciliation Legislation." Washington, DC: Congressional Budget Office, August 4, 2022.

Swagel, Phillip. "Letter to the Honorable Sheldon White Whitehouse." Washington, DC: Congressional Budget Office, March 17, 2023.

Swagel, Phillip. "The Effects of Increased Funding for the IRS." Washington, DC: Congressional Budget Office, September 2, 2021.

Szatmary, David P. *Shays' Rebellion: The Making of an Agrarian Insurrection.* Amherst: University of Massachusetts Press, 1980.

Talbot, Donald and Ross Hadwiger. *The Policy Process in American Agriculture.* San Francisco: Chandler Publishing, 1968.

Taylor, Carl. *The Farmers' Movement: 1620-1920.* Westpoint: Greenwood Press, 1953.

Taylor, Jacob. "Rep. Waters Calls for Harassing Admin Officials in Public, Trump Calls Her 'Low IQ.'" *NBC News*. June 25, 2018.

Timm, Jane. "Democrats Gain 40 House Seats, as NBC Projects TJ Cox Wins California's 21st District." *NBC News*. December 6, 2018.

Tocqueville, Alexis de. *Democracy in America.* Translated by George Lawrence. Garden City: Anchor Books, 1969.

Torgerson, Randall. *Producer Power at the Bargaining Table.* Columbia: University of Missouri Press, 1970.

Troy, Leo. *Trade Union Membership: 1897-1962.* Washington, DC: National Bureau of Economic Research, 1965.

Trudo, Hanna. "Restless Progressives Eye 2024." *The Hill*. November 28, 2021.

Truman, David. *The Governmental Process*. New York: Knopf, 1951.

Turner, Grace-Marie. "Build on Success." *American Healthcare Choices*, Newsletter Issue No. 188. Paeonian Springs: Galen Institute, January 13, 2023.

Turner, Grace-Marie. "Epic Errors." *American Healthcare Choices*, Newsletter Issue No. 206. Paeonian Springs: Galen Institute, July 14, 2023.

Turner, Grace-Marie. "Looking Forward." *American Healthcare Choices*, Newsletter Issue No. 186. Paeonian Springs: Galen Institute, December 16, 2022.

Turner, Grace-Marie. "Marching Toward Socialism." *American Healthcare Choices*, Newsletter Issue No. 177. Paeonian Springs: Galen Institute, August 12, 2022.

Turner, Grace-Marie. "Quick Takes." *American Healthcare Choices*, Newsletter Issue No. 157. Paeonian Springs: Galen Institute, February 4, 2022.

Turner, Grace-Marie. "What It's All About." *American Healthcare Choices*, Newsletter Issue No. 225. Paeonian Springs: Galen Institute, January 26, 2024.

US Department of Commerce. *Bicentennial Edition: Historical Statistics of the United States, Colonial Times to 1970*. Washington, DC: Department of Commerce, 1975.

US Government Accountability Office. "A Glossary of Budget Terms Used in the Federal Budget Process." Washington, DC: US Government Accountability Office, September 2005.

US Government Accountability Office. "The Nation's Fiscal Health: Federal Action Critical to Pivot toward Fiscal Sustainability." Washington, DC: US Government Accountability Office, May 2022.

US Inflation Calculator. "Current US Inflation Rates: 2000-2024." CoinNews Media Group Company, 2024.

Vankar, Pretti. "U.S. National Health Expenditure as Percent of GDP from 1960 to 2022." *Statista*. February 16, 2024.

Vaughn, Jessica and Nathan Desautels. "Still Subsidizing Sanctuaries." Washington, DC: Center for Immigration Studies, July 13, 2023.

Vincent, Nicholas. "Consequences of Magna Carta." London: British Library, March 12, 2015.

Vitiello, Domenic. "As Red States Send Migrants to Blue States, Sanctuary Cities are Crucial." *The Washington Post*. September 15, 2022.

Walker, Jack L. "The Mobilization of Political Interests in America." In *Mobilizing Interest Groups in America: Patrons, Professions, and Social Movements*. Ann Arbor: University of Michigan, 1991.

Walker, Jack L. "The Origin and Maintenance of Interest Groups in America." *American Political Science Review* 77 (1983): 390-404.

Walker, Jack L. *Mobilizing Interest Groups in America: Patrons, Professions, and Social Movements*. Ann Arbor: University of Michigan, 1991.

Warren, Joseph. The Suffolk Resolves. Suffolk: *Essex Gazette*, September 20, 1774.

Weigel, David. "Hickenlooper Denounced Socialism—and Then Got Booed in San Francisco." *The Washington Post*. June 2, 2019.

Weisman, Steven R. *The Great Tax Wars*. New York: Simon and Schuster, 2002.

Weitzman, Murray, et. al. *The New Nonprofit Almanac: The Essential Facts and Figures for Managers, Researchers, and Volunteers*. New York: Wiley and Sons Inc., 2002

The White House. "Fact Sheet: The American Families Plan." Washington, DC: The White House, April 28, 2021.

The White House. "Fact Sheet: The American Jobs Plan." Washington, DC: The White House, March 31, 2021.

White, Matthew. "The Turbulent 17th Century: Civil War, Regicide, the Restoration and the Glorious Revolution." London: British Library, October 5, 2018.

White, Theodore H. *The Making of the President 1972*. New York: Atheneum Publishers, 1973.

Wilson, Woodrow. "Message to Congress." 63rd Cong., 2nd Sess., Senate Doc. No. 566 (Washington, 1914), pp. 3-4.

Wood, Gordon S. *The Radicalism of the American Revolution*. New York: Vintage Books, 1991.

World Bank Group. "Military Expenditures (% of GDP)." Washington, DC: World Bank Group, 2022.

World Population Review. "Highest Taxed Countries: 2024." Walnut: World Population Review website, 2024.

Zeballos-Roig, Joseph. "Bernie Sanders Seeks $6 Trillion Infrastructure Package, Which Senate Democrats are Considering Passing Without the GOP." *Business Insider*. June 17, 2021.

Zedong, Mao. "Report on an Investigation of the Peasant Movement in Hunan." In *Selected Works of Mao Tse-tung, Volume I*, 28. Peking: Foreign Languages Press, 1967.

ACKNOWLEDGMENTS

No book is ever written by just one person. A book is truly a case of *e pluribus unum*. It takes the contributions of many—many who doubtless do not know the contribution, or the extent of the contribution, they made. So, it is, in the case of this book, and so it is at this juncture that I attempt the impossible task of trying to name a few of the many.

First, there are many who made the writing of this book, if not possible, certainly better. At the top of this list is Rachel Stout whose timely and tireless editing sped the book along and improved it at every juncture. Natasha Simons gave me well-aimed editorial pointers early on and shaped its path in important ways. And of course, there are those at RealClear Publishing—Dan Gerstein, Naren Aryal, and Carl Cannon—and at Amplify Publishing—Lauren, who keeps the trains running and Will Wolfslau—who were so encouraging along the way.

There are those who gave expert advice which served as a compass when I worried that I was lost. In health care, there was Chuck Blahous at Mercatus and Robert Moffit at Heritage. Then there were those, Doug Badger and Grace-Marie Turner, who were more than experts, but friends too when I needed both. In that same category of expert and friend I put David Hobbs and Steve Moore, both of whom helped on tax and politics.

The list of those who gave support is the one I am most worried about cutting short because the list is simply too long. To those who do not know how many true friends they have, I offer this advice: write a book, because you will certainly find out who they are in the process. Jamie Brown, Tevi Troy, Laura Dove, Shahira Knight, Tucker Eskew, Steve Pinkos, Christin Baker, Alison Jones,

Tony Roda, and Emma Doyle—all were there when I needed them.

Over three decades, I have been fortunate to have written for many conservative publications. The guidance of countless editors helped shape what appears in these pages. To these publications and people, I am immeasurably indebted: *American Spectator, Barron's, Daily Caller, The Federalist, Forbes, The Hill, Investor's Business Daily, Human Events, Issues & Insights, National Review, New York Post, Roll Call, Townhall, Wall Street Journal, Washington Examiner*, and the *Washington Times*—where I do want to mention Frank Perley, who has been a constant from the beginning.

While there were many sources that proved invaluable in my work on this book and cited accordingly, a few appeared in repeated chapters, and I think warrant special mention. John Cogan's *The High Cost of Good Intentions* provides a unique overview of federal entitlement programs. Daniel Flynn's *A Conservative History of the American Left* does the same in its topic. MeasuringWorth's calculator for nominal and real GDP was exceptionally helpful for giving comparisons of America's economy over time and allowed me to put federal spending in a graspable context to the economy. And the incomparable *Socialism* by Ludwig von Mises was used as a touchstone throughout.

Finally, which is really firstly, there is family. They are the ones who must endure the hardest part of any book: the author. Jennifer, Eliza, Jimmy, and Jeremy have been through it all, and of course my parents Carolyn and James, who truly set me on my path.

To all of you, and to all those who I did not mention but am no less indebted, I say, thank you.

Undoubtedly, I have failed to capture everyone who deserves mention, just as I undoubtedly have failed to capture everything that should have been said on this topic. For any omissions and errors, I apologize. Rest assured: these oversights were unintentional, and while this book is due to the contributions of many, any errors are mine alone.

J.T. Young
July 2024

ABOUT THE AUTHOR

J.T. YOUNG has worked for over three decades in and around DC politics, immersed in economic advising and policy legislation from Capitol Hill. Alongside degrees from the University of Chicago (B.A.) and Cornell University (M.A., Ph.D.), Young's writing has appeared in the *Wall Street Journal, Washington Times, Washington Examiner, The Hill, American Spectator, The Federalist, Washington Post, New York Post, Barron's, Forbes, Chicago Tribune, San Francisco Chronicle, Cleveland Plain Dealer*, and elsewhere.

With a fondness for motorcycles and scuba diving in his youth, he now considers himself a responsible adult with a wife and family. His adventures today consist of attending baseball games, visiting national parks, and photography.

INDEX

New Deal, 188–91
overview, 179–82
Post-World War II, 193–94
World War II, 192–93
See also small-government
model
Bismarck, Otto von, 8
Black, Conrad, 169, 189
Black Lives Matter, 2
association with socialist Left,
30
and Marxist agenda, 31
socialist roots of, 10
Blahous, Charles, 63
Bloomberg, Michael, 20
Bonus Marchers, 165, 167, 170
Bonwick, Colin, 97
Booker, Cory, 27
Boston Tea Party, 100
Bowman, Jamaal, 65
Bradford, William, 73, 74, 149
Bryan, William Jennings, 157
Build Back Better, 14
Bull Moose Party. *See* Progressive
Party
Burgoyne, John, 110
Burke, Edmund, 14
Burton, David, 311
Bush, George H. W., 57, 279
Bush, George W., 58, 202
Buttigieg, Pete, 20, 33

C

CAA. *See* Community Action
Agencies

Cabet, Etienne, 247, 272
CAP. *See* Community Action
Program
capitalism, 3, 87–90, 111, 116, 120,
177, 194, 273, 265, 277, 279
English, 293
freedom permeated, 87
free-market, 71, 74, 120, 198,
86, 244, 246, 249
mercantilism *vs.*, 118
millennials and, 27
within socialist system, 249
state-monopoly, 85
traditional Left divergence
from, 250
Capitol Hill Autonomous Zone
(CHAZ), 30
Capper-Volstead Act, 161
Caro, Robert, 52
Carson, Ben, 31
Carter, Jimmy, 5, 55, 65, 279
CBO. *See* Congressional Budget
Office
centrism, 230–31
CFPB. *See* Consumer Financial
Protection Bureau
Charles, King II, 77
CHAZ. *See* Capitol Hill
Autonomous Zone
Chernow, Ron, 182
China, 9, 175, 194, 263, 269, 271,
282, 286, 299
Belt and Road Initiative, 284
Cold War, 171, 172
replicating the USSR's legacy,
283–84

T

Taft, Philip, 136, 164, 274

Taft-Hartley Act, 173

taxes
    1919-1929, during, 140, 142
    colonial, 124–25
    income *see* income tax
    invisible, 304
    payroll *see* payroll tax
    rich and corporations, 311–15
    wealth *see* wealth taxes

Temperance Movement, 160

Ten Days that Shook the World
    (Reed), 259–60

Thomas, Norman, 170, 294

Thoreau, Henry David, 144

Tlaib, Rashida, 26

Tocqueville, Alexis de, 3, 143,
    150–52, 176
    "equality of conditions," 151
    on federal government, 126
    on interest groups, 213
    predicted raise in taxes, 131

totalitarianism, 120

Townshend Acts in 1767, 99

A Tract on Monetary Reform
    (Keynes), 250

traditional Left, 4–5, 43–66, 289,
    297, 300, 321
    and Biden nomination, 20
    contemporary, 51–53
    Democrat Party and, 5, 23, 44,
    229–36, 291
    direct political power, 240
    divergence from capitalism, 250
    forty years of, 53–56

legitimization of, 45
Obama, return under, 59–61
opposition of, 19–20
original dynamic, impact of,
    320
policies supported by socialist
    Left, 17
Trump's 2016 electoral victory,
    23–24, 25
See also socialist Left

Truman, David, 161, 222

Truman, Harry S., 57, 173, 196, 221

Trump, Donald, 5, 8, 20
    2016 electoral victory, 23–24
    businesses of, investigation of,
    29
    impeachment, 24
    Solid Liberals and, 232–33
    Trump administration, 20,
    24–25
    CFPB during, 8
    health care, 15–16
    Obamacare and, 202
    targeting of, 25

Tugwell, Rexford, 169

Turner, Grace-Marie, 16

Turner, Nina, 42

two-party system, 20, 40, 47–48,
    161, 164, 177, 241, 280

U

UN Charter (of July 1945), 195

unemployment benefits
    during COVID, 13, 303

duing Nixon administration, 199

unionization, 173–74

unions, 155, 214–216, 237–38, 309
1865-1900, during, 153–54
certified, 168
collective bargaining, 177
company, 162
private-sector, 173
United Auto Workers, 49, 221
See also cooperatives

United Auto Workers, 49, 221

United States Department of
Agriculture (USDA), 211
Extension Service, 216, 219
under Roosevelt, 166–67

United States Steel Corporation, 167

US Immigration and Customs
Enforcement, 303–4

US Postal Service (USPS), 253

USSR, 9, 174, 194, 221, 246, 259,
271, 282–83
Cold War with, 171
collapse, 172
Communist Party of, 274
follow traditional Marxist
ideology, 175
poor record, 275
undermining American
Communist Party, 269

V

Venezuela, 283

Vietnam War, 9, 21, 44, 54, 175

Vincent, Nicholas, 76

Virginia Company of London, 72

Volpe, John Della, 22

Voyage in Icaria (Cabet), 247

W

Wagner Act, 168

Walker, Jack, 223, 225, 227, 228

Wallace, George, 49, 177

Wallace, Henry, 169, 174, 210, 211,
218, 219, 221

War Industries Board, 137, 139

War Manpower Commission, 193

War of 1812, 127, 128, 132

War on Poverty, 52–53, 223, 317

War Production Board, 193

Warren, Elizabeth, 8, 20, 27

Warsaw Pact, 9, 298

Washington, George, 103, 108–9,
117, 127, 206

Watergate scandal, 55–56, 239
See also Nixon, Richard

Waters, Maxine, 25

Wattenberg, Ben, 54

Wayland, J. A., 163

wealth, 256–57

The Wealth of Nations (Smith), 71

wealth taxes, 1, 10, 29, 256–57,
311–12
proposals, 290
rising calls for, 246
socialist Left and, 29
unprecedented, 245
See also income tax; payroll tax

Weaver, James B., 157